Society for Promoting Christian Knowledge

Martyrs and Saints of the First Twelve Centruies

Studies From the Lives of the Black Letter Saints of the English Calendar

Society for Promoting Christian Knowledge

Martyrs and Saints of the First Twelve Centruies
Studies From the Lives of the Black Letter Saints of the English Calendar

ISBN/EAN: 9783744719865

Printed in Europe, USA, Canada, Australia, Japan

Cover: Foto ©Lupo / pixelio.de

More available books at **www.hansebooks.com**

MARTYRS AND SAINTS

OF THE

FIRST TWELVE CENTURIES

Studies from the Lives

OF

THE BLACK LETTER SAINTS

OF THE

ENGLISH CALENDAR.

BY THE AUTHOR OF
CHRONICLES OF THE SCHÖNBERG-COTTA FAMILY

PUBLISHED UNDER THE DIRECTION OF THE TRACT COMMITTEE

LONDON:
Society for Promoting Christian Knowledge,
NORTHUMBERLAND AVENUE, CHARING CROSS, W.C.
43 QUEEN VICTORIA STREET, E.C.
BRIGHTON: 135 NORTH STREET.
NEW YORK: E. & J. B. YOUNG & CO.
1887

CONTENTS.

	PAGE
INTRODUCTION	1

PART I.

THE MARTYRS.

CHAPTER I.

THE MARTYROLOGIES 7

CHAPTER II.

THE PERSECUTIONS OF THE FIRST CENTURY.

St. John before the Latin Gate.	25
St. Nicomede	26

CHAPTER III.

MARTYRS OF THE SECOND CENTURY.

St. Clement	28
St. Perpetua	41
The Passion of SS. Perpetua and Felicitas, with their Companions	50

CHAPTER IV.

THE THIRD CENTURY.

St. Fabian, Bishop and Martyr	70
St. Cyprian (Thascius Cæcilius Cyprianus)	73

CHAPTER V.

LEGENDS OF THE EARLY MARTYRS.

	PAGE
St. Laurence	96
St. Vincent	103
The Legend of St. Alban, Protomartyr, and in early days Patron of Britain	112
St. Denis, Patron of France	117
St. Lucian	123
SS. Crispin and Crispinian, Brothers	125
St. Blaise, Bishop and Martyr	128
St. George, Patron of England and of Soldiers	132
St. Valentine, Bishop and Martyr	139
St. Sylvester, Bishop of Rome	141
St. Nicholas of Myra	146

CHAPTER VI.

THE LEGENDS OF THE VIRGIN MARTYRS.

St. Cæcilia	154
St. Agnes	162
St. Agatha	166
St. Lucy	169
St. Prisca	173
St. Faith (Fides)	175
St. Margaret	178
St. Catharine	182

CHAPTER VII.

MARTYRS IN THE WARFARE WITH THE BARBARISM OF THE NORTH.

St. Lambert	189
St. Boniface (Winfried of Crediton)	196
St. Edmund the Martyr	216
King Edward the Martyr	222
St. Alphege of Canterbury	227

CONTENTS

PART II.
SAINTS NOT MARTYRS.

CHAPTER I.
THE FOUR LATIN FATHERS AND ST. BENEDICT.

St Ambrose	236
St. Augustine	260
St. Jerome	302
St. Benedict	323
St. Gregory the Great	334

CHAPTER II.
SAINTS OF FRANCE.

St. Hilary	346
St. Martin	352
St. Britius	362
St. Enurchus or Evortius	364
St. Remigius	366
St. Leonard, Patron of Prisoners	370
St. Machutus (St. Malo)	373
St. Giles or Egidius, Patron of Lepers, &c.	376

CHAPTER III.
SAINTS OF ENGLAND, WALES, AND IRELAND.

St. Augustine of Canterbury	379
St. Patrick, Apostle of Ireland	391
St. David (Dewi), Patron of Wales	403
St. Chad	407
St. Etheldreda (St. Audrey)	414
The Venerable Bede	420
St. Swithun	427
St. Dunstan	429
St. Edward the Confessor	442
St. Hugh of Lincoln	448
St. Richard of Chichester	459

CHAPTER IV.

OTHER MINOR FESTIVALS	463

BLACK LETTER FESTIVALS

ACCORDING TO THE PRAYER BOOK CALENDAR OF THE CHURCH OF ENGLAND.

January.

		PAGE
8.	St. Lucian, Priest and Martyr	123
13.	St. Hilary, Bishop and Confessor	346
18.	St. Prisca, Virgin and Martyr	173
20.	St. Fabian, Bishop and Martyr	70
21.	St. Agnes, Virgin and Martyr	162
22.	St. Vincent, Deacon and Martyr	103

February.

3.	St. Blasius, Bishop and Martyr	128
5.	St. Agatha, Virgin and Martyr	166
14.	St. Valentine, Priest and Martyr	139

March.

1.	St. David, Archbishop and Confessor	403
2.	St. Chad, Bishop and Confessor	407
7.	St. Perpetua and her Companions, Martyrs	50
12.	St. Gregory the Great, Bishop of Rome	334
17.	St. Patrick	391
18.	St. Edward, King and Martyr	222
21.	St. Benedict, Abbot	323

April.

3.	St. Richard, Bishop and Confessor	459
4.	St. Ambrose, Bishop, Confessor, and Doctor	236
19.	St. Alphege, Bishop and Martyr	227
23.	St. George, Martyr	132

BLACK LETTER FESTIVALS

May.

		PAGE
3.	Invention of the Holy Cross	465
6.	St. John Evangelist before the Latin Gate	25
19.	St. Dunstan, Archbishop and Confessor	429
26.	St. Augustine, Archbishop and Confessor	260
27.	Venerable Bede, Priest and Confessor	420

June.

1.	St. Nicomede, Priest and Martyr	26
5.	St. Boniface, Bishop and Martyr	196
17.	St. Alban, Martyr	112
20.	Translation of St. Edward, King and Martyr	222

July.

2.	Visitation of the Blessed Virgin Mary	463
4.	Translation of St. Martin, Bishop and Confessor	352
15.	Translation of St. Swithun, Bishop and Confessor	427
20.	St. Margaret, Virgin and Martyr	178
22.	St. Mary Magdalene	464
26.	St. Anne, Mother of the Blessed Virgin Mary	463

August.

1.	Lammas Day [or the Chains of St. Peter]	465
6.	Transfiguration of our Lord	466
7.	The Holy Name of Jesus	466
10.	St. Laurence, Deacon and Martyr	96
28.	St. Augustine, Bishop, Confessor, and Doctor	260
29.	Beheading of St. John Baptist	466

September.

1.	St. Giles, Abbot and Confessor	376
7.	St. Enurchus, Bishop and Confessor	364
8.	Nativity of the Blessed Virgin Mary	463
14.	Exaltation of the Holy Cross	465
17.	St. Lambert, Bishop and Martyr	189
26.	St. Cyprian, Archbishop and Martyr	73
30.	St. Jerome, Priest, Confessor, and Doctor	302

October.

		PAGE
1.	St. Remigius, Bishop and Confessor	366
6.	St. Faith, Virgin and Martyr	175
9.	St. Denis, Bishop and Martyr	117
13.	Translation of St. Edward, King and Confessor	442
17.	St. Etheldreda, Queen, Virgin, and Abbess	414
25.	St. Crispin, Martyr	125

November.

6.	St. Leonard, Deacon and Confessor	370
11.	St. Martin, Bishop and Confessor	352
13.	St. Britius, Bishop and Confessor	362
15.	St. Machutus, Bishop and Confessor	373
17.	St. Hugh, Bishop, Confessor, and Abbot	448
20.	St. Edmund, King and Martyr	216
22.	St. Cæcilia, Virgin and Martyr	154
23.	St. Clement, Bishop and Martyr	28
25.	St. Catharine, Virgin and Martyr	182

December.

6.	St. Nicholas, Bishop and Confessor	146
8.	Conception of the Blessed Virgin Mary	463
13.	St. Lucy, Virgin and Martyr	169
16.	O Sapientia	466
31.	St. Sylvester, Bishop and Confessor	141

MARTYRS AND SAINTS

OF THE

FIRST TWELVE CENTURIES.

INTRODUCTION.

ALL Calendars of Saints can but present us with types and samples, specimens more or less casual, of the great treasure of holy lives in the Church. The selection can but be as if the hands of a child had dived into a casket of precious ores or costly jewels, and taken up a few chance specimens of the contents. However many are gathered, the larger number, and often, perhaps, the choicest treasures, must be left behind. For the treasure is too large for any human hand to grasp; and the quality which makes it precious is in its deepest sense known only to Him who is the true Refiner of the silver, the true Sculptor of the gems. And, moreover, the metal is still in the ore; the jewels are but partially cut, and none of them is yet in its true setting. Yet, it must be admitted, at a first glance, our own Anglican Calendar does seem to have a peculiar casualness of its own.

That the Calendar should close altogether in the thirteenth century may not seem so unaccountable when we think that 1250 was not further from its revision in 1561 than the great Elizabethans are from us. Three hundred years is perhaps not too wide a distance to enable us to distinguish the relative level between the 'little hills' and the 'mountains of God.' The omissions within the space included are more difficult to understand. For the more perplexing there seem, however, to be two explanations: firstly, the comparatively insular character of the ancient English Calendars, on which our own is based; and secondly, that it is a partial restoration of a treasure for a time altogether lost.

Until the twelfth century, when canonisation became (like the conferring of a military order) more systematically the sole prerogative of the central sovereign authority, the additions to the Calendars seem to have rested with the bishop and council of each diocese, sacred names being added like birthdays in a family Bible. With the more organised centralisation came at once restriction and expansion; a sifting of mere local celebrity, and a wider grasp of choice.

Our own English Calendars, moreover, seem always to have had rather a peculiarly local and inexpensive character. Comparatively few names were added to the English Calendars from the eleventh or twelfth to the sixteenth century, though many were added to the Roman.[1]

And we must also remember that our Black Letter Festivals are a Restoration. In two Prayer Books of Edward VI. they were left out altogether. That some great names are still omitted may be a chance, but it is no mere chance that those remaining are there. It is the witness to the triumph of that wider sympathy, that fearless recognition of the continuity of life in the Church through all exaggerations and deficiencies, which seems characteristic of our Anglican Communion. It is the confession that the demands of the Master are unrelaxed, and the possibilities of the highest achievement undiminished throughout the ages; that the saints and martyrs are not an extinct species; that the Creator Spirit did not cease to create

[1] Blunt, *Annotated Prayer Book.*

saints at the close of the Apostolic Age, or at the great Division of Eastern and Western Christendom, or at the Reformation; on both sides of all the barriers, 'moving on the face of the waters,' and giving men and women love and courage to live and to die martyrs for Christ,—in the darkest ages, as to-day in Africa, in Melanesia, or among the lepers of the Sandwich Islands,—in the streets of our own cities now as outside Jerusalem 1800 years ago. It is the recognition that the Day of Pentecost is 'fully come,' and come for ever. It is indeed comprehensible how an intense sense of the imperfection of all human holiness may, to souls freshly awakened to the supremacy, and the nearness, of Him who alone is at once the Spotless Sacrifice and the Priest for ever, have made the application of the title 'saint' to any human creature seem a presumption. The great Eucharistic hymn 'Thou only art holy, Thou only art the Lord' absorbs all other strains. Or, again, when we consider the entirely derivative and dependent character of all human goodness, we can understand how it can be doubted whether the name 'saint' should be given to any one redeemed and forgiven child rather than to another. All, all, it may be said, are chosen in that Holy One to be holy; all or none are called to be saints, nothing lower and nothing less. As in our Eucharistic service, all are called to adore with angels and archangels and all the company of heaven, while all confess themselves below the dogs, *not* worthy to gather the crumbs under the Master's table.

But if *any* are to be thus honoured and set apart as heroes and leaders of the armies of heaven by this great title, it is surely of high moment that this distinction should not be limited to any era in the history of the Church, that the records of the highest Christian life should not be supposed to be closed with the New Testament.

A comparative study of the various Calendars brings out many points of interest.

The Oriental Calendar begins not centuries, but millenniums before any other, embracing the prophets of the

Jewish Church, such as Job, Isaiah, and Haggai. It contains also a most touching commemoration of 'the Holy Poor' three times a year—on June 28, July 1, and our All Saints' Day.

The modern Roman Calendar extends much further, through the great saints of the later Middle Ages to our own times.

This extension on opposite sides into the past and towards the present is very characteristic. The ancient Church of the East, conservative and steadfast, embraces in her reverent recollection those elder Apostles and Prophets on whose foundation the Christian Church acknowledges herself to be built by Him who came not to destroy but to fulfil, recognising the continuity of the present with the earliest past of those 'who through faith subdued kingdoms.'

On the other hand, the Latin Church, with her westward gaze and onward step, gathers into her starry crown the latest lights, scarcely yet sunk beneath our earthly horizon, recognising the identity of the first creative Inspiration with the last holy life breathed out but yesterday in our midst.

And between these two stands our own brief Calendar, based on the earliest used in England; in itself, like so many things in our most conservative and also most progressive England, an untouched relic and witness of the historical past swept on in the current of the present.

For, as has been said, the Sarum Calendar, on which our own is based, virtually closes before the irregular and natural growth of the local and national Calendars had been replaced (in the twelfth century) by the regular system of canonisation organised at Rome, with its 'Devil's Advocate' and forms of legal investigation.

In earlier days the names of the saints to be commemorated, being fixed by the Bishop of the Diocese, or the Diocesan Council, naturally vary according to the nationality to which they especially belong, Spanish, Gallican, or English, our own Calendar bearing witness to the early relations of our Church with France and Italy.

The centralisation of authority would naturally tend to

widen the range of vision and to lessen the vividness of local colouring.

The modern Roman Calendar, whilst omitting some of the local saints, adds more systematically the great names of the East—for instance, Polycarp, Ignatius, and the great Greek Fathers, Basil, Gregory, Chrysostom, and Athanasius. It also remains open for the admission of new names from century to century,—a power of expansion which the English Church, having dropped (with the rest of Latin Christendom) the simple, old, uncritical method of the early martyrologies, and not accepting the authority of Rome, has naturally lost. But for that very reason our Calendar possesses a distinct historical interest of its own.

Of the omissions, the Sarum Calendar is responsible for the absence of St. Polycarp, St. Ignatius, and the martyrs of Lyons and Rome, of the four Greek Fathers, and of St. Aidan, St. Anselm, and St. Bernard, who lived within its chronological limits. For the absence of St. Cuthbert the Commission of Revision have to answer.[1]

On the whole, about two-thirds of the names in the Sarum Calendar are left out, chiefly, it is said, because the Festivals being kept as holidays withdrew too much time from daily work. Nevertheless a goodly number remain to us. The range of time embraced is from the first century to the thirteenth; the range of secular callings extends from the king to the shoemaker; the countries embraced are Asia Minor, Egypt, the shores of Carthage, Italy, Dalmatia, Greece, Spain, France, and Flanders, besides our own; so that the scope of subject and of sympathy is by no means narrow. To follow the footsteps of one after another of these moulders of Christendom is like climbing the slopes of a

---

[1] The name of Thomas à Becket (St. Thomas of Canterbury), once commemorated three times a year, and erased, it is said, in deference to the vehement dislike of Henry VIII.; the festival of St. Patrick, left out, we must hope, by accident; and All Souls, the Commemoration of the Departed, were restored in a Calendar published by the Stationers' Company, with the authority of the Archbishop of Canterbury, up to the year 1832. It is interesting to observe the recognition of two of the Greek Fathers, St. John Chrysostom and St. Athanasius, in the Prayer Book, although not in the Calendar.

mountain by an unusual road, to house after house on its slopes, and whilst we make acquaintance with the inmates of each dwelling, finding in each a new point of view from which we see the whole land around and below in a new aspect.

And, after all, the inspiring conviction abides with us that in all the Calendars what is left out must be infinitely more than what is included. No calendar yet existing includes the names of Alfred the Great or Joan of Arc; while, curiously enough, *all* include St. Catherine of Alexandria—of whom Tillemont says not a fact in her legend is certain—and St. George, of whose history a writer of devout meditations says its chief lesson is that saints of whom man can know nothing at all may yet be great before God. And all the Catalogues of Saints, like the first muster-roll of the 11th chapter of Hebrews, have to stop at one point or another with 'The time would fail me to tell.' All the numbered 'twelve thousands' have to expand at last into the 'great multitude which no man can number.' All the calendars have to be supplemented by an All Saints' Day.

PART 1.

THE MARTYRS.

CHAPTER I.

THE MARTYROLOGIES.

ONE of the first characteristics of the Calendar that must strike us all is the foundation of the Christian Church on martyrdom. The 'Vincit qui patitur' is emblazoned around it all. Half of the whole number in our Prayer Book were martyrs; the Corner Stone, the Crucified Christ; the foundation stones, those who follow Him, obedient unto death. The walls of the city do not seem able to rise except on this basis. From the first glorious forlorn hope apparently broken, but really all the while prevailing against the first 'gates of the enemy,' the old paganism of Asia, Carthage, and Rome—to the brave Devonshire man who fell in the ninth century leading the attack against the barbarism of the Teutonic North, and the English king and archbishop who fell under a fresh onrush of the heathen Norsemen—up to our own days in Africa and the Southern Seas, not only is the whole fabric of the Christian Church founded on martyrdom, but every fresh conquest over every fresh foe seems to be thus necessarily consecrated by fresh sacrifice.

Not, indeed, that any book of spiritual peerage can include all who were truly martyrs. We all know, indeed, that the voluntary sufferings and sacrifices of Christian life may often be as great in themselves and as triumphant a witness for Christ as any sufferings of death. But the great principle of conquering by suffering is emphatically asserted through the martyrs. Not by wars such as those of Joshua, nor by prosleytising armies such as those of the early Mahometans, but by martyrdom is Christianity as Christianity, the Church as the Church spread. The army of the Church is the 'noble army of martyrs.' With the martyrs, therefore, these sketches of the Black Letter Saints must begin.

The history of the martyrologies, the Acta Martyrum, on which all the calendars are based, is in itself a most characteristic portion of ecclesiastical history. The stories of the martyrs seem naturally to divide themselves into historical and legendary, and a borderland between the two.

The very history of the word *legend* itself is full of significance. The legends of the martyrs were the *legenda collecta* of the martyrdoms to be read on the day of commemoration. About this the ancient Church of Rome was especially careful and cautious, forbidding any stories of doubtful origin, of whose authors and witnesses the names were not known, to be accepted among the *legenda* in the churches.[1]

But this reverent care was not followed in all directions; a town, village, or afterwards monastery, in its eagerness to glorify its own especial local saint, might accept too easily, on little authority, any words, or deeds, or miraculous interpositions which seemed to give colour and detail to the marvellous story; and so probably by degrees the word *legend* grew to mean not a carefully attested history, but the imaginative story which sprang up around it; the growth of legend becoming most exuberant where the fact around which it entwines is feeblest. Possibly scarcely one of the old stories, often so picturesque, so quaint, and so beautiful as parables, exists without some germ of actual history. But it is not around such natural and characteristic

---

[1] De Smedt, *Introductio in Historiam Ecclesiasticam*, p. 115. The religious romances or mediæval tracts for edification constructed *out of the legend* or history are of course on another level altogether.

histories as that of Perpetua and Felicitas, of Polycarp and Ignatius, or Cyprian, that the wealth of legend accumulates; it is rather around such brief and momentary glimpses of fact as gleam through the stories of Agnes or Agatha, St. George or St. Catherine.

In the early ages there must have been a large accumulation of Christian documents relating to the martyrs. It is the destruction of these documents in the persecution of Diocletian which swept such a wide field clear for the subsequent growth of romantic legend. And if the records thus destroyed were like the stories still preserved to us in the *Acta* of Perpetua and Felicitas the loss is great indeed.

The faith and courage which upheld the martyrs in death must evidently have represented a large amount of faith and love equally ready for the sacrifice. The martyrologies so lovingly and carefully compiled while the persecution was still in force were as really a witness to the faith as the martyrdoms. Not only did the Christians visit their confessors in the prison, acknowledge them at the torture and executions, reverently recover the torn and tortured bodies, bearing them as sacred treasures to the catacombs, and then in intimate converse gather together and record the faithful words they had heard and the patient sufferings they had seen. They went to the public notaries and obtained when they could copies of the official records of the trial, often purchasing these—so precious historically from the prosaic coldness of their official accuracy—at a considerable cost.

And thus from these records of Roman persecutions, pieced together with the recollections of the Christians who had dared to witness the sufferings they were so likely to share, or who knew certain details of the life given up for Christ, were slowly collected the story, the earliest Legenda or Lections, which were the historical treasure of each city which possessed them and of the whole Church, to be *read* when the brethren assembled by their graves in the catacombs, on the birthday of the martyr, or in connection with the Eucharistic commemoration of the Master.

So the Acts of the Apostles flowed on into the Acta Martyrum, and the Church history, which is from beginning to end founded not chiefly on *teaching*, but on *living* and *dying*, was slowly growing from age to age, until at last the pagans began to learn the power of this historical faith, and, not being able to quench the life which created the history, directed their assaults against the history which nourished the life.

In the great persecution of Diocletian, the last Imperial and general attack on the Church, the force of the enemy was directed towards the destruction of the Christian documents: the Sacred Scriptures, which were the history and law of the whole Church, happily too universally diffused to be destroyed; and the Acta Martyrum, which were the especial glory and heritage of the various cities and villages where the martyrs had suffered.

As regards these precious local contemporary records, the attack seems to have been sadly successful. In many cases there may have been only one manuscript copy, carefully laid up in the church or place of assembly with the sacred vessels and vestments, to be read on the days of commemoration, the sacred 'Birthdays.'

In too many instances this one precious record seems to have been destroyed. Afterwards, no doubt, efforts were made to recover the story from memory; but the authenticity of the official legal record, the quiet force of its bare statements of word or fact, the vivid touches of those who heard and saw, and told what they had heard and seen, at a moment when every detail of words and looks remembered was infinitely more sacred than any eulogistic phrases about them, the individuality, the local colouring, the naturalness, were lost irreparably; and instead came the story dim through the distance of ages, and also through the halo of the very fervour of the reverence which enshrined it, magnified by worship, stunted to the stature of the narrator, dwarfed and dimmed from a great and simple human, Christian story into a mere religious lesson-book; until, in place of the far deeper poetry of the history, that other literature arises, not, indeed, without its own fantastic beauty and its own high teaching, which we call Legend.

The faith and love of later ages takes the beloved names out of the mist, and clothes them with its own ideal in a new world of Christian legend. St. Margaret, the type of womanly purity, destroys the dragon that devours her. St. George, type of the true chivalry which is not only to keep itself pure, but to save, rescues the maiden from the dragon; St. Cæcilia wins her bridegroom from earthly joys to holy works of charity, and by her touch and heavenly singing consecrates music as the great Christian art; St. Catherine with her eloquent lips is the mighty maiden Athene of Christian science; St. Christopher with his lovely parable story of the strong serving the weak, finds in the helpless childhood he serves the Divine Lord who saves. Greece and the wild North pour their gold into the crucible of Christian legend, and it comes forth the 'pure gold, like transparent glass' of the heavenly city. Thus the history of the martyrologies is the history of much besides the martyrs.

But the 'Acta Sincera Martyrum' brings us down to the very rock on which the City is built.

In attempting to make a distinct division between the legendary and the historical it must be remembered that there must often be a borderland between the events of each life, and between the various lives so classified, where both elements meet. But, practically, without subtle critical dissection the distinction is sufficiently apparent.

Clement of Rome, Nicomede, Fabian, Perpetua, Cyprian, stand out, veiled, indeed, and seen but in glimpses, but solidly individual and historical, in the struggle of the first three centuries against the classical paganism of Greece and Rome; as Boniface, Alphege, and Edmund, in the later conflict with the heathen barbarism of the North. The Christian warfare of those centuries is represented in their life and death. Between these, legend and history intertwined inextricably in their stories, are Alban, Denys,

Crispin, Lawrence, and Vincent, yet still giving the impression of individual historical growth, garlanded with legend. And on the other hand, from those three first martyr centuries a radiant band shines on us, surely also representing lives lived and sacrificed for Christ, yet so blended with the ideals of purity, and charity, and Christian grace they no doubt helped to create, that Agnes with her lamb, Margaret, daisy and pearl of Paradise, Catherine with her royal state, her Plato, her mathematics, and her stars, Cæcilia with her beauty and her music, Lucy and Agatha, stand before us rather as symbols of the purity and chivalry they embody than as men and women of mortal mould; the individuality is lost in the type.

CHAPTER II.

THE PERSECUTIONS OF THE FIRST CENTURY.[1]

THE first pagan or imperial persecution has left us no definite names of martyrs, except those of the Apostles Peter and Paul.

Those living torches in the gardens of Nero on the Vatican flash on the pagan world, as they would have wished, not their own names, but the name of Jesus only, and the existence of His Church.

The seal which that persecution set on the Church may no doubt be read in the Apocalypse, written a few years afterwards: the 'souls under the altar,' 'the white-robed multitudes who came out of great tribulation and washed their robes and made them white, not in those rivers of their own blood, but in the blood of the Lamb,' ' the armies of heaven on white horses riding after the Crucified, conquering and to conquer.'

A flood of light is thrown on the Apocalypse by connecting it with that first persecution.

Within the imperial eternal city a new city was being silently built, Imperial indeed and Eternal, the City of God.

Beside this corrupt and degraded civilisation, which was 'corrupting the whole earth,' a new ideal of purity, not dreamt of before, was dawning. The 'Bride, spotless and radiant, 'clothed in fine linen, pure and white,' was in the world. Every martyr in the arena, every strong young life yielded up to death rather than sin, proclaimed this new

[1] The two festivals in our Calendar belonging to this century are St. John ante Port. Lat. and St. Nicomede.

purity, not merely passive but saving, this new love, not only patient but passionate, which had come into the world.

Most expressive is the fact that no new individual name has come down to us from that first persecution of Nero, but to the world and to the Church a new Apocalypse of Christ, the Lamb that was slain, and the Bride of the Lamb; and also (as urgently needed) an Apocalypse of the wrath of the Lamb. It declares in the 'voices of many thunders' that cruelty and lust, injustice and oppression, tyranny of the strong against the weak, are *not* inevitable evils which the easy gods regard, or disregard, with indulgent indifference; that they are abhorred in heaven, that the Christian heaven is no mere serene supernal abode of smiles and sunshine; thunders and lightnings are in it, the severity of love, the vengeance of patience, the wrath not of the lion, but the Lamb.

For beyond all that diseased imagination can conceive, the diseased imagination of that wretched madman who had Rome and the Roman Empire in his grasp seems really to have inflicted on the Christians of Rome in that sixty-fifth year of the Christian era.

'The world,' it is said, 'was abandoned to a monster. There was no means of getting rid of him. His German Guard, which had all to lose if he fell, defended him with rage. At once grandiose and grotesque, as Nero was literary his madness was chiefly literary. The dreams of all the ages, all the poems, all the legends, Bacchus and Sardanapalus, Ninus and Priam, Troy and Babylon, Homer and the faded poesy of his own times floated like a chaos through that poor brain of a mediocre artist, on whom chance had bestowed the power of realising all his chimeras.

'It was after the murder of his mother, Agrippina, that cruelty began to invade his active life. Every year was marked by fresh crimes. Nero proclaims daily that the only serious thing is art; all virtue is a lie. The dilettante threatens men with torture if they do not admire his verses. The madness of Caligula was short; he was a buffoon, but had wit. On the contrary, the madness of Nero, usually weak and frivolous, was at times frightfully tragic. Yet with all his cruelty this wretched being had a sentiment for art.

In those days art had indeed lost its way. 'The gigantic passed for great; it was an age of colossal statues, of art, materialistic, theatrical, falsely pathetic.'

'There was an ignoble taste for tableaux vivants.' The most ferocious and impure myths were actually represented on the stage, by criminals, who amused the people by deaths of frightful, ignominious torture.

'Nero had a mania for magnificent buildings. His Golden House was a world; with its porticoes three miles long, its parks with flocks, its solitudes, its vineyards.'[1]

But this was only a preparation. He desired and planned to rebuild the whole city of Rome. To rebuild, it was necessary to clear the ground; and to clear the ground no means would be so efficacious as a conflagration.

'It is known that the burning of Troy had acquired a terrible power over his fancy. He had been accustomed to act it from his childhood.'[2]

The legend that Nero set fire to Rome in order to imitate the burning of Troy, and that he contemplated the flames, lyre in hand, in a theatrical costume, from a tower, represents the contemporary conviction that he used, and probably promoted, the spread of the conflagration to make space for rebuilding Rome, as he did, with wide spaces and imperial magnificence.

On July 19, A.D. 64, the fire broke out. 'It began at the Porta Capena, in the Circus Maximus, near the Palatine and the Cœlian, a quarter which contained many shops full of inflammable material. Thence it raged round the Palatine, ravaged the low ground of the Velabrum and the Forum, climbed the hills, descended again into the valleys, raged six days and seven nights among those compact and winding streets. The conflagration seemed to arise at several points at once. Of the fourteen quarters into which the city was

[1] Renan, *L'Antéchrist*.   [2] Ibid.

divided four only remained entire; three were entirely destroyed.[1]

'To Nero the old sacred associations of the Republic, the old patriotic memories of the patrician houses, were less than nothing. But to every true heart in Rome they were unutterably dear. All the most precious antiquities were gone; the most sacred trophies, ancient ex-votos and monuments, the most honoured temples, all had disappeared. The whole city was in mourning for its most cherished recollections.'[2]

The city was cleared for his rebuilding. But the flames were raging in the hearts of the citizens.

Nero had to appease the storm he had roused, and it seems clear that, whoever first made the suggestion, he sought to fill the gulf he had opened by throwing into it the infant Christian Church of Rome.

In the midst of that luxurious, corrupt city, with its cruel pleasures, its lawless crimes, its base servilities, had silently arisen a band of men and women, of all ranks, and people, and kindred, and tongues, Greek slaves, Roman women of the noblest families, Jews and Jewesses, bound to each other, and separated from the rest of the world, by a faith and a worship which made them abandon all other worship as a crime, and seek to make others abandon it, which made them chaste, and true, and good, yet open to admit and save the lowest and worst. A secret society, dangerous therefore on political grounds; a secret society moreover claiming, it was said, to be a universal kingdom, into which they called on its subjects to enter as a supreme duty and privilege for all.

Ties of country, even of kindred, seemed feeble to the ties which bound them to each other. To the world outside their bearing was austere. The social gatherings, with the customary national religious rites, they carefully avoided. The amphitheatre they detested. The combats of men or beasts did not amuse them.

They were said to be 'atheists.' They rigidly avoided

[1] Gibbon, *Decline and Fall.*   [2] Renan, *L'Antéchrist.*

all religious rites, spoke of all the gods of Rome as 'nothing,' mere dreams, or worse, as evil dæmons, confounding Olympus and Tartarus.

Yet, in spite of all this moroseness to the outside world, there was something in them, or among them, which every now and then fell on the best and sweetest and loftiest souls like an irresistible spell.

Those doors so open to all who would enter seemed to those who entered to shut in a home of warmth and light, a world of love and hope and peace, compared with which all the world outside was as a cold Hades of shades and dreams. There was a love there, a purity undreamed of elsewhere, love ready to sacrifice all to succour or to save each other; love as of mothers for young children, of children for aged parents. They called each other brothers and sisters. And there was worship there. One Name was spoken among them which seemed to have over them the power of the name of Athens to the Athenians of her prime, of Rome to the Romans of the old patriotic days, the power of the name of a bridegroom to the chaste matrons of earlier Rome, the power of the name of a great general to the soldiers he leads to victory, the power of the name of God to a devout Jew. And yet this Name belonged to One whose countrymen had persecuted Him to death, who had led no one to victory, who, so far from leading His followers to triumph or success, had Himself ended His life in the most utter defeat, and who promised His followers no destiny more glorious than treading in His steps. They spoke, indeed, of His returning; but also of going to Him by dying, which made death to many of them no menace, but a promise. Immortality with these enthusiasts was no mere slight overweight of carefully balanced arguments, no mere dim dream of an ancient faith shrouded in mysteries. It was simply a swallowing up of death in life, which made death to them but an incident in life, their own individual life and the life of the society.

This society, moreover, invaded the philosophers' schools,

professing to make the Divine Ambrosia of elect intelligences the common bread of common men, women, and children. It troubled social and family life by its dreams of brotherhood. It undermined political life by its claim to be a universal kingdom.

And withal it was a religion not simply entreating toleration, but demanding universal allegiance, and aiming at nothing less than the abolition of all other religions, or at least the absorption of all into itself. For above all, and beneath all, and through all, it was an absorbing personal devotion to this Jesus, the Lord Christ, who they admitted had died, whom all men knew to be dead, but whom they affirmed to be alive. Brothers, disciples, believers, all these names they accepted; but the only name which really defined them, in which they gloried, was the name of Christian.

'I am a Christian,' was a bond which they acknowledged among each other as a claim to any amount of mutual succour and sacrifice, all over the world, from Syria to Britain.

'I am a Christian' was a confession they would maintain, it was said, through any amount of torture unto death. It was also said that they often threatened the destruction not of the city only but of the whole world, especially by fire. That they should have sought to hasten the consummation by setting fire to this Rome which they thought so wicked was at least conceivable. It was a suspicion which, kindled designedly, scattered recklessly, might spread as easily as the conflagration itself, which Nero had probably found it so easy to promote and now found it as easy as it was convenient to turn to the disadvantage of this mysterious, dreaded, despised society.

And if he could succeed in fastening this suspicion upon them many other advantages would follow. Not only would the anger of the people be turned from himself, but for them and himself, out of the conflict with this new fanaticism might be created a drama, a theatrical entertainment, more realistic, more passionate, more artistic, and more wildly exciting than any yet dreamt of.

For those Christians, while ready to die, eager even to die for this Name, which was to them as a magic spell, had something which, in spite of their fearlessness of death, made life and its pure affections, the freedom of men, the chastity of women, not less but more sacred and precious to them than to all beside.

Depths of anguish, therefore, were possible to them in seeing each other suffer, which might make a persecution of Christians a spectacle more pathetic, more tragic, more capable of exciting varied emotions than any poem or drama ever conceived by Homer or Æschylus.

The wildest horrors of the most diseased imagination were actually perpetrated above the charred ruins of those devastated hills.

'The victims were kept for a *fête* to which, no doubt, was given the character of an expiation.' 'The day may be fixed as about August 1, A.D. 64, a day after the day when Jesus expired on Golgotha, the most solemn in the history of Christianity.'[1]

The *ludus matutinus*, the morning performance of that day, was to be the torture of the first Christian martyrs in the Circus Maximus; the evening entertainment, their being burnt alive in the Vatican gardens.

For that August day also had its morning, and its evening, and its night like all other days.

They were clothed in skins, driven in troops into the arena, torn by wild dogs, dragged like Dirce on the horns of bulls; crucified. Many were suspended to gibbets, covered with resin or oil; and when that day of torture and massacre, of shame and glory was over, were set on fire in the gardens of Nero on the Vatican, flashing thence across the waste spaces of Rome.

Thus opened that Book of the Acts of the Martyrs called by one who saw its grandeur without sharing its inspiration 'that extraordinary poem of Christian martyrdom, that epic of the amphitheatre, which will last 250 years, and from

---

[1] Renan, *L'Antéchrist*.

which will spring the ennobling of woman, the emancipation of the slave.' One day of agony and shame, and one night. But that living illumination on the Vatican flashed not only over the waste spaces of ancient Rome; it began an illumination for the whole world, and all the ages, never since extinguished, to be extinguished never more.

This was in A.D. 64. The great muster-roll of the Epistle to the Hebrews was probably written about one year, the Apocalypse, with its visions of the Lamb and the Bride, Babylon, and the Holy City, the New Jerusalem, about four years afterwards. And characteristic indeed it is of the first strain of that new song from the earth that it gives us no names of individual sufferers, but only two names, the name of the Christ for whom they suffered and of the Christian Church.

But not only did that first persecution begin the 'glorious epic of 250 years;' it sets a stamp on suffering, on all that is meant by martyrdom, as the eternal foundation of the Christian Church and the Christian character in all ages.

For the Church is not an institution founded on a fact in the past. Eternal life thrills through every throb of her being at every moment. She is for ever being created, being founded. Every age, every character, every one of the living stones is built down to the living Rock, the Corner Stone; and, therefore, the martyr ages and the martyr spirit are never past.

The foundation of every fresh conquest is fresh sacrifice; the foundation of every Christian character is willing sacrifice. And this gives such endless interest to the story of the ancient martyr ages. They typify in eternal forms, grand and clear, the little conflicts and victories of the complicated struggles of each age. The age or the character which has not this imperial stamp on it can never conquer, can never found.

What do we mean by martyrdom? This great word, like all others, may be degraded; but the great word and fact remains. And it is good to ask ourselves every now and then what those foundation words mean. For this word is at the foundation of Christian thought, as the fact is at the foundation of the Christian Church.

The word martyrdom is in a sense peculiar to Christianity. The faith of the Jewish nation, when its people were in exile among idolaters, certainly could and did lead to death. Daniel at his prayers at the open window, in the lions' den, the three children in the fire were martyrs of the noblest. But in each of these stories it is interesting to observe that the supernatural intervention resulted not in sustaining the sufferers in suffering and death, but in saving them from death, and even from suffering.

In these persecutions, indeed, we know, some 'were tortured, not accepting deliverance,' but the very essence of Christian martyrdom is that the sufferers are not saved from suffering or death, but strengthened to suffer and to die.

It is also possible, no doubt, that Mahometanism, or any real religious conviction, especially any theistic faith, may have its martyrs in the protest against idolatry.

But Mahometan conquest is professedly founded on the victory of force rather than of patience. It is no exaggeration to say that the Moslem spread his faith by wielding the sword, the Christian by submitting to it.

Three things seem essentially involved in this word martyrdom: bearing witness to truth; passive endurance; and voluntary sacrifice. Mind, heart, and will are blended in it, in the whole and in every part.

The truth witnessed to, at all events with the martyrs we have now to do with, is no mere assertion of an intellectual proposition; it is loyalty to a Person. When Perpetua, laying her hand on a pitcher that stood near, said, 'Can you say this pitcher is not a pitcher? No more can I say I am not a Christian,' she meant not only that she could not tell a lie, but that she could not betray a trust. Her words had really a similar significance with those of Polycarp: 'These seventy years I have found Him a true Master, and can I deny Him now?'

Fidelity to truth, loyalty to the Person, proved by suffering to death, this is the essence of martyrdom. For that the suffering should issue not in rescue but in death is essential to the enrolling of any name as martyr in the Christian Calendar. Others are confessors, and many perhaps have suffered more. But to be a martyr in the sense of the Martyrologies the sufferer must die. The issue must be into the immortal life, not back into this.

And in this there is nothing to make these high examples inaccessible to our own following in these days of peace. Independent of the fact that actual death in our own days has been encountered and is again and again embraced by men who have fought against the especial wrongs of our own especial battle, it is well to have the endurance all are called to set before us, in its extremest form by some.

Any age, any character, which stops short of the quick decision for right at any cost, the determined carrying out of conviction at any peril, which leaves out the soldierly qualities, renunciation, austerity, readiness to endure hardness (call them 'ascetic' or 'Puritan,' or what we will), can only end in failure, in effeminacy, and in barrenness. Without the discipline, the hardness, the endurance as of the most devoted love of woman, the courage as of the most heroic of men, of which the spirit of martyrdom is the culmination and the type, Christian life, human life, would soon lose not merely its strength but its beauty, would cease to be luxuriant and free and fruitful.

We must never lose hold of the possibility of death and apparent failure—of the Cross, as the possible issue of our own especial conflict—if our warfare is to be part of the world's great battle, not a mere faction fight, and our victories not mere triumphs but conquests.

And martyrdom must involve patience—the glorifying of the passive side of virtue. It has been made a reproach of Christianity that it brings out too exclusively this passive, feminine side of our nature. That it does bring out the passive graces as never before there can be no doubt.

Losing sight of them we lose sight of the essence of Christ's life. But in all true patience there is as much courage as endurance. And in Christian martyrdom the extreme of patience in enduring is inextricably blended with the most unconquerable strength of will. It is of the essence of Christian martyrdom that there is a choice in it; that the sufferer is free to escape; that the sacrifice is voluntary. The whole effort of the persecutor is to subdue the will of the sufferer; at any moment of the trial the sufferer, by a single word, belying his convictions, by the smallest act of compliance, such as throwing a few grains of incense on a shrine, could be set at liberty. In other words, the martyr is essentially no helpless victim, but from beginning to end a willing sacrifice. And thus the ages of martyrdom result in no passive community of bondsmen, but in a force of individual life, a freedom of thought and conscience, down to the lowest ranges of society, never before known except in the loftiest character on the highest levels.

The contemporary records of the martyrdoms are, it is most interesting to remark, not called the sufferings of the martyrs, but their 'Acts.' And yet again, this voluntariness, this freedom of choice, this absolute exertion of will, need not prevent the stories of the martyrs from being the consolation of the lowliest sufferer helplessly laid on a sick bed. 'To accept is to resign;' to resign willingly is to sacrifice. Interior acts, acts of the soul, are certainly not less real than those of the body. Faith and hope and love can transform inflictions of suffering into acts of sacrifice, because at the bottom the essence of martyrdom, as of all Christian life, all true human life, all Divine life, is love; love faithful unto death to truth and trust; love patient to endure; love mighty to resist, to overcome evil with good.

Nevertheless we do and will glory in having leaders who scaled the citadel of the enemy, carrying the common standard through the breach. The nobleness of that 'noble army' does not dwarf our little lives; it raises and ennobles them. For those lives also were lived by moments, in hours and days, from morning to evening.

In the space between one morning and the next the first Great Persecution was accomplished. Three Hours gave us the story of the Cross.

St. John Evangelist ante Portam Latinam.

May 6.

(Sarum Epistle : Ecclus. xv. 1-6 ; Gospel, St. John xxi. 19-24.)

The tradition of 'St. John before the Latin Gate' is, that outside the Latin Gate—that is, the gate leading to Latium—he was thrown, by order of Domitian, into a caldron of boiling oil, which was to him no place of torture, but as a refreshing bath, in which the old man seemed to renew his youth; so that Domitian, seeing him come forth full of life and strength, attributed his deliverance to magic, but nevertheless was so far restrained by fear of the power which had sustained his victim that he dared not inflict any further sufferings on him, but banished him to Patmos, where he remained till the Emperor's death, when he returned to Ephesus.

There is also a legend that at the same time before the Latin Gate the Apostle was given a cup of poison, which he drank unhurt.

On the spot of his deliverance has stood a church from the days of the first Christian emperors. It is called S. Giovanni in Olio.

The Festival is in all the Calendars, and has given a name to 240 churches.[1]

---

[1] St. John before the Latin Gate was honoured in many places as their patron by printers, coopers, candle and lamp makers.

St. Nicomede

Of Rome.

June 1.

(In most Western Calendars. Martyred A.D. 81, under Domitian. Sarum Epistle, Ecclus. xiv. 20 and xv. 3-6; Gospel, St. Matt. xvi. 24-28.)

Two saints are enumerated in the Calendar of the first century, and both stand on its extreme verge. One, Nicomede, has the title of martyr (A.D. 90); the other, Clement (A.D. 100), is simply said to be bishop, but his name is in the ancient canon of the Roman Mass and he is often ranked among the martyrs.

Of Nicomede very little seems certainly known.

But it is interesting to observe that in the little known to us of the lives of both St. Clement and St. Nicomede the characteristic of each seems to have been Christian love, manifested in Nicomede especially in serving and honouring the martyrs, and by Clement in his endeavours to heal divisions in the Church of Corinth.

It was in the persecution of Domitian (A.D. 81) that St. Nicomede suffered. He was a priest at Rome, seized in the persecution for his assiduity in assisting the confessors and for his zeal towards the martyrs, whose bodies he searched out in order to bury them.[1]

To the last moments of life he must have attended them, and when the tortures were over and the victory won, secretly, probably at night, he must have come to search for the poor despised bodies, tossed out to perish, in order to bear them away to some place of honoured rest. He did it secretly, that he might not be hindered in these services of love, not that he himself might be hidden and might escape. At last this succourer of many was himself arrested.

---

[1] Morone, *Dizionario ecclesiastico*, and Alban Butler.

The usual choice was offered to him of sacrificing to the gods and thus denying Christ ; and then having refused to sacrifice to idols, he was beaten to death with blows of a stick.

Formerly his tomb could be seen in the Via Nomentana. In the Sacramentary of St. Gregory and the Martyrologies of St. Jerome and of Bede his festival is, as in our Calendar, on September 15.

Brief as his biography is, there is not a little in it. Perhaps his name indicates that he, like so many of the first Christians at Rome commemorated in the catacombs, was by birth a Greek. Not a word has come down to us from his lips ; only quiet deeds of reverent lovingkindness, such as Joseph of Arimathea and Nicodemus had rendered of old to the Master. The eyes that searched out the martyred dead for burial had certainly sustained them by faithful sympathy while they still suffered. It was no rash determination to die, no passionate, fanatical self-immolation which caused his martyrdom. His faith was betrayed by his love. It is a happy beginning of our martyrology (taken in the order of the centuries) that the first enrolled on the glorious list was a martyr for charity.

CHAPTER III.

MARTYRS OF THE SECOND CENTURY.

St. Clement
OF ROME.
November 23.

(Martyred, according to general tradition, A.D. 100. Sarum Epistle and Gospel: Phil. iv. 1-3; St. Luke xix. 12 28.)

It is remarkable that while of Nicomede not one spoken or written word has come down to us, but only the memory of his acts and sufferings, of Clement's life we scarcely know anything except through his writings. Every circumstance recorded of him seems to have been made a subject of contradiction and debate.

By one account he was of pagan descent, from a Roman patrician family. By some he is identified with Clement the fellow-labourer of St. Paul, whose name is in the Epistle to the Philippians, and, as the Apostle says, 'in the Book of Life.' By others he is spoken of as the devoted companion and disciple of St. Peter.

By many it is questioned if he suffered martyrdom at all. In our own Calendar he is not reckoned among the martyrs, nor is anything said of his martyrdom by Eusebius or any earlier writer.

But in the canon of the Roman Mass he is ranked among the martyrs, and in the eighth century a church stood at Rome dedicated in his name, at a time when it is said none but martyrs were thus honoured.

Besides these historical debates about him there is a religious romance, or rather a whole 'Clementine' literature, founded on his life, and there is also a legend recorded in the sixth century by Gregory of Tours describing his death in the Tauric Chersonese (the Crimea), with the subsequent miracles attending it.

But the very gathering of this literature around him proves the reality and importance of his personality and the weight attached to his name, for at the heart of it are those unquestioned and characteristic writings of his own—the fact that they are included in many ancient MSS. of the New Testament, and were certainly read of old in the Church services—and the fact that the author lived and died at Rome at the close of the first century in a position of honour and responsibility.

Bishop Lightfoot, after weighing the traditions, chiefly from the internal evidence of the epistle, arrives at the conclusion that St. Clement was a man of Jewish parentage, a Hellenistic Jew brought up not on the classics but on the Septuagint Bible, a freedman of Flavius Clemens [1] (the cousin of Domitian, who was undoubtedly martyred for his Christian faith on the charge of atheism and neglect of social and political duties) and Flavia Domitilla, his wife, also a cousin of the Emperor, who after her husband's death was banished to an island in the Mediterranean, to whom belonged the Cœmeterium Domitillæ, in the Tor Marancia, near the Ardeatine Way, unquestionably a Christian catacomb in the second century.

'Is it possible to consider this letter as written by one who had received the education and who occupied the position of Flavius Clemens, who had grown up to manhood, perhaps to middle life, as a heathen, who was imbued with the thoughts and feelings of the Roman noble; who about this very time held the most ancient and honourable office in the State (Roman Consul) in conjunction with the Emperor; who lived in an age of literary dilettanteism and Greek culture; who must have mixed in the same circles with Martial and Statius and Juvenal, with

[1] By some he was identified with the Flavius Clemens, cousin of Domitian.

Tacitus and the younger Pliny, in whose house Quintilian lived as the tutor of his sons, then designated by the Emperor as the future rulers of the world? Would not the style and diction and thoughts, the whole complexion of the letter, have been very different? It might not, perhaps, have been less Christian; but it would certainly have been more classical—at once more Roman and more Greek—and less Jewish than it is.

'The writer, indeed, like the author of the Book of Wisdom, is not without a certain amount of classical culture; but this is more or less superficial. The thoughts and diction are alike moulded on 'the Law and the Prophets.' He is a Hellenist indeed, for he betrays no acquaintance with the Scriptures in the original tongue; but of the Septuagint version his knowledge is very thorough and intimate. It is not confined to any one part, but ranges freely over the whole. He quotes profusely, and sometimes his quotations are obviously made from memory. He is acquainted with traditional interpretations of his text. He teems with words and phrases borrowed from the Greek Bible. His style has caught a strong Hebraistic type. All this points to an author of Jewish or proselyte parentage, who from a child had been reared in the knowledge of this one book.

'Jews were found in large numbers at this time among the slaves and freedmen of the great houses, even of the Imperial palace.

'I venture, therefore, to conjecture that Clement the bishop was a man of Jewish parentage, a freedman or the son of a freedman, belonging to the house of Flavius Clemens, the Emperor's cousin. It is easy to imagine how, under these circumstances, the leaven of Christianity would move upwards from beneath, as it has done in so many other cases; and from their domestics and dependents the master and mistress would learn their perilous lesson in 'the Gospel. Even a much greater degree of culture than is exhibited in the epistle would be quite consistent with such an origin; for among these freedmen were frequently found the most intelligent and cultivated men of their day. Nor is this social status inconsistent with the position of the chief ruler of the most important Church in Christendom. More than a century after Clement the Papal chair was occupied by Callixtus, who had been a slave.'[1]

We may, therefore, picture to ourselves the Rome in which St. Clement lived and wrote as the Rome of the Flavian emperors, Domitian, Vespasian, Titus, and Trajan.

The ruins of Nero's conflagration must have left traces, though, as the great Rebuilder, he had filled up many of the waste spaces. His Golden House by the Palatine, the beautiful Greek statues of which he had ruthlessly rifled the cities of conquered Greece, were adorning Rome. The Palatine, with its stately palaces, thronged with soldiers, with the Imperial Court and with slaves, looked down on the Forum, girt round with temples and basilicas, and across to the Capitol with its diadem of temples.

It was an era of great conflagrations. Five years after the fire of Nero, in the civil war between Vitellius and Vespasian, the great Temple of the Capitoline Jove had caught fire, and blazed up like a sacrificial Ara Cœli to the December sky; and seven months afterwards the rumour came to the colony of Jews at Rome that the sacred shrine of their law, of which they had deemed the destinies eternal, had been burned to ashes amidst the death agonies of fallen Jerusalem, captured by Vespasian; to the Jewish colony at Rome a bewildering destruction of sacred hopes, to the Christians a terrible fulfilment.

Along that Sacred Way to the Capitol the Jewish captives had been driven, bound and laden with the sacred vessels of their own desecrated temple, afterwards as captives forced to build the triumphal arch in which their defeat was commemorated, and the Coliseum, where the Christian martyrs suffered.

Emperor after emperor had been slavishly obeyed, more slavishly worshipped, and afterwards ignominiously slain. Twice within ten years the dreadful solitude of despotic

[1] Dr. Lightfoot's *St. Clement of Rome*, Appendix, p. 3.

power had ended in the madness, and then in the murder, of the despot.

Yet through all these tragedies the hundred thousand citizens of crowded Rome, leaving work to the foreign slaves, feasted, and bathed, and criticised, and debated in the stately corridors of the Baths and on the seats of the Amphitheatre.

There was no malaria then on those peopled hills; and instead of the desolate Campagna a fertile undulating plain, gay with cities and villages and country houses, spread on all sides of the City. Caravans of merchandise came from Ostia, and trains of captives along the great northern roads. Centre of empire and commerce and of conquest, from which all power went forth, to which all wealth flowed back, in the midst of all this activity and idleness and corruption the little Christian community lived and grew; a little germ of imperishable hope in the midst of this despairing and crumbling world. To this new living youthful society the things that betokened death to others were promises of a new life and dawns of a new era. The burning of the temple on the Capitol[1] might be to them as a beacon of promise, prophetic of a true Ara Cœli to be erected over its ruins; the burning of the Temple of Jerusalem but the scattering of the sacred light and fire, the diffusion of the Shechinah throughout the world.

A little community, scarcely now to be ignored, least of all at Rome, since a husband and wife of the Imperial Family—Flavius Clemens and Domitilla—had been among its martyrs; in which all ranks and stations were fused into one by the fire of Divine love, since while Domitian's cousin german died for Christ in the palace, Alexamenos, the slave, was being mocked for Him in the slaves' quarters of the Palatine, caricatured gazing up at the Cross, 'Alexamenos is worshipping his God.'

For the most part Greek, many of them of Jewish extraction, their language in their liturgy and in their funeral inscriptions was Greek; the names inscribed in the cata-

---

[1] By the soldiers of Vitellius, December 19, A.D. 69. Smith's *Dictionary of Greek and Roman Biography and Mythology*.

combs are often Hebrew. Yet this little community appears also to have been endued with the ruling faculty of the imperial Roman race and with the worldwide sympathies of the Central City of the world, sending out her words of wise and dignified guidance to the earlier Church of Corinth, not as a daughter to a mother, but rather as a wise mother to a refractory and unwise child, in answer to counsel asked by the child.

All this shines through this epistle 'from the Church of God sojourning at Rome to the Church of God sojourning at Corinth,' which is called in the title added at the close (though never in the text) the First Epistle of Clement to the Corinthians. For the autobiographical interest of the epistle is twofold: it is not only the unconscious autobiography of St. Clement, but of the Church of which he was the leader and representative.

The fact of the persistent recognition of his personality from age to age in spite of the effacement of it in the circular heading of the epistle, combined with the vagueness as to his personal history, seems to imply that this personality was *representative* rather than *exceptional*; gathering into itself and giving out the characteristics of the society around him rather than towering above them on some solitary height.

In reading the epistle we see St. Clement. In seeing St. Clement we see the Roman Church for which he lived. We hear its language, the Greek language of its prayers and hymns; we see its literature. The classical fable of the phœnix rising from its funeral pyre of frankincense and myrrh, and flying to the City and Altar of the Sun, is alluded to as a type of the Resurrection; but not a name of Greek poet or hero occurs throughout, whilst scarcely one of the great names of the Old Testament is absent. Abraham and David are its heroes, the psalms and prophets its poems. The master-key of classical culture is in the hands of the writer, in the language he lisped in infancy. But the sacred stories of his infancy are those of Abraham, Job, David, and Daniel.

As we listen we seem to stand by the twin fountains of

Christian thought. But it is the moral ideal of St. Clement and of that early Roman Church revealed in the epistle which is more than all else to us.

In the first place this comes out of its whole scope and purpose when seen in connection with the circumstances under which it was written.

It is an answer to an appeal for counsel from the Church of Corinth ; and as an explanation for delay in answering it begins with the words, 'By reason of the sudden and repeated calamities and reverses which *are* befalling us.' Only a few years before, two members of the Imperial family of Domitian had suffered for the faith. And, after an allusion to the persecution of Nero it is said, 'We are in the same lists ; the same conflict awaits us.'

In another place, after speaking of the continuity of the sufferings of the saints from Abel to the present, the writer says, 'Unto these men of holy lives are gathered a vast multitude of the elect *among ourselves*, who through many sufferings and tortures, being the victims of jealousy, give a brave example. Matrons and maidens and slave girls being persecuted, after they had suffered cruel and unholy insults' (another version alludes to the tossing by wild bulls, like Dirce), 'safely reached the goal in the race of faith and received a noble reward, feeble though they were in body.'

They were thus evidently in daily peril of the most cruel wrongs and death ; but the peril and the wrong strike from them no note of terror, no word of murmur or retaliation. They are not embittered by their wrongs. The epistle mounts up at the close into a liturgy of intercession for the fallen, the weak, the hungry, and for prisoners ; but also for the rulers and governors who were their oppressors.

They are not bewildered by their own peril ; they are not even occupied with it. After that brief allusion to it, as an excuse for the delay in replying, the whole thought of the writers goes out to the wounds they want to heal. It is no school defending a opinion. It is an universal kingdom caring for every one of its subjects, its compatriots, throughout the world.

It is interesting also to see how the epistle is written from a society of *families* to another society of families; not to a mere religious community or party, a conglomeration of individuals united only by a religious bond. It is no mere creation of an army of conquest detached from the race that is aimed at, but a restored and hallowed humanity; it is to husbands and wives, parents and children, brothers and sisters, that the letter is addressed.

And this, again, makes the heroism under persecution so much nobler. It is no sullen endurance, no over-strained fanaticism of those who believed human affections forbidden and the joys of human life a barren thing. It was over homes made dear and sacred, as never before, that the peril of the desecration and anguish of persecution hung, and might at any moment fall.

All through, it is the *contrasts* which make the moral ideal so beautiful; it is an interweaving of the richest colour, no mere washing in of neutral tints, that makes its harmony; it is the assertion of the principle of order and obedience as the remedy for the Corinthian divisions by those who were daily asserting the principle of liberty by life and death; the opposition to anarchy of those whose unconquerable freedom of conscience was revolutionising the world.

In other words, the liberty springs from the loyalty, the resistance from the obedience; it is as subjects of the King of kings that they are citizens of the 'Mother City, which is free.'

And again, the social, and moral, and spiritual are inextricably intertwined throughout. The order, the courage, the freedom are based on purity, and truth, and love; and on the two graces so new to the conquering Roman State, humility and patience; the patience not of submission to the inevitable, but of hope; the humility not of servility, but of love. And the moral is rooted deep in the spiritual, the ethics in the theology, the human in the Divine. The source of all is the faith in the supreme goodness of the Father and the Saviour they adore.

'Let us be good one towards another, according to the compassion of Him that made us,' is the keynote.

The patience he exhorts the Corinthians to follow is the patience of the saints of all time—of Elijah and Ezekiel; of 'Peter, who by reason of jealousy endured not one or two but many labours ; of Paul, who when he had suffered bonds, and had been stoned, had taught righteousness in all the world, and had borne testimony before kings, went into the Holy Place, being found in patient submission ;' of 'the vast multitudes of holy lives, brave examples, *among ourselves*, who have reached the goal.' But the eye of the writer ever looks steadfastly on through the long procession of those patient ones to the patience of Him, the Just One, who beareth our sins, whose sufferings are before our eyes, ' the Sceptre of the majesty of God, even our Lord Jesus Christ, who came not in the pomp of pride, but in lowliness of mind, the pattern given unto us ; for if the Lord was thus lowly of mind what should we do, who through him have been brought under the yoke of His grace ? '

'Let us hasten to return unto the goal of peace which hath been handed down to us from the beginning, and let us look steadfastly unto the Father and Maker of the whole world ; let us behold Him with our mind ; let us look with the eyes of our soul into the depths of His long-suffering will ; let us note how free from anger He is to all His creatures.

'The heavens are moved by His direction and obey Him in peace ; the sun and the moon and the dancing stars, according to His appointment, circle in harmony within the bounds assigned to them. The earth beareth fruit at her proper seasons, putting forth the food that supplieth abundantly both man and beasts and all living things, making no distinction.

'The inscrutable depths of the abysses are constrained by the same ordinances. The basin of the boundless sea, gathered by His workmanship into its reservoirs, passeth not the barriers wherewith it is surrounded ; the winds in their several quarters at the proper season fu'fil their ministry without disturbance; and the ever-flowing fountains, created for enjoyment and health, without fail give their breasts, which sustain the life of man. Yea, the smallest of living things come together in concord and peace. All these things the great Creator and Master of the universe ordered to be in peace and concord, doing good to all things, but far beyond the rest to us who have taken refuge in His compassionate mercies through our Lord Jesus Christ, to whom be the glory and the majesty for ever and ever.'

And as to love, it is the same; he never pauses till the highest Love is reached. Beginning with commendation before proceeding to the necessary rebukes (as the Master in the Epistle to the Seven Churches), he speaks of the magnificent hospitality of the Corinthians, 'their insatiable desire to do good,' their delight to give rather than to receive, ' the practical services of love of those ' who are neighbours to each other, as the good Samaritan was to the wounded stranger; of their conflict for the brotherhood, of the outpouring of the Holy Spirit on them; of the stretching out of the hands for forgiveness of the least sin." But the root of all this love is always traced to God and to the sacrifice of Christ.

'Let not the strong neglect the weak,' he says, 'and let the weak respect the strong. Let the rich minister to the poor; let the poor give thanks to God because He hath given them one through whom their wants may be supplied.' Also, working out the exercise of love into detail :—

'The young are to be modest; elders are to be honoured; women to perform their own duties, to show forth the beauty of purity; to be gentle, manifesting their moderation through silence . . . . The children are to be partakers of the instruction which is in Christ.' But then again, mounting to the 'source, who is sufficient to tell the majesty of the beauty of the love of God? The height to which love exalteth is unspeakable. Love joineth us to God; love covers the multitude of sins; love endureth all things, is long-suffering in all things. There is nothing coarse, nothing arrogant in love; love hath no divisions; love maketh no seditions; love doeth all things in concord. In love were all the elect of God made perfect; without love nothing is well-pleasing to God; in love the Master took us to Himself; for the love He hath toward us Jesus Christ our Lord has given His blood for us by the will of God, and His flesh for our flesh, and His life for our lives.' 'You see, dearly beloved, how great and marvellous a thing is love; and there is no declaring its perfection. All the generations from Adam to Moses have passed away, but they that by God's grace were perfected in love dwell in the abode of the godly.'

Thus this letter stands before us in the midst of all the haze of legend (and also of romance which does not even claim to be legend) which has gathered around it, a solid, unquestioned piece of historical fact. Through all the contradictory voices debating who is this invisible speaker the voice itself reaches us, clear and intelligible across the centuries; an individual, distinct human voice, not to be confused by those who know it with any other voice, its volume indeed lessened, but its individuality never lost through that long telephone of the eighteen hundred years. No mere impersonal chant of a multitude speaking in unison, but a personal human voice revealing the speaker as well as the things spoken.

It is the entire absence of intentional prominence on the part of the writer, that makes this unintentional translucence of his personality all the more remarkable. Unlike all the epistles canonically included in the New Testament, there is no mention of the writer's name. Even the Epistle to the Hebrews, with its contested authorship, beginning like an impersonal treatise, ends with an 'I beseech you' and 'I will see you.' But in the epistle called St. Clement's not once does the writer use the personal pronoun.

Yet surely we know this Bishop of Rome, this one saint of renown who links our English Calendar with the early Greek ages of the Church, better than many the external details of whose life are familiar to us. Greek in speech,

Jewish in training and sacred patriotic memories, Roman in world-wide sympathy, in love of law and order, and in tact of ruling. If we do not know the circumstances of his life we know its inspirations, what he loved, what he hoped, what he lived for. And if the conjecture that he was a freedman of the Flavian family is true, it is a beautiful prophetic intimation of the great reconcilings of Christianity, that Jew and Gentile, bond and free, should actually be blended in the person of this earliest of the Apostolic Fathers, that this great peace-making bishop of the great imperial city should once have been a slave.

The Legend of the Martyrdom of St. Clement weaves these historical recollections into a touching kind of allegory. It tells us that a fierce persecution of the Christians arose in Rome in the reign of Trajan, and Clement was accused; but many of the people so honoured him for his benevolent and holy life and his kindness to the poor that they wished to save him. When he was brought before the tribunal, Mauritius, the prefect, could find no fault in him and pleaded for him with the Emperor. But Trajan said Clement must sacrifice to the idols, and as nothing would induce him to betray his faith he was banished to the Tauric Chersonese. Mauritius wept when he pronounced the sentence. 'God will not abandon thee,' he said. But Clement was banished to the Crimea, where he found two thousand Christians who had been banished thither before, and were working in the mines. These the good bishop greatly encouraged, so that his exile proved a blessed mission. He found the captives in great distress from want of water, which they had with great toil to bring from ten miles off. He encouraged them to pray for help, and himself knelt down and prayed with them. And as he prayed he lifted up his eyes and saw on a mountain a Lamb which pointed with its right foot to the place of a spring of water. None else saw this lamb, but Clement knew it must be the Lamb of God. At once he went to the spot, stuck his spade into the ground, and an abundant fountain of water gushed up immediately to satisfy the thirst of this company of Christian confessors. The water of life also flowed forth there through Clement's word from the Eternal Fountain of Life, at the touch of the Lamb of God, and multitudes of heathen believed and were baptised.

The Emperor, indignant at these conversions, sent soldiers to seize the new converts. They yielded themselves joyfully to martyrdom. And at length St. Clement himself was thrown into the sea with an anchor round his neck— that no precious relics might be left for his people to honour. But the Christians prayed that they might yet find the martyred bishop's body. And suddenly the sea retired three miles, and the body of the saint was found in a fine white marble shrine, which the angels had built over it, in the depths of the sea, and beside it the anchor, the instrument of his martyrdom.

And every year afterwards at his festival the sea retired for seven days, that the Christians might worship at his tomb.

Thus it happens that the living fountain and the anchor are the characteristic symbols of St. Clement in sacred Art.[1]

---

[1] An anchor on the buttons of the beadles and on the weathercock is the device of the parish of St. Clement's in the Strand. There are forty-seven churches dedicated in his name in England. See Mrs. Jameson, *Sacred and Legendary Art*.

St. Perpetua[1]
Of Carthage.
March 7.

(Martyred 203 A.D. Sarum Epistle and Gospel: 1 Cor. vii. 25-34; St. Matt. xxvi. 1-13.)

It seems best to include in the second century the story of the Carthaginian martyr St. Perpetua, who, though she suffered in the third century, A.D. 203, lived the longer portion of her brief life of twenty-two years in the second.

Not only in date but in character her story forms a link between the early days of the origins and the later times of fuller organisation, and also between Eastern and Western Christendom.

Between the deaths of St. Clement of Rome and Perpetua come the three great martyr stories of St. Ignatius, St. Polycarp, and the martyrs of Lyons and Vienne, all written by eye-witnesses.

But while the stories of Ignatius, Polycarp, and Blandina are told in Greek, the 'Acts of St. Perpetua, St. Felicitas, and her associates' are in Latin.

It seems well, therefore, to place her thus apart from the great cluster of martyrdoms under Decius and Diocletian in the third century, because while her birth and her mother tongue link her with Latin Christendom, the occasion of her death and the character of her confession seem to associate her rather with earlier days.

The great persecutions of Decius and Diocletian in the third century are named naturally after the emperors who promoted them. They were the last conscious, determined, organised struggles of the central Imperial power, awakened

---

[1] Sketches of the martyrdoms of St. Ignatius, St. Polycarp, and the martyrs of Lyons have been introduced as preparatory to the Acts of Perpetua.

to perceive the imperial and universal claims of the religion with which it had to do.

The persecutions of the second century were local and accidental, the results of outbreaks of personal irritation or of popular jealousy. They arose not at Rome but at Antioch, at Smyrna, at Carthage, or at such colonial cities as Lyons and Vienne, in Gaul.

The persecution which led to the martyrdom of St. Ignatius is said in the ancient story to have arisen out of the impatience of the triumphant Emperor Trajan at encountering in the midst of his victories a small new religious society, which professed allegiance to a Sovereign whose commands were superior to his, and dared to resist his will. It was on his way from victories over the Scythian Dacians and as he pushed on to further conquests over the Armenians and Parthians, that he was thus irritated by the resistance of the little community of the Christians, yet lacking to complete the subjugation of all things to himself; and he threatened them with persecution unless they 'worshipped the dæmons, as did all the nations.'

'Then Ignatius, Bishop of Antioch, the noble soldier of Christ, who had piloted his people through the persecution of Domitian and other dangers by the helm of prayer and fasting, by the earnestness of his teaching, and by his constant spiritual labours, was by his own desire confronted with the Emperor.'[1]

It was rather as a voluntary champion of his flock than as a victim he stood forth.

Two desires possessed him, as a good shepherd desiring 'not to lose the faint-hearted and the defenceless, and also himself to enter into a closer relation with his Lord by the confession of martyrdom.'[1]

Ignatius was called Theophorus, a name translated by tradition into a legend that he was the little child borne by Christ in His arms to set before the disciples the example of

---

[1] Ruinart, *Acta Sincera Martyrum*, pp. 62, 63 (the Greek version).

what they must be to enter the Kingdom of Heaven; but by Ignatius himself, according to ancient story, interpreted to mean not that he was borne, but that he bore the Christ in his heart.

This illuminated moment of conversation between the emperor of the world and the servant of Christ, recorded for us in the contemporary Greek 'Acta,' gives us a wonderfully vivid glimpse into the past.

Trajan: 'Who are those cacodæmons (evil dæmons) hastening to transgress our commands, and persuading others also that they should miserably perish?'

Ignatius: 'No one calls Theophorus an evil dæmon, for all the dæmons have departed from the servants of God; but if indeed I am grievous to these, and if thou callest me evil to the dæmons, this I confess; for having Christ, who is the heavenly King, I do indeed dissolve their devices.'

Trajan: 'And who is this Theophorus?'

Ignatius: 'He who has Christ in his breast.'

Trajan: 'Do we, then, seem to thee to have no gods in our mind, we on whose side the gods fight against our enemies?'

Ignatius said: 'The dæmons of the nations, in an illusion, thou proclaimest to be gods; for there is one God who made man and earth and the sea and all things therein, and one Christ Jesus, the only begotten Son of God, for whose kingdom I am longing.'

Trajan: 'Dost thou speak of Him who was crucified under Pontius Pilate?'

Ignatius: 'I speak of Him who has crucified my sin, with him who devised it, and has put all delusion and evil under the feet of those who bear Him in their hearts.'

Trajan: 'Then thou bearest the Crucified in thy heart?'

Ignatius: 'Yes, for it is written, "I will dwell in them and walk in them."'

Then Trajan answered, 'This Ignatius, who says he bears about within him the Crucified, we command to be taken, bound, by soldiers to Great Rome, to become the prey of wild beasts for festivity to the people.'

Then Ignatius exclaimed with joy, 'I thank Thee, O Supreme Lord, that Thou hast deigned to honour me with the perfecting of love to Thee, permitting me, like thine Apostle Paul, to be bound with chains.'

And so with great eagerness and joy the longing of his heart to suffer for his Redeeming Lord was fulfilled, and Ignatius was carried bound to Rome. On his way he poured out his heart in his Epistle to the Romans. 'Now I begin to be a disciple. Fire and cross, troops of wild beasts, rending of every limb, dire torments of the Devil, let them come to me, if only I may follow Jesus Christ. . . . Living I write to you, longing to die. My Love is crucified. I long for the Bread of God, the Bread of heaven, the Bread of Life, which is the flesh of Jesus Christ, the Son of God. I long for the wine [1] of God, His own blood, which is love incorruptible, and eternal life.'

At last, having reached great Rome, 'and there on his knees called on the Son of God that the persecution might cease, and that the brethren might love one another, he was thrown to the cruel beasts in the amphitheatre; and, as he wished, gave no trouble to the brethren in collecting his relics, for nothing was left but a few hard bones.' 'These they gathered with reverence and many tears; and some that very night in a vision saw the blessed Ignatius praying, whilst others saw him coming forth with the sweat of the travail of his agony on him, and beside him the Lord, sustaining him.'

And having with much joy seen these visions, the brethren then 'sang hymns of praise to God, Giver of all good things, and called the martyr holy and blessed.'

This was at Rome, A.D. 107, on the 20th day of December.

As individual is the story of Polycarp, to whom, while yet in his prime, the martyr Ignatius wrote one of his letters.

---

[1] (Drink, πόμα θεοῦ) Ruinart, 67

MARTYRS OF THE SECOND CENTURY

This almost the earliest of the martyr stories can be read by all in the words of the members of the Church of Smyrna, who saw the venerable bishop die, and 'would gladly each of them have died as he died.'[1]

A local popular tumult seems to have been the occasion of the persecution, intensified by the hatred of the Jews.

No passionate longing to suffer seems to have moved Polycarp or the Church he ruled, but only the quiet determination to do and suffer the will of God. 'We do not commend those who give themselves up,' they write; the one of them who did thus give himself up, they observe, was the one who failed in courage, and denied.

The aged bishop would have stayed in the city to await what might come. It was the wish of the people not to lose him that persuaded him to take refuge in the country house where he was arrested.

The magistrates evidently were more favourable to him than the mob. Among these were some infuriated, apparently, by fear of loss to their religion or their craft, and besides these the Jewish colony, the old hatred from which St. Paul suffered further embittered by the destruction of their Temple.

'This is the master of Asia,' the crowd cried scornfully when he was led into the Stadium, 'the father of the Christians, the enemy of our gods.' And to these Polycarp cried, indignantly retorting their accusation, 'Away with the godless!' and spoke of the 'enduring fire,' so different from the 'transitory flames' to which they condemned him.

At every stage of his trial his dignity and gentleness seem to have touched his enemies.

The soldiers sent to arrest him willingly suffered him to finish his prayer; and for two hours they listened while he stood and prayed; and many repented that they had come forth against so godly and lovable an old man.

The Irenarch and his father took him up in their chariot with all honour, and would have persuaded him there could

[1] Ruinart.

be no harm in sacrificing to the genius of Cæsar. But when their persuasions failed, they pushed the old man down from the chariot, so that he strained his ankle and limped quietly along on foot without a complaint.

Then the Proconsul entreated him to respect his age. 'Swear and denounce the Christ, and I will set thee at liberty,' he said, thus calling forth the tender, loyal answer which has rung through all the ages since.

'*Eight and sixty years have I served Him, and He has done me no injustice. How, then, can I blaspheme my King, who has saved me?*'

When Polycarp asked the Proconsul, if he wished 'to know what Christianity is, to fix a day of public audience, the only reply was that he might "persuade the people."' 'And when he saw that no threats of wild beasts or fire terrified him, but that he was filled with confidence and joy, the Proconsul was astonished, and sent his herald to proclaim three times in the Stadium, "Polycarp has professed himself to be a Christian."'

Thus the feeble, tremulous tones of the old man's confession were taken up by the herald's cry.

The Asiarch refused to yield to the cry of the populace that Polycarp should be given to the lions, the regular games being over, and he was sentenced, as he had foretold, to be burned alive. He submitted gently to all the preparations, only resisting when they would have fixed him with nails to the stake, saying, 'He who gives me to suffer by fire will enable me to stand unmoved by the pyre.'

There also the persecutors waited for him to finish his prayer. As he lifted up his eyes to heaven he said, standing before the pyre, 'Lord God Omnipotent, Father of Thy beloved and blessed Son Jesus Christ, through whom we have received the knowledge of Thee; God of the angels and the heavens, and of the whole creation, and of all the generations of the just ones who live before Thee, I bless Thee that Thou hast thought me worthy of this day and hour, that I should have a part in the number of Thy martyrs, and the cup of Thy Christ, unto the resurrection of eternal life, of soul and body, in the incorruptible life of the Holy Spirit; among whom (Thy martyrs) I desire to be received to-day before Thee, a ripe [fat] and acceptable sacrifice, as Thou hast prepared and foreshown and fulfilled, Thou the true God who canst not lie. Wherefore for all things I bless Thee, I glorify Thee, with the eternal and heavenly Jesus Christ, Thy beloved Son, with whom to Thee and the Holy Spirit be glory now and in the ages to come. Amen.'

And 'after that Amen the men of fire kindled the fire,' and it seemed to those who saw him that the flames formed themselves above his head into a triumphal arch into the heavenly city he was entering, and a fragrance as of Paradise floated round him; that his body shone like silver and gold; and the fire could not burn him, so that the death stroke was given by the executioner; and his blood extinguished the flames, and a dove, gentle as his spirit, came forth thence and flew to heaven. But some of the Jews cried out that the Christians would abandon the Crucified to worship Polycarp, and the unconsumed body was thrown again into the flames. 'For they are ignorant that we are not able to abandon the Christ who suffered for the salvation of all that are saved through the whole world, the Blameless for the sinful; Him, being indeed the Son of God, we worship; but the martyrs as disciples and followers of the Lord we love on account of their surpassing fidelity to Him our King and Master, with whom may it be given to us also to be partakers and fellow disciples.'

So at last the poor scorched bones were taken up and laid up 'as precious treasures dearer than gold.'

'Now the blessed Polycarp suffered martyrdom on the seventh day before the calends of May, on the great Sabbath at the eighth hour, Statius Quadratus being Proconsul; but Jesus Christ being King for ever, to whom be glory, honour, majesty, and an eternal throne. 'These things Gaius copied from Irenæus, a disciple of Polycarp, who himself

[1] Ruinart, p. 93.

was intimate with Irenæus ; and Socrates copied it again in Corinth from Gaius. God be with all ! '[1]

This was at Smyrna, on the hill above the Mediterranean Sea, A.D. 140.

The next of these earliest martyr stories leads us to the heart of France, to the banks of the Rhone, though the sufferers were many of them also of Asiatic birth, and the letter of the survivors was written in Greek from the Churches of Lyons and Vienne to their brethren in Asia and Phrygia.

Equally local, and apparently accidental, is the persecution, equally genuine the record, but in this instance it is no well-known names of veteran leaders of the flock which shine out most gloriously, but those of a boy of fifteen and a slave girl, Saturus and Blandina.

Their glory is in the mighty grace of God, which enabled the weak to resist, 'like firm and stable columns,' all the assaults of the enemy.

Some indeed of higher degree were among them, and Bishop Pothinus was the first to suffer, being beaten and dragged through the streets without respect for his ninety years.

'But the eyes of all were especially directed to the boy of fifteen, the neophyte Saturus, who endured unutterable tortures for days, and the girl Blandina, racked, scorched, tossed by beasts, and finally fixed to a stake in the amphitheatre, where the brethren, as on this her cross she most contentedly pleaded for them all, beheld in her, stretched in anguish there, with their bodily eyes a visible image of the Crucified Lord, and were sustained as by the sight of Him.

'For with such strength was that feeble one endued that the torturers, succeeding each other from the first light to evening, wondered at her capacity for suffering. But that blessed one, like a noble athlete, drew strength and courage from her own confession, and found refreshment

[1] Ruinart.

and rest, and lost all sense of the present pain, in simply repeating these words: "I am a Christian, and nothing evil is done amongst us."[1]

The courage of some did indeed fail through those long days of torture; but those who had stood firm through all had not a word of reproach for the lapsed, but only sought tenderly to encourage and restore them, which indeed they did, 'the measureless mercy of Christ shining on them again through the forbearance of those who loved Him.' And as they died, like Stephen, the first martyr, the sufferers prayed for their persecutors.

'So,' the survivors write, 'last of all, as a noble mother, who had inspired her sons to a noble conflict, and sent them victors before her, Blandina herself went by the same path they had trodden, exulting, not as one thrown to the beasts, but as a guest at a marriage feast.'[1]

This was in A.D. 177, in the reign of Marcus Aurelius.

And as Blandina suffered and overcame, not only did her heroism manifest again the Crucified, for whom she suffered; she proved for all time that a Kingdom, a heavenly City, had come, in which the noblest battles could be won by womanhood and the highest honours might rest on the head of the slave.

'Brave athlete' the brethren call this weak woman; 'noble matron and mother' they felt her to be, this helpless slave girl.

Around the writings of the great martyred bishops Ignatius and Polycarp many controversies have gathered. They, as men building up in order and solidity the kingdom which was to absorb all that was high in Greek culture and Roman law, had, besides their higher conflicts, to wage war also on earthly ground, among things temporal, for law and order, and the great framework of the City of God.

But the lives of women, because of their lowliness and simplicity, sometimes lead us to the deeper sources, the things human and Divine which underlie the things ecclesiastical, the moral and spiritual depths common to all

[1] Ruinart.

lands and ages, common to earth and to heaven, in the kingdom which is righteousness and peace and joy in the Holy Ghost.

The roll of the earliest martyrs of this period may therefore well close with the story of that tender and noble Carthaginian woman who is commemorated in our Anglican Calendar.

The Passion of SS. Perpetua and Felicitas, with their Companions.[1]

'There were arrested the young catechumens Revocatus and his fellow slave Felicitas, Saturninus and Secundulus; and among these also Vivia (Ubia) Perpetua, honourably born, liberally educated, a freeborn matron, married according to the most honourable rites (*matronaliter nupta*); having a father and a mother and two brothers, one of these a catechumen like herself; and also an infant son at the breast. Her age was about twenty-two. *She herself narrated the whole order of her martyrdom, and left it written by her own hand*, in her own sense and meaning.

'"When," she says, "we were with the persecutors, and my father would persevere in turning me aside and casting me down" [i.e. from the faith] "out of his affection for me, 'Father,' I say, 'thou seest, for example, this vessel lying on the ground, a little pitcher, or whatever else it may be?'

'" And he said, 'I see.'

'" And I said to him, 'Can I call it by any other name than what it is?'

'" And he answered, 'No.'

'"' So also I cannot say of myself that I am anything else but a Christian.'

'" Then my father, moved by that word, cast himself on me as if he would have torn out my eyes, but he only hurt me, and, overcome by the arguments of the devil, he departed. Then when for a few days I had been severed

---

[1] Translated from Ruinart's *Acta Sincera Martyrum*.

from my father I gave thanks to the Lord and was comforted for his absence.

' "In that interval of a few days we were baptised; and to me the Spirit suggested to ask nothing else in the water save patience to suffer in the flesh.

' "After a few days we were received into the prison, and I was sorely terrified, because never before had I experienced such darkness. O bitter day—from the great heat of the multitudes shut up there, and from the violence of the soldiers! I was also fretting with anxiety for my babe. But then Tertius and Pomponius, the blessed deacons who ministered to us, obtained, for a price, that, for a few hours each day, being sent into a better part of the prison, we might be refreshed. Then going out all together from the prison, they were at leisure and had space by themselves; whilst I could suckle my babe, already weak from want of food. I spoke anxiously about him to my mother and I encouraged my brother, and I committed the little son [to them]. For their sakes I was myself pining away, because I saw them pining away for my sake. From such solicitudes I suffered many days, and at last I prevailed to have my baby with me in the prison; and at once I regained strength and was relieved from the travail of soul and anxiety for the babe, and the prison became to me as a palace, and I had rather be there than anywhere else.

' "Then my brother said to me, 'Lady, my sister, now already thou art in great honour, so great that thou mayest well ask for a vision; it may be shown to thee whether our passion is to be accomplished or whether we shall yet go freely hither and thither again.' And I, who knew that I held converse with the Lord, from whom I had already received so many benefits, fearlessly promised this to him, saying, 'To-morrow I will bring back word to thee.'

' " And I asked, and this thing was shown to me : I see a golden stair of wonderful height reaching up to heaven, and withal so narrow that only one could go up at a time; and in the sides of the stair were inserted all kinds of implements of iron. There were daggers, spears, hooks, swords [a Greek word], so that if anyone climbed those steps carelessly, or not looking upwards, he would be wounded and his flesh would be left on the iron weapons. And there was beneath that staircase a dragon crouching, of wonderful size, who was always devising traps and stratagems against those who were ascending that stair, and seeking to terrify them, that they might not dare to ascend at all. Saturus ascended first, who was not with us when we were apprehended, but gave himself up freely afterwards; and he reached the top of the stair and turned to me, and said to me, 'Perpetua, I am sustaining thee. But see that that dragon seize thee not.' And I said to him, '*He will not hurt me, in the name of the Lord Jesus Christ.*' And from beneath the stair, as if he feared me, the dragon slowly raised his head; and when I trod the first step, I had trodden on his head; and I went up, and I saw a boundless space of a garden, and in the midst of the garden, sitting, a Man, hoary-headed and tall, in the clothing of a shepherd; great and stately, and He was milking the sheep; and around Him were standing many thousands clothed in white. And He lifted up his head and looked at me and said to me, 'Child [a Greek word], thou art welcome.' And He called me, and of the cheese of the milk He gave me a small mouthful, and I received it with joined hands and ate, and all those who stood around said, 'Amen.' And at the sound of that voice I awoke, still eating something of I know not what sweetness; and I brought back word at once to my brother, and we understood that our passion was to be; and we began to have no hope in this world.

' " After a few days the rumour came that we were to be tried. But my father also arrived from the city, and he came up to me and sought to cast me down, saying, 'Have compassion, my daughter, on my grey hairs; have compassion on thy father, if I am worthy to be called thy father. If, with these hands, I have brought thee up to the flower of thy age, if I have loved thee beyond all thy brothers, give me not to be dishonoured among men. Have regard to thy brothers; consider thy mother and thy mother's sister; consider thy son, who will not be able to live without thee. Lay aside thy purpose, lest thou destroy us all, for none of us will be able to speak freely if thou shouldst suffer.'

"'These things my father said, in his fatherly affection, kissing my hands and throwing himself at my feet; and with tears he went on calling me not 'child,' but 'lady' and 'mistress.' And I was full of pain, grieved at heart for the grey hairs of my father, who alone of all my kindred would not be able to rejoice in my passion [martyrdom]; and I comforted him, saying, 'On the scaffold (at the tribunal), that will be done which God has willed; for know that we are not placed in our own power, but in God's.' And he departed from me very sorrowful.

"'The next day, while we were at our morning meal, suddenly we were laid hold of, that we might be examined, and we came to the Forum. At once the tidings spread through the neighbourhood of the Forum, and there was an immense gathering of the people. We went up to the tribunal. The others were questioned and made their confession. Then it came to my turn, and my father appeared there with my little son, and he drew me down from the step and said entreatingly, 'Have mercy on thy babe;' and Hilarianus, the prætor, who then, in the place of the proconsul Minucius Timinianus, lately dead, had received the power of the sword, said, 'Spare the grey hairs of thy father; spare the infancy of the boy; make the sacrifice for the Emperor.' And I replied to him, '*I do it not.*' Hilarianus said, 'Art thou a Christian?' and I answered, '*I am a Christian.*' And as my father still stood there to cast me down" [from the faith] "command was given by Hilarianus that he should be cast down and smitten with a rod; and it grieved me that this should happen to my father, as if I had been smitten myself, so was I grieved for his sorrowful old age. Then he sentenced us all together and condemned us to the wild beasts; and rejoicing we descended to the prison.

"'Then, because my babe was wont to take the breast

and to remain with me in the prison, immediately I sent Pomponius, the deacon, to seek the babe; but my father would not give him up, and, as God willed, neither did the child much long for the breast, neither did much suffering ensue to me, that I should be weakened by the longing for the child, and by pain.

'"After a few days, whilst we were all together praying, suddenly in the middle of the prayer a voice came to me, and I uttered the name of *Dinocrates*;[1] and I wondered much, because never had he come into my mind except then, and I mourned, remembering his sufferings; and I recognised immediately that I was considered worthy to pray also for him; and I began to make much prayer for him and to groan for him to the Lord. And continuously through that night he was shown to me in a vision. I see Dinocrates going forth from a place of darkness where many were gathered, oppressed with burning heat and thirsting; his countenance wretched, pallid in hue, and the wound in his face which he had when he died. This Dinocrates was my brother in the flesh, seven years of age, who suffered from a terrible cancer in his face, so that his death was a horror to all men. For him I made supplication; and between me and him there was a great interval [gulf], so that I could not come to him nor he to me. And there was in that place where Dinocrates was a pond full of water; but its edge was too far down for the child to reach, and Dinocrates stretched himself down as if to drink. I grieved because that pool had water, and yet because of the depth of its margin the child could not reach it; and I woke, perceiving how my brother was toiling. But I was confident that my prayer would help his toil, and I prayed for him every day until we went into the prison of the Castle. That was on the birthday of Geta Cæsar, and I prayed for him night and day, groaning and weeping, that he might be given to me.

'"But on the day on which we were kept in fetters this vision was manifested to me. I beheld that place which

---

[1] Her little brother who had died in childhood.

before I had seen all in darkness now full of light, and Dinocrates, the child, clean and fair in body, clothed in fine raiment, his thirst refreshed ; and where the wound had been I saw a scar, and in that pool of water which I had seen out of his reach the boy standing to his waist; and he drew water from it without ceasing ; and on its margin was a vessel full of water, and Dinocrates went up to it and began to drink of it, for that vessel failed not nor grew empty. And his thirst assuaged, he went away from that water full of glee to play, as little children are wont ; and I awoke. Then I understood that he was translated out of his torment.

'"Then after a few days Pudens, an officer placed over the prison, who began to make much of us, perceiving the great power of God in us, admitted many of the brethren to see us, that we might refresh each other in turn.

'" But when the day of the festival drew nigh my father came in to see me, consumed with grief, and began to tear his beard, and to throw himself on the ground, and to prostrate himself on his face, and to upbraid his age, and to say words which would have moved the heart of any creature. I indeed mourned for his unhappy old age.

'" The day before we were to have our conflict I saw in a vision Pomponius, the deacon, come to the door of the prison and knock vehemently. I went out and opened the door to him. He was clothed in white raiment adorned with a multitude of pomegranates ;[1] and he said to me, 'Perpetua, we expect thee : come !' and he took my hand and we began to go by a narrow, winding way. We had scarcely arrived, panting for breath, at the amphitheatre, when he led me into the middle of the arena and said to me, 'Fear not ; I am here with thee, and with thee I share the labour.' And he departed. And I beheld around me an immense astonished multitude ; and because I knew I was to be given to the wild beasts I wondered that no wild beasts were sent to me. And there came forth a certain

[1] Referring, probably, to the vestments of the High Priest (Ruinart).

Egyptian, foul in face, with his assistants to combat with me; and there came also to me noble youths to stand on my side and aid me; and I was unclothed of my womanhood and became as a man; and my friends anointed me with oil, as it is wont to anoint the wrestlers for the conflict; and on the other hand I saw the Egyptian rolling in the sand.[1] And there came forth a man of marvellous stature, so that he rose above the top of the ampitheatre, having a flowing purple garment, with two keys in the middle of his breast, and a multitude of gold and silver pomegranates, of many forms, bearing a rod like the captain or trainer of the gladiators, and also a green bough, on which were golden apples; and he demanded silence, and said, 'If this Egyptian overcomes her let him slay her with the sword, but if she overcomes him she shall receive this bough;' and he retired, and we came to the encounter and began to deal blows. He sought to seize my feet, but I struck him in the face with my heels; and I was lifted up into the air, and began to smite him as if I trampled on the earth. But when I saw a pause in the fight I clasped hands, finger against finger; and I seized his head and he fell on his face, and I trod on his head; and the people began to cry out and my friends to sing with joy. And I went up to the captain [*lanista*] and received the bough; and he kissed me and said to me, 'Daughter, peace be with thee.' And I began to go, with glory, towards the Sanevivarian Gate. And then I awoke; and I understood that not with the wild beasts but with the Devil my combat was to be; but I knew that victory was before me. This I did the day before the gladiatorial games; but when the games are over, if anyone will, let him describe it."

'But the blessed Saturus [Perpetua's brother] also described his vision, which he also wrote: "We had suffered," he said, "and we went forth from the flesh and began to be borne by four angels, whose hands nevertheless touched us not, towards the east. But we went not up-

---

[1] I.e. the sand with which the wrestlers were sprinkled after being anointed (Ruinart).

wards reclining, but as if we were ascending a gentle slope. And being set free, we saw the primal boundless light; and I said, "Perpetua" (for she was by my side), this is what the Lord promised us; we have received the promise.' And whilst we were still borne onward by those four angels a great space opened around us which was like a green garden, having rose trees in it and all kinds of flowers.

'"But the height of the rose trees was as that of cypresses, and their leaves were falling ceaselessly to the ground. And there, in that green garden, were other four angels, brighter than the first four, who when they saw us paid us honour, and said, wondering, to the other angels, 'Lo, they are here! Lo, they are here!' And the other angels who were carrying us were astonished, and set us down; and with our own feet we walked a mile on a broad road. There we found Jocundus and Saturninus and Artaxius, who, suffering in the same persecution, were burned alive; and Quintus, who went forth a martyr from the prison. And we asked them where were the rest; but the angels said to us, 'Come ye first, enter, and salute the Lord.'

'"And we came near to a place of which the walls are as if they were built of light; and before the gate of that place stood four angels who, as we entered, clothed us in white raiment. And we, thus clothed in white, entered in and saw the boundless light, and heard one united voice of those who said continually, 'Holy, Holy, Holy' [in Greek, 'Agios, Agios, Agios,' the great Eucharistic hymn]. And we saw in the midst of that place, sitting, One like a hoary-headed man, having hairs white as snow, and with youth in His face, whose feet we did not see. And on the right hand and on the left stood four-and-twenty elders, and behind them many others.

'"We entered with great wonder, and we stood before the throne. And four angels lifted us up, and we kissed Him, and He passed His hand over our faces. And the other elders said, 'Let us stand.' And we stood and gave the kiss of peace. And the elders said to us, 'Go and play.' And I said, 'Perpetua, thou hast what thou desirest.' And she said to me, 'Thanks be to God; for whatever gladness I had when in the flesh my gladness is greater now.'

'"And we went forth and saw outside Optatus, the bishop, on the right, and Aspasius, the presbyter, on the left, apart and sad, and they placed themselves at our feet and said to us,[1] 'Keep together with us, for ye are going forth and leaving us behind." And we said to them, 'Art not thou our father, and thou our presbyter? Wherefore do ye place yourselves at our feet?' and we went forward and embraced them. And Perpetua began to talk with them in Greek, and we gathered together in the garden under a rose tree. And whilst we were speaking to them, the angels said to them, 'Let them alone, that they may refresh themselves; and if ye have any dissensions among you dismiss them mutually from among you.' And they reproved them ("conturbaverunt eos"), and they said to Optatus, 'Correct thy people, because they gather to thee thus as if they were returned from the circus and as if they were contending in the factions.'[2]

'"And it seemed to us as if they (the angels) were about to close the gates. And then we began to recognise many brethren, also martyrs. And we were each and all nourished with an unutterable fragrance, which satisfied us. . . . . Then full of joy I awoke."

'These are the famous visions of the most blessed martyrs Saturus and Perpetua, which they wrote together. But God called Secundulus by an earlier departure, whilst still in the prison, not without favour; that he might have the gain of being thrown to the wild beasts without enduring the anguish—a relief to the flesh, if not to the soul.

'But concerning Felicitas (the slave) she was in great grief as the day of the spectacles approached, lest, being pregnant for eight months, for her the day of the conflict should be deferred, because it is not lawful for pregnant women to appear in the amphitheatre, and lest afterwards she should have to shed her innocent blood amongst other common malefactors.

---

[1] There seems in this vision some echo of divisions in the Church.
[2] Ruinart and Böhringer, *Kirchengeschichte*.

'And her fellow martyrs also mourned sorely with her, lest they should have to leave so dear an associate and companion alone behind, not having attained her hope. And so with one united sigh of supplication they poured forth prayer to the Lord before the third day of the festival. Immediately after the prayer her travail came upon her. And when, with premature labour, she was suffering great anguish, one of the servants who kept the iron gates of the prison said to her, "If thou sufferest thus now, what wilt thou do when thou art thrown to the wild beasts, which thou hadst in such contempt, refusing to sacrifice?" And she answered, "*Now it is I only who suffer what I suffer; then Another will be in me who will suffer for me, because I also shall be suffering for Him.*" So she travailed and brought forth her child, whom a certain sister brought up as her own daughter.

'Since, therefore, the Holy Spirit has permitted, and so permitting has willed, that the order of that festival should be recorded, although unworthy to supplement the story of so great glory, nevertheless as a mandate from the most holy Perpetua, as a trust committed to us by her, we follow up her words, adding this record of her constancy and greatness of soul.

'When they were treated with greater severity by the tribune because he feared, from the warnings of foolish men, lest they should be withdrawn from the prison by magical incantations, Perpetua answered to his face and said, "Why dost thou not permit us, most noble of criminals, belonging forsooth to Cæsar and about to celebrate his birthday by our combat, to have some refreshment ordered? Is it not thy glory if we come forth well fattened for his festival?" The tribune was shocked and blushed, and at once gave orders that they should be treated more humanely, and that their brethren should be allowed free access to them, that same officer Optio (who had been favourable to them) being entrusted with the prison.

'Also on the eve of the games, when that last supper

is given which is called the "free supper,"[1] they held no "free supper," but celebrated indeed, as far as they could, the supper of the Agape. And faithfully they spoke to the people, warning them of the judgment of the Lord, bearing witness to their joy in their sufferings and smiling at the curiosity of the spectators. Saturus said, "To-morrow seems not enough for you that ye may gaze on us at your pleasure and listen to us; to-day friends, to-morrow enemies. Nevertheless observe our faces diligently, that ye may recognise us in the Day of Judgment." And at this all departed thence, astonished; and out of these many believed.

'At length the dawn of their day of victory shone in upon them, and they went forth from the prison to the amphitheatre as to heaven, glad, and with a grave dignity in their countenances; trembling, perhaps, but for joy and not for fear. Perpetua followed with a placid countenance and with a step and bearing as of a matron beloved by the Christ of God; looking down, withdrawing the power (*vigorem*) of her eyes from the gaze of all. So also Felicitas, rejoicing that her babe was born, went forth from her travail to the gladiatorial strife as if to be purified by a second baptism. And when they reached the gate, and were to have been compelled to put on, the men the vestments of priests of Saturn, the women those of the priestesses of Ceres, their noble constancy, faithful to the end, refused to be thus arrayed; for they said, ' Freely we have thus come hither by our own will, lest our liberty should be taken from us. For this we have surrendered our lives, that we might not do such things as this: this compact we have made with you; in this you are in justice bound to yield to us."[2] Injustice itself acknowledged the justice of this; the tribune conceded that they should be simply clad, just as they were. Perpetua sang hymns, already trampling on the

---

[1] Those who were condemned to the wild beasts the day before the games had a magnificent public supper (Ruinart, from Tertullian).

[2] Some MSS. say Perpetua spoke in the name of the rest (Böhringer).

head of the Egyptian (the Devil). Revocatus, Saturninus, and Saturus warned the people once more as they looked on. When they came in sight of Hilarian they began to speak to him by sign and gesture. " Thou now judgest us," they said, " but God will judge thee." At this the people were exasperated, and demanded that they should run the gauntlet and be scourged. And they exulted in this as a following of the passion of the Lord.

'But He who said *"Ask and ye shall receive"* gave to each that which each had desired. For when they had discoursed together as to their wish how to be martyred, Saturninus said that he desired to be cast out to all the wild beasts, that he might bear away a more glorious crown. And it came to pass in the ordering of the spectacle that he and Revocatus were tested by a leopard, and also on a stage were worried by a bear. Saturus, on the other hand, abhorred nothing more than a bear, but imagined beforehand that he might be demolished by one bite of a leopard. Accordingly when a wild boar was let out, the huntsman who supplied that wild boar was torn and pierced by him, and himself died the day after the games, whilst Saturus was only dragged along by him. And when he was drawn up on the stage to a bear, the bear would not come forth from his den. And thus the second time Saturus was called back unharmed.

'But for the women the Devil had provided a ferocious cow, eager to make them suffer by a creature of their own sex. Accordingly they were unclothed and brought forth wrapped up in the nets. Then the people were horror-stricken, seeing one in the tenderness of her youth, and the other recently a mother. And they were recalled and clothed in loose garments. Perpetua was first brought in: she was tossed and fell on her side; and as she saw her tunic rent from her side she folded it around her, more mindful of modesty than of her pain. After this, finding it needful, she bound together with a clasp her dishevelled hair; for it did not become a martyr to suffer with dishevelled hair, lest she should seem to mourn on her day of glory as one at a funeral. Then she rose, and when she saw Felicitas lying crushed she went to her and stretched out her hand to her and lifted her up. And both of them stood up, and the hardness of the people was melted and they were recalled to the Sanevivarian Gate. Then Perpetua, being received by a certain catechumen who was devoted to her, and roused, as it were, from sleep (for she had been in the Spirit and in ecstasy), began to look around; and to the amazement of all she said, as if questioning, "I know not when we are to be brought forth to that cow." And when she heard that it was over, at first she did not believe it until she recognised some signs of hurt in her body and in her garments. Then having summoned to her her brother and that catechumen she addressed them and said, "Stand fast in the faith, and all of you love one another, and be not shaken by our sufferings."

'Just so Saturus, her brother, at another gate exhorted the soldier Pudens, saying, "I am here indeed" (present at the roll-call, *adsum*), "as I promised and foretold. Hitherto I have felt nothing from any beast. And now do thou believe with all thy heart. Lo! I shall be *brought forth*, and at one *bite I shall be destroyed by the leopard.*" And immediately, at the end of the spectacle, being thrown to a leopard, with one bite he was so bathed in blood that the people called out to him as he turned back (bearing witness to this second baptism), "Washed and saved! washed and saved!" ("Salvum lotum! salvum lotum!"[1])

'Truly indeed was he saved who shone thus gloriously in that spectacle. Then he said to Pudens the soldier, "*Farewell (Vale); and remember my faith, and let not those things move thee, but confirm thee.*" And at the same time he took the ring from his finger, and dipping it in his own wound,

---

[1] 'The cry of the people mocking the Christian sacred rites. It was known to the populace that the Christians believed men to be saved through baptism, and thus the people seeing, from the theatre, a Christian bathed in blood, proclaimed him "saved," who was thus washed or baptised' (Ruinart).

restored it to him, leaving to him the inheritance of that pledge and the memory of his blood. Then fainting away, he was laid with the rest in the usual place where the final stroke is given. And when the people demanded them to be set in the midst, that as the sword pierced their bodies they might with their own eyes, as it were, be accomplices of the murder, they rose up spontaneously and went whithersoever the people would; but first they kissed each other, that their martyrdom might be consummated with the kiss of peace. The rest indeed immovable and in silence accepted the sword. But Saturus did much more, who both was the first to ascend the stair and the first to yield up his spirit. He also upheld Perpetua. But Perpetua, that she also might taste something of pain, cried out when her side was pierced by the sword, and she herself guided the erring right hand of the inexperienced gladiator against her throat. Perhaps such a woman could not otherwise be slain, because she was feared by the impure spirit and could not be slain unless she willed it.

'O most strong and most blessed martyrs! O truly called and elected to the glory of our Lord Jesus Christ! which glory whosoever magnifies and honours and adores ought to read these not less than the earlier examples given for the edification of the Church, since these new manifestations of power bear witness that One and the Same Holy Spirit is ever working, even until now, with the Omnipotent God the Father and His Son Jesus Christ our Lord, to whom belong brightness of glory and boundless might for ever and ever. Amen.'

We may well rejoice that this sacred story of Perpetua is embalmed in our Calendar.

So natural, so supernatural, so childlike, so sisterly, so motherly, so matronly, how well we seem to know her through those few days illuminated by her own writing! The delight of her father's heart, the friend and scarcely yet having ceased to be the playmate of her young brother! In his vision Perpetua is by his side; the celestial elders say to them both, 'Go and play,' whilst she speaks of the gladness she had on earth and the greater gladness now.

She shrank, like any girl cherished in a loving and luxurious home, from the darkness of the prison, its stifling heat, and the discourtesy of the soldiers, though the prison became like a palace when her little son was left with her there; and yet there was a matronly majesty about her which made the tribune blush with shame when she remonstrated with him on the harshness with which they were treated, and spoke with a high spirit and a fine scorn of the meanness of the additional insults heaped on them; and at the same time there was in her a glowing ardour of devotion which made those who knew her expect that especial visions would be vouchsafed to her.

Not a touch of self-pity; but for the bereaved old age of her father an anguish of compassion. Tossed and gored, and thrown wounded on the ground of the arena, she rose again, calm as in her own chamber, to arrange her dishevelled hair, lest she should seem to be a mourner at the festival of her own martyrdom; and when at her first glance around she saw her fellow sufferer the slave Felicitas lying helpless near, she went and took her hand and lifted her up. The simplicity and gladness, the dignity and calm, the mystic fervour, with the quiet, truthful seeing and speaking of things as they are, we see them all! We see even the 'vigour,' the vivid power of the eyes which she cast down on her way to the amphitheatre.

Whatever else her visions reveal they reveal Perpetua; her sympathy for the little brother thirsting for the living water he cannot reach, the fervour of intercession with which she wins it for him; the putting off as a robe of the womanhood of that most tender woman's heart in her combat with the enemy.

And through all, not apart as rival and contending forces, but pervading and glowing through all, through the Roman matron's dignity, through the child's and mother's tenderness, through the gladness and the anguish, always that supreme, all-pervading, all-mastering passion of loyal love to Christ which made her go forth to the wild beasts, as to heaven, with the bearing and the step of a *matrona dilecta Christi Dei*.

In the vivid record of those few days of Perpetua's life in her own handwriting the whole of the little group around her seem to live and speak and weep and smile. We hear the very tone of their voices. So real is the story, so beautiful, so abounding in individuality of life, that no legend has been able to gather around it, to melt all into a colourless halo. Art itself has had to let her alone. But it is good to have a right to commemorate as the sacred name of one of our beloved taken from our home in all the freshness and glow of youth, the young matron and mother Vivia Perpetua, martyred for Christ at Carthage A.D. 203. Hers is the last of those individual contemporary stories belonging essentially to the second century.

With Ignatius, whose writings are so full of order and discipline, like a general of a great National Army of Liberation, who knows how the freedom of all is depending on the order and obedience of the few who are to fight for the whole, the two sides of his character, as is so often the case, seem represented respectively in his life and in his writings. He shows himself at once the champion of order and the daring herald of individual freedom of conscience and thought, confronting the emperor of the world with fearless courage because of his enthusiasm of loyalty to the crucified King whom he bore in his heart, which made him passionately long to confess Him by the martyr's death.

Polycarp, on the other hand, stands quietly with the calm of his eighty-six years, awaiting the will of God whether to live or die, moving the rulers by his dignity, and encountering the fury of the mob with a spirit as lofty as that with which Ignatius met the emperor.

Blandina, the slave girl, from her stake sustains the courage of all sufferers as a 'noble mother' and a 'brave athlete,' acknowledged as the leader of the martyr band at Lyons. And lastly the young matron Perpetua encourages her friends and kindred in the prison and in the amphitheatre. All are so different and yet so alike. It is the common inspiration breathing through all the varieties of character and circumstance which makes these stories so inspiring, the personal devotion to the crucified Redeemer and King.

For the Christ crucified under Pontius Pilate, who had also crucified and nailed to the Cross his sins, 'the' Christ 'borne in his heart,' Ignatius Theophorus went with eager joy across land and sea to be thrown to the wild beasts in the Roman amphitheatre.

'*Polycarp confesses himself a Christian*' rang out through the stadium at Smyrna in the thrice-repeated proclamation of the herald as he went to stand unbound and erect at the stake, full of confidence and joy.

Blandina found food and refreshment and renewal of strength through all her prolonged tortures in the joy of confessing again and again, 'I am a *Christian*, and among us nothing evil is done.'

At Autun, A.D. 180, the young Symphorian, whom his mother encouraged to die, saying, 'My son, born to-day to heavenly life,' answered with exultation to his judges, 'I am *called* Symphorian. *I am* a Christian.'

Perpetua *could not* say she was not what in her deepest being she was, '*a Christian.*'

For Christ, 'known and tried through the eighty-six years,' Christ crucified, Redeemer, Lord, Son of God, coming to judge the world ; for Christ by their side, in their hearts, Source of all goodness and strength, these Christians died. And so dying for Him they brought to the world for which He died order and freedom ; the largest liberty for the development of all individual life ; the recognition of the unity of humanity ; the breaking down of all barriers that *divide* nations, or class, or sex, the intensifying of all the individual ideals that *distinguish* ; supplementing the needs of each with the gifts of all. They brought order, liberty, unity to the world, a new ideal, for each man and woman, and for the whole. Yet it was not for order, or liberty, or unity they died, or merely for any lofty ideal of humanity, but simply for the love of Christ their Lord. They serve all humanity through their devotion to the Son of Man, the Second Man, the Lord from heaven. Ignatius is more essentially Ignatius, Polycarp Polycarp, Perpetua Perpetua, for being Christian; but it is in Christ that their own true individual life is developed; it is as Christians they have strength to die.

CHAPTER IV.

THE THIRD CENTURY.

WE approach the era of the systematic persecutions ; when the Roman Empire had waked up to the might of the Kingdom which had been silently growing up within it and undermining it by the simple force of life. Once more it is an Emperor who leads the attack, but not now, like Nero, the tyrant in chase of helpless prey, nor even the ruler of the world gathering his strength to crush the society which disputed with him the universal empire. Decius seems rather to have assailed the Church on the grounds which made him revive the censorship, than as the military chief. He was determined to stem the corruption of morals which he saw was sapping the life of Rome, and as a means to this end, in his brief reign of two years, he re-established the office of censor in the city, and sought to revive the religious sanctions of morals, which he believed to be the ancient reverence of the gods. The Christians probably appeared to him enemies of the State, because of their contempt for the ancient religious order of the State.[1]

The cruelties of his persecution seem to have arisen not in the first place from intentional ferocity, but from the determination at any cost to vanquish the resistance of the victims, in an age and a society terribly inured to spectacles of bloodshed and torture. All the practical lessons of history are lost if we represent the enemies of the best as

---

[1] Eusebius speaks of him as a monster of wickedness, but, as in so many other cases, it seems to have been fear of the ruin of what he knew to be good that made him the enemy of the better which he knew not.

monsters. They are so often only the lovers of the second best. From the Decian persecution three martyrs are enrolled in our Calendar—Fabian, Laurence, and Agatha—and we may include St. Cyprian, virtually suffering in consequence of it, although his actual martyrdom occurred under Valerian.

St. Fabian, Bishop and Martyr[1]
OF ROME.
January 20.

(Chosen Bishop of Rome A.D. 236, martyred A.D. 250. Sarum Ep. and Gosp. : Heb. xi. 33-39 ; St. Luke vi. 17-23.)

Fabian was contemporary with the emperors Maximin, Philip the Arabian, Gordian, and Decius. Gordian by his marriage with Fabia Orestilla had entered that great House of the Fabii of which Fabian was a member.

'Fabian, Roman in origin, was the son of Fabius. It is said that Fabian had come to Rome with some others from the country just after the death of Anteros, the bishop, and there, in the most remarkable manner, by Divine and celestial grace, was advanced to be one of the candidates for the vacant office. When all the brethren had assembled in the church (in the catacombs) for the purpose of ordaining him that should succeed Anteros in the episcopate, though there were many eminent and illustrious men in the estimation of many, Fabian being present, no one thought of any other man.

'It is related further that a dove, suddenly flying down from above (through one of the openings—*lucernaria*—of the catacombs), sate upon his head, recalling the scene of the Holy Spirit descending upon our Saviour in the form of a dove (on the banks of the Jordan).

'Upon this the whole body exclaimed, in all eagerness and with one voice, as if moved by the Spirit of God, "He is worthy," and without delay they took him and placed him on the episcopal throne. He was the first elected as a simple layman to be raised to the summit of the hierarchy.'

Cyprian, writing to Fabian's clergy after his death, speaks of the 'glorious departure of the good man his colleague,' and the Roman clergy lament the want of a

---

[1] In all the Calendars associated with St. Sebastian.

bishop to control all things in times of difficulty, and to treat the Lapsed with authority and wisdom, 'since the departure of Fabian, of most noble memory.' He assigned to each of the seven districts of Christian Rome a deacon, and placed under them also seven sub-deacons to direct the notaries previously appointed by St. Clement, charged with collecting the Acts of the Martyrs and completing the arrangements originally made by St. Clement. By his orders numerous constructions were made in the cemeteries and galleries of the catacombs. He brought from Sardinia the body of his predecessor Pontianus, and buried it in the Catacomb of Calixtus, in the Appian Way. There was a tradition that he baptised the Emperor Philip the Arabian; there is also another tradition of his having founded, by missions in Gaul, the seven Churches of Toulouse, Arles, Tours, Paris, Narbonne, Clermont, and Limoges (sending amongst other missionaries St. Denys to Paris); but this also is not insisted on as historical.

His martyrdom (though many of the early Bishops of Rome are in the martyrologies) is, it is said, the first really authenticated of a Roman bishop. The sub-deacon Crementius was sent to Carthage with a letter relating his sufferings in detail. This letter has perished, and all we know now is the fact of his being beheaded under Decius at Rome, January 20, 250, the first victim of the Decian persecution, dearly loved and honoured by his flock. His epitaph, in Greek, is in the Catacomb of Calixtus, in the Appian Way :

FABIANOC+EΠΙ+MP.[1]

Thus, though the facts recorded of him may have to do chiefly with external things, the character which lies underneath—which made it seem no strange thing that the dove-like Divine Spirit should rest upon him, bearing witness to him, the simple layman, as fittest for the highest office —which made Cyprian and his own clergy feel that when he

[1] The MP, for 'martyr,' is less deeply graven in the stone, and is supposed to have been added afterwards.

fell, no other man could be found to deal with the 'authority and wisdom' which he had shown towards the Lapsed, seems essentially that of the true Priest and Good Shepherd, able to restore the fallen, not because He has Himself fallen beneath temptation, but because He has felt the temptation and yet not fallen.[1]

[1] Represented as Pope; at a block, kneeling; with dove, sword, or club.

St. Cyprian (Thascius Caecilius Cyprianus),
Of Carthage.
September 26.

(Martyred A.D. 258. Sarum Ep. and Gosp.: Wisdom v. 15-19;
St. Matt. x. 23-25.)

In all the Calendars the life and work of Cyprian link in so naturally with the story of his contemporary Fabian of Rome that it seems best to place him next in order, although his actual martyrdom took place not under Decius but Valerius.

It is remarkable that three out of the brief roll of saints in our Calendar lived and died on that northern shore of Africa so long since swept bare of Christianity and civilisation by Mahomedan fanaticism and Turkish misrule. After Perpetua, Cyprian, and Augustine, the next vivid page of Christian history associated with North Africa is the story of the capture of St. Vincent de Paul, in the seventeenth century, by the Barbary corsairs.

Of Cyprian's life the only portion really brought into light for us are the ten years between his conversion to Christianity and his martyrdom. For these we have his own letters and treatises,[1] his 'Life and Passion,' by his deacon Pontius, and the 'Acta Proconsularia' of his martyrdom.[2]

His letters are not familiar letters like many of those of St. Ambrose, speaking naturally of his own life and family, or letters of spiritual counsel, like those of St. Jerome, revealing the counsellor's heart in the counsel; they are rather the despatches and orders of a general. There is no allusion in them to father, mother, or kindred, not from any ascetic crushing of natural affections, but because he was, before all things, during those ten years which we see of his life, a bishop and shepherd of the flock. They were years of

---
[1] *Writings of Cyprian*, translated by Rev. Robert Ernest Wallis, Ante-Nicene Christian Library.
[2] Ruinart, *Acta Sincera Martyrum*.

war and pestilence, of frequently recurring persecution and of difficulties brought on by lapses and weaknesses during the persecutions. The whole natural tenderness of his heart went out to the martyrs, to the confessors, to the plague-stricken, the poor, the captives, the lapsed and fallen; these were his kindred and family. All the patriotism and loyalty of his character were spent in expanding and consolidating the Kingdom of Christ; this was his fatherland.

The unity of the City of God was his passion, and yet never unity at the expense of truth and holiness; if he erred, it was in severity on the side of what seemed to him the cause of holiness and truth.

His history begins for us, as his deacon and biographer, Pontius, says, 'with his heavenly birth.'

He was forty-six years of age when the aged presbyter Cæcilius found him and led him to the Christian faith. 'This man he loved with entire honour and all observance, regarding him with an obedient veneration, not only as the friend and comrade of his soul, but as the parent of his new life.' And Cæcilius, on his part, dearly loved Cyprian, and when he was dying confided to him the care of his wife and children. That he could inspire devoted affection is shown by the story of his life and passion by his deacon Pontius, whose heart can be felt through all the draperies of his rhetoric full of a love to which it would have been easier indeed to die with his bishop than to live without him.

His earlier friendships were not broken off by his conversion. To the day of his martyrdom the friends of his earlier years, still pagan, clung around him and sought to save him.

Cypriote in origin, his family were of high standing in the African province in which they had settled; he inherited lands and beautiful gardens along those fertile shores; he was also a trained rhetorician and a professor of philosophy.

There were a high-bred authority and dignity about him; his countenance was 'grave and joyous.'

In dress, and speech, and bearing, and mode of living he disliked exaggeration and eccentricity, though he could appreciate the force of character or genius which led to eccentricity. He would not, as a Christian, assume the 'philosopher's pall,' though Tertullian, whom he called his 'master,' approved of it. If the tropical fire, the vehement rush, the original imagery, the fine incisive point of Tertullian are not in his writings, there are in them a grace and gentleness, a dignity and moderation equally individual and perhaps as rare.

His own account of his conversion and baptism in a letter to Donatus is full of instruction. Christian influence must have been around him before it definitely reached him.

'While I was still lying in darkness and gloomy night, wavering hither and thither, tossed about on the foam of this boastful age, and uncertain of my wandering steps, knowing nothing of my real life, and remote from truth and light, I used to regard it as a difficult matter, and especially as difficult in respect of my character at that time, that a man should be capable of being born again—a truth which the Divine mercy had announced for my salvation—and that a man quickened to a new life in the laver of saving water should be able to put off what he had previously been, and although retaining all his bodily structure should be himself changed in heart and soul. "How," said I, "is such a conversion possible, that there should be a sudden and rapid divestment of all which, either innate in us has hardened in the corruption of our material nature, or acquired by us has become inveterate by long-accustomed use? These things have become deeply and radically ingrained within us. When does he learn thrift who has been used to liberal banquets and sumptuous feasts? And he who has been glittering in gold and purple, and has been celebrated for his costly attire, when does he reduce himself to ordinary and simple clothing? One who has felt the charm of the fasces and of civic honours shrinks from becoming a mere private and inglorious citizen. The man who is attended by crowds of clients and dignified by the numerous association of an officious train regards it as a punishment when he is alone. It is inevitable, as it ever has been, that the love of wine should entice, pride inflate, anger inflame, covetousness disquiet, cruelty stimulate, ambition delight, lust hasten to ruin, with allurements that will not let go their hold.'

'These were my frequent thoughts. For as I myself was held in bonds by the innumerable errors of my previous life, from which I did not believe that I could by possibility be delivered, so I was disposed to acquiesce in my clinging vices; and because I despaired of better things I used to indulge my sins as if they were actually parts of me and indigenous to me. But after that, by the help of the water of new birth, the stain of former years had been washed away, and a light from above, serene and pure, had been infused into my reconciled heart; after that, by the agency of the Spirit breathed from heaven, a second birth had restored me to a new man, then in a wondrous manner doubtful things at once began to assure themselves to me, hidden things to be revealed, dark things to be enlightened; what before had seemed difficult began to suggest a means of accomplishment, what had been thought impossible to be capable of being achieved; so that I was enabled to acknowledge that what previously, being born of the flesh, had been living in the practice of sins, was of the earth, earthly, but had now begun to be of God and was animated by the Spirit of Holiness. . . . All our power is of God; I say, of God. From Him we have life, from Him we have strength. Only let fear be the keeper of innocence, that the Lord, who of His mercy has flowed into our hearts, in the access of celestial grace, may be kept by righteous submissiveness in the hostelry of a grateful mind, that the assurance we have gained may not beget carelessness and so the old enemy creep upon us again.

'But if you keep to the way of innocence, the way of righteousness; if you walk with a firm and steady step; if, depending on God with your whole strength and with your whole heart, you only *be* what you have begun to be, liberty and power to do is given you in proportion to the increase of your spiritual grace. For there is not, as is the case with earthly benefits, any measure or stint in the dispensing of the heavenly gift. The Spirit freely flowing forth is restrained by no limits, is checked by no closed barriers within certain bounded spaces; it flows perpetually, it is exuberant in its affluence. Let our heart only be athirst, and be ready to receive: in the degree in which we bring to it a capacious faith, in that measure we draw from it an overflowing grace.'

The keynote of the life is evidently struck here. Even before his conversion to Christianity it was power to overcome sin of which he felt the need; it was new life, it was holiness for which he longed.

He set himself from the beginning of his Christian life to aim at its highest ideal, and this at a time when the Church around him had grown in some measure cold and feeble through thirty years of peace. And all through it was the same. His love for the Church was for the 'Spotless Spouse,' the 'Holy Mother,' the ideal saintly society.

The strictest purity of life was to him identical with Christianity, and at once he recognised the law of brotherhood by selling his beautiful gardens and two of his estates to distribute among the poor.

His love for the garden he sold (afterwards bought back for him by the Church) is shown in his description of it in the letter to Donatus. 'This vintage festival invites the mind to unbend in repose. Moreover the place is in accord with the season, and the pleasant aspect of the gardens harmonises with the gentle breezes of a mild autumn, in soothing and cheering the senses. In such a place as this it is delightful to pass the day in discourse. That no unrestrained clatter of a noisy household may disturb our converse, let us seek this bower; the neighbouring thickets secure us solitude, and the trailings of the vine branches, creeping in pendent mazes among the reeds that support them, have made for us a porch of vines, a leafy shelter.'

'His house,' Pontius says, 'was open to every comer. No widow returned from him with an empty lap; no blind man was unguided by him as a companion; none faltering in step was unsupported by him as a staff; none stripped of help by the hand of the mighty was not protected by him as a defender."

'Such things ought they to do,' he was wont to say, 'who desire to please God.' A revelation surely of countless quiet acts of kindness in the streets or quiet paths among the vineyards, and in the home, from one who walked day by day by his side.

He had not long been baptised when the Bishop of Carthage died, and the general appreciation of his character was shown by the people crowding round his house, and, though he desired to give place to older men, vehemently insisting on his becoming their bishop.

Some jealousy was felt by a few of the presbyters at his election, but by degrees he won most of those who had resisted; and soon came the fierce test of persecution to prove how true and faithful a leader had been chosen in this wise and gracious man.

Four years after his conversion the Decian persecution broke on the Church throughout the Empire. It soon reached Carthage. The assault was systematically planned. Five commissioners were to sit in every town, and the proconsul was to go on circuit giving judgment. The object was to induce the Christians to deny Christ by open assault, by scourges, racks, wild beasts, and also by subtle wiles, by which many were deceived. A few grains of incense on a shrine of what was really 'nothing at all,' or even a purchase of false certificates that sacrifice had been offered when it had not—and all could be escaped! And hundreds, thousands (in one bitter moment; Cyprian even says, 'the majority') did deny and escape.

Some even rushed to sacrifice at the pagan altars, anticipating their arrest; many of the bishops and clergy lapsed; for the Christians had begun to grow cold and to live at ease. The luxurious life of that delicious climate, the licentiousness of that corrupt society had invaded the Church; and in too many instances the persecution only revealed a lapse into heathenism, and even into the lower depths of heathenism, already begun.

Cyprian was proscribed by the State. The persecution was especially directed against the chiefs of the Church; and his blood was also demanded by the populace of Carthage. 'The bishop to the lions!' was their cry.

He retired into concealment in a place within reach. Deliberately, knowing what calumny might say, and did say, of his flight, he chose *not* to forsake his people by a death which afterwards he proved convincingly he did not fear, but to cleave to them; that so from his hidden post of observation he might be able to direct their movements, to encourage the combatants, to recall the stragglers, to guard against the too easy restoration to posts of trust of those who had proved cowards,—and at the same time to restrain the unforgiving severity of some who had themselves stood firm.

From his retirement Cyprian guided the policy of the whole West upon the tremendous questions of Church communion which now arose.

To comprehend the value of such combined moderation and firmness as he showed, and helped to make prevail, we must remember that the treatment of the lapsed at that time was no question of technical arrangement of detail; it concerned the consolidation, and therefore the very existence, of a community beleaguered on all sides by the enemy, and endangered by treachery within, by the laxity of those who had fallen, and also by the pride of those who had held their ground.

There was a positive danger in those days of the martyrs becoming dictators or rulers of the Church, although the enthusiasm which enabled them to suffer by no means necessarily implied the calmness and wisdom which would fit them to be guides of the community. Cyprian's letters must be studied as a whole to see fully how he honoured the martyrs and confessors, without weakly yielding to their judgment; and what fatherly severity was blended with **tenderness** in his treatment of the lapsed.

'With what praise can I commend you, most courageous brethren,' he writes to the confessors at Carthage in the Decian persecution, 'the strength of your hearts and the perseverance of your faith! The multitude saw with admiration the manly contest, the battle of Christ, saw that His servants stood with free voice, with unyielding mind, bare indeed of weapons of this world, but armed with the weapons of faith. Beaten and torn, they overcame; the scourge, often repeated, could not conquer. What a spectacle was that to the Lord, how acceptable the allegiance and devotion of His soldiery! He was present at His own contest. He animated the champions of His name. He who once conquered death on our behalf always conquers it in us. He Himself also, in our conflict, not only crowns but is crowned.' Then, to encourage those not called to martyrdom, he adds, 'Nor let any one of you be saddened as if he were inferior to those who have suffered tortures. The Lord is the Searcher of hearts. O blessed Church of ours which the honour of the Divine condescension illuminates! She was white, before, in the works of the brethren; now she has become purple, in the blood of the martyrs. Among her flowers are roses and lilies. 'Now let each one strive for crowns, white as of labour, or purple as of suffering. In the heavenly camp both peace and strife have their flowers, with which the soldiers of Christ may be crowned for glory.' And again, speaking of those who had suffered least, 'As far as they could,' he writes, 'they bore whatever they were prepared and equipped to bear.'

Again and again he entreats those who are free, to manifest all care and honour for those who are kept in prison, and sends money to help. And of the martyrs he writes, 'Let us take note of the day on which they depart, that we may celebrate the commemoration.' Yet on the other hand he warns the Confessors that their having borne witness for Christ does not save them from the future temptation of the enemy, but renders them more exposed to his hatred and seductions; he points out that some of those who had faithfully confessed had afterwards fallen into open sin; and faithfully he warns them to be on their guard.

Most precious are these words of warning from one of the martyrs, as to confession or martyrdom in itself being no safeguard from temptation. It is like a vision straight into the heart of the fiery furnace, and a voice from the midst of the fire saying that even there the purifying power comes, not from the fire, but from the Son of God walking within it beside His faithful ones.

And with regard to the lapsed, while he blames their *demanding* to be received again, he tenderly excepts 'some who have lately written to me, who are of the lapsed, but who are meek and humble and fearing God.'

Again, to the presbyters and deacons, guarding against a too hasty restoration to communion, he writes, 'The wounded and unhealthy mind of the lapsed suffers what those who are bodily diseased often suffer; so that while they refuse wholesome food and beneficial drink as bitter and distasteful, they crave those things which are sweet for the present, thereby inviting to themselves mischief and death.'

And again, on the other hand, to the Novatianist confessors, who would have refused remission to the lapsed, he writes these golden words (said to be three times cited by St. Augustine [1]), congratulating them on their return from schism: ' For although there seem to be tares in the Church, yet neither our faith nor our charity ought to be hindered, as if because we see there are tares in the Church we ought to withdraw from the Church. We ought only to labour that *we* may be wheat, that when the wheat shall begin to be gathered into the Lord's barns we may receive fruit for our labour and work. The Apostle in his epistle says, "In a great house there are not only vessels of gold and silver but also of wood and of earth, and some to honour and some to dishonour." Let us strive, dearest brethren, and labour as much as we possibly can that we may be vessels of gold or silver. But to the Lord alone it is granted to break the

---

[1] Dr. Benson (Archbishop of Canterbury), Smith's *Dictionary of Christian Biography.*

vessels of earth, to Whom also is given the rod of iron. The servant cannot be greater than his lord, nor may anyone claim to himself what the Father has given to the Son alone, so as to think that he can take the fan for winnowing and purging the threshing-floor, or can separate by human judgment all the tares from the wheat.'

Greatly, it is said, through the influence of Cyprian's words and character, the decision arrived at by the Council of Carthage and accepted by the whole Church with regard to the lapsed, was that 'the intercession and merits of the martyrs as affecting the conditions of restoration are set aside; whilst, on the other hand (as against Novatian), no offences are to be considered beyond the regular power of the whole Church to remit.[1]

Throughout this difficult navigation it is most interesting to see the Churches of Rome and Carthage in constant consultation, the Roman clergy appealing to Carthage and Cyprian for counsel, during the interval after the martyrdom of Fabian; and Fabian's successor Cornelius and Cyprian working together for mercy and justice.

In another controversy which occupies a large portion of Cyprian's letters, Cyprian and the African episcopate arrived at a decision different from that of Rome, which was subsequently annulled by the decision of the Church.

In all ecclesiastical history there is scarcely anything more interesting than the manifestation through this controversy how the insight of the whole Church proved truer than that of any section of it, and the heart of the Church penetrated deeper than the intellect of the wisest of her sons.

This was the controversy about the rebaptising of heretics. The Churches of Asia Minor and of Africa decided —at least their official heads decided—that the baptism of heretics was void. And Cyprian writes most strongly on the subject. It was no doubt his horror of division and love of consolidated unity which led him to this conclusion.

It must be remembered he was always acting in presence of the enemy. Stephen of Rome, with the harsher temper, came to the gentler decision, which was ultimately

[1] Dr. Benson, Smith's *Dictionary of Christian Biography*.

followed by the whole Church, on the ground that 'the grace of baptism is of Christ and not of the human baptiser.' The Council of Carthage was unanimous in following Cyprian.

'The unanimity of such early councils, and their erroneousness, are a remarkable monition. Not pushed; not pressed; the question broad; no attack on an individual; only a principle sought; the assembly representative; each bishop the elect of his flock, and all 'men of the world' often christianised, generally ordained late in life; converted against their interests by conviction formed in an age of freest discussion; their chief (Cyprian) one in whom was rarely blended intellectual and political ability, with holiness, sweetness, and self-discipline. The conclusion reached by such an assembly uncharitable, unscriptural, uncatholic—and unanimous.

'The consolation as strange as the disappointment. The mischief silently and perfectly healed by the simple working of the Christian society. Life corrected the error of thought.'

'It may be noted, as affording some clue to these one-sided decisions, that the laity were silent in the council. It was a parliament of officials, of provincial governors. It must have been among the laity that there were in existence, and at work, those very principles which so soon not only rose to the surface, but overpowered the voices of the bishops for the general good.'[1]

We return to the story of Cyprian, as told in his letters and his 'Passion,' by Pontius.

Yet it is not difficult to see how Cyprian, in his passion of patriotism for the Church, for his heavenly fatherland—the city of his heavenly birth and of his King—regarding the heretics as deserters and the schismatics as traitors (and that in presence of a besieging enemy), would find it impossible to recognise any religious act of theirs as other than the continuance of disloyalty.

It is pleasant to turn from this campaign, in which

[1] Dr. Benson, Smith's *Dictionary of Christian Biography*.

the Church of Rome at the time, and the whole Church afterwards, decided against him, to his direction of his Carthaginian flock in the perpetual Christian work of mercy.

He himself, we must remember, in an age of almost fanatical homage to the martyrs, wrote that the 'white rose of the crown for faithful labour might be as fair as the red rose of martyrdom;' and to such labour he led the African Church, going always before his flock as an example both in giving and suffering.

The Berbers, native African tribes, untouched by Christianity or civilisation, began to press in on the little rim of light of the African province. They advanced their frontier steadily during the next few years and reconquered much territory.

In a raid made during the session of the Council of Carthage which discussed the rebaptisation of heretics, these Berbers carried away a great number of Christians from eight of the African sees. The bishops appealed to Cyprian, and he writes—

'Christ is to be contemplated in our captive brethren; and He is to be redeemed from the peril of captivity who redeemed us from the peril of death; He is to be rescued from the hands of barbarians for a sum of money who redeemed us by His cross and blood. He will say now, "I was captive and ye redeemed me."

'We give you the warmest thanks that you have wished us to be sharers of your anxiety in so great and necessary a work; that you have offered us fruitful fields, in which we might cast the seeds of our hope. We have, then, sent you a sum of 100,000 sesterces [about 800*l.*] But that you may have in mind in your prayers the brethren and sisters who have laboured so promptly and liberally, I have subjoined their names.'

But in A.D. 252 the greatest call to works of mercy came on the Church as a great organisation of charity.

A dreadful plague which devastated the whole Roman Empire for twenty years, in 252 broke out in Carthage. Cyprian was in Carthage again at his post. 'All were shuddering, fleeing, shunning the contagion, impiously exposing their own kindred ; the bodies of those who had died by the pestilence lay unburied over the whole city.'

Cyprian gathered the Christians together, and by word and example showed them that it was not enough to cherish their own people. 'There was nothing wonderful in that ; if they would be more than the publican in the matter, they must do kindness to others also—to their enemies' (to the enemies who had so recently said, ' The Christians and Cyprian to the lions'). 'God makes His sun to rise on the evil and the good,' he said ; 'if a man professes to be a son of God, it becomes us to answer to our birth.'

He believed the world to be 'very old, corrupt, and about to perish ;' yet he laboured as much for its immediate succour as if his horizon were bounded by it.

Nobly he writes about it in his treatise on 'The Mortality.' 'The kingdom of God, beloved brethren,' he says, 'is beginning to be at hand, the perpetual gladness and possession, lately lost, of Paradise ; already heavenly things are taking the place of earthly and great things of small, and eternal things of things that fade away. What reason is there for anxiety ? It is for him to fear death who is not willing to go to Christ. What else is the world but a battle against the Devil ? Our warfare is against avarice, immodesty, anger, ambition. The mind of man is besieged. So many persecutions the soul suffers daily ! Who would not desire to hasten to Christ, since to see Christ is to rejoice ?

'But, nevertheless, it disturbs some that this disease attacks us equally with the heathen, as if a Christian believed for this purpose, that he might have the enjoyment of this world and this life, free from the contact of ills, and not as one who undergoes all adverse things here and is reserved for future joy.

'It disturbs some that this mortality is common to us with others, and yet what is there in the world that is not common to us with others according to the law of our first birth? So long as we are in the world we are associated with the human race in fleshly equality, being separated in spirit. When the earth is barren, famine makes no distinction; in the invasion of an enemy, captivity desolates all; when clouds withhold rain the drought is alike to all; when the rugged rocks rend the ship, the shipwreck is common to all, so long as this common flesh of ours is borne by us in the world.'

'This, in short, is the difference between us and those who know not God: that in misfortune they complain, whilst adversity strengthens us by suffering.' Then, after enumerating the loathsome symptoms of the present plague, he adds, 'What a grandeur of spirit to struggle with all the powers of the mind against so many assaults of death!'

'Many of our people,' he continues, 'die in this mortality —that is, are liberated from this world.'

Then addressing those who grudged to depart by a common disease instead of by the glorious fate of martyrdom, he says, 'We should do not our own will, but God's. It is one thing for the spirit to be ready for martyrdom and another for martyrdom to be ready for the spirit. Such as the Lord finds you when He calls you, such also He judges you. For God does not ask for our blood, but our faith. How preposterous that when we ask daily that the will of God should be done we should not at once obey the command of His will! We struggle and resist, and after the manner of froward servants. Who that is exiled in foreign lands would not desire to return to his country? We regard Paradise as our country. There a great number of our dear ones are awaiting us. To return to their presence and their embrace, what a gladness both for them and for us! There are the glorious company of the apostles; there the host of the rejoicing prophets; there the innumerable multitude of martyrs, there the triumphant virgins; there are merciful men rewarded. To these, brethren, let us hasten with an eager desire; let us crave to be with them and quickly to come to Christ.'

Six years passed from the breaking out of the plague to Cyprian's martyrdom. Some of these he passed in banishment in the neighbouring small seaside town of Curubis.

The 'Acta Proconsularia'[1] give this account of his banishment :—

'The Emperor Valerian being consul for the fourth and Gallienus for the third time, on the third of the calends of September, in the secretariat of Carthage, Paternus, the proconsul, said to Bishop Cyprian—

'"The most sacred Emperors Valerian and Gallienus have thought fit to give me letters, in which they have commanded that those who do not observe the Roman religion must recognise the Roman ceremonies. I have enquired, therefore, of thy name. What dost thou answer me?"

'Bishop Cyprian said, "I am a Christian and a bishop. I know no other gods but the One True God, who made heaven and earth, the sea and all things that are therein. This God we Christians serve; to Him we pray day and night for ourselves and for all men, and for the prosperity of our Emperors."

'Paternus, the proconsul, said, "Dost thou persevere in this determination?"

'Bishop Cyprian replied, "A good determination which recognises God cannot be changed."

'Paternus, the proconsul, said, "Art thou, then, prepared, according to the command of Valerian and Gallienus, to go into exile in the town of Curubis?"

'Bishop Cyprian replied, "I go."

'Paternus, the proconsul, said, "Not only concerning the bishops but also concerning the presbyters they have thought fit to give orders to me. I desire therefore to know from thee who are the presbyters who are in this city."

'Bishop Cyprian replied, "In your laws you have well and usefully judged that there shall not be Informers. Therefore these cannot be revealed and given up by me. But they will be found in their own cities."

'Paternus, the proconsul, said, "To-day I am making inquisition in this place."

'Cyprian said, "If discipline forbids that any should give himself up, this must also be open to thy censure; neither

[1] Ruinart.

can they give themselves up; but if sought for by thee they will be found."

'Paternus, the proconsul, said, "They shall be found by me." And he added, "They have also commanded that private assemblies (*conciliabula*) shall not be held in any places, nor shall they meet in cemeteries. But if any will not observe such a salutary precept he shall lose his head."

'Bishop Cyprian replied, "Do what is commanded thee."

'Then Paternus, the proconsul, commanded Bishop Cyprian to be banished.'[1]

It is remarkable throughout the Roman legal proceedings what knowledge is shown by the officials of the Christian customs, and with what courtesy and respect the rank and character of Cyprian are regarded.

What his life was in this banishment may be filled up from his own letters and treatises, especially the treatise on the Lord's Prayer; from the 'Life and Passion,' by the deacon Pontius, who was always with him; and from the 'Acta Proconsularia.'

'In the morning,' he writes, 'we must pray; that the Lord's resurrection in the morning may be celebrated. At the sunsetting and at the decline of day, of necessity, we must pray again. For since Christ is the true Sun, when we pray that the light may return to us we pray for the advent of Christ, who shall give us the grace of everlasting light. But if, in the Holy Scriptures, the true Sun and the true Day is Christ, so we that are in Christ—that is, in the true Sun and the true Day—should be instant throughout the entire day in petitions.

'Let us not, then, who are in Christ—that is, always in the light—cease from praying even in the night. Let us, beloved brethren, who are always in the light of the Lord, who remember and hold fast what, by grace received, we have begun to be, reckon night for day. New created and new born of the Spirit by the mercy of God, let us imitate what we shall one day be. Since we are to pray and give thanks

[1] Ruinart, *Acta Sincera Martyrum*.

to God for ever, let us not cease in this life also to pray and to give thanks.'[1]

The time of repast was doubtless not without heavenly benediction : ' the temperate mind would often be gladdened with psalms and the sweetness of religious music.' And in his walks along the Roman roads or the vineyard paths many a blind and feeble wayfarer would remember the sound of his sympathetic voice, the glance of his observant eye, the touch of his kind hand. Many widowed and destitute would go away relieved and gladdened from his doors by alms ; for kindnesses were always with him the accompaniments of prayer.

The Eucharist was celebrated daily.

Such was his delight in sacred discourse that he prayed he might be put to death ' in the very act of speaking about God.' But since, chiefly and perpetually, he was shepherd and bishop of souls, wherever he was, the condition of the Church, of his own Carthage, and throughout the world, was on his heart.

From his exile he writes of the persecution then going on at Rome, and encourages his own clergy and people. In A.D. 257, the last year of his life, he writes to the martyrs in the mines, speaking in sympathetic detail of all their sufferings—' beaten, chained, fettered.'

' O feet blessedly bound, which are bound not by the smith, but by the Lord ! O feet bound for the present time in the world that they may be always free with the Lord ! O feet, lingering for a while among the fetters and cross bars but to go quickly to Christ on a glorious road !' And he asks that they will pray that ' God will perfect the confession of us all.' They respond thus to his letter, from the mines :—

' You speak, dearly beloved Cyprian, always with deep meaning, as suits the condition of the time. For by whatever good things you have introduced in your many books you have described yourself to us. And you know, beloved, that our eager wish was that we might see you, our teacher

[1] *Epistle to Donatus.*

and friend, attain to the crown of a great confession. As a sounding clarion you have stirred up God's soldiers. You have also marshalled the troops of the brethren with your words. Believe us, dearest, that your innocent spirit is not far from the hundredfold reward.'

And at last it came.[1]

'A messenger came to him from the city, from Xystus, the good and peace-making priest; the coming execution was instantly looked for; he was in daily expectation of dying. In the meantime many eminent people gathered around him, of most illustrious rank and family, and noble, who, on account of ancient friendship with him, repeatedly urged his withdrawal, and also offered places where he might retire. But he had now set the world aside, though he would even then have done what was being asked by so many and so faithful friends, if it had been bidden him by Divine command. He continued instructing God's servants to tread underfoot the sufferings of this present time by the contemplation of the glory which was to be revealed.

'These were the daily acts of a priest destined to be a Sacrifice well-pleasing to God. When, by the command of the proconsul, the officer with his soldiers came unexpectedly on him (or rather imagined he had come unexpected), they came to his gardens, which he had sold in the early days of his faith, and which, when restored by the kindness of God, he would have sold again for the use of the poor, if he had not wished to avoid ill-will from his persecutors. He went forward with a lofty and erect bearing, gladness in his countenance and courage in his heart. Having reached Carthage, the trial being delayed till the next day, he was brought back from the prætorium to the officer's house.

'Then all at once the news spread through Carthage that Thascius was brought forth; there was not one who did not know him—glorious to us for the devotion of faith, and also to be honoured by the Gentiles.

---

[1] The rest is translated from Ruinart, the Passion by Pontius, and the *Acta Proconsularia*.

'At last that next day dawned, that destined, that promised, that divine day; the day glad with the consciousness that it was to be the festival of a martyr. He went forth from the house of the chief officer (*princeps*) (it was Aug. 13, 258), he himself a prince of Christ and God, amongst the assembly of a mixed multitude, walled in on all sides by that mass of people.

'On the way he had to pass the stadium (racecourse)— for him to tread a fit way, who having finished his course was speeding to the crown of righteousness. When he came to the prætorium, as the proconsul had not yet come forth, and as he sat bathed in sweat with no quiet around him (though the seat was covered with white fine linen, as if under the very death-stroke of martyrdom he was to be honoured with episcopal symbols), one of the officers who had formerly been a Christian offered him his own dry clothes in exchange, desiring nothing in return for his proffered kindness but to possess the martyr's clothing.

'Cyprian replied, "We apply remedies to inconveniences which probably to-day will cease for ever."

'Suddenly he is announced to the proconsul. He is brought forward; he is placed before him; he is interrogated as to his name.'

So far Pontius. In the 'Acta Proconsularia' it is related thus :—

'Galerius Maximus, the proconsul, said to Bishop Cyprian, "Thou art Thascius Cyprian?"

'Bishop Cyprian replied, "I am."

'Galerius Maximus, the proconsul, said, "The most sacred Emperors have commanded thee to sacrifice."

'Bishop Cyprian replied, "I do it not."

'Galerius Maximus said, "Take counsel with thyself."

'Bishop Cyprian replied, "Do what is commanded thee. In so just a cause there is no need for consultation."

'Galerius Maximus, having spoken with the council, said words to this effect: "Long hast thou lived with a sacrilegious mind, and many men hast thou gathered to conspire with thee, and hast constituted thyself an enemy to the Roman gods and the sacred laws ; nor have the pious and most sacred princes Valerian and Gallienus, the Augusti, and Valerian the most noble Cæsar [1] been able to recall thee to the observance of the ceremonial due to them ; and since now thou art apprehended as the author and standard-bearer (*signifer*) of abominable crimes, those will be instructed whom by thy wickedness thou hast gathered to thee. By thy blood discipline will be restored."

'And having said this he recited the sentence from the tablet : " It pleases that Thascius Cyprian be beheaded with the sword."

'And Bishop Cyprian said, "*Thanks be to God.*"'

The Deacon Pontius writes of the proconsul's sentence, 'Nothing could be more complete than this sentence, nothing truer. All things therein said, though said by a Gentile, were divinely said ; and this is no marvel, since the High Priest [alluding to Caiaphas] prophesied of the Passion [of Christ]. A standard-bearer, indeed, had he been, who was ever teaching how to bear the standard of Christ ; and by his blood, discipline did, indeed, begin to be established ; but it was the discipline of martyrs.'

The 'Acta Proconsularia' go on :—

'After his sentence a multitude of the brethren said, " And we also will be beheaded with him."

'A tumult arose among the brethren, and a great crowd followed him.

'And when Cyprian was brought forth into the field of Sextus he himself laid aside his upper garment and knelt down on the ground and prostrated himself in prayer before the Lord. Then he divested himself of his dalmatic and stood in his linen garment, and desired that twenty-five gold pieces should be given to the executioner.'

'And when he left the doors of the prætorium,' Pontius writes, ' a multitude of soldiers accompanied him ; and, that nothing might be wanting in his passion, centurions and tribunes guarded his side. Now the place where he was to suffer is level, so that from the trees thickly planted

[1] Thus in the *Acta Proconsularia*, Ruinart.

all around a sublime spectacle could be seen. And lest, on account of the crowds that thronged the place, those who revered him should miss the sight of him, they climbed, like Zaccheus, into the trees.

'And then, having with his own hands bound his eyes, he tried to hasten the slowness of the executioner, whose office it was to wield the sword, and who could scarcely clasp in his trembling hands the weapon which was to bring about the death of that man so dearly prized.'

It seems he had thought he would have been given to utter some prophetic words at his death; but his eloquent lips and his holy life had spoken already; and no better last sermon could be left to thrill through the hearts of his people than the words with which he accepted his sentence of death: '*Deo Gratias.*'[1]

---

[1] St. Cyprian is in art represented with a gridiron and sword. Dedication of churches: one church in England, Chaddesley, in Worcestershire; at Carthage two great basilicas. It was in an oratory of St. Cyprian on the shore that Monica was praying when St. Augustine secretly abandoned her to go to Rome.

CHAPTER V.

LEGENDS OF THE EARLY MARTYRS.

WE come now for a time out of the wider region of history into that of individual story and of legend.

Clement, Fabian, Cyprian, and Perpetua, and even Nicomede come before us with a wide historical surrounding and a definite local and historical colouring. They touch the world at many points; they tread the common earth. To understand them we must understand something of their age, of the place and people, the cities, the empire amidst which they lived. Clement, while supremely Christian, was also Jewish, and Greek, and Roman; the world he touched was the historical Rome and Corinth. Cyprian was a great provincial. In studying his life we learn the life of his time; of the Carthage and Rome of his times; its everyday ways and customs; its society, amusements, dress, gardens, table, as well as its especial temptations and controversies. The light of these biographies illumines in a measure a wide space around them. But in the cluster of saintly lives—or rather deaths—now opening before us we see each as by a flash of lightning at one supreme moment of martyrdom; or as by a lamp, throwing its circle of intense light on one point and leaving all around in darkness.

Each story might, in a sense, have happened anywhere, at any time. There is one vivid dramatic scene—the persecutors, the victim, the incidents of torture, the spirit victorious over the flesh; the surrounding crowds, like a tragic chorus, either sharing the rage of the persecutor or in sympathy, more or less, with the sufferer. But, whether the world surrounding that little spot of light is Rome, Spain,

Carthage, Antioch, Nicomedia, or Verulamium makes no difference to the story. All around the immediate actors is in darkness.

Of all the biographies in this section no details are given at all in the contemporary 'Acta Martyrum,' except of St. Vincent, who suffered in the persecution of Diocletian in Spain. But even these contemporary Acta of St. Vincent are scarcely to be distinguished from the other more obviously legendary stories; and yet of the existence of those martyrs, of their confession, their fidelity to death, their share in the conquests of the kingdom of Christ, for whom they suffered, there seems no doubt. Their names are in the earliest martyrologies. The homage paid them began when those who had seen them die were still living.

Of these fourteen martyrs the greater number suffered in the persecution under Diocletian, early in the fourth century. It may be best to begin with St. Laurence, who suffered under Valerian, in the same persecution as Cyprian of Carthage.

St. Laurence

Of Spain.

August 10.

(Martyred A.D. 258. In all the Calendars. Sarum Ep. and Gosp.: 2 Cor. ix. 6–10; St. John xii. 24-6.)

The name of St. Laurence is in all the Calendars. Pope Leo the Great said that his patronage was for Rome what that of St. Stephen was for Jerusalem. He seems to have been naturally associated with the first martyr on account of his being, like him, a deacon. The Emperor Constantine built a basilica at Rome over his tomb, in the cemetery outside the gates of Rome. The Empress Pulcheria built a beautiful church in his name; another was raised on the Pincian Hill in early days. 'There is scarcely a city in Christendom which does not contain a church or altar dedicated in honour of him.' In England there are 280 churches bearing his name. Scarcely one among the martyrs is more frequently represented in devotional pictures—young, 'with a look of calm sweetness almost angelic,' in the vestments of a deacon, with the gridiron, or iron bed, on which he was tortured; sometimes with a plate full of the gold and silver treasures which it was his office to dispense; sometimes carrying a cross, or swinging a censer, as a deacon in a procession.

And this is, briefly, the legend of the brief life of service and the death of torture which have so held the heart of Christendom.

Laurence was a Spaniard. His father, Orentius, and his mother, Patience, lived in a country house two or three miles from the town of Huesca, still called from him Loretto. Their holy lives are still commemorated on the 1st of May near their native town. Their son was educated

[1] Ruinart.

at Saragossa, and either there or at Genoa, on the way to Rome, began that friendship between the young Laurence and St. Sixtus, afterwards of Rome, which lasted until the martyrdom of both within three days of each other.

When Sixtus became Bishop of Rome he appointed his young countryman and friend Archdeacon, or head of the seven deacons originally appointed by Clement, and further organised by Fabian to collect and certify the Acts of the Martyrs and otherwise serve the Church. The century and a half which had elapsed since Clement, had added largely to the material riches of the Roman Christians; they were in possession, as common ecclesiastical property, of houses, gardens, even palaces, chalices and vessels of gold and silver richly embossed and jewelled, embroidered vestments. But they also numbered among them many poor, widowed, and crippled, and sick, to whom it was Laurence's office and delight to minister. His office thus combined the administration of considerable property in lands and money, and much personal care of the poor, of whom 1,500 were on the lists of the Church to be relieved.

There was nothing to indicate the approach of persecution. The Emperor Valerian's palace was so full of Christians, openly known to be such, that Eusebius says it was like a church; and he himself at the beginning showed them a courtesy and regard not yet experienced in the history of the Church.[1]

On this tranquil and expanding life of increasing wealth, and benevolent use of it, burst suddenly, as an earthquake, a new edict of persecution. It was thought the riches of the Roman Christians were one occasion of it, but chiefly it was attributed to a superstitious terror which seized the Emperor lest the twenty years' pestilence which was wasting city after city—the same which called forth Cyprian's noble beneficence at Carthage—and also the inroads, on all sides, of the barbarians might be the consequence of the dis-

---

[1] From Eusebius, *Les Petits Bollandistes*, Mrs. Jameson's *Sacred and Legendary Art*, and Alban Butler.

pleasure of the ancient gods at the desertion of their altars and contempt of their rites by the Christians.

Once more the decree went forth that the Christians were to be compelled to sacrifice to the gods or to die, but not to be suffered to die until every means had been exhausted to make them apostatise.

The blow fell first on the head of the Roman Church. Sixtus was arrested, and on his refusal to offer incense to the gods was loaded with chains, thrown into the Mamertine prison, and sentenced to death.

The young deacon Laurence followed him weeping and said, 'Whither are you going, O my father, without your son? What would you do without him whom you have chosen to minister with you at the altars? In what have I displeased you? Do you think me capable of cowardice? Did not St. Peter yield to Stephen the glory of being first of the martyrs? Shrink not from the offering up of a child whom you have nurtured. His triumph will be yours.'[1]

'Far from me, my son,' was the answer, 'to abandon you; but the faith of Jesus Christ calls you to greater combats than mine. I am already broken with old age, and for me they prepare but light trials. But to you, who are in the flower of your age and the vigour of your youth, the tyrants will grant a more glorious triumph. Cease, then, to weep. If I am to shed my blood for the Gospel, you also shall pour forth yours. Three days more of patience and you shall follow me. Why would you only have a portion of my victory, since you shall have a victory altogether your own? Why so crave my presence? Elijah mounting to the heavens left Elisha on the earth, and the disciple did not lose courage. Go now and take

---

[1] It is said in *Les Petits Bollandistes* that St. Ambrose 'puts these words into the mouth of St. Laurence.' This dramatising of the stories of the martyrs, in a way sanctioned by the classical historians, gives the greater value to such narratives as those of Perpetua and Cyprian. In the poems of Prudentius, in the fifth century, on St. Laurence and St. Vincent we naturally expect this.

care, and distribute the treasures of the Church which I have left you.'

And then he gave him the kiss of peace and was parted from him, and Laurence went in obedience to that farewell commission to search out the poor Christians of Rome.

First he hasted to the Cœlian Hill, where lived a holy widow called Cyriaca, who had given refuge in her house to many of the faithful priests and other ministers.

It was already night when Laurence entered this house, and there he washed the feet of the brethren.

Cyriaca whilst ministering to the wants of all had herself been suffering for a long time from grievous pain in her head. Laurence (says the Legend) laid his hands on her head, making the sign of the Cross, and she was cured perfectly; then he distributed alms according to the need of each.

The same night he went on to the quarter near the Cloaca Maxima, into the house of Narcissus, where again he found a great number of Christians who had taken refuge there. There he did the same works of humility and charity as in the house of Cyriaca; and also restored sight to a blind man, making the sign of the Cross.

Thence he directed his steps towards the Viminal, in the quarter of the patricians, and descended into a catacomb, where he found sixty-three Christians, men and women. He entered with tears in his eyes, gave them the kiss of peace, and distributed to them the succour he had brought. In this place he met a holy priest called Justin, who had been ordained by Sixtus. Laurence, knowing his character, would have kissed his feet. Justin forbade him, but Laurence vanquished in this combat of humility, kissed his feet and washed them, and also washed the feet of all the brethren.

Having spent the night in these services of love, and fulfilled the intentions of Sixtus, he saw him once again on the last steps of his last journey towards his execution. As soon as he perceived him he cried out from afar, 'Ah, holy father, forsake me not. I have done all you bade me;

the treasures with which you entrusted me I have given to the poor.'

The soldiers who were guarding St. Sixtus, hearing the word 'treasures,' seized Laurence, and he was brought before the Emperor and questioned about the treasures, but, as he refused to say a word, he was given into the custody of Hippolytus, a Roman knight, with the command that he should be examined about those treasures of the Church.

Hippolytus took him to his own house on the Viminal, and there shut him in a prison with many other prisoners on the spot which can be seen in our days under the Church of S. Lorenzo in Fonte.

Among these he found a man called Lucillus, who had been long imprisoned there, and had become blind by weeping over his miseries.

Laurence spoke to him of Him who had healed the man born blind. 'If you will believe in Jesus Christ,' he said, 'I promise to cure you;' and then he found that Lucillus had long been wishing for baptism. Laurence baptised him then and there, and in receiving light into his soul the light of his bodily eyes came back.

The fame of this miracle soon spread through the city, and many other blind men came and threw themselves at the feet of Laurence and received sight.

Hippolytus began to be moved by these wonders, and courteously entreated Laurence to tell him of those 'treasures' of which he had spoken.

'O Hippolytus,' he said, 'if you will believe in God, the Almighty Father, and in His Son Jesus Christ, I can engage to show you great treasures, and I can promise you eternal life.'

These words, and the grace of God, worked so mightily in the heart of Hippolytus that he turned to the faith and received baptism from the hands of Laurence, with all his household, consisting of nineteen persons.

Summoned once more before the Emperor and interrogated about his 'treasures,' he asked three days to collect them, and this was granted him, with the order that Hippolytus should accompany him everywhere. Laurence collected as many as he could find of the blind and lame and other afflicted ones, and went with this company to the palace of the Emperor. 'August prince,' he said, 'these are the treasures of the Church which I have brought to you; treasures which ever increase and never grow less, which are to be found everywhere and which everyone may share.'

The Emperor, enraged, commanded him to be tortured, and that all sorts of instruments of torture should be brought to show him what could be inflicted on him.[1]

But Laurence said, 'Unhappy one, these may seem torments to thee, but not to me; for long have I desired to eat at this table.'

Then he was dragged to tribunal after tribunal, from the Palatine to the Capitol, until he reached the Viminal, where he died. Beaten, lacerated, his limbs dislocated, scorched with slow fire, he prayed, 'Adorable Lord Jesus, have mercy on Thy servant, who has not been cowardly enough to deny Thy name;' and thinking he was dying of the anguish, he asked God to receive his soul. But it is said that a voice from heaven told him he was not yet at the end, but had a hard battle still to fight.

'Blessed be Thou,' he said, 'my Lord and my God, who showest such mercy to me, unworthy. Grant me grace, my Saviour, to make known to all around that Thou never forsakest Thy servants.'

To the unjust judge he spoke of the fire which burns without consuming.

At last the tribunal was set up at the Baths of Olympius, on the Viminal, near the house of Sallust. The examination began again from the beginning. He was interrogated as to his birth and his country.

'As to my country,' he said, 'I am a Spaniard, though I have been at Rome from my youth. They made me a

---

[1] The legends vary, some making the prefect his judge and another (which is adopted in *Les Petits Bollandistes*) attributing the cruelties to the Emperor Valerian himself.

Christian from my cradle, and I have always been brought up in the knowledge and practice of the Divine laws.'

Fresh menaces and mockeries followed, until he was stretched on the iron bed of torture and slowly scorched to death.

It is said his countenance was radiant with light and joy, and that he said, jesting with his anguish, 'Don't you see that my flesh is roasted enough on one side? Turn it to the other.'

And so at last his victory came, and thanking God for opening to him the gates of heaven, he yielded up his spirit.

And the next day the newly baptised Hippolytus and the priest Justin carried the poor lacerated body to the cemetery near the Via Tiburtina, two miles from Rome, where not a hundred years afterwards Constantine raised the Basilica over his tomb.[1]

---

[1] Dedications of churches : 280. Represented as a Deacon, with gridiron, thurible, church, and book, long cross, staff, or alms-bag.

St. Vincent

OF SPAIN.

January 22.

(Martyred A.D. 304. Sarum Ep. and Gosp. : Ecclus. xiv. 20 and xv. 4-6 ; and St. John xii. 24, 25. In all the Calendars.)

One legend links St. Vincent to St. Laurence by a tie of kindred. It is said that his mother Enola, of Huesca, was the sister of Laurence. At all events they were fellow-countrymen and fellow-townsmen, both born at Huesca, a town among the mountains of Granada ; both brought up from the cradle by devout parents in the Christian faith ; both young, both filling the humble office of deacon ; both united in reverent friendship with the bishop called with them to confess their Lord ; both called home by a terrible similarity of tortures. Between the martyrdom of Laurence, A.D. 258, on the Viminal Hill at Rome and of Vincent, A.D. 303, at Valencia, in Spain, only forty-five years elapsed. Vincent was only twenty years of age when he suffered. Enola, the mother of Vincent, might recall the news from Rome of the heroic endurance of her young brother the deacon Laurence. The story of that martyrdom would be a sacred inheritance and an inspiring memory in that Christian family. From his earliest years the parents dedicated their son to God, and, as soon as he was old enough to learn, committed him to the charge of Valerius, Bishop of Saragossa (where, according to one legend, St. Laurence first met St. Sixtus). As between Sixtus and Laurence, a close friendship seems to have grown up between Valerius and Vincent, one of the many holy and mutually sustaining friendships between the young soldier of Christ and the veteran. Before he reached twenty years Vincent was ordained deacon.

Valerius was a man of learning and influence and high

character, but he had an impediment in his speech, which hindered his preaching. Thus it happened that Vincent, fervent, brave, and eloquent, was early appointed to preach to the people in his stead.

The Church throughout the world had long been at peace. Diocletian had been reigning eighteen years—since 285—and not an assault had been made on the Christian faith.

Since the martyrdom of Laurence, in A.D. 258, much had happened in the Roman world. Valerian, the occasion of the last persecution, had died of grief and shame, a vanquished captive, led about in mockery and exhibited in triumph to the multitude by the Persian victor Sapor.

The Empire had been engaged in more than one mortal combat with the Gothic invaders, in Bithynia, in Thrace, in Greece. Aurelian had defeated and captured Queen Zenobia at Palmyra. For eighteen years the strong hand of the soldier Emperor, once a slave, who had fought his way to the Imperial throne, had ruled the State and kept its foes at bay.

Meantime the Christian faith during forty tranquil years had been steadily spreading and visibly triumphing.

The temples of the ancient gods, the schools of the philosophers were more and more deserted. In every city and town, large, and, in some places, richly decorated buildings arose for the worship of Christ.

The strength of the new faith no more lay in its obscurity, but in the manifestation of its strength. The only daughter of Diocletian had embraced it. Still the old State religion kept its hold on the officials and bound with superstitious terrors the scattered pagan dwellers in the villages. And still the philosophers resented the defection of their disciples. The country people dreaded what seemed to them an impious atheism likely to draw down vengeance from the deserted gods. The philosophers detested a theory which sought to replace their theories by a doctrine which seemed to them a new superstition under the guise of a philosophy. It is from the *peasants* and the *philosophers* hat the last great persecution seems to have sprung.

Galerius and Maximian, whom Diocletian associated with him in the empire towards the end of his reign, were soldiers of fortune, men sprung from the peasantry, and at his new Eastern capital of Nicomedia the two peasant Cæsars, with the philosophers, especially the Neo-Platonists, worked on the mind of Diocletian until he reluctantly consented to issue an edict against the Christians.

Unhappily, the forty years of tranquillity had produced the too frequent effect of outward prosperity in lulling the Christians to sleep, in the increase of luxury and worldliness, in divisions among themselves.

This persecution, the tenth and last ('*the* persecution,' as Eusebius calls it), was as well-directed as it was ferocious. The vehement hatred of the peasant soldier emperors was only too skilfully guided by the philosophers. The objects of attack were the clergy, the Church buildings, and the sacred books; more especially the Holy Scriptures, which were recognised as the historic source of the faith, and the contemporary Acts of the Martyrs, so precious from their local associations and as a witness that Pentecost was not a close but a starting-point—the Incarnation the beginning of a new life in humanity.

This especial aim of the persecution is indicated by the name given in the Church to those who failed to hold fast their confession. They were called not only 'lapsed,' but 'traditores,' betrayers of the sacred treasures of the Scriptures.

With regard to the Holy Scriptures, diffused everywhere, the effort could have no success. The impossibility of eradicating these is among the proofs of their universal diffusion and recognition as something apart, and especially Divine.

But there can be little doubt that Christian biography has suffered much by the destruction of the contemporary 'Acta,' often so carefully collected and compiled from the testimony of those who beheld the martyrdoms.

The persecution lasted six years. Then the emperors virtually declared themselves defeated, and in a few years more Christianity, under Constantine, became the recognised religion of the State. But this result—the nearness of this shore so soon to be reached—must not make us doubt the reality of the last storm, the strain of the last struggle with the surges before the haven was won. *We* know how near the shore was ; not so those who were dashed to death among the breakers.

The persecution very soon reached Spain.

The edict was promulgated A.D. 303. In 304 the conduct of the prosecutions seems to have fallen into merciless hands. Dacian, the proconsul, ordered the arrest of the bishops and clergy in various cities ; and among them the aged bishop Valerius and his young deacon Vincent were taken from Saragossa to Valencia, chained hand and foot, loaded round the neck with heavy weights, and left in prison many days, solitary and half starved.

At the end of these days, when they were brought before the tribunal, instead of finding them worn and cowed Dacian was surprised to see them vigorous and full of spirit, so that he said to his people, 'Why have you given them so freely to eat and drink?' He addressed Valerius with courtesy. 'Do you not know,' he said, 'that those who despise the Imperial decrees will lose life? The rulers of the world have commanded that you should offer libations, not willing that the dignity of the ancient worship should be profaned with new laws.'

And then turning to Vincent, son of the 'most noble consul' Agrestes, he added, 'And thou also, Vincent, hearken wisely to my words, distinguished as thou art by thy noble birth and by the beauty and grace of thy youth, before thou choose between being loaded with honours and subdued by tortures.'

Then the gentle old bishop, of wonderful simplicity and guilelessness, full of learning, but with an impediment in his speech, was silent and made no reply.

Vincent said, 'If thou commandest me, my father, I will make answer to the judge.'

And Valerius said, 'I have long entrusted thee, my

dearest son, with the Divine Word; and now to thee I commit the answer for the faith, for which we stand here.'

Vincent made his defence, or rather accusation, in words which recall the tremendous rebuke of St. Stephen, the first martyr deacon, convicting the Sanhedrim of being idolaters, uncircumcised in heart, betrayers and murderers of the Just One promised by the prophets they professed to revere.

'Know,' Vincent said, 'that it is held among Christians to be a nefarious prudence to blaspheme by denying the worship of the Godhead. And, not to detain thee, we Christians profess to be worshippers, servants, and witnesses of the One True God, who abideth for ever. In His name we must ever take spiritual weapons to contend with the subtleties of your elaborate arguments, fearless of your threats and punishments; yea, rather most gladly embracing death for the truth. For thy torments do but bring us home to our own country; through death we are conducted into life. It profits that the flesh should perish by diabolical cruelty, since the inner man fearlessly preserves his faith. For that most poisonous and murderous serpent, who first envied man his paradise and, robbing him of immortality, made him subject to death, is now constraining you to assault the innocence of Christians. He by his malice substituted the worship of idols for the worship of God. It is he and his satellites that we, by calling on God, banish from poor possessed human bodies, it is he whom you honour with the vain praises of a profane adoration, with madness preferring the creature to the Creator. For the devil burns with rage against the Christian faith, and when he sees himself despised he groans.'[1]

Then Dacian sentenced the Bishop to banishment for contempt of the imperial edict. But the young 'rebel' who had offered the public insult he singled out for especial torments. 'Stretch him on the rack,' he said, 'before the other torments;' and then, 'What wilt thou say now, Vincent? How wilt thou take care of thy wretched body now?'

[1] *Acta Sincera Martyrum* (Ruinart).

But Vincent, strengthened by the presence of God, with a cheerful countenance answered, 'This is what I have ever desired ; nothing is more friendly, more familiar to me than this (perhaps recalling from childhood the familiar martyr story of his mother's brother, the young deacon Laurence). 'Lo, I am going on high, and on those princes of thine I shall look down from a higher world. The servant of God is ready to suffer all for his Saviour.'

And then began the combat between force and faith, the outer and the inner man, the whole might of the empire of the world and one believing human spirit, of which we must not lose the sublimity and far-reaching power in our horror of the atrocious details of the torture.

The martyr stories too often seem to take us out of a human world altogether into some wild underworld of wicked gnomes and sprites ; into some horrible circle of a medieval Inferno, lurid with fires and peopled with devils ferocious and grotesque.

But these racks, these iron beds of torture were realities, and their remains still exist. The coals which scorched the flesh of our brethren burn on our hearths now, and the torments which they endured were as real as the changed world their heroic faith has wrought for us.

It does seem as if the courage, the obstinacy, the refusal even to acknowledge that they felt the suffering, excited the persecutors to an insane fury of cruelty, in the vain effort to subdue the spirit which thus defied them.

And it must be confessed that, though not a few of the martyrs reached the height of a courage faithful and unconquerable as that of St. Stephen before the Sanhedrim, perhaps not many penetrated to that depth of patient forgiving love with which amidst the murderous stones he looked up and said, 'Lord, lay not this sin to their charge.'

Their aim sometimes seems to have been rather to show how mighty the Lord they confessed was to sustain them in suffering than how gracious to forgive those who made them suffer.

And yet even Stephen, with 'his face like an angel's'

and his dying prayer like the Lord's, did not soften the hearts of his enemies—did not, at once, soften even the heart of the Apostle Paul !

Something in the bearing of these later martyrs did unquestionably make their confession the conversion of multitudes.

Again and again the tortures of the young Vincent were renewed, with intervals of repose just sufficient to make further torment possible. Again and again the proconsul Dacian was exasperated at his failure to subdue the young spirit. Once he had the torturers themselves punished for the feebleness of their work.

'What are you about?' he said. 'I do not recognise your hands to-day. Ye have succeeded in breaking the silence of parricides, in wrenching from him the secrets of the adulterer, and now ye cannot compel this despiser of the Emperors to silence.'

But Vincent said, 'What you say is not reasonable. I confess Christ to be the Lord, the Son of the Highest Father, the Only One of the Only One; Him with the Father and the Holy Spirit I confess to be the One Only God. Because I say what is true thou wouldst have me deny. Rather shouldst thou torture me if I declared thy princes to be gods. The gods thou wouldst have me confess are idols of wood and stone. Thou, their witness, makest thyself the dead pontiff of the dead. But I sacrifice to the One Living God, who is blessed for ever.'

Then Dacian appealed once more to his youth. 'Have pity,' he said, 'on the flower and beauty of thy years!'

But Vincent replied, 'O poisonous tongue of the devil, to what wouldst thou not move me, who hast dared to tempt our Lord? Better far than beauty is that which thou feignest to pity. By thy bitter poison thou wouldst crush the sweet faith and courage from a Christian soul.'

Again the seductions gave place to the scourges and the fire, till every form of torture had been exhausted, and at last he was stretched, like Laurence, on the iron bed, above the flames; yet the countenance remained glad, the spirit grew braver, the confession of Christ the Lord more persistent than ever, until at last Dacian exclaimed, 'Alas! we are vanquished!'

Then Vincent was thrown into a dungeon, among broken potsherds, but there, it is said (the only external supernatural manifestation recorded in the story of this martyrdom), the angels filled the night with light and the silence with their songs.

'Know, O Vincent unconquered,' they say, 'He for whose name thou hast fought so faithfully, who has made thee victor in thy sufferings, has prepared for thee a crown, and thou shalt be joined to our society.'

So they sang, and the modulated sweetness, like a resounding organ, was diffused afar. The gaolers, astonished, approached the closed doors, and saw the boundless light, and the very edges of the broken potsherds bright like flowers, and the blessed martyr of God walking about, his bonds loosed, and singing. And, moved by fear, wonder, and reverence, they gave up their heathen faith for the Christian religion.

Then the multitude of the faithful, so long mourning for his sufferings, but now rejoicing in his heavenly glory, came around him, and to these he said, 'Fear not, for darkness I have light. Him whom you believed to be groaning in torments you find rejoicing in the praises of God. Wonder rather and be sure that Christ will ever be victor in His servants.'

And Dacian, hearing of this, trembling and confounded, said, 'What further can we do? We have been vanquished.'

The weary, lacerated limbs were laid at last, by the proconsul's permission, to repose on a soft bed. His friends gathered around. It is said he was but reserved for further suffering, but Christ determined the reward should come. When the martyr of God was laid on the couch and kind and pious hands were softening it for him, with fixed resolve he yielded up his spirit to heaven.

Prudentius in his poem on St. Vincent records the

quaint and poetical legends which gathered round the tortured body, through which he had made such a good confession.

'Throw it into the open fields,' said Dacian, 'lest the Christians should gather his remains.'

It was therefore carried some way off and cast out at the foot of a mountain in a desert place, where the reverent hands that would so willingly have honoured it could not touch it. But all nature, the Christians believed, was friendly to the mortal relics of him who had made such a good confession for his Lord. A crow, a minister of grace, like the ravens of old to Elijah, constituted herself guardian of the outcast corpse, and, 'offensive' and slow and lazy creature as it was, flew vehemently at any bird or beast of prey which dared approach, perching on the head of a wolf which sought to prowl too near, and pecking at his eyes until he fled.

Baffled in his first attempt, Dacian then commanded the body to be taken far out in a boat and thrown into the deep sea, weighted with a heavy stone. But the obedient waves swept the stone and the saint back to the shore and laid him gently on the beach, and even, some said, scooped out a temporary grave in the ribbed sand. But at last it was given to the tender human hands of a poor widowed woman, called Ionica, to lay the body in his resting-place. She took it from its wave-worn sandy sepulchre, and bore it to a little obscure church near the shore, where it remained until in brighter days it was translated with all honour to its place before the altar of a church outside the walls of Valencia.

Poetical illustrations of a most real combat. Soul and body the young deacon martyr had been one of the bulwarks of the City of God. Soul and body he had helped to win the victory for the souls and bodies of liberated Christians through all after years for ever.

Dacian was right. By that fragile tortured frame he himself, the emperors, the world, *had* been 'vanquished.'[1]

---

[1] Dedications of churches: 4. Represented as a Deacon, holding an iron hook, or a boat, or a palm, with an angel breaking his chains; on a gridiron, with a wolf and a crow, and a millstone.

The Legend of St. Alban, Protomartyr and in early days Patron of Britain.[1]

June 17.

(Martyred circa A.D. 283. In the Calendars of Sarum and York. Sarum Ep. and Gosp.: Wisdom iv. 7–11, 13–5; St. Matt. xiv. 24–8.)

The course of history leads us next to Roman Britain, to Verulam, on the banks of the little river Ver, in Hertfordshire, one of the many Roman towns scattered then throughout England, connected with each other by the straight and solid and well-repaired Roman roads, linked with Rome by their chain of military stations.

In one of those well-built, well-warmed Roman houses, whose mosaic floors and hot-water baths remain to this day, lived St. Alban, the heir of a wealthy Roman House.

He was sent to Rome to be educated, the Rome of the beginning of the fourth century, with its palaces on the Palatine Hill still full of the splendour of the imperial court; its temples on the Capitol, with its Sacred Way, still frequented by pagan processions and worshippers; its magnificent Baths, the resort of the idle citizens; its Forum, with the stately Hall of Justice, the Senate House, and the

---

[1] The story is combined from the old legend in the Venerable Bede, and *Les Petits Bollandistes*, who intertwine with it the later twelfth century story of Amphibalus, which seems not so much a popular legend as one of the religious romances or medieval Tracts written in the monasteries for the edification of the people, generally of little true historical interest as records or as literature, as giving the life of the saint, or as reflecting the popular ideal of the legend; but in this case containing one or two points which seem worth remembering.

In Ruinart's *Acta Sincera Martyrum* there are these two brief notices of St. Alban: 'Gildas Sapiens, who in the fifth century wrote of the slaughter in Britain, among other English martyrs reckons Alban of Verulam, Aaron, and Julian. Of the same Alban Constantius has various things in his *Life of St. German of Autun*.'

Venantius Fortunatus (fifth century) joins Victor of Marseilles with him in this distich:—

'Egregium Albanum fœcunda Britannia profert;
Massiliâ Victor martyr ab urbe venit.'

shops, still a place of busy commerce and eager litigation; its schools of philosophy and rhetoric thronged by students.

Alban came back to his provincial home at Verulam. Rich and cultivated, and hospitable and travelled, to his house on the banks of the Ver were welcomed travellers and strangers who passed through the place, because his heart was generous and open to those in need of help. And so one day the stranger came to his hearth who became to him the 'angel entertained unawares.'

A Christian priest (called by the later story Amphibalus from his teacher's-cloak), pursued by his persecutors, was received like other unfortunate people into the house of Alban. There he remained hidden for many days. The young host observed him and was touched by his piety.[1] The stranger spent much of the day alone in prayer, and was often found in adoration of his unseen God.

At last Alban asked the meaning of his worship. The priest spoke of the Son of God, the Incarnate Saviour; of the miraculous birth, prophesied for ages; of the Virgin Mary; of the manger and the stable. He also frankly told his young host that if he followed the Christ he would probably end his life by martyrdom, and that this would be the reward for his generous hospitality.

He attracted him by no seductive promises; it was the old trumpet call to believe and follow, to sacrifice and suffer, which penetrates so much deeper, and leads so much higher. Alban retired much moved, but rather in anger than in acquiescence, and would not listen to another word. But the priest remained alone all night in prayer.

And in the night a dream was sent to Alban, which on the next morning he told his guest. His dream completed the teaching of the stranger.

'If what you say is true,' he said, 'explain to me this mysterious dream. I saw a Man descend from heaven, and a great crowd of other men seized Him, bound Him, smote Him with rods, stretched Him on a cross, pierced His hands and feet with nails, His side with a spear, and mocking Him

[1] From the story of Amphibalus, not in Bede.

for hours bade Him descend from the cross. But He, without answering them, only uttered a great cry, "Father, into Thy hands I commend my spirit!" And then at once He died. Then I saw them take down the lifeless body from the cross, lay it in a sepulchre, sealed fast and surrounded by guards. But, oh wonder, this corpse comes back to life! He comes forth from the grave without breaking the sealed doors. I have seen with my eyes how He rose from the dead. Men clothed in garments white as snow came down from heaven; they returned to heaven together. An innumerable multitude of men in white robes follows this Conqueror of death, never ceasing to sing His praises and to bless the Father, saying, "Blessed be God the Father and His only Son." Explain this dream to me.'

Full of joy, the priest continued his instructions, and afterwards baptised his host. Then, having given his message there, he would at once have gone on to spread the glad news elsewhere. But Alban entreated him to stay a while, that they might worship God together; and when, at length, a final search was made by the soldiers for the stranger, Alban insisted on changing clothes and putting on his teacher's-cloak, and giving himself up to death in his stead.

He was dragged before the judge, who was at the moment before the altars of the gods. The judge threatened that, as he had concealed a sacrilegious rebel in his house, all the punishment due to the fugitive should fall on Alban's head if he abandoned the worship of the gods.

St. Alban, who had voluntarily confessed himself to the soldiers to be a Christian, declared distinctly that he would not obey the judge's command.

Then said the judge, 'Of what family and race are you?'

'What does it matter of what stock I am?' answered Alban. 'If you desire to hear the truth of my religion, be it known to you that I am now a Christian, and bound by Christian duties.'

'I ask your name,' said the judge. 'Tell it me immediately.'

'I am called Alban by my parents,' he replied, 'and I worship and adore the True and Living God who created all things.'

Refusing to sacrifice, he was seized and cruelly tortured, and then led into the arena beyond the river to die.

But so dense was the crowd which thronged to see the sentence executed on this man of wealth and rank, and so new a convert, that the bridge was filled. Then Alban turned aside to ford the river, and lifting up his eyes to heaven, the legend says, it dried up at his prayer. The executioner who was to have beheaded him, seeing the miracle, threw down his sword at the martyr's feet, desiring rather to suffer with him than to inflict death on him.

And so the martyr passed on out of the old Roman town up the opposite hill, then called Holmhurst, 'adorned,' says Bede, 'or rather clothed, with all kinds of flowers, having its sides neither perpendicular nor even craggy, but sloping down into a most beautiful plain, worthy from its lovely appearance to be the scene of this martyr's sufferings. Here, therefore, the head of the most courageous martyr was struck off, and here he received the crown of life, which God has promised to those that love Him.'

Bede adds two miracles: one, like a beautiful parable, of a fountain springing up at his request on the top of that fair, flowery, wooded hill; the other a miracle of vengeance, the blinding of the soldier who gave the fatal stroke, yet this also perhaps as true parable, suggesting how those who misuse the power of seeing cease to see.

The other soldier, who had refused to be the cause of Alban's death, was also beheaded at the same time, baptised, Bede says, in his own blood (willingly shed, for mercy, and for the little fragment of truth he had learned), and so rendered worthy to enter the Kingdom of Heaven.

'The blessed Alban,' Bede concludes, 'suffered death on June 22, near the city of Verulam, where afterwards, when peaceable Christian times were restored, a church of wonderful workmanship and suitable to his martyrdom was erected.'

The old pagan city on the plain, with its walls and temples, has passed away, though leaving many remains which we can trace. The city and church on the flowery hill remain a memorial of this our first English martyr, led by his own merciful deeds to the Merciful, a martyr for Christ and for mercy.[1]

[1] Dedications of churches: 8. Represented as a layman, with a tall cross and with a sword.

St. Denys, Patron of France.

October 9.

(Martyred in 3rd Century.)

From the first patron saint of England we pass to the patron of France. And here we come into the midst of historical controversies which were hot enough at one time to imperil life to the combatants, and in our own days seem scarcely to have altogether cooled. The monks of St. Denys, near Paris, are said to have nearly killed Abelard for denying their saint to have been St. Paul's convert, Dionysius the Areopagite ; and their aged abbot is reported to have died of the debate.

Of the legend of St. Denys there seem to be three versions ; one identifying him with Dionysius the Areopagite, and also with the author of the writings called the 'Pseudo-areopagitica.' This is adopted by 'Les Petits Bollandistes,' and is the tradition of the Greek Churches, and of France and Italy, by which he is called 'Bishop of Athens and Paris.' The second, while accepting much of the same tradition, drops the identification with the Areopagite and represents him as sent on a mission to Gaul by St. Clement of Rome, with six others. The third, following Sulpicius Severus (410) and Gregory of Tours (594), (as adopted by Alban Butler) attributes his mission to St. Fabian of Rome, places his martyrdom under Decius, A.D. 250, and contains very little detail.

Although, as we know from early contemporary documents, especially from the Greek letters concerning the martyrs of Lyons and Vienne, written by the Church of Lyons to the Churches of Asia Minor, Christianity made

---

[1] Authorities : Smith's *Dictionary*, *Les Petits Bollandistes*, Alban Butler, &c.

very early conquests in Gaul, the converts seem to have been chiefly Greek or Oriental colonists, and afterwards Romans. Dionysius is said to have carried the Gospel farthest. In the 'Acts' of his martyrdom (not contemporary) we are assured 'that he built a church at Paris and converted great numbers to the faith, and that after a long and cruel imprisonment he was beheaded for the faith, together with Rusticus, a priest, and Eleutherius, a deacon.'

The 'Acts' add that the bodies of the martyrs were thrown into the river Seine, but taken up and honourably interred by a Christian lady named Catalla, not far from the place where they had been beheaded. In 459, by St. Geneviève's suggestion and direction, a chapel was built over the remains; and King Dagobert, who died in 638, founded there the great Abbey of St. Denys, which was for centuries the burial-place of the Kings of France outside the walls, until in the French Revolution the gorgeous tombs were opened and the royal remains removed and cast out.

There is also a tradition that the first burial-place of these martyrs was at Montmartre (Mons Martyrum).

The longer and more popular tradition floats in and out of ancient stories, Scriptural and apocryphal, like a dream, piecing together in a curious mosaic fragments of various histories. According to this, St. Denys of France, identified not only with Dionysius the Areopagite, but with the author of the mystical books which so deeply influenced medieval thought, was born of a family of high, even royal rank, and was educated by his parents in all the wisdom of the Athenians at Athens, and then was sent to learn all the wisdom of the Egyptians at Hierapolis, in Egypt.

At Heliopolis (the legend says) he saw an eclipse of the sun, 'marvellous and contrary to nature,' during the full moon. He asked his friend, Apollophanius, an astrologer, what this could mean. 'It is a sign that some change is taking place in things Divine,' was the reply. 'Either the God of nature is suffering,' he exclaimed, 'or all the machinery of the world is being destroyed and will return into its ancient chaos.'

He was then twenty years of age, and he marked the exact day and hour.

When, with Damaris (said by the legend to be his wife), he was converted by St. Paul at Athens, he found that the time of this eclipse was the very hour of the darkness during the Passion of Calvary.

St. Dionysius became Bishop of Athens, lived a life of devout and often ecstatic contemplation, wrote books on the celestial hierarchy, and was the type and model of mystical poetry. He was at Jerusalem at the time of the death of the Blessed Mother of our Lord, A.D. 50–60, and formed a close friendship with the beloved disciple John, to whose care she had been committed. There is one episode full of significant touches in this legend. St. Dionysius, besides being a great Christian writer, was a most diligent shepherd and bishop of souls, restraining the harshness of less tolerant, because less saintly, men towards the straying sheep.

Once, in order to censure the undue severity shown by Demophilus, a member of his Church, in his absence, Dionysius wrote him a letter, telling him a touching story of one of his disciples called Carpus. This Carpus was a very holy priest, and often had wondrous heavenly visions at the altar; but it happened that once he was so incensed at the perversion of a Christian by an infidel that he prayed the thunderbolts of heaven might destroy them both. When he had made this prayer he went to bed, full of indignation. But when at midnight he rose, as was his wont, to sing the praises of God, it seemed to him as if the house were rent in twain : the heavens opened ; Jesus Christ appeared with His angels and a fiery rain fell from His judgment seat to burn up all sinners.

When he looked below, Carpus saw a horrible chasm, out of which were coming a multitude of serpents, which, entwining themselves around the limbs of those two miserable sinners against whom he had prayed, were dragging them down over the precipice into the abyss. This spectacle gave him 'much joy,' and he was longing to see the end, when they must fall into the burning flames.

While with this immoderate zeal for (what seemed to him) justice he was waiting for the fulfilment of this wish, looking up a second time to heaven, he saw our Lord descend from His throne, and come with the company of His angels, and give His hand to one and another of those on the edge of the abyss to deliver them from the envenomed rage of the serpents.

Carpus was much surprised at a charity so contrary to his own rigour; but he was more so when our Lord, turning to him, said, 'Strike Me, if thou wilt, Carpus, and unburden thy wrath on My own Person. I am ready to receive thy blows and come to die a second time for man. What I demand is not that they may be punished, but that they may cease to sin, and so to render themselves worthy of eternal penalties.'

St. Denys had a fervent desire to win to Christ his old friend Apollophanius, the Egyptian astrologer at Hierapolis, who had been enraged at his conversion, and continued to say the fiercest things against him and his new faith. St. Polycarp, Bishop of Smyrna, endeavoured to convince Apollophanius, and St. Denys wrote him a letter, furnishing St. Polycarp with weapons of argument wherewith to vanquish the astrologer. They were successful. Apollophanius became a Christian, and St. Denys wrote a letter of joyful welcome to his old friend. It began, 'I address these words to you, O love of my heart,' and it ended, 'Now I shall die joyful in Jesus Christ, who is my Being and my Life, since you also have received life.'

From Sparta he is said to have written to St. John during his exile at Patmos, assuring him that he should yet live to return to Ephesus and to write his gospel. And at Ephesus he once more saw St. John and had heavenly converse with him.

After this, aged as he was, he left Athens with a purpose of carrying the good news to nations who knew it not. At Malta he found Publius, once governor of the island, like himself a convert of St. Paul. And by the direction of St. Clement of Rome he went westward to preach the Gospel in Spain and Gaul, where he became Bishop of Paris, in which city he was at last called to suffer martyrdom with long and cruel torments.

The whole legend, which seems to ordinary modern understanding as completely out of the region of historical investigation as a dream, is nevertheless most interesting. As a rich and curious mosaic piecing together into one fabric countless scattered fragments, it links together the East and the West, St. Paul and St. John. The mystical writings attributed to Dionysius the Areopagite, given by a Byzantine Emperor to Louis the Pious of France, translated by John Scotus Erigena, the Irishman, in the ninth century, endowed with a mysterious sacredness and charm by their supposed link at once with ancient Athens and with St. Paul, are said to have influenced more than anything the highest thought of the Middle Ages. The triple (or threefold triple) hierarchy of the angels encircling that Triune Light and Love on which 'dipende il cielo e tutta la natura,' and mediating between this and the threefold hierarchy on earth, captivated the imagination of those twilight days at once with its vague grandeur and its quaint limitations. St. Thomas Aquinas is said to have been so steeped in these writings that if lost they could be recovered entire from his quotations.

Dante drinks deeply through them of Platonic visions of light and good as the only reality, and evil and darkness as mere negations, in that Paradise of ever-changeless, ever-changing joy where the 'ceaseless Hosanna makes perpetual spring, with three melodies in those three orders of bliss, where the vision penetrates into the depths of truth—'nel vero in che si queta ogni intelletto'—into the truth in which every intellect is at rest.

The echo reaches to Milton's

 Thrones, Dominations, Princedoms, Virtues, Powers.

So that this legend of St. Denis is not merely, like others, a reflection of the medieval Christendom from which its rich, quaint colouring is drawn. It is a window through which Greek thought and Oriental contemplation flicker in for centuries on the Western world.

We are translated by it for a moment from the Latin world, with its Roman roads, its law, its military rule and order and its Latin rhetoric, into the Greek world, with its poetry, its art, its philosophy, its Homer, Æschylus and Plato, and the language which grew out of their thinking, which is also the language of the New Testament.

St. Lucian, Priest and Martyr,[1]

OF BEAUVAIS.

January 8.

(Martyred A.D. 290.)

It seems to be concluded that the St. Lucian of our Calendar comes to us through the Gallican martyrology, and is St. Lucian of Beauvais, 'priest' and martyr in our Prayer Book; at Beauvais honoured as bishop.

He was one of the companions of St. Denys of Paris. He is said to have come of a noble Roman family. He made Beauvais the centre of his mission, but was always making missionary journeys among the neighbouring scattered hamlets and villages. The country, although subject to Rome, was still in a wild state, almost covered with forests. And besides the old Roman 'demons,' such as Mercury and Ceres, St. Lucian and his companions had to contend against earlier local superstitions and rites, often fierce and sanguinary. Antiquarian researches in this district show us statues of Mercury and Ceres side by side with the massive stones of the earlier worship, hollowed to receive the blood of human victims.

To the Romans and Gauls alike the young Christian from Rome addressed his teaching, showing them of the one Creator of the whole world, the One Saviour of all men. 'To the vices of pagans,' says a nearly contemporary funeral sermon, 'he opposed the virtues of Christianity—to egoism charity, to the spirit of vengeance the law of pardon, to the fires of hatred the gentleness of the Gospel, to disorder of manners the wonders of chastity, to covetousness detachment from the things of earth.' His own diet was water and a little bread, and roots. And so he taught and

[1] At Beauvais honoured as Bishop, a very different bishop of Beauvais from him to whom Jeanne d'Arc said on the day of her death, 'It is you that have made me die.'

lived from youth to old age, till the whole of the region was penetrated with his words and holy example, and was changed. Many souls were won to the fold of Christ; among these he trained two to be his fellow-labourers in the priesthood. His own spirit was refreshed from time to time by converse with other missionaries, and the path by which St. Denis came from Paris to visit him was pointed out long after his death.

His vigour continued to very old age. It is always interesting to trace at what various ages the gates of heaven through martyrdom open on the saints of old. At length his success roused opposition. Two of his young converts went before him on the heavenly road. They were beheaded. And then the old man himself was called to follow those who had so long followed him. Imprisoned, insulted, beaten with rods, he declared himself 'a Roman citizen, but by a far more noble title, the servant of Christ,' and throughout his torments the old dying strain of the martyrs was heard again and again from his lips, 'I believe with my heart and confess with my mouth that Jesus Christ is the Son of God,' until he was silenced by the headsman's axe.[1]

---

[1] The story of St. Lucian, of Samosata, in the Greek martyrologies has some incidents so touching that they may well be given here. He was born at the beginning of the second century at Samosata, in Syria. Left an orphan at twelve, he distributed his goods to the poor. He took refuge with St. Macarius of Edessa, who taught him from the Holy Scriptures the things of eternal life. He opened a school at Antioch. He was ordained priest, and laboured diligently at procuring a correct version of the Holy Scriptures by comparing different Hebrew copies. His version of the Holy Scriptures was much used by St. Jerome. In the persecution of Maximin he was taken to Nicomedia. On his way he restored forty Christian soldiers, who had lapsed, to the faith. Tortured in the stocks, dislocated in every limb, laid on sharp potsherds in the prison, he was left to die of starvation, prostrate and helpless. When the great Greek Feast of Epiphany drew near he desired the Holy Eucharist. Many disciples gathered round, and the gaolers did not oppose. But how could a table be brought into the prison? The dying saint solved the difficulty. 'This breast of mine shall be the table,' he said, 'and I deem it will not be less esteemed of God than one of inanimate matter. And ye yourselves shall be a holy temple, standing round about me.' And so he said the appointed prayers. The next day the officers of the Emperor came to see him. Three times he said, 'I am a Christian,' and then he died.

SS. Crispin and Crispinian, Brothers
OF SOISSONS.
October 25.[1]

(Martyred A.D. 288.   Sarum Ep. and Gosp. : 1 Cor. v. 9-14;
St. Matt. x. 16-22.)

Crispin and Crispinian,[2] missionaries and martyrs at Soissons during the Persecution of Diocletian, are again links between the Anglican and Gallican Calendars.

They were brothers, and in these monastic medieval biographies a glimpse of family life and affection is always precious. Of a noble Roman family, together they believed, together gave up all for Christ, and together went as missionaries to the North of Gaul, and there, at Soissons, together they worked (like St. Paul at his tents) at the trade of shoemaking, not choosing to be of charge to anyone. Sitting at the shoemaker's last, they welcomed all who came, listened to their questions, taught them of Christ and all the time went on making excellent shoes.

Their courteous, polished manner, their easiness of access, and their good shoes, attracted many to their workshop. And so they remained living at their humble post in the city, sowing, unobtrusive and undisturbed, far and wide, the good seed ; until the seed sprang up and bore fruit a hundredfold ; and then the enemy, seeing the harvest of conversions, at last searched out the hidden sowers, found the brothers at their quiet work, and brought them before the tribunal.

'Is it Jupiter, or Diana, or Apollo, or Mercury, or Saturn that you adore?' they were asked.

'We adore the One Only God,' was the reply of the brothers.

'Whence came you, and what are you doing in Gaul?'

[1] The day of the battle of Agincourt in Shakespeare's *Henry V.*
[2] Shakespeare's Crispin, Crispian.

'We are of a noble Roman family. We came to Gaul in the name and for the love of Jesus Christ, True God, One with the Father and the Holy Spirit.'

Riches and honours were promised them if they sacrificed; and they were menaced with all kinds of tortures if they continued faithful.

'Your threats alarm us not,' they said. (The 'they' is the touching feature throughout the story of these brothers, undivided in life and death.) 'The Christ is our Life; death to us is gain. Your silver and your honours, give them to those who serve you. Long since we renounced all these with joy for Christ.' Then summoning their judges before the higher tribunal, they warned them of the judgment to come and held out to them the promises of eternal life.

The place of their imprisonment is still shown at Soissons; it was part of the residence of the Roman governors.

They endured prolonged torments by fire and in other ways, during which they sang in the words of the old Hebrew Psalmist, 'Help us, O God, for the glory of Thy name. Wherefore should the heathen say, Where is now their God?'

At last their sufferings were ended by their being beheaded.

It is said that their persecutor, maddened by his failure to conquer them, threw himself into the flames which had been kindled for the martyrs.

The heart goes back affectionately to that open shoemaker's stall at Soissons, from which so much that is bright in its picturesque streets, pleasant walks, and noble churches sprang.[1]

---

[1] It is interesting to read in Alban Butler's *Lives*, in connection with the shoemaker saints, a sketch of Le Bon Henri, founder of a religious guild of Brother Shoemakers—Frères Cordonniers. Henry Michael Buch was born of poor parents early in the seventeenth century at Erlon, in Luxembourg, and was apprenticed to a shoemaker, and early set before him SS. Crispin and Crispinian as examples of doing all work to God. He spent much of his leisure in prayer, in visiting the sick in hospitals and in their own houses, in rescuing wild boys and restoring them to their parents, in saving dissolute apprentices and

For not only as patrons of shoemakers may we think of Crispin and Crispinian, but as leaders of all co-operative labour, setting a saintly and royal stamp on all faithful work of the hands, heralds of a day when all men may be not lowered to a monotonous level, but lifted on different levels to infinite varieties of soil and aspect and climate, as in the mountain ranges, by each doing his best, and by all receiving their due; when all work may be ennobled by being done to the One Father, and for all the brothers, and therefore done well.[1]

reconciling them to their masters. Often he lived on bread and water, and would give his own food and clothes to feed the hungry and clothe the naked. Some of the tailors hearing the hymns and songs of praise of the shoemakers Henry had associated with him, and seeing their good and peaceful lives, founded a similar guild of their own. Henry was much honoured by the excellent Baron de Renty.

[1] In the sixth century a basilica was dedicated to them at Soissons, where they were buried. Represented shoemaking, with shoemaker's tools or strips of hide, or with a cornucopia full of boots and shoes.

St. Blaise, Bishop and Martyr, Patron of Wool-combers

OF ARMENIA.

February 3.

(Martyred A.D. 316. In all the Calendars. Sarum Ep. and Gosp. Heb. v. 1-6; St. Matt. x. 26-32.)

The martyr stories once more return from the East, and we find ourselves at large in the open country of allegory and legend, where the history as well as the beauty of the story seems best learned not from a narrative feebly clipped into a semblance of history, but from the most popular form of the legend most frankly and simply told.[1]

St. Blaise was born at Sebaste, in Armenia, the child of wealthy parents. Gentle and modest from his childhood, he grew in favour with God and man. When he grew up he especially studied medicine, being always full of longing to help all kinds of sickness and suffering. All the people loved him, and he was elected bishop.

He loved to retire to solitary places among the mountains, not so much for their solitude as because of their beauty and the companionship of the wild creatures, birds and beasts, who were at home there, and grew to be at home with him. He used often to retire alone to a cave in Mount Argus, near the city. There the wild beasts of the neighbourhood came to him every day to pay him homage, and to receive his blessing and be cured of their diseases. If he was at his prayers when they arrived they never interrupted him, but waited till he had finished, but never were content to go away without having in some way taken courteous leave of him.

Agricola, governor of Cappadocia and of Lesser Armenia

---

[1] Bollandists, *Acta Sanctorum*, also *Les Petits Bollandistes*, Alban Butler, Mrs. Jameson's *Sacred and Legendary Art*.

under the Emperor Licinius, having come to Sebaste, began by the commands of his master to persecute the flock of Jesus Christ like a cruel and famished wolf, whilst the wolves themselves were licking the feet of Blaise, their shepherd. This wicked judge, not wishing to spare any of the Christians he had thrown into prison, determined to kill them all at once by exposing them to the wild beasts in the arena.

To accomplish this he sent his people into the forests to capture lions and other fierce beasts. But it came to pass that as they were surrounding Mount Argus they came to the cave where Blaise lived, and found around him a great number of lions, tigers, bears, wolves, and other similar animals who kept him company.

Surprised at this adventure, they entered further into the cavern, and finding the saint seated, rapt in meditation on the greatness of God, they were still more astonished, and returned to the town to make known to the governor what they had seen. What they told him led him to send more soldiers to this mountain, to hunt out the Christians and to bring back all they could find. The soldiers therefore went there, and having found St. Blaise, who was praying and praising our Lord, they told him what the governor demanded. The saint answered joyously, 'My children, you are welcome. I have long sighed for your coming. Let us go in the Name of God.'

On his way to the town a poor woman came to him and laid at his feet her only child, who was dying from swallowing a bone.

'O servant of Christ,' she cried, 'have mercy on me.' And Blaise had pity, and he laid his hand on the child's heart and prayed, and restored him, cured, to his mother. Then another poor woman came and besought his help. She had no property in the world but one pig, which a wolf had carried off. This was naturally no difficulty at all to Blaise, the friend of wolves and all wild creatures. He told the poor woman to be of good cheer; her pig should be restored to her; and having given his orders to the wolf, the pig was at once brought back.

It seems rather a prosaic conclusion to this story that the good woman afterwards killed this miraculously rescued pig and brought it to Blaise in the form of pork when he was perishing of hunger in the dungeon.

As soon as Blaise and his companions reached the city of Sebaste the governor had them thrown into prison, and the next day summoned him to his presence. 'I am charmed to see you, Blaise,' he said, 'dear friend of the immortal gods.'

'God keep you, O governor,' replied Blaise. 'But give not the name of gods to those miserable spirits who can do you no good.'

The governor, enraged, had the Bishop beaten with a stick for two or three hours; but he continued joyful in the midst of the suffering, and only said (apparently to the devil), 'O senseless deceiver of souls, dost thou think to separate me from God by torments? No, no; the Lord is with me. It is He who strengthens me. Do with me therefore what thou wilt.'

One instrument of his torture was a sharp comb, such as wool is carded with. At last he was beheaded.

Several Christian women and little children were martyred with him.

These women, being ordered to sacrifice to the gods, said they would first take them to a neighbouring lake and wash them, that the offering might be purer. The governor, pleased at their apparent submission, acquiesced and gave them the idols, which they caused to be taken and thrown to the bottom of the lake.

The women were then burned to death, the little Christian children encouraging their mothers to die.

Then the governor threw Blaise into the lake where the idols had sunk; but he made the sign of the Cross and walked tranquilly on the waters, and sat on them as on a throne. The waves, like the wild beasts, recognised the servant of Christ as their master and their friend. But the officers of the cruel governor essaying to do the same were drowned. At last the Bishop floated back to the shore of the lake radiant in dazzling light ; and Agricola, the governor, seeing that all efforts to subdue him by torture were vain, had him beheaded.

There are three churches dedicated in his name in England; and at Bradford, in Yorkshire, to this day a festival is held every seven years, where Prince Jason, of the Golden Fleece, and Princess Medea, with Bishop Blaise and his chaplain, walk in procession.

In Ruinart's 'Acta Sincera Martyrum' merely his name is given, as one who is said to have suffered under the governor Agricola ; but his name occurs early in all the Calendars. And surely underneath all this rich tangle of legend is hidden some beautiful helpful life, trusted by children and by animals and beloved by all. One day, perhaps, we shall know the true story, and find it richer and greater than the legend.[1]

---

[1] In art represented as a bishop with crosier and book, and with wool and comb, or torch and taper, restoring a dead pig ; birds bringing him food.

St. George, Patron of England and of Soldiers.

April 23.

(Martyred A.D. 303. Called 'Our Lady's Knight,' and by the Greek Church the 'Great Martyr and Trophy-Bearer.' April 23. In all the Calendars. Sarum Ep. and Gosp. : St. James i. 2-12 ; St. John xv. 1-7.)

The legend of St. George also comes to us from the East. The Greek Church honours him as the Great Martyr, Captain of the Noble Army of Martyrs.

His 'cult' began very early. Constantine built a church in his name only twenty years after his death.

In the West his apocryphal legend was not accepted, and was in fact repudiated from the offices of the Church by Pope Gelasius in 494, when he reformed the Calendar. It was then decided that St. George should be placed among those saints 'whose names are justly reverenced among men, but whose actions are known only to God.'[1] But his 'cult' was especially promoted in England by Richard Cœur de Lion, who invoked his name in his crusading wars in Palestine.

The 'Petits Bollandistes' give his legend thus :—

St. George came into the world at Diospolis (280), or Lydda, in Palestine. His parents were rich, and good Christians. His father was in the Emperor Diocletian's service ; the education of George was therefore entrusted to his mother.

At the age of seventeen George embraced the profession

---

[1] In one book of devout meditations (Challoner) the meditations on St. George are given under three heads to this effect :—

'1. It is clear no one *does* know anything about St. George.

'2. It is clear no one *can* know anything about St. George.

'3. It is, therefore, good to meditate on him as one of those hidden saints who, although unknown to man, are glorious before God.'

of arms; the loyal services of the father, who had lately died, were recompensed in the son. George, moreover, had beauty of person and much intelligence, and was of an exquisite courtesy. He pleased the Emperor Diocletian, who quickly raised him from rank to rank and made him military tribune of his guards.

One day when 'the Cæsar Diocletian,' much devoted to Apollo, was consulting the god on an affair of much importance to the State, from the dark depths of his cave, it is said, a voice came forth in reply: 'The just who are on the earth prevent my telling the truth. By them the inspiration of the Sacred Tripod is reduced to a lie.'

Full of consternation, the Emperor asked who were these just ones, and one of the priests of Apollo answered, ' Prince, they are the Christians.' And thus the persecution, which had begun to relent, was rekindled.

From the first the cruelties against the Christians, and the decree of the Senate ordering them, excited the indignation of the young soldier, and he boldly denounced these cruel edicts against his brethren. In vain did his friends recommend him to be prudent and recall to him the favours of the Emperor. He knew well that his own call to confess and suffer might come at any moment; and so he distributed his money and wardrobe among the poor, at once set free the slaves who were with him, and left directions to provide for those who were absent.

Thus prepared for death, George approached the Emperor, and himself pleaded for the innocent Christians, demanding as the least that could be granted them liberty, 'since this liberty could hurt none.'

'Young man,' was all Diocletian's reply, 'think of thine own future.'

But as he was about to reply the benevolence of the tyrant changed to fury. The guards were commanded to take him to prison; he was thrown on the ground, his feet placed in the stocks, and an enormous stone laid on his chest. But the blessed one, always patient in the midst of his tortures, ceased not to give thanks to God.

The next day he was stretched on a wheel with sharp spokes. But a voice from heaven came to comfort him and said, 'George, fear nothing, for I am with thee.' And also there appeared to him a Man brighter than the sun, clothed in a white robe, who stretched out his hand to embrace him and encourage him in his anguish. Two of the prætors who saw it were converted and gave their lives for Christ.

The Emperor, seeing the constancy of George, once more sought to move him by entreaties. But this generous confessor would no more reply in words, but in deeds, and demanded to go to the temple to see the gods Diocletian worshipped. The Emperor, believing that at length George was coming to himself and was about to yield, caused the Senate and people to be assembled, that all might be present at the grand sacrifice George would offer.

Then the eyes of all being fixed on him to see what he would do, he drew near the idol of Apollo; and stretching out his hand and making the sign of the Cross, he said, 'Wouldst thou that I should offer thee sacrifices as to a god?'

The demon who was in the statue made answer, 'I am not God, and there is no other God but Him whom thou preachest.'

At the same hour were heard horrible wailing sounds coming out of the mouths of the idols, and they all at last fell crumbling into dust.

Then the priests of the temple conjured the people to lay hands on the martyr, crying to the Emperor that he must rid himself of this magician and cut off his head.

He was therefore taken to the place of execution, and, having said his prayers, was beheaded, April 28, A.D. 303.

The 'Petits Bollandistes' do not give the dragon story, saying it is an allegory.

But St. George cannot be left without his dragon.

The more popular legend [1] is that St. George on his

---

[1] Mrs. Jameson, Rev. S. B. Gould, and others, chiefly drawn from the *Golden Legend*.

knightly travels came to a certain city in Libya, called Silene. The inhabitants of this city were in great trouble and consternation in conseqnence of the ravages of a monstrous dragon, which issued from a neighbouring lake or marsh and devoured the flocks and herds of the people, who had taken refuge within the walls; and to prevent him from approaching the city, the air of which was poisoned by his pestiferous breath, they offered him daily two sheep ; and when the sheep were exhausted they were forced to sacrifice to him two of their children daily, to save the rest. The children were all taken by lot (all under the age of fifteen), and the whole city was filled with mourning, with the lamentations of bereaved parents and the cries of the innocent victims.

Now the king of the city had one daughter exceedingly fair, and her name was Cleodolinda. And after some time, when many people had perished, the lot fell upon her, and the monarch, in his despair, offered all his gold and treasures, and even the half of his kingdom, to redeem her ; but the people murmured, saying, 'Is this just, O king, that thou by thine own edict hast made us desolate, and behold now thou wouldst withhold thine own child ? '

And they waxed more and more wroth, and threatened to burn him in his palace unless the princess was delivered up.

Then the king submitted, and asked only a delay of eight days to bewail her fate, which was granted ; and at the end of eight days the princess, being clothed in her royal robes, was led forth as a victim for sacrifice ; and she fell at her father's feet and asked his blessing, saying that she was ready to die for her people ; and then, amid tears and lamentations, she was put forth, and the gates were shut against her.

Slowly she walked towards the dwelling of the dragon, the path being drearily strewn with the bones of former victims, and she wept as she went on her way.

Now at this time St. George was passing by, mounted on his good steed, and being moved to see so beautiful a virgin in tears, he paused to ask her why she wept. She told him, and he said, ' Fear not, for I will deliver you.'

And she replied, 'Oh, noble youth, tarry not here, lest thou perish with me ; but fly, I beseech thee.'

But St. George would not, and he said, 'God forbid that I should fly. I will lift my hand against this loathly thing, and I will deliver thee through the power of Jesus Christ.'

At that moment the monster was seen emerging from his lair, half crawling, half flying towards them. Then the virgin princess trembled exceedingly and cried out, 'Fly, I beseech thee, brave knight, and leave me here to die.'

But he answered not; only making the sign of the Cross and calling on the name of the Redeemer, he spurred towards the dragon, and after a terrible and prolonged combat he pinned him to the earth with his lance.

Then he desired the princess to bring her girdle, and he bound the dragon fast, and gave the girdle into her hand, and the subdued monster crawled after them like a dog.

In this guise they approached the city. The people being greatly terrified, St. George called out to them, saying, 'Fear nothing; only believe in that God through whose might I have conquered this adversary, and be baptised, and I will destroy him before your eyes.'

So the king and the people believed and were baptised —twenty thousand people in one day.

Then St. George slew the dragon and cut off his head; and the king bestowed great rewards and treasures on the victorious knight. But he distributed all to the poor, and kept nothing, and went on his way and came to Palestine.

At that time the edict of the Emperor Diocletian was published, and it was affixed to the gates of the temples and in the public markets; and men read it with terror and hid their faces. But St. George, when he saw it, was filled with indignation; the spirit of courage from on high came upon him and he tore it down and trampled it under his feet. Whereupon he was seized and carried before Dacian, the proconsul, and condemned to suffer during eight days the most cruel tortures.

And when Dacian saw that St. George was not to be vanquished by torments he called to his aid a certain enchanter, who after invoking his demons mingled strong poison with a cup of wine and presented it to the saint. He having made the sign of the Cross, and recommended himself to God, drank it off without injury. When the magician saw the miracle he fell at the feet of the saint and declared himself a Christian. Immediately the wicked judge caused the enchanter to be beheaded ; and St. George was bound upon a wheel full of sharp blades, but the wheel was broken by two angels who descended from heaven. Thereupon they flung him into a cauldron of boiling lead ; and when they believed that they had subdued him by the force of torments they brought him to a temple to assist at the sacrifice, and the people ran in crowds to behold his humiliation, and the priests mocked him. But St. George knelt down and prayed, and thunder and lightning from heaven fell upon the temple and destroyed it and the idols ; and the priests and many people were crushed beneath the ruins, as at the prayer of Samson in ancient times. Then Dacian, seized with rage and terror, commanded that the Christian knight should be beheaded. He bent his neck to the sword of the executioner and received bravely and thankfully the stroke of death.

And so he shone for ages, the Perseus of Christendom, scorning earthly rewards as well as earthly torments ; the conqueror of the dragon, the liberator of the maiden from death, and of the city from heathenism ; yet not ending, as the conquerors of old, by a joyful marriage with the rescued maiden and the inheritance of the kingdom. From the victory over the slain dragon, from the fair princess, from the city at his feet, he passes on to another combat and another victory, but this time a victory won through torture and humiliation. So deeply had the Cross stamped itself on the heart of the Church that she could not crown her young victor on those lower levels.[1]

So he stands for ever before the young manhood of

[1] There is, however, also a legend on a lower level of his appearing at the head of an army, as one of the 'Seven Champions of Christendom,' a glorious celestial knight, and of a great victory won over a Moslem host.

Christendom, one of its great champions, the type of courage shown in brave intercession for the oppressed; of purity, not merely spotless in whiteness, firm to endure, but fiery, with chivalrous manhood, mighty to save; true soldier of Christ, rewarded for victory in one combat by being sent forth to another harder fight—the martyr soldier, whose order and decoration is not a crown but a cross.[1]

[1] Dedication of churches, 162. Represented in art, as an armed knight, standing, or on horseback, fighting a dragon with a spear; a cross on his armour and shield.

St. Valentine, Bishop[1] and Martyr[2]

Of Rome.

February 14.

(Martyred A.D. 270. In all the Calendars. Sarum Ep. and Gosp.: Ecclus. xxxi. 8-11; St. Matt. xvi. 24-28.)

St. Valentine was a priest in Rome in the reign of the Emperor Claudius II. His good deeds, and especially his generous care of the martyrs, caused him to be widely known. He was brought before the Emperor, who asked him why he did not worship the gods. 'If you, sire, knew the gift of God,' was the reply, 'you would abandon the worship of these impure beings, and you and your empire would be happy.' One of the judges asked what he thought of Jupiter and Mercury, and Valentine replied that they seemed to have spent their time in low pleasures. The Emperor seemed moved by Valentine's eloquence and courage, so that the prefect of the city said to him, 'Shall we forsake the religion of our ancestors?' whereupon Claudius, dreading sedition, gave Valentine up to the prefect, who placed him under the charge of the judge Asterius, whose house became his prison. On entering the house, Valentine, intent, not on his own peril, but on saving all he could, prayed that God would make those who were still in the darkness of heathenism know Jesus Christ to be the Light of the world. Asterius heard him. 'How,' he asked, 'dost thou say that Jesus Christ is the True Light?' 'Not only the True Light,' replied Valentine, 'but the only Light, who lighteth every man that cometh into the world.'

'If this be so,' said Asterius, 'I will now test it. I have a little adopted daughter who has been blind for two years; if you can restore her sight, I will believe that Jesus Christ is the Light and is God, and I will do all thou sayest.'

---

[1] In some Calendars priest.
[2] In art represented as a priest with a sword.

Then they brought the young girl to Valentine, and he laid his hands on her eyes and said, 'Lord Jesus Christ, who art the True Light, enlighten this Thy servant.' At these words the child received sight, and Asterius and his wife threw themselves at the feet of Valentine and entreated him, since through him they had attained to the knowledge of Jesus Christ, to tell them what they must do to be saved. He commanded them to break all their idols in pieces, to fast three days, to forgive all who had injured them, and then to be baptised. Asterius did all this; set free all the Christians in his keeping, and was baptised with all his household of forty-six persons.

These new Christians almost immediately proved their faith by martyrdom; and soon Valentine, their father and master, after being thrown into a dungeon and beaten with rods, followed these his children to Christ.

A church was built in his honour near the Ponte Mole, in Rome, and the gate now called the Porta del Popolo, near this church, was long called after the martyr, the Gate of Valentine.

He is regarded as the patron of young girls, and a pagan festival to Juno for boys and girls occurring about the time of his martyrdom was intended to be transformed through his patronage, and was called by his name, St. Valentine's Day.

St. Sylvester, Bishop of Rome.

New Year's Eve.

(Died A.D. 335. In all the Calendars. Sarum Ep. and Gosp.:
1 Ecclus. i. 1, 4, 5-12, 15, 21-23 ; St. Matt. xxv. 14-23.)

ALTHOUGH not among the martyrs it seems for some reasons best to place the legends of St. Sylvester and of St. Nicholas next to those of St. George and St. Valentine.

Although both no doubt historical, having made by real life that deep incision in the history of Christendom which imagination afterwards made a fountain of romantic story, it is by their legends rather than by their histories that they are known.

St. Sylvester is called a confessor.

Historically he bridges over the period between the last persecution of the Church under Diocletian and its triumph under Constantine.

Legends (and also the forged decretals) connect him with Constantine. He was the son of Rufinus and Justina, early taught by a Christian mother. In his youth he delighted to minister to the pilgrims who came to the various sacred shrines at Rome, washing their feet, serving them at table, and caring for them in every way.

One of these, Timotheus of Antioch, was martyred, and Sylvester is said to have been himself thrown into prison by the pagan prefect of Rome, not so much for his Christian faith as from a rumour that the wealth of Timotheus, reported to be great, had fallen into the hands of Sylvester.

He seems therefore to have been almost in the ranks of the 'Noble Army.' The days of imperial persecution were, however, over for ever. Sylvester seems to have had much influence over the life of Constantine, which embodied itself in a tradition that he baptised the Emperor. He certainly induced the Emperor to build basilicas and churches and to destroy pagan statues and temples. The great basilica of the Lateran was, it is said, begun at his suggestion. He also made many regulations as to ritual, the consecration of churches, the order of baptism, and the period of ordination.

And for many centuries it was believed that the famous donation of Constantine, the foundation of the papal claims to the temporalities, was made to him.

He was Pope for twenty-one years, died on December 31, 335, and was buried in the Cemetery of Priscilla, on the Salarian Way, a mile from Rome.

The incidents by which he is commemorated in Christian art are taken from his legend.

He is represented, first, translating the body of St. Peter to a place in the church called the Confession of St. Peter; baptising Constantine; binding the jaws of a dragon in the midst of flames; standing in the act of benediction; or on his knees, before an Apostle holding a cross, in allusion to the invention of the Holy Cross by the Empress Helena in his time.

The chief incidents in his legend are these two, both full of allegorical significance.

According to the legendary 'Acta' Sylvester was compelled by the persecution of the pagan magistrates of Rome to take refuge in a cave near Soracte.

Constantine having defeated his pagan colleagues, Maximin and Licinius, came to Rome, and was there smitten with leprosy and elephantiasis. The remedy for this dreadful disease was a bath in the blood of several little children. A number of the little helpless victims were collected. But when the Emperor was being drawn in his chariot to the place where this bath was to be prepared, the mothers threw themselves before him, weeping and entreating for mercy on their babes. Touched with compassion for the mothers of the babes, the Emperor at once relinquished the purpose, and with it the hope of recovery. 'Better I should die,' he said, 'than cause these innocents to perish. Let the children be spared;' and the Emperor went back to his palace with the leprosy still on him. But, in the night, God, moved by this act of mercy of the pagan Emperor, sent to him the two blessed Apostles Peter and Paul. They stretched their hands over him and said, 'Because thou hast feared to shed innocent blood Jesus Christ has sent us to bring thee good counsel. Send to Sylvester, who lives hidden in Mount Soracte, and he shall show thee a font, in which having washed three times thou shalt be clean of thy leprosy; and henceforth thou shalt adore the God of the Christians.'

Then Constantine awoke and sent his soldiers in search of Sylvester. And when they took him he supposed it was to lead him to death. Nevertheless he went cheerfully with them and was led into the presence of the Emperor. And when Constantine saw him he saluted him and said, 'I would know of thee who are those two gods who appeared to me in the night.' And Sylvester said, 'They are not gods; they are Apostles of the Lord Jesus Christ.' Then Sylvester showed the Emperor the images of the Apostles, and Constantine said they were the same who had appeared to him in the vision.

Then Sylvester baptised him, and he came out of the font with his flesh fresh as that of a little child.

The second story from the legend is that once the Empress Helena, mother of Constantine, having a leaning to the religion of the Jews, commanded that the wisest rabbis should come to Rome, that Sylvester might meet them in debate. Two Greek philosophers, Crato and Zeno, were appointed arbitrators.

The Jewish rabbis were defeated by Sylvester's arguments, but one of them, being a magician, defied Sylvester to a trial of the power of the gods. 'Dost thou know the name of the Ineffable,' he said, 'that Name which no creature can hear and live? I know it. Let them bring me a wild bull, the fiercest to be found, and when I have uttered that Name in his ear he will fall dead.'

Then they brought in a fierce bull, which it took over one hundred men to restrain. And when Zambri, the magician, had whispered the awful Name in his ear, he fell dead.

Then the Jews triumphed and would have slain Sylvester; the two Greek philosophers were perplexed, and even Constantine was staggered.

Only Sylvester was unmoved. He said quietly, 'The name which Zambri has pronounced must be the name of the devil, not of God; for *Christ our Redeemer came not to kill but to make alive.* Men and wild beasts, lions, tigers, and serpents can *kill*. If Zambri's power is from God, let him *restore to life* the creature he has slain.' Thereupon the judges commanded Zambri to restore the bull to life; but he could not. Then Sylvester made the sign of the Cross and commanded the bull to rise and go in peace. And the bull rose up, as gentle and tame as a beast used to the yoke. Then all the Jews and the Greeks, and all others who were there, convinced by this miracle of mercy, believed and were baptised.

The third incident of the legend is that after the baptism of the Emperor Constantine the pagan priests came in a body and complained to him. 'Most sacred Emperor, since you have embraced the Christian faith the great dragon that dwelleth in the moat has destroyed every day 300 men by his envenomed breath.' The Emperor consulted Sylvester, who said, 'Only have faith and I will subdue this beast.' Then he went down 142 steps into the moat, and exorcised the dragon in the name of Him who was born of a virgin, was crucified and buried, and rose from the dead. And then he closed the mouth of the dragon and with a thread bound it round, twisting the thread three times and sealing it with the Cross. And so the people were delivered at once from the dragon and from the idols.

Three glorious Christian truths to be embodied in one legend. The Emperor choosing to sacrifice himself rather than the children. He that loseth his life shall save it, saved body and soul by the sacrifice.

The miracles of Christ miracles of life, not of destruction. The mighty dragon bound with the feeble thread, held by the hand of him that dares to resist, and sealed with the cross he not only signs, but himself bears.[1]

[1] Dedications of churches : one at Chevelstone, Devon. In art represented as a pope baptising Constantine ; and also with a bull. The 'St. Sylvester Festival' is still the popular name in Germany for New Year's Eve.

St. Nicholas[1]

OF MYRA.

December 6.

(Died circa A.D. 343.   Sarum Ep. and Gosp.: Ecclus. xliv. 17-23;
xlv. 5, 7, 15, 16; St. Matt. xxv. 14-23.)

One of the few saints whose name is in all the Calendars, whose praise is in all the Churches, the patron of the little children, of friendless maidens, the saint of the people, of the oppressed, and of strangers, the 'Santa Claus' of the children, of sailors, of scholars; chief patron of Russia; with more churches dedicated to him than any Saint in the Calendar. In England there is said scarcely to be a town without a church dedicated in his name.

St. John Chrysostom calls him 'father of the friendless and standard of the faith;' St. Peter Damian, 'the joy of the aged, the glory of the young, the light of priests.'

Justinian built a church in his name at Constantinople, A.D. 560, 200 years after his death.

Such a memory of graciousness, gentleness, insight into sin and sorrow, and power to succour has that life shed forth east and west, north and south, bearing witness to the presence of a real star at the heart of the prismatic halo of quaint wild legend which is all we see of it.

The date of his life is the beginning of the fourth century, and he is said to have been imprisoned and tortured in the persecutions of Diocletian and Maximin, and afterwards to have been among the confessors who appeared, with their glorious scars, at the Council of Nicæa.

In Greece, Russia, and the East generally his name was

---

[1] Also called St. Nicholas of Bari, on account of the translation of his body from Myra to Bari, in the Neapolitan territory, by a daring band of Neapolitan sailors, after Mahomedanism had swept over Asia. The boy-bishop pageants of the Middle Ages began on St. Nicholas' Day and lasted till 'Childermas,' or Holy Innocents' Day.

always honoured from the date of his life and death. His legend appeared in the West in the tenth century.

These are some of the incidents of his legend :—

He was born at Panthea, in Lycia. Like St. John the Baptist, he was the child of his parents' old age.

As soon as he was born he at once stood upright, and, turning eastward and looking upwards, joined his baby hands in prayer. He knew how to fast as soon as he knew how to feed, and kept the fasts of Wednesday and Friday.

His parents died when he was a boy. He at once embraced the command, as if given directly to him, to sell all his inheritance, which was large, and give it to the poor. His wants were few indeed, for after his ordination as a priest he never tasted wine or flesh; he went barefoot, and his couch was a plank, or the bare earth.

He did not distribute his possessions at random, but carefully watched where the need was greatest and then gave succour.

Among his countless other works of mercy one is recorded in all the legends and painted in all the pictures of his life.

A nobleman of the city, who had three fair young daughters, had fallen into misery so abject that he saw no way for his children to exist but through a life of sin. St. Nicholas heard of this, and putting together in three portions money enough to apportion each of the maidens, he determined to rescue them.

Desiring not to be known in his good deeds, he went one night secretly to their house, found a window open, and the wretched father sitting weeping inside; the young maidens meanwhile peacefully sleeping, unaware of the perils that threatened them.

St. Nicholas threw one of the portions, in a money bag, in at the window and crept noiselessly away. The father took it up, and at once gave a dowry to one of the maidens.

The next night the saint came again to the window, threw in another money bag, and crept away unobserved.

The third night he tried to do the same, but the father, who was watching to learn his benefactor, found him out, threw himself at his feet in an ecstasy of gratitude for his children and in an agony of penitence for his own sinful distrust.[1]

The uncle of the saint, also called Nicholas, was Archbishop of Myra, and, greatly honouring his nephew, he founded a monastery near the city, of which he made Nicholas abbot.

At this uncle's death Nicholas desired to retire into the deserts, to perfect himself amongst the 'anchorites' in solitude. But it was revealed to him in a vision that he was to stay amongst the multitudes and be the shepherd of the people and their saint.

He made a voyage to Egypt and the Holy Land, and saw St. Anthony and the Fathers of the Desert, but, obedient to the heavenly vision, resisted his longing to live amongst them. On this voyage a fearful storm arose and all was given up for lost, when at his prayers the storm became calm and all were saved, one sailor who had fallen overboard being restored to life. Hence St. Nicholas is also the patron of sailors.

He visited the sacred places of Palestine, bathed with his tears the soil of Gethsemane and Calvary, always, in the Holy Land, walking barefoot and bareheaded, and often creeping on his knees for reverence and tender gratitude and love.

In the cave where the Virgin and St. Joseph and the Child Jesus were said to have spent a night on the flight into Egypt he stayed many hours, and when he died a church was built over it in his name.

Then he quietly returned to his monastery at Myra, to the great joy of his monks. And soon after he was elected Archbishop. His election came about in this wise : A good old priest had been told in a dream that the first who entered the church on the morning of the election was the man designed by God to be Archbishop. Nicholas as usual,

[1] Therefore three purses or three golden balls are the symbols of St. Nicholas in art, as in the Ansidei Madonna of Raphael.

spending most of his nights in prayer, was the first to be at the door of the church in the morning, and he was chosen, to the great joy of all the city.

Then soon after his election a dreadful famine laid all the region waste. Other incidents among those commonly rendered in the pictures of his life are connected with this famine.

It was told St. Nicholas, to whom the sorrows of his flock were always his own, that a merchant with corn ships was waiting in one of the ports of Sicily, not having decided where to sell his corn.

In a dream, St. Nicholas appeared to him, telling him of the great profits he might reap by bringing his corn to Myra, and placing three gold pieces under his pillow as a pledge.

In the morning the merchant found the three gold pieces under his pillow, and hastened at once to Myra with his corn ships. But the famine still continuing, St. Nicholas induced the owners of some other corn ships who were on their way to Constantinople, where their corn was already due, to sell a portion to his people, promising them that the amount should not fall short when they reached their destination. They believed him, sold him a portion of the grain, and found when they came to the market at Constantinople their cargo undiminished, according to his promise.

Another terrible consequence of the famine was that an innkeeper near the city was tempted to murder children, place their bodies in a salting-pan, and serve them to his guests.

One day St. Nicholas was passing, and the voices of the murdered little ones cried to him from the cellar where they had been laid.

He went down to them at once, and at the prayer and words of faith these children stood up alive and whole and gave thanks to God and their deliverer, St. Nicholas.

Two incidents also are given showing the union of fire with his gentleness, that he also was a son of thunder as well as a son of consolation. One is the tradition that he was so indignant with Arius the heretic, at the Council of Nicæa, that he dealt him a heavy blow on the jaw.

The other is the story of his rushing to the place of execution to deliver two innocent men who had been unjustly condemned to death. Finding the victims on their knees, their eyes bandaged, ready to receive the fatal blow, St. Nicholas stopped the executioner, took away his sword, sent for the judge, reproved him for his mercenary cruelty, in virtue of his authority as bishop reversed his sentence, and sent the unjustly condemned men to their homes free and rejoicing.

And so this gracious vision of the protector of the weak and the oppressed, with a fire of indignation in his heart against all injustice and a tender glow of pity for all the suffering, shone on the toiling people through the stormy medieval days of oppression and tumult and of the rule of the strongest.

East and West, North and South, innocent little children at their Christmas festivals, brave men in peril on the sea, maidens in worse peril at home, saw shining on them this vision of mercy and charity and homely kindness and sympathy with common joys and sorrows, this Saint of the People, disciple, and reflection of the gracious light of Him who took the little children in His arms, proclaimed the opening of the prison to them that are bound, stilled the storms of Galilee ; of Him of Whom it is said that 'the common people heard Him gladly.'[1]

---

[1] Dedications of churches : 372. In art represented with three children in a tub or kneeling before him, with three golden balls or purses, with an anchor or a ship in the distance.

CHAPTER VI.

THE LEGENDS OF THE VIRGIN MARTYRS.

IN the Church of St. Apollinaris at Ravenna the mosaic of the stately procession of the Virgin Martyrs fills one side of the great basilica, ending in the manger where they cast down their crowns before the Infant Saviour in the arms of His Virgin Mother.

On the other side the men of the martyr host are seen advancing towards the enthroned Redeemer, sitting in majesty between the grand forms of the 'angels that excel in strength.'

For twelve hundred years those stately forms have looked down unchanged on the changing worshippers beneath them. When those mosaics were fresh the saints represented in them had but lately fought the good fight and passed away. Scarcely a century elapsed between the martyrdom of St. Cæcilia, St. Agnes, St. Agatha, and St. Lucy, and their being enshrined in the basilica at Ravenna ; scarcely a longer interval than between ourselves and the French Revolution with the saintly heroine Madame Elizabeth.

Legend has grown luxuriantly around those early martyrs since; but that the men and women whose names those mosaics commemorate lived, confessed their Lord, and died for their confession, is certainly no dream.

Those stately figures are strangely typical of their stories even as legend has expanded it.

Alike, with a majestic monotony, like the ancient chants which resounded through the church around them, there is yet a delicate variety, when we examine carefully, which breaks the sameness with individual distinctness. They stand before us types of many kinds of womanly endurance and womanly character.

Yet, it must be admitted, of womanhood in one aspect; courageous and pure and self-sacrificing, full of high aspiration and devotion, they follow the Lamb whithersoever He goeth; they banish by their presence the earthly and sensual gods and goddesses they denied and dethroned.

But of all that side of womanhood which creates homes, not a trace is here. For this we must go back further, to Bethany, and the mothers who brought their little children to the Lord. These stories glorify not so much the great virtue of chastity, which is for all human creatures, as the circumstance of celibacy, which cannot be for all.

And, however this assertion by living and dying of a high, independent feminine ideal, devoted to the service of no one special family, but to God and to all humanity for His sake, may have been needed to quench the evil fires which so consumed the corrupt Roman world, it is well not to forget that the medieval popular secular poetry, which sprang out of medieval popular sacred legends, too often glorified not the passionate purity of married love, but the romance and devotion of unlawful passion. It cannot but be at great risk that any ideal is set higher than the Divine creation of the family.

And this we cannot but bear in mind, as we reverently approach the four great Virgin Martyrs of the Latin Church, and the two great Virgin Patronesses, who, with the less known maiden Fides and the child Prisca, the martyred child, constitute the feminine side of our Anglican martyrology. Moreover it may help us, to think of the hidden saints whose lives so often are the foundation of those we see.

The glorious maiden martyrs Cæcilia and Agnes and Agatha and Lucy had mothers and fathers, who taught them the faith for which they suffered, and when for the faith they had taught, their children died, *suffered with them*, inevitably, and also rejoiced with them, encouraging them to be faithful unto death, yielding them up willingly like the blessed Mother who stood by the cross.

'Only my father' (he being a heathen still), said Perpetua, 'of all my family *will be unable to rejoice at my death.*' *And her mother was living.*

If we compare the saints with the stars, are not the stars we see like our own sun, globes of fiery vapour, spending themselves in giving forth light and heat to others, whilst the worlds around them, illuminated by these suns, the abodes of life, inhabited earths, where the human history goes on, must be invisible? And so perhaps it may be in a measure in the spiritual heavens. Each burning, fiery, light-giving star may involve a family of illumined inhabited worlds, homes of life and love, with all their moral conflicts and victories.

St. Cæcilia [1]

OF ROME.

November 22.

(Martyred circa A.D. 280. In all the Calendars. Sarum Ep. and Gosp.: Ecclus. xli. 9-12; St. Matt. xiii. 44-52.)

St. Cæcilia 'came of Romans and of noble kind,' of the family of the Cæcilii, descended from Caia Cæcilia Tanaquil, wife of Tarquin the Elder, a family illustrious through high achievements, its members being distinguished by their conquests over various races, as Cæcilius Macedonius, Balearicus, Numidicus, Creticus. Of the same house came the Cæcilia Metella whose tomb, erected by her husband, Crassus, is still the most prominent feature of the Appian Way.

From early childhood the faith and love of Christ possessed her heart. Her parents were still pagan, but they loved the gracious, gentle girl, and did not oppose her. They lived, an ancient tradition says, in the Campus Martius, in a palace full of the trophies and pomps of their ancestors. But all the splendour was nothing to her. Underneath her gold-embroidered robes she wore a garment of hair. She, 'heaven's lily,' had her home and palace in paradise.

And all the people saw in her 'the great light of wisdom, the magnanimity of faith,' and sundry works 'bright of excellence.' 'Swift and busy was she in every good work, and round and whole in persevering,' and burning ever in charity full bright.

And from her cradle she was fostered in the faith of

---

[1] In Ruinart's *Acta Sincera Martyrum* only her *name* is given as among the martyrs early commemorated. Alban Butler gives only a few lines to the story. In *Les Petits Bollandistes* the legend occupies twenty pages, from which, with Chaucer's *St. Cæcilia* and Mrs. Jameson's *Sacred and Legendary Art*, her story, as given here, is taken, the words of the narrative being frequently from Chaucer.

Different dates; according to the earliest A.D. 170, 180, and 230; Greek menology, A.D. 305. She was venerated very early, and her epitaph is probably in one of the catacombs. The legends connecting her with music are later.

Christ, and bare His Gospel in her mind, and never ceased in her prayer to love and dread God, 'beseeching Him to keep her a chaste maiden.'

The Book of the Gospels, hidden under her dress, rested always on her heart. From those words, which are spirit and life, she received a force beyond nature. Underneath her gold-embroidered robe she wore the garment of hair; and she fasted often.

Day and night she lived in hidden communion or in loving service of Him who died for her on the Cross. To Him her whole being was consecrated. She loved to pray in the churches of the catacombs and to celebrate the feasts of the martyrs, and to attend to the needs of His poor, who knew and loved the gentle maiden.

Her voice was of a ravishing sweetness, and she played on all kinds of instruments; but so full was her heart of joy that no instrument could utter it all, and so she invented the organ to pour forth in full tides the gladness of her soul in the praises of God.

In those days martyrdom was always a possibility. The Christians had still often to hide in the catacombs. But to her martyrdom was but a fire-guarded gate of the paradise of her Lord.

At last she was betrothed by her parents to Valerian, young, virtuous, and rich, but a pagan. She was married with all the solemn old Roman rites, in the tunic of pure white wool and with the girdle of white wool (but underneath was the hair garment of penance), and her hair plaited in six tresses like the vestals'.[1] And so this Christian vestal, vowed to Christ, veiled in the flame-coloured veil, was lifted over her husband's threshold into the house which she was to transform into a house of prayer and a house of mercy.

At once she told him of her vow and of the good angel who always guarded her. He listened to her with tender reverence, and asked to see the holy angel; but she told him that to have this granted his eyes must be opened by the well of living waters which springeth up for ever.

[1] *Les Petits Bollandistes.*

'Go,' she said, 'to the Appian Way, that is but three miles from this town, and say to the poor folks there what I shall tell you. Tell them that I, Cæcilia, sent you to them to show you the way to the good Urban the Old; and when you shall see him tell him the words I told you. And when he has purged you from sin then shall you see the angel.'

Urban was much moved when he saw Valerian come thus to him, 'quiet as a lamb with its ewe,' ready to learn. And suddenly a majestic old man, clad in white, shining clothes, appeared to them; and in his hand was a book written with letters of gold. And at first Valerian fell down before him as one dead; but he lifted him up by his hand, and then in this book he began to read of our Lord, and faith, and God, and Christianity, and of the Father of us all above, everywhere, over all.

And when he had read, the old man said, 'Believest thou this thing?'

And Valerian said, 'I believe all this.'

Then the old man vanished, and Urban christened Valerian. And he returned to his house. In their chamber he found Cæcilia, and with her an angel with two crowns, of which he placed one on the head of Cæcilia and one on that of Valerian.

And the angel told him that for his accepting of the will of God as to the vocation of Cæcilia he might ask what he would and it should be given him.

Then Valerian replied, 'I have a brother whom I love as I love no other man. I pray, then, that my brother may have grace to know the truth as I do, in this place.'

The angel, his face radiant with heavenly joy, said, 'God liketh thy request. As Cæcilia has won thy heart thou shalt win thy brother's, and both with the palm of martyrdom shall come into God's blissful rest.'

Then he went back to heaven and left the spouses full of joy, each admiring the crown on the brow of the other.

And scarcely had the angel left when Valerian's brother, Tiburtius, now become also the brother of Cæcilia, came into the room.

And when he smelt the fragrance of their celestial crowns he began to wonder, and said, 'I wonder whence the sweet smell of roses and lilies comes at this time of the year? For if I held them in my hand they could not be sweeter. I find the fragrance in my heart, and it hath changed me into another kind. Is it a dream?'

'All our life till now has been a dream; now we are in the reality,' Valerian replied. 'We have two crowns, snow white and rose red, that shine clearly, which thine eyes have no power to see; but as thou smellest them, through my prayer, so shalt thou see them clear, if without sloth thou wilt believe aright and know the very truth.'

Then he told his brother of the angel and of their Lord; and Cæcilia showed him all, open and plain, and that 'idols are but a vain thing, for they are dumb and also deaf,' and she spoke with such a fervour of eloquence that her voice was as heavenly music; and Tiburtius said, 'He that would not believe what you say would be but a beast.'

And then, full glad that he could see the truth, she embraced him as her brother and said ('this blissful maiden dear'), 'So as the love of Christ made me thy brother's wife, so this day I take thee for my ally.'

And then he also went to Urban, who baptised him 'with a glad heart and light,' and he became God's knight, and saw the angel of God.

And thus most blissful was the life of these three blessed ones for the mutual society, help, and comfort Cæcilia and Valerian had each of the other and of this beloved brother to them both. The fragrance of Paradise filled their home. Cæcilia sang sacred hymns with such sweetness that the angels came down to listen.

And they went about doing good, full of works of mercy towards the families of Christians bereaved by persecution, seeking out the bodies of their martyred brethren, embalming them and preparing them honourable sepulchres.

And so their good deeds reached the ears of the prefect of the city, Almachius. He would have stopped them, but they said, 'How can we desert our duty for anything man can do to us?' And they were seized and brought before the tribunal, and given the alternative of sacrificing to the gods or being put to death.

'Every day we offer sacrifices to God,' they said.

'To which of the gods?' asked Almachius.

'Is there more than one God?' said the brothers.

'Then the whole world is wrong and you and your brother alone are right!' said the prefect.

But Valerian said, 'Deceive thyself not, Almachius. The Christians who have embraced this doctrine cannot any longer be numbered. It is you who are as the planks which float in the water after a shipwreck.'

Their patrician dignity did not save them from ignominious punishment. But their sufferings and heroism touched the hearts of the officers of Almachius, especially of his attendant Maximus. Weeping for pity he said, 'O flower of Roman youth, and brothers united by an affection so tender, why will ye despise the gods and thus go to death as to a feast?'

They told him of immortal life, 'of the soul laying aside the vesture of the body at death, as the body lays aside its clothing at night.'

Maximus took them to his house, and there Cæcilia also came at night, and Maximus and many others turned from their false faith to God alone, and were christened; and afterwards, when day waxed light, Cæcilia said to them with steadfast cheer, 'Now, Christ's own knights "leve" and dear, cast away the works of darkness and arm yourselves in the works of brightness. You have fought the good fight, your course is done, and have kept the faith. Go to the crown of life that may not fail. The rightful Judge shall give it you.' And when this was done men led them forth to do sacrifice.

Then were they led along the Appian Way, these new Christians, Maximus and his soldiers, with the dew of baptism fresh on their brows—along the Appian Way, by the tomb of the Cæcilia Metella, who was of the young bride's ancient house.

But when they were brought to the place, no incense nor sacrifice would they offer, but fell on their knees with humble heart and glad devotion, and lost both their heads in that place; and their souls went to the King of grace.

And Maximus saw their souls glide to heaven with the angels, 'full of beauty and light, as if going to a nuptial feast.' And as he told this with piteous tears many were converted; and he was beaten to death.

The Christians she had so long served rescued the bodies of her heroes for Cæcilia, and she herself buried them, with tears of farewell and hope, and with sacred perfumes, and placed above them the stone tablet engraven with the crown and palm.

Maximus also she reverently buried, and on his memorial stone she engraved a phœnix, in tender memory of the words concerning the resurrection and the deathless life by which Valerian had won him to the faith.

Not many days were the three blessed ones separated. Martyrdom soon reunited them in one home.

The prefect sent officers who brought Cæcilia before the tribunal, covetous, it was said, of her wealth.

But her gentle and gracious ways melted the hearts of those sent to take her.

They bewailed her being thus sacrificed in her youth. But she said, 'To die for Christ is not to lose youth but to renew it.' And her wise and eloquent words as, standing on the marble steps of her house, she spoke to them of their Lord and of immortal life with Him, won these also to the faith.

She asked a few days' delay, and during that time many more were turned to Christ, until at last she was brought before the tribunal.

'What manner of woman art thou?' said Almachius.

'I am a gentlewoman born,' she said; 'among men I am called Cæcilia, but my noblest name is Christian.'

'Knowest thou not,' he said, 'that I have the power of life and death?'

'Not of life,' she said; 'but thou canst indeed be a minister of death. The power of man is but as a bladder which a needle can pierce and burst.'

The prefect himself was smitten with a reverence which prevented his ordering her to a public execution.

She was taken to his house to perish by heat and suffocation in the calidarium of the baths. But through the long night and the day also, for all the fire and the heat of the bath, 'she sate all cold, and felt it no woe.'

' But in that bath she was to leave her life.' At last the headsman came and smote her neck three times with his sword.

More than three strokes were not lawful. And so half dead, with her fair neck bent, ' he left her lie, and on his way he went.'

The Christian people gathered round her, and three days she lived in that torment; and never did she cease to teach the faith to those she had fostered and led to believe, and all the time her sweet voice sang the praises of God. And quietly and with thought for everyone she distributed her wealth among those who had need, and for her house she prayed it might be made a temple to the Lord for ever.

And so at last, laid down like a lamb for the sacrifice, her head softly resting and her hands clasped together, she breathed out her soul to God, to the Lord, to whom in her childhood she had given her whole heart.

> Her house the church of Saint Cecile hight;
> Saint Urban hallowed it, as he well might;
> In which unto this day in noble wise
> Men don to Christ and to his saint servise.

And in the church built over her house, beyond the Tiber, lies her statue above the tomb in which her body was removed from the Cemetery of St. Calixtus, where she had been laid beside the two brothers she had won to Christ. The spotless marble represents her lying as, Baronius says, her body was found, not as one dead and buried, but on her right side, as one asleep.

And in the sacristy is an ancient sarcophagus with the inscription, 'This is the house in which St. Cæcilia prayed.'[1]

[1] Dedications of churches : 2. In art represented crowned, bearing wreaths of roses or other flowers ; a palm, a sword, an almond branch, a sprig of flowers. In later representation with a portable organ or harp, and playing on an organ.

St. Agnes

OF ROME.

January 21.

(Martyred A.D. 304. In all the Calendars. Sarum Ep. and Gosp. : Ecclus. li. 1-8; St. Matt. xiii. 44-52.)

'Genuine Acts of this most celebrated martyr we do not possess,' Ruinart says, 'but the loss may be in some measure repaired from the witness of the Fathers.'

St. Ambrose had an especial veneration for her; Prudentius also has a hymn in honour of her. St. Jerome writes of her to Demetrias, 'In the writings and tongues of all nations the life of Agnes is praised in the churches, the blessed martyr Agnes, who overcame her own youth and the tyrant, and consecrated her chastity by martyrdom.'

Constantine built a Basilica over the place of her martyrdom outside the walls, near the Porta Pia. St. Gregory preached to the people his homilies on St. Matthew, on her festival.[1]

The Basilica on the Via Nomentana is known to all, where every year it is the custom to bless twin lambs, from whose wool is woven the pallium of the Archbishops.

Agnes, like St. Cæcilia, came of a noble Roman house, and is the favourite saint of the Roman women, and was called to her confession at an earlier age than Cæcilia, at thirteen, when scarcely more than a child. She was the child of Christian parents and wealthy. From her earliest childhood her whole heart was given to the Saviour who died for her. But the son of the governor of Rome fell passionately in love with her. He sought her hand in marriage from her parents ; but they respected the feelings of their daughter and received his advances with hesitation. Impatient of delay, he sought an interview with the young maiden to plead his own cause.

[1] Ruinart.

But Agnes would not listen to his suit. Her heart was already bound to 'One,' she said, 'by whose love alone my soul lives. Such is His beauty that the brightness excels all the brightness of the sun and the stars; the heavens are ravished with His glory and say in their language that they are as darkness to His light. He has given me a treasure beyond all the wealth of the Roman Empire. Those who serve Him are loaded with riches. He is so powerful that all the forces of heaven and earth cannot vanquish Him; the sick are healed by His touch, the dead rise at His voice, and I love him more than my soul and life and am willing indeed to die for Him.'

Her words and her disdain incensed her suitor and turned his love to bitter jealousy and rage. His father, Sempronius, the governor, made every possible effort to change the mind of Agnes with regard to his son, until one day one of his people told him she was a Christian, and it was to Him the Christians called their Lord and King her heart was given.

Then the prefect was glad, because if he could not win her heart for his son he could avenge her disdain on the unconquerable maiden without seeming to be acting from private resentment.

He therefore summoned her before his tribunal.

'Be married, Agnes,' he said, 'or, if thou wilt not, then sacrifice to the goddess Vesta, and serve her all thy life among the virgins who keep the sacred fire for Rome.'

And as she refused he threatened her with the direst insults. But she said, 'If I will not be faithless to my Lord for thy son, who nevertheless has my esteem and who is a living creature of God, still less will I abandon His service for lifeless forms that can neither hear nor see. And as to thy threatened wrongs, my Lord Jesus can send His angels, or be Himself around me an impenetrable citadel.'

And her trust was rewarded. He whom she loved and trusted preserved her inviolate in the midst of every attempted outrage.

The fair tresses of her own hair enfolded her like a vestment of cloth of gold, and moreover a heaven-sent robe whiter than snow enfolded her, not white only but luminous, so that the darkness shone like heavenly day around her; and those who approached her with evil intent grew pure and chaste in heart by the sweet purity of her presence, and went away penitent and renewed, with a new vision of what life, womanhood, and holy love could be.

Only the prefect's son, the cause of all her suffering, blinded by his passion, seemed unable to be raised by the vision of her purity, and he fell, smitten by the wrath of Heaven, blinded and convulsed and stiffened in death, at her feet.

Then the prefect, his father, mad with grief and anger, called her sorceress and murderess.

But Agnes made the wretched father understand that his son had perished not by her will, but from the wrath of heaven, so that he entreated with tears her prayers.

And she prayed so fervently to God for the life of her persecutor that it was given back. The son was brought back indeed to a new life in every sense, and went as a herald of the Cross through Rome, declaring that there was no god in heaven or earth, in the heights or the depths, but the God whom the Christians adored.

Then the prefect would have gladly saved the saviour of his son; but it was too late.

The tide of priestly and popular fury he had raised swept him on. 'She is a sorceress! a witch!' cried the people and the priests of the idols, 'and she must die!'

They made a pile of fagots and kindled them, and set her on them as on a funeral pyre. But the flames divided and encircled her like a rainbow, and moreover they blazed forth all around and consumed those who had kindled them.

At last the executioner mounted the pyre; and the young girl knelt down and prayed. 'Blessed be Thy holy name, O Lord. I see what I have longed for. I hold fast what I have loved. My heart and tongue and soul praise Thee. I go to Thee, O Thou eternal God, who reignest with Him only, Jesus Christ, for ever and ever.'

The executioner trembled and turned pale, but Agnes quietly gathered her robe around her, covered her face with her hands, and bent fearless to the mortal blow.

The Christians of Rome laid her to rest in a catacomb which still bears her name, in the Via Nomentana, outside the gates of Rome, fearlessly following her to the grave not with wailings and lamentings, but with joy and triumph. And among them were her father and mother, who had trained her for Christ and whose home she had never left. Day and night her parents prayed beside the sacred grave; and eight days after her martyrdom, when they were in prayer together there, on the winter day, they saw, in a vision, a company of virgins, clothed in cloth of gold, with precious stones, crowned with garlands, pearls, and diamonds; and in the midst of them came forward St. Agnes, triumphant and glorious, with a lamb whiter than snow by her side.

She stopped, and begged her companions also to stop, and turning to her parents, she said to them, 'My beloved parents, weep not for me as for one dead, but rejoice rather with me that I have now in heaven the crown of glory in such a holy company, and that I am with Him whom when on earth I loved with all my heart and soul and strength.'

Then she was silent, and passed on with the heavenly choir who bore her company.

This was on January 28.

And ever since the vision of St. Agnes, the pure and saintly maiden, and her snow-white lamb have shone on Christendom amidst the winter and the snow, a type of the love which purifies and the purity which is the purity not of ice, but of fire, the sacred vestal fire of the City of God.[1]

---

[1] Dedications of churches: 3. Represented in art with a lamb, or angel; in a fire; angels covering her with a garment; a sword in her hand or in her throat; a dagger; a palm; a short cross; a dove bringing her a bridal ring.

St. Agatha
Of Sicily.
February 5.

(Martyred A.D. 251. Sarum Ep. and Gosp. : Ecclus. li. 1–8 ;
St. Matt. xiii. 45–52.)

The current of the story leads us again to the borders of the old Greek world. Through all the contests of Carthage and Rome, the touch and memory of Greece seem to linger among the old Greek colonies founded, before Rome began to be, on the coasts of Sicily and Southern Italy.

The name of Agatha is in the martyrology of the Carthaginian Church, so early swept away that every mention of any name among her commemorations is a sure title of ancient pedigree.

Her praises are sung among those of other martyrs by Venantius Fortunatus. Palermo and Catania dispute the honour of being her birthplace, but it was at Catania that she lived and suffered.

Her martyrdom, according to the legend, though it took place under Decius, was due not to any general edict, or to the popular fury, but to the special wickedness of the governor Quintianus.

She was of an illustrious family. Quintianus, hearing of her beauty and her holiness, determined to tempt her from Christianity and purity. Unable to make any impression on her, he gave her into the keeping of a wicked woman and her nine yet more wicked daughters.

For nine days the good and gentle maiden was left in the hands of those lost ones, themselves altogether gone over to the side of the tempter and become tempters. But in the end they confessed it would be easier to melt rocks than to tear Christianity from her heart.

'My soul,' she said, 'is founded and built on Christ. Your words are but wind, your persuasions like a stormy rain, your threats like a rushing river. But this wind, this rain, this river, let loose against the foundations of this house of mine, cannot shake it, for it is founded on a rock.'

Quintianus, enraged at his failure, summoned her before his tribunal and said, 'What is thy condition?'

'I am free-born,' she replied—'indeed, of noble birth.'

'Why, then, if of a noble and illustrious family, dost thou show by thy conduct the baseness of a slave?'

'Being a servant of Christ, I am in this sense of servile condition.'

'If thou wert indeed noble, wouldst thou take the name of slave?'

'The service of Christ is perfect freedom and the highest title of nobility.'

'Are not we, then, who despise the service of Christ and worship the gods, of noble rank?'

'Your nobleness has sunk to a slavery so low that not only are you slaves of sin but subjected to wood and stone.'

He threatened her with torture unless she would sacrifice to the gods.

'Take care,' she said, 'that you do not become like the gods you worship—thyself like thy Jupiter, thy wife like Venus. What worse curse could we wish to anyone than to wish them to follow those execrable lives?'

'To what end this torrent of words?' he replied. And he commanded her torments to begin.

All the suffering only wrung praises of God from her lips, except once, when in the agony of her wounded breast she asked if no mother's breast had nurtured her persecutor.

Thrown back again into the dungeon, at midnight a venerable old man appeared to her, bearing a vase, and before him an angel carrying a wreath. The venerable man offered to heal her. But she hesitated. 'If it is the will of my Saviour Christ to heal me,' she said, 'He will heal me Himself.' And she drew her veil around her and would accept no alleviation of her pain until the old man told her he was the Apostle Peter, and said, 'Fear not, my daughter, for Christ has sent me to minister to thee.'

Not only were her wounds healed, but the prison was filled with a light so brilliant that the gaolers fled in terror and her fellow prisoners counselled her to escape. But she refused and said, 'Tempt not me to lose my crown and be a cause of trouble to my guards. With the aid of my Lord Jesus Christ I will keep my confession to the end.'

Four days afterwards she was summoned again before the judgment seat, and came forth again fresh and strong, and healed of all her wounds.

'Who has healed thee?' Quintianus asked.

'It is the Christ, the Son of God.'

'Dost thou dare still to speak of thy Christ?' he cried.

'My lips shall never cease to confess Him nor my heart to call upon Him.'

Then Quintianus had a great fire kindled, and, bound and helpless, the maiden was flung on it. But a great earthquake shook all the city, and the people rose against the governor, and said this was sent for his cruelty to the maiden Agatha.

And as they took her back to her prison and would have laid her on burning coals, she stretched out her hands to heaven and said, 'O Thou who hast won my heart from earth and made me victorious over tortures, and given me courage and patience, I pray Thee now to receive my soul.'

Then, having made this prayer, she rendered up her spirit.

And it was said that as they buried her in a new tomb, with balms and perfumes, a young man suddenly appeared, clothed in rich raiment, with a troop of more than a hundred beautiful children in magnificent robes.

No one had ever seen him in Catania before. But he entered the tomb where they had laid the virgin's body and placed near her head a marble tablet on which were inscribed these words: 'Holy, devoted soul, the glory of God, the protector of thy city.' And then he disappeared and was never seen again.[1]

[1] Dedications of churches: 3. Represented with a knife at her breast, and various tortures.

St. Lucy

OF SYRACUSE.

December 13.

(Martyred A.D. 303. Sarum Ep. and Gosp. : Ecclus. li. 9-12 ; St. Matt. xiii. 44-52.)

Fifty years had passed away since the young maiden Agatha had been laid to rest in the new tomb in fair Catania, at the foot of Etna, whose fiery floods the maidenly veil she had drawn around her in her dungeon (preserved as a precious relic) was believed to have turned aside from her city, when, at Syracuse, another persecution arose under Diocletian, and another Christian maiden, as young and fair, of the same race as Agatha, was found ready to die for the Lord to whom she had consecrated her life.

Lucy—St. Lucia—lost her father early, and lived with her mother, Eutychia. Lucy had been early trained as a Christian, but her mother and her relations had betrothed her in her childhood to a young man of her own city, rich and noble, but a pagan.

Lucy had desired never to marry at all, but this marriage to a pagan was an especial desecration and terror to her, and from day to day she entreated it might be put off.

Meantime her mother had been suffering for years from a disease no physician of the many she consulted was able to cure.

The fame of the wonders wrought at the tomb of St. Agatha at Catania reached Syracuse, and Lucy persuaded her mother to make a journey with her to Catania and implore the intercession of the saint, their young country-woman.

While they were at Catania, in the church there happened to be read from the Gospels the story of the woman with the issue of blood, who, like her mother, 'had suffered many things of many physicians, and grew nothing better, but rather worse,' and who was healed by touching the hem of the garment of Christ.

This encouraged Lucy to hope for her mother, and she told Eutychia her hope, and the mother and young daughter together, after everyone else had left the church, stayed prostrate in prayer before the tomb of Agatha.

And as they thus knelt for a long time, the young girl fell into a sweet sleep, and in a vision she saw St. Agatha in dazzling lustre of diamonds and pearls, amidst a troop of angels. She said, 'Lucy, my dear sister, virgin consecrated to God, well art thou called Lucia, who art a light to the faithful. Why dost thou ask of me what thou canst obtain at once thyself for thy mother? Know that thy faith has won back health for her, and that as Jesus Christ has rendered Catania famous for my sake, Syracuse also shall be made glorious through thee.'

Lucy awoke at these words, and turning to Eutychia said, 'You are healed, my mother; but, as God has given you health, grant me this grace : never more to speak to me of marriage, but to leave me free to give myself wholly to the Lord.'

Eutychia consented, and then Lucy asked another favour.

'I pray you, also, my mother, to give me what would have been my dowry, that I may use it to help the poor who are the members of Him who possesses all my heart.'

Eutychia, with some natural pride in her good administration of her daughter's inheritance, and with a natural clinging to her worldly goods, which gives additional value to her giving them up, replied, 'You know, my daughter, that during the nine years since your father died I have increased rather than diminished the wealth he left you. I will give you all this, and you shall do with it what you will. Only for what belongs to me I should be glad to keep it while I live, and when you have closed my eyes this also will be yours.'[1]

But Lucy wished her mother to share in her willing

[1] *Les Petits Bollandistes.*

offering, and persuaded her that it was little to do for God to give Him what we are no longer able to keep. And so together, with one mind, when they had returned to Syracuse the happy mother and child began to distribute their wealth among the poor. By degrees they sold their jewels and their costly furniture and their estates, and spent the price in ransoming captives, delivering prisoners, succouring widows and orphans and all who had need.

The young nobleman to whom Lucy had been betrothed hearing of this was much irritated, and complained to Paschasius, prefect of the town, that Lucy, who ought to have been his wife, being misled by the superstitions of the Christians, was thus wasting his substance.

The judge summoned her at once before his tribunal and spared no efforts to make her sacrifice to the gods; but Lucy said, 'The perfect and holy sacrifice that we have to offer is to visit the fatherless and the widows and the afflicted, and to succour them. For three years I have been offering this sacrifice to the living God, and there remains nothing now but for me to offer Him myself.'

Then he threatened her with the edicts of the Emperor.

She replied that if he had to please his sovereign, she feared only to displease Him—the Lord—who had the keys of hell and death.

He would not listen to her further, but said, 'You will not speak thus when you come to suffer.'

But she said it would not then be she that would speak, but the Holy Ghost, who would speak through her.

'You think, then, that the Holy Ghost is in you?' he said.

'I believe,' she replied, 'that those who live pure lives are temples of the Holy Ghost.'

Then he threatened her with insult and outrage.

But she replied, 'The Holy Ghost will not abandon me for that. My body may be in thy power, but no violence to *that* can destroy the purity of my soul. That can neither be sin nor stain to which the soul does not consent.

If thou wouldst cut off my hand, and with it offer sacrifice to idols, God would not impute that to me.'

Paschasius, enraged, commanded his officers to take her away; but the power of God came on her and made her immovable, so that not all the force they could bring, with many oxen bound to her by ropes, could move the young girl from where she stood.

Then they kindled a great fire around her, but the flames had no power over her, any more than over the three Hebrew children in the furnace of old.

She, in the midst of the flames, consoled the Christians around, and predicted the end of the persecution; and so, succouring and comforting all around her to the last, her life was ended at length by the stroke of a poniard.

And in a few years—less than twenty—Constantine became Emperor; St. Lucy's dying words were fulfilled, and the Christians were persecuted no more.

Whether the mother who had first trained her martyred child for Christ, and then so meekly followed her on the higher way of service and sacrifice, survived her, and lived to see, according to her daughter's prediction, the Christian religion triumph throughout the Empire, the legend does not say. Beside the few whose names are visible to us are always multitudes of the hidden ones, whose canonisation is at another tribunal.[1]

---

[1] The incident from a later legend that her eyes were taken out and then miraculously restored, which is represented in many of the pictures of St. Lucy by her eyes being carried on a dish, is considered by *Les Petits Bollandistes* to be a kind of allegorical play on the name Lucia, or to refer to the story of another St. Lucy (the Chaste) with whose beautiful eyes a young man fell so madly in love that to save his soul she plucked them out.

Dedications of churches: 2. Represented with a sword through her neck; oxen unable to drag her along, &c.

St. Prisca

OF ROME.

January 18.

(Martyred A.D. 270. Sarum Ep. and Gosp.: Ecclus. li. 9–12;
St. Matt. xiii. 44–52.)

Among the virgin martyrs in our Calendar are two who may be called children.

The sacred aureole rests on every age as well as kindred, on the white hair of Polycarp, and also on the innocent heads of the young girls Prisca and Faith.

The name of Prisca, and only her name, is in the 'Acta Sincera Martyrum.' Her legend is very confused as to chronology; it seems to have become entangled with the story of Prisca or Priscilla, the wife of Aquila.

The Church of St. Prisca is on the Aventine Hill, in Rome, and stands, according to an old tradition, on the site of the house of Aquila and Priscilla.

Her story may be given thus :—

She was a maiden of an illustrious Roman house. Her parents were Christians. She was apprehended and brought as a Christian before the Emperor Claudius. He thought it would be easy to persuade the gentle and beautiful child to change her faith. She was, therefore, led into the Temple of Apollo and commanded to offer incense; but she said she would never bend her knees to any but the One God who made heaven and earth, and His Son Jesus Christ our Lord.

Then she was subjected to blows and tortures such as it seemed impossible her childish frame could bear, so that all who saw it wondered and were touched with pity. But none of these things moved her. She seemed clothed in heavenly light.

Finding the child unconquerable, the Emperor sent her back to prison, and thence they brought her forth to the amphitheatre to be devoured by a lion. But the lion forgot his savageness and would not touch the child, but fawned at her feet, gentle as a lamb.

After other torments, and after shutting her up a long time in one of the temples of the gods, all in vain, she was led to the Ostian Gate and beheaded on January 19.

It was said that an eagle watched over the body of the child until the Christians were able to come and bury it; the king of beasts and the imperial bird both paying homage to the martyr child, whom Jesus the Lord had indeed taken up in His arms and blessed.

Great honour was paid to her memory in ancient days in England.[1]

---

[1] Ruinart in the *Acta Sincera* does not even give St. Prisca's name. It was honoured in Europe in the fifth century, but the legend was rejected as not trustworthy by Pope Gelasius in 494.

Represented with a lion near her; with an eagle guarding her in death.

St. Faith (Fides, Foi)

Of Aquitaine.
October 6.

(Martyred late in 3rd Century. Sarum Ep. and Gosp. : Ecclus. li. 9-12 ; St. Matt. xiii. 44-52.)

The other child martyr in our Calendar links us with the ancient martyrologies of France.

Her name (only her name) is found in the 'Acta Sincera' of Ruinart, with that of St. Caprasius.

In the 'Petits Bollandistes' she stands among a glorious company of fellow martyrs, the martyrs of Agen (in Aquitaine), St. Caprasius, St. Faith, St. Alberta (sister of St. Faith), St. Felician, and a great number of others massacred by the crowd.

They suffered in the persecution of Diocletian, under the same ferocious persecutor who put St. Vincent to death at Valencia—Dacian, the governor of Spain.

From Spain, whence, according to the local legends, had first come to Agen missionaries of the Cross, Dacian swept across into Aquitaine. Arriving at Agen, he threatened death to all Christians who would not worship the gods, and spread before their eyes the instruments of torture he had used in Spain. Horror seized the Christians, and they fled to the neighbouring hill of St. Vincent, where they found a refuge in the cave near the top, surrounded with wild rocks. The Bishop Caprasius went with them, to protect and minister to his flock.

And so it happened that the glory of leading the forlorn hope of Agen fell on the little maiden Faith, still but a child ; 'for God has chosen the weak things of the world to confound the things that are mighty.' Of noble blood and gentle courtesy of manners, the beauty of the soul exceeded the beauty of her form. From her cradle she loved the Saviour, her God, and would have no other master.

Left in Agen whilst the other Christians had taken refuge amongst the rocks, she was summoned before Dacian. As she went to the tribunal signing herself with the Cross, as it had been signed at baptism, on brow, lips, and breast, she prayed, 'Jesus Christ, my Lord, Thou never forsakest those who call upon Thee. Help Thy servant and send my lips words worthy of the questions I have to answer before the tyrant.'

'What is your name?' said Dacian.

'My name is Faith,' she replied.

'And your religion?'

'I am a Christian from my infancy. I serve the Lord Jesus Christ with all my heart and soul.'

'Sacrifice to our gods,' the governor said, 'or you shall die under the torture.'

She heard these threats without fear. Looking to heaven she said in a clear strong voice, 'In the name of Jesus Christ my Lord not only will I not sacrifice to your gods, but I am ready to suffer all kinds of torments.'

She was stretched, like Vincent, on the fiery bed of torture.

But all the people were touched with pity to see a young and noble maiden thus tortured and suffering with such courage. 'What cruelty, what injustice,' they cried, 'to torment thus a young maiden of an illustrious house, who has done nothing amiss, whose lips have not been polluted with an evil word, whose only crime is adoring her God!'

And that day a multitude whose names we know not confessed the faith of Jesus Christ and won the palm of martyrdom.

But on the mountain with his fugitive flock among the rocks, the Bishop Caprasius, ever bearing in his heart those of his people still left in the city, saw in a vision how the young maiden Faith was suffering. And as he prayed for her and looked again towards heaven he saw the young maiden crowned with a crown of precious stones, brilliant and of many colours, and from the clouds he beheld a dove descend and rest on her head, and from the wings of the dove fell a soft dew which quenched the flames.

Then the bishop felt his place was beside the sufferers, and returning to the city, his mother met him and encouraged him to suffer for his Lord. And he also made a good confession.

And many hearts were turned from heathenism to Christ by the cruelty of the persecution and the patience of the martyrs, and numbers came to the Temple of Diana and refused to do sacrifice, and therefore were beheaded, and multitudes more were massacred in an assault of the heathen crowds, instigated by Dacian.

Thus a great multitude was added to the noble army of martyrs from the city of Agen. But at the head of that heroic company was the young maiden Faith, revered for ages in England as well as in her own Aquitaine, in London as well as in Agen. And to this day to a little island of silence and peace in the midst of the roar of the tide of the great city we give the name of 'St. Faith's, under St. Paul's,' in memory of the young girl who gave her life for her Lord at Agen, in Aquitaine, fifteen hundred years ago.[1]

[1] Dedications of churches: 16. Represented in art; three sisters, as children, holding swords.

St. Margaret [1]

OF ANTIOCH.

July 20.

(Martyred A.D. 306.   Sarum Ep. and Gosp. : Ecclus. li. 9-12 ;
St. Matt. xiii. 44-52.)

Once more from the West back to the East—from Rome and Spain and England and France to Alexandria and Antioch, not only for the saints but for the legends.

With St. Margaret and St. Catharine we step out of the region of historical research altogether, into the world of religious romance and sacred ideals. What history there is in the matter is concerned not with the life but the legend.

Two of the four great virgin patronesses, St. Catharine, St. Barbara, St. Margaret, and St. Ursula, are in our Calendar ; St. Catharine and St. Margaret belonging both to the East and West.

They stand, these two types of ideal womanhood, Margaret, daisy of Paradise and pearl of the heavenly city, with her dragon, feminine counterpart of St. George, conquering, according to one form of the legend, by being sacrificed, and in the strength of purity destroying the destroyer ; Catharine, queenly in rank and in intelligence, satisfied with nothing but the loftiest love and the highest wisdom, keen to search into the secrets of the universe and the laws of the stars, and finding the secret of secrets to be the Divine love, at the heart of all the secrets and at the root of all the laws.

The 'cult' of St. Margaret was brought back by the crusaders with that of St. Catharine from Syria to Europe, in the eleventh century.

And from that time the two beautiful ideals and allegories

---

[1] The legend is given from *Les Petits Bollandistes* and in Mrs. Jameson's *Sacred and Legendary Art*.

rose higher and brighter before Latin Christendom, and especially England. The name of Margaret becomes one of our most familiar names, partly also through the honour paid to Margaret, Queen of Scotland. There are 238 churches dedicated in honour of St. Margaret amongst us.

The legend has many forms; it changes like a summer cloud. By the Greeks she is called Marina. She was the daughter of a priest of the old gods, of high rank and reputation, called Ædesius, and was born at that Antioch, in Pisidia, where St. Paul confirmed the souls of the disciples, exhorting them to 'continue in the faith, and that we must through much tribulation enter the kingdom of God.' The echo of the Apostolic words had not died away. Margaret's mother died early, and the child was committed to the care of a poor woman six miles from the town, and grew up with her foster mother amongst the fields and flocks.

This foster mother was a Christian, and from her infancy Margaret learned to love the Saviour, and gave herself to Him as her only Master and Lord. When her father heard that she had become a Christian he was very angry and drove her from him; and she went back to the foster mother and lived content and humble with her as a child and servant, thinking nothing of her noble birth, and in all things gentle and obedient; and the two loved each other as mother and daughter. And Margaret used to keep her foster mother's few sheep, like the peasant girl who a thousand years afterwards was inspired, as she believed, through Margaret's voice to rescue France. So the peaceful days passed on until Olybrius, the pagan governor, happening to pass that way, saw the young maiden watching the little flock, and, smitten by her gentle grace and beauty, fell in love with her.

'If she is a slave by birth,' he said to his attendants, 'she must be purchased for me. If she is free-born I will make her my wife.'

The attendants made haste to seize Margaret and bring her to the prefect's house; but as they took her thither, fearing the torture and her own weakness, she prayed to the Lord to keep her, body and soul.

And the officers who had captured her said to the prefect, 'This young maiden is an enemy of the gods of the Empire. She adores Jesus, who was crucified by the Jews, and no promises nor threats of ours can move her.'

When she appeared before Olybrius he said, 'Fear nothing, young maiden; tell me whether thou art slave or free-born.'

She answered, 'My family is well known in the city and I am of no obscure house. But, since thou speakest of freedom, know that I depend on no man. I am a servant of Jesus Christ. From my earliest years I have learned to revere and honour Him, and Him I will adore for ever.'

'What is thy name?' said the prefect.

'Men call me Margaret,' she said, 'but in holy baptism I received a more illustrious name. I call myself a Christian.'

Then, furious with anger and passion, the prefect had a great tribunal erected and summoned all the city to witness the trial of the young girl, hoping the terror of such publicity would subdue her. The day of trial came, and the multitude being assembled he began by offering her the choice between life and death, joy and torments.

She replied, 'Life and joy, thanks to God, I have indeed found. They are in the strong citadel of my heart.'

The words she spoke in confession of her faith were so eloquent and forcible that the prefect said they could not be her own; she was entangled in a net of sophism and magic enchantment.

She said the words and wisdom were not indeed her own, but that if he or any would believe the Christ they would at once see and understand as she did.

Then, proceeding from persuasion to punishment, by the prefect's orders she was subjected to torture after torture, till she herself could not bear to behold what she was strengthened patiently to endure, and covered her eyes with her robe.

She was finally thrown into a dungeon, where the great adversary himself assailed her with his wiles and his terrors.

The wiles which her simplicity of heart penetrated she despised. And when at last he rushed on her in the form of a terrible dragon, breathing out sulphurous flame, she vanquished him by holding up before him the cross of her Lord. Or, according to the more popular story, she was actually devoured by the monster, who then burst asunder and vanished, leaving the young maid unhurt and the prison full of a great glory of light, in the midst of which appeared the Cross, and resting on it a heavenly dove, whiter than snow, with a heavenly voice encouraging her to persevere.

The next day the tortures were renewed, but neither fire nor water nor any of the elements created could injure this servant of the Creator or subdue her soul. Through all the torments she spoke to the people of the Saviour she loved, so that multitudes came to Christ and to the crown of martyrdom through her.

And to silence the eloquent preaching of her lips and of her patience, at last, she was borne outside the city, and when she had knelt and said her last prayer she was beheaded.[1]

---

[1] Dedications of churches : 238. Represented crowned ; piercing a dragon with a long cross or spear ; with dragon and lamb ; with dragon chained ; bursting through body of dragon ; trampling on dragon, grasping its head.

St. Catharine
OF EGYPT.
November 25.

(Martyred A.D. 307. Sarum Ep. and Gosp. : Ecclus. li. 1–8 ;
St. Matt. xiii. 44–52.)

The legend of St. Catharine does not date further than the eighth century even in the East, and it does not rise above the horizon of Western Christendom until after the Crusades in the eleventh century.[1]

It is curious as an evidence of the common life which throbbed through medieval Christendom and of the flowing back of the East on the West through the Crusades, to find, by the beginning of the fourteenth century, Venice taking her as patroness of her colleges ; fifty churches dedicated in her name in England; and in France the heroic peasant girl of Domremy, dreaming in her childhood among the forests of Catharine and Margaret as the foremost saints in Paradise, and believing she received that inspiration of 'great pity' by which she rescued France, through their voices.

When Joan of Arc was asked, during that six months' trial at Rouen, 'Did she know she was to be wounded at Orleans ? '

' I did know it,' she said, 'but I told the king nevertheless not to desist from action.' And 'St. Catharine heartened her,' she said, ' so that she rode on in spite of her wound.'

They asked her how she knew St. Michael and the angels from St. Margaret and St. Catharine.

' By their voices,' she said, 'and because they told me.'

They asked her details as to their forms.

[1] Ruinart (and Alban Butler, quoting Joseph Assemani) come to the conclusion that all the particulars we have on which we can depend are a passage in Eusebius about a Christian lady of Alexandria, illustrious for her high birth, great wealth, and likewise for her singular learning, who having resisted all the temptations and menaces of the tyrant Maximin, was by him despoiled of all her estates and goods and sent into banishment.

She would only say she saw the glorious faces, always the same ; and a great light, and that the voice was 'beautiful, gentle and humble, and spoke French.'

And, as no other saints except the mother of the Lord, the names of Catharine and Margaret have stamped themselves on our common speech—Margaret giving her name to the daisy with its golden heart and 'crimson-tipped' rays, the little children's flowers, commonest of all ; and Catharine to this day flashing in the Catharine wheels.

The legend of St. Catharine may be given thus :—

St. Catharine was the daughter of Costis and Sabinella, King and Queen of Egypt. From her earliest childhood she was the wonder of all for her beauty of mind and face. She studied Plato, and would have answered the questions of the Queen of Sheba better than Solomon.

Her father built her a high tower with many fair chambers full of books and mathematical instruments. And from the top she would study the stars in that clear sky of Egypt, and all the creation to her was full of wonder and delight.

Her father and mother were excellent and most loving to her, but they died early and left her a queen at fourteen, and wiser than all around her, but an orphan and alone. She was more beautiful than any princess in the world, but she did not care for any pomp, or dress, or all her precious things. God's golden stars seemed to her more magnificent than all the treasures of earth, and she shut herself up in her palace and studied philosophy, Plato, and the stars, till she grew wiser than all the wise men of the East.

Then the people of the country grew disturbed, and came to her and entreated her to marry, that she might have one by her side to share the cares of government and lead them forth to war.

When she heard this she was much troubled.

'What manner of man is this that I must marry ?' she said.

'Madam,' the spokesman of the people said, 'you are our most sovereign lady and queen, and you have four notable gifts: the first, that you are come of the most noble blood in the whole world; the second, that you are a great inheritor; the third, that in wisdom you surpass all others; the fourth, that in bodily shape and beauty there is none like you. Wherefore we beseech you that these good gifts with which the great God has endowed you may induce you to take a lord to your husband, to the intent you may have an heir to the comfort and joy of your people.'

Then the young queen Catharine, with a grave countenance, said that if God had indeed so endowed her she must the more love Him; and if they would have her wed, her husband also must possess four noted gifts. 'He must be of blood so noble that all men should worship him; so great that he shall never think I have made him king; so rich that he shall pass all others; so full of beauty that angels of God shall desire to behold him; and so benign that he will gladly forgive all offences done to him. Him, if you find him, will I take for my lord and husband of my heart.'

Then the councillors and people despaired, for they said, 'Such a one as she has desired there never was nor ever will be.'

But she said, 'If I do not find him he shall find me, for other will I none.'

Now, near the queen's palace there lived a poor old hermit in a cave, and that very night the Holy Virgin Mother of our Lord appeared to him and told him that the King who should be Lord of the queen's heart was none other than her Son. Then the hermit went to the palace and presented the queen with a picture of the Virgin and her Child; and when St. Catharine saw it her heart was so filled with its holy beauty that she forgot her books, her spheres, and the stars. Plato and Socrates became tedious to her as a twice-told tale, and she kept the sacred picture always before her.

That very night she had a dream. She met on the top of a high mountain a glorious company of angels, clothed in white, with chaplets of white lilies. She fell on her face before them, but they said, 'Stand up, dear sister Catharine, and be right welcome.' Then they led her by the hand to another company of angels, more glorious still, clothed in purple, with chaplets of red roses. Before these she fell on her face, dazzled with their glory; but they said, 'Stand up, dear sister Catharine; thee hath the King delighted to honour.' Then they led her by the hand to an inner chamber of the palace of heaven, where sate a Queen in state. The angels said to her, 'Our most gracious Sovereign Lady, Empress of Heaven and Mother of the King of Blessedness, be pleased that we present unto you this our sister, whose name is in the Book of Life, beseeching you to accept her as your daughter and handmaid.' Then our Blessed Lady rose and smiled graciously, and led St. Catharine to her beloved Son. But He turned from her and said sadly, 'She is not fair enough for Me.' Then St. Catharine awoke, and in her heart all day echoed the words, 'She is not fair enough for Me.' And she rested not until she became a Christian.

And when Catharine was baptised the Blessed Virgin appeared to her again in a dream with the Divine Child, and presented her to the Lord of Glory and said, 'Lord, she hath been baptised, and I myself have been her godmother.' Then the Lord smiled on her and held out His hand and plighted His troth to her. When she awoke she saw the ring on her finger, and thenceforth despised the world and all its pomps for Him.

Soon after this Maximin, the cruel tyrant, came to Alexandria from Italy full of rage against the Christians, and made an edict that there should be such a sacrifice to the gods as had never been known before. And from all the country they brought oxen and sheep to sacrifice, and the city was full of their lowing and bleating and of the preparation for the sacrifice and feast.

Then Catharine, the queen, knowing that after the blood of rams and oxen would flow rivers of the blood of the Christian brethren, did not wait to be summoned, but with her royal heart, taking the people under her protection, went herself to the great temple of the god Serapis, where Maximin was celebrating his wicked rites, and confronted him and demanded to be allowed to plead for the Christians and to show the glory of the Christian faith.

And her beauty of countenance and majesty of bearing being as great as her rank the Emperor was subdued, and permitted that a great assembly of the people should be called, and that also the priests and philosophers should appear to defend the gods and Catharine should speak for Christ her Lord.

And the assembly was convened, and fifty of the ablest sophists were called on to defend their gods; and they began with scorn, saying that the least of the scholars was able to answer this royal maid. Catharine, full of humility, had prepared herself by prayer and fasting, knowing that she had no strength but of God.

And such was the wisdom and majesty of truth and tender pleading with which she spoke, quoting their own wisest, such as Plato and Socrates, to prove there was one God, and only one, Creator of the glorious stars she knew so well, and of heaven and earth and all men, showing by Greek philosophers and Hebrew prophets, astronomers and sybils, that Christianity not only brought to them something glorious and new, but restored to them the old treasures of their forefathers which they had lost,—that the fifty opponents laid down their weapons of argument and confessed that she was right and that Christ the Lord was God. And with them a great multitude of the people believed.

But the rage of the cruel Maximin knew no bounds. He ordered the new converts to be massacred. And they went to the Christ they had confessed consecrated by the baptism of blood; and the glorious princess herself was both racked and tortured, and then laid with her bruised and wounded limbs in a dungeon, with no one to wait on her, to die of hunger. But her eloquence and her patience had touched the heart of the Empress Faustina, Maximin's wife, and in a dream she saw Catharine come to her and offer her a crown from Christ the Lord. Therefore the Empress Faustina and Porphyry, the Emperor's chief captain, came to her in the dungeon. And then the captive princess spoke to them of the Christ who had died for all, and for whom she suffered, so that the Empress and Porphyry believed. Catharine had no earthly promises to give them, none but the promise of following the Lord to death. She said they should go to their Lord by the path of martyrdom in three days if they were faithful to the end. Wounded, she healed their wounded souls; captive, she set them free; in the darkness of the dungeon she brought them light. In three days the tyrant had the Empress and Porphyry put to death. And then once more he began the combat of torments with Catharine. Four wheels were made with spikes, between which she was to be torn in pieces; and to these she was bound. But fire came from heaven and broke the wheels in pieces, so that the fragments flew far and wide and injured many. But Catharine stood in the midst untouched.

And at last she was led outside the city of Alexandria and beheaded by the sword.

But the angels came and bore her body tenderly in their arms across the Red Sea and across the sandy desert, which the children of Israel had trodden of old, and laid her to rest on the top of the holy mount that must not be touched—Mount Sinai.

And thus after many hundred years she was found, her raiment indeed waxen old with the ages, but her body folded as in silken robes by the rich tresses of her fair hair, an aureole around her brow, and a heavenly fragrance breathing from the tomb. And meanwhile the blessed spirit had long dwelt with Him who had made her 'fair enough for Himself.'

And so these two, Margaret and Catharine, shone on the West from the Eastern lands where they lived and suffered, the two great Virgin Patronesses; two highest types of womanhood: Margaret meek and patient and strong to suffer; Catharine queenly and wise, with her keen and cultivated intellect and her royal, fearless eloquence ; going forth to encounter danger for her people as a mother bird for her brood, and from the depths of her dungeon bringing light and liberty even to those who had bound her there.[1]

[1] Dedications of churches : 51. Represented with a wheel ; with a sword, book, a lamb, a palm ; carried by angels to Mount Sinai.

CHAPTER VII.

MARTYRS IN THE WARFARE WITH THE BARBARISM OF THE NORTH.

St. Lambert

OF MAESTRICHT.

September 17.

(Martyred A.D. 709. Calendars : all except Roman. Sarum Ep. and Gosp. : Heb. v. 1-6 ; St. Matt. ix. 35-38, and x. 7, 8, 16.)

WE come with St. Lambert into an altogether new world, or rather into what looks like a new chaos without form and void before the creation of a new world—from a world penetrated with the art and literature of Greece, ruled by the laws of the Empire and city of Rome, to the chaos out of which Christendom was struggling into existence in the days of the Merovingian kings. Rome was gone for ever, with its temples, its emperors, its armies, swept away by the northern invasion. And the invasion of the Franks in Gaul seems to have been in a sense more disintegrating than any other, being rather a wild irruption of bands of warriors under their captains than the emigration of tribes under their chiefs. All the wonderful centralised web of roads was broken off from the centre, and had become meaningless, reduced to mere interrupted tracks between town and town or village and village, and when out of repair no one could any longer be found who knew how to restore them. And not only were these material means of communication shattered ; the great Latin language was replaced by countless dialects, not one of which had yet grown into a recognised or written language.

Only the Church remained intact out of all that shattered ancient world; the germ of the new life which had done so much to shatter it. The clergy still sang psalms and chanted liturgies, wrote homilies, letters, and hymns in Latin. The bishops were princes or magistrates in their episcopal cities; through them the cities were linked with the Central See of Rome. The clergy also stood between the invaders and the invaded, the chiefs and the people; and when the Frankish chiefs forbade any freeman to become a priest, lest he should thus become exempt from military service, the clergy laid all the deeper and wider the foundations of freedom by consecrating the serfs, who were not free men, to the priesthood, thus liberating and educating at once, and turning the edict of prohibition into an act of emancipation.

The sole survivor and heir of the old civilisation, bearing in her heart the regenerating force of the new nations, never, perhaps, did the Church hold the whole future of the world more in her keeping than in that turbulent period represented in France by the Merovingian kings.

And the high standard of purity and righteousness held up by the Church in these darkest times is well reflected in the life of St. Lambert.

St. Landebert, or Lambert, was born about 640, during the reign of Childeric II. His parents were of high degree, and possessed of large property in the county of Liège. His father, a great seigneur, his mother, of an illustrious family, both sought to train their son in the Christian faith and life. St. Remaclus, Bishop of Maestricht, was his godfather. From his childhood he showed a fervent piety and a generous care for all around him. His legend records two characteristic miracles, full of symbolism. When serving at the altar as a young acolyte he is said to have carried burning coals without injury in the folds of his surplice to rekindle the incense. And one day, when some workmen who were building a church wanted water to drink, by his prayers a spring gushed forth close at hand, satisfying their thirst.

When his godfather, St. Remaclus, died, St. Lambert's

parents put him under the charge of St. Theodard, who had succeeded to the bishopric; and in the city of his birth, under the guidance of the good bishop, he grew up, delighting in the sacraments and services of the Church and in solitary prayer, despising the things of the world and full of zeal for the good of his neighbours.

When he was twenty-one years of age his bishop, Theodard, was murdered in a neighbouring forest by some men of power and influence, men who had unjustly seized estates belonging to the Church, of whom he had demanded restitution. And then his fellow citizens, who had known Lambert's blameless and benevolent life from his infancy, claimed him; and he was forced rather than elected to the bishopric.

It was useless or him to plead his youth as a reason against the choice. The burden was fastened on him, and his house, bare of all luxuries for himself, became a hall of justice and a house of mercy for all the needy and afflicted of the city. Always gracious and courteous, the serenity and kindliness of his face, his frank bearing and conversation attracted all. Daily he ministered at the altar and delighted to preach in his church. Justice and a thoughtful consideration marked his rule in the city and on his estates; from the pulpit and in private he never failed boldly to rebuke vice, and at the same time tenderly to encourage and restore the penitent. His holy presence and his just and gentle government helped to keep alive, in those distracted times, the ideal of justice and mercy, which might enable men to understand the existence of God.

To him it was personally no distress on his own account to have this burden of place and rule torn from him, as it was, when his patron, Chilperic II. (who, though weak and cruel himself, had upheld Lambert), was deposed and he was driven from his bishopric.

But to the people it was as the loss of a father. What would become, they said, of the feeble and the poor, the orphans and widows, now that he was torn from them? And in his stead was placed over them a man of hard nature and lawless life—a ravening wolf instead of the good shepherd.

For seven years this usurping bishop, Pharamond, misruled and misused the Church of Maestricht.

But to Lambert those were years of sacred calm, and of precious discipline and growth in humility and grace. He spent them in the monastery of Stavelot, on the borders of his diocese, refusing to be treated with any distinction, taking the place of the humblest of the brethren; and if, unconsciously to himself, still a leader of others, a leader simply by his close following of the Leader of all—most earnest in prayer, most patient in hardships, most ready in service.

One anecdote expresses what his life among the brethren was. One cold winter night when he rose to his private devotions he let fall his sabot, or wooden sandal, which made a noise. The abbot heard it, and to punish this breach of the silence of night he ordered the delinquent, not knowing who it was, to go and pray before the cross outside the church. Lambert obeyed without a word, and went barefoot and without his outer garment. There he prayed three or four hours on his knees. When the monks came in to warm themselves at the fire after Matins the abbot asked if all were present. 'All,' was the reply, 'except the one who was sent to pray before the cross.'

At once he was called in, and great was the surprise of the community when Bishop Lambert entered, covered with snow and stiff with cold.

The abbot and the monks threw themselves at his feet, asking his forgiveness.

No one was to blame, he said. Was it not good for him to learn to serve God, like St. Paul, in cold and nakedness?

The reflex lesson was not lost, let us hope, on the giver of the order.

Seven years passed, of silence and obedience, of peace and prayer, the preparation for the years of combat, of faithful guiding and difficult rule to come. At the end of the seven years Pharamond was driven, for his crimes, not only from the city but the province, and Ebroin, Mayor of the Palace, a cruel persecutor of Lambert, died a violent death.

Pepin d'Héristal, a man who, whatever his own shortcomings, could recognise and honour good men, sent an embassy to the monastery to entreat Lambert to return to his diocese. And wonderful was the joy with which the city of his birth and his pastoral rule welcomed him back; the same as of old save for the seven years' pruning and ripening; more humble, more gracious, more faithful than ever in rebuke, more wise and tender than ever to restore.

Numbers of holy men and women gathered around him to serve God and His Church, in the city, or to found monasteries in the regions around. Many saints were inspired and trained through him. He went about doing good through the least known and remotest villages of his diocese. He became the first missionary apostle to the Island of Zealand, an outlying district where the people were still given to idolatry, and at much personal toil and peril he won the greater part of them to the faith, so that he was called their 'apostle.'

But it was not among the heathen but among those who professed the Christian name that he found his martyr's crown.

Pepin d'Héristal, by a license terribly common among kings and Mayors of the Palace in those Merovingian times, had repudiated his wife, Plectrude, and taken instead to his house a beautiful woman called Alpaïs, who became the mother of Charles Martel, and thus grandmother of Pepin le Bref and great-grandmother of Charlemagne. Neither Pepin nor Alpaïs intended by this sin to cut themselves off from the communion of the Church.

Pepin continued to honour Lambert, and Alpaïs made every effort to win his favour. Not one of the clergy or bishops, aware as they were of the crime, dared to open their lips to rebuke the great captain and to say, 'It is not lawful for thee to put away thy wife and marry another.

Lambert alone, never able to compromise where the glory of God and the salvation of souls were concerned, boldly and faithfully showed the prince the horror of his sin, called it by its true name, and warned him of the scandal he was causing and of the judgment to come.

Pepin listened, and was so moved that Alpaïs began to dread that he would give her up, and after using in vain every method she could think of to bend the conscience of the Bishop she resolved on his destruction.

Pepin continued to defer to the counsels of Lambert in all things except this one passion, and invited him to his court to consult him about some affairs of state.

Alpaïs entreated him, if he could not change his mind, at all events to spare her the humiliation of public rebuke.

Lambert could only say he dared not flinch from his duty as a bishop.

Pepin gave a great banquet, and entreated the Bishop to be present, and when the wine cup was presented to him he offered it first to Lambert to bless it and then to replace it in his hands.

The Bishop thought himself bound to do what Pepin asked. The courtiers followed the prince's example. But when Alpaïs presented the cup to him he refused to sanction her presence by taking it, and complaining to Pepin of his attempt to entrap him into compliance he rose from the table and left the room and resolved to retire from the court.

Pepin followed, to entreat him to relent; but Lambert said frankly and faithfully he was grieved at heart that the prince should thus cause a scandal to all France and draw on him the anger of God.

And from that time, it is said, Alpaïs did not rest until she had him put to death, dreading lest at last Pepin would be persuaded to take back his wife. She seems to have turned the anger of certain lawless chiefs who were already irritated against some relations of St. Lambert, in one of the many quarrels of those fierce days, against the Bishop himself. They found him sleeping in a little village, since grown into the city of Liège. They surrounded the house on all sides. The Bishop could have summoned defenders; and two nephews who were with him and his domestics were eager to defend him, but he would not suffer a blow to be struck on his account. 'If you love me truly,' he said, 'love Jesus and confess your sins to Him. As for me, it is time that I go to live with Him.' When the assassins broke into the house he threw himself prostrate on the ground in an attitude of penitence, his arms outspread in the form of a cross. And after massacring his nephews and some of his servants the assassins killed the Bishop with the sword.

And so St. Lambert died a true martyr for Christ, for daring to rebuke vice in high places and for defending the purity of Christian homes.[1]

[1] There is another version of the story of Alpaïs.
Dedications of churches: 2. Represented in art with spear or dart in his hand or at his feet; sometimes a palm branch; stabbed with javelins; beaten with a club.

St. Boniface (Winfried of Crediton).

June 5.

(Born A.D. 680; martyred June 5, A.D. 755. Sarum Ep. and Gosp. :
1 Cor. iv. 9-14; St. Matt. x. 23-26, during Eastertide St. John xv. 5-7.)

The first English missionary bishop martyred among the heathen, but not the last. From the cold snows of Friesland to the heart of Africa and the islands of the Southern Seas, from the eighth century to the nineteenth, our English Church has sent her sons to join the 'noble army' with which she daily praises God. And she is sending them still.

Winfried, afterwards named Boniface, was born at Crediton, among the pleasant hills of Devonshire, near Exeter. One wishes he had not changed his beautiful Old English name with its sweet breathing of peace for any other.

At five years old the little child's heart seems to have been awakened by a heavenly touch never forgotten. Good monks from the monasteries near were in the habit, according to the custom of the Celtic or Irish communities, of going on missions through the neighbouring countries, sometimes preaching on the village green and resting under lowly cottage roofs, at other times accepting the hospitality of the great men of the place, and then hallowing the houses of their hosts with their prayers and teachings. And the child Winfried listening (as a thousand years afterwards the boy John Coleridge Patteson listened to Bishop Selwyn), with wondering eyes, to the words of the strangers, probably himself unnoticed, drank them in until the Spirit speaking through them became in him a well of living water, springing up and flowing forth as a fountain of life for the great German land. Thenceforth it seemed to the child that the home where those good men lived must be as the very gate of heaven; and there he desired to live. At first his father opposed, but the boy's purpose continued steadfast until at last, when he was about thirteen, he was brought to the verge of death by a serious illness ; and then the father accepted his son's desire as a Divine vocation, and gave him to God with an acquiescence as generous and unreserved as in after days the father of John Coleridge Patteson.

He passed many years in the abbey at Exeter, and then he removed to the abbey of Nutcell, in the diocese of Winchester, one of the great schools of the time. There he studied diligently, and learned all that was to be learned—poetry, rhetoric, history. There also, above all, he steeped his heart and mind in the Holy Scriptures, and was in time appointed a teacher of literature and history, having always much delight in being among the young. At thirty he was ordained priest, and from that time was chiefly occupied in preaching to the people around, and in the cure of souls. His ability and judgment were early recognised, and he was sent on a deputation to the Archbishop of Canterbury. He was also much consulted in the councils of his Church and was honoured and courted by all.

But deep in his heart all the time was burning a fire of missionary zeal, fed doubtless by the stories told from monastery to monastery of the work of Willibrord in Friesland, and of other missionaries. Especially he longed to carry the Gospel to those ancient German lands from which his own forefathers had come.

And in A.D. 716 his friend Abbot Wimbert gave his sanction to his going forth as a missionary to the heathen of Friesland. He needed not to learn a new language to make himself understood. For a hundred years, from the coasts of Great Britain the tide of Christian life had been flowing back in missionary enterprise to the Continent of Europe ; and through what is now the North of France, Switzerland, Belgium, Bavaria, and Hesse, on the mountains, and among the primeval forests, and on the sites of abandoned Roman cities, were founded monasteries peopled by men from Great Britain, followers of Columban, St. Gall, and other adventurous spiritual pioneers.

It is interesting to remember that as regards England the first missionary impulse seems to have been given by a young priest named Egbert, by one who, like so many others, had found instruction and inspiration among the monastic communities in Ireland, and had devoted himself to evangelising the Continent, but just as he was starting on his voyage he was arrested by illness, was left behind by his companions, and was never able to follow.

Friesland was then in a state of wild turmoil on account of the war between King Radbrod and Charles Martel.

(It is of Radbrod that the story is told that once, when considering the possibility of becoming a Christian, he asked a missionary as a preliminary enquiry what had become of the kings his ancestors who had not believed, the missionary replied that they were in torments in the other world; whereupon Radbrod said, 'I see no good in my going to heaven with a few poor people. I shall keep to the religion of my fathers.' And he became a violent persecutor.)

After remaining the summer in Friesland, where Willibrord of Yorkshire, trained in the northern monasteries, had long been labouring, Boniface returned to England, the steadfastness of his purpose tested, as so often, by disappointment. Two years he remained at his monastery, where, on the death of his old friend Abbot Wimbert, he was elected abbot. But the passion for clearing new ground, which has always been such a large element in English life, was not to be quenched in the heart of Boniface; he longed to penetrate new lands, found new churches, monasteries, schools; to bring the good news for the first time to new tribes of men, yet allied to his own in speech and blood. He was moved, as he said, 'by the love of travel and the fear of Christ;' the loving fear of selfishly hoarding a treasure which was meant to enrich the world, and the *Wandertrieb* of our race.

Boniface had reached the sober age of thirty-eight when he set out on his missionary career again, this time never to return. His thirty-seven remaining years were to be devoted to the glorious work given him to do.

No doubt his first unsuccessful missionary expedition, with the interval of rest in the English monastery afterwards, had been no lost or wasted time for him. He had learned, at all events, one of the first lessons in all work, to see its especial difficulties.

Before proceeding again on a pilgrimage to the field of foreign missions he went to Rome, with a letter from his bishop, Daniel of Winchester, to Pope Gregory II. A very different journey for Boniface from what it had been when four centuries before Alban of Verulam went to Rome (according to the legend) to complete his education there;—the Roman roads broken into disconnected fragments, the military stations and post-houses gone, the way beset with perils from wild tribes of invaders, none of which recognised each other or themselves as the germs (which nevertheless they were) of future nations; a world without form and void, of chaotic ruins and chaotic beginnings; the only organisation left standing throughout it the Church, like a highly developed vertebrate organism amidst a floating mass of molluscous or crustaceous creatures, which wore whatever bony substance they had mainly outside, in the form of bristling armour wherewith to destroy each other.

He went with a band of English pilgrims, and on the way through Gaul and Italy they made their devotions at the shrines of the martyrs, who had mostly belonged to the old vanished Roman world.

And when he reached the city what a different Rome!

In Alban's Rome Christians might still be thrown to the wild beasts in the Coliseum; on the Capitol and all around stood the temples of the gods, basilicas, theatres. For Boniface all that ancient world had vanished—emperor, 'Senate and people,' gods and goddesses; basilicas transformed into churches, pillars of temples into pillars of Christian shrines, statues which could not be transformed broken up, or only saved by being lost.

Yet still, still more than ever, to Boniface Rome was the Imperial and Metropolitan city: imperial because

Christian; metropolis because the citadel of the City of God.

Every church, on the Capitol of the dethroned Jove or in the catacombs of the martyrs, was a trophy of victory over a whole ancient world of vanquished foes, and might become a triumphal arch into a new world of conquest over the new heathenism of the North, which Boniface had vowed his life to overcome.

From the Vatican, where the martyrs now venerated throughout Christendom had illumined Rome in their agony as living torches from Nero's gardens; from the Capitol, where the Ara Cœli, the altar of Heaven, had replaced the altar of Jove; from the Aventine, whence the great Gregory had sent Augustine to convert Boniface's own heathen forefathers, the English Winfried might well gather inspiration to go forth and fell any sacred oak of Thor the Thunderer or to encounter any perils among the heathen of the North.

At Rome moreover he touched the historical past of Christianity.

The language which for him was the language of the Church and the sacred books was still, at Rome, as for St. Agnes or St. Cæcilia, St. Augustine or St. Gregory, the speech of everyday life. The Devonshire Winfried did not need to learn a new language for Thuringia and the Rhineland. But in Rome he distrusted his scholastic Latin which he had learned as a foreign tongue, and feared to express his creed except in writing.

From Rome also the monk from remote Devonshire could gain a new, wide outlook over the Eastern and Western world.

Severed as the Church was, even then, the great destructive tide of Mahomedanism, which had laid waste the Churches of Asia Minor and Africa, of Polycarp and Augustine, and was rolling up through Bulgaria on the east and through conquered Spain on the south into the heart of Europe, could be felt from the Seven Hills surging against the whole of Christendom.

Unity, external unity, might well seem to him, looking from that central height over the devastated East and the stormy heathen North, not a mere dream of some far-off paradise, but a necessity of bare existence.

Three times in his missionary life of thirty-eight years Boniface came to Rome; first in 719 with a letter from his friend Bishop Daniel of Winchester to introduce him to Pope Gregory II. and to receive his sanction and counsel; secondly, in 722, summoned by the same Pope to report results of his three years' labour and receive consecration as bishop (*regionarius*) of the new mission; thirdly, seventeen years afterwards, in 739, at his own desire, to see the new Pope, Gregory III., to tell of his 100,000 German converts, and to receive fresh powers as Archbishop of Mainz.

Gregory, with the true tact and instinct of the ruler, perceived at once his capability for his vocation, and sent him away with the encouragement of his sympathy and the sanction of his authority, armed also with letters to Charles Martel, then the great ruler of the christianised Franks, entreating him to aid the English missionary in converting the Saxon tribes Charles was endeavouring to subdue, and also empowering Boniface to restore to the faith the half-lapsed Christians, remnants of the Christianity of the old Roman frontier, and to organise or gather together the scattered communities founded during the past century by the Irish missionaries.

For from the beginning to the end the work of Boniface was twofold: winning new converts from the outside barbarian world; and gathering into unity of communion and discipline the lapsed or disorganised Christians already there.

He went first to Thuringia, and there, through the great Thuringian forest, then all forest (afterwards Martin Luther's land), our Devonshire Winfried went up and down, preaching and baptising, often in hunger and poverty and peril of life, but never weary of gathering into the fold the lost and wandering sheep altogether outside, or of gathering together the scattered sheep from solitary hermitages or small communities who were in danger from their isolation of being again absorbed into the heathen world around.

From Thuringia he made an expedition to Friesland, the first scene of his missionary labours, never forgotten by his heart, and so strangely interwoven with his missionary life from its beginning to its martyr close.

It was opened again now to Christian work by the death of the heathen king Radbrod, and Boniface laboured there for two or three years, assisting his countryman Archbishop Willibrord. Willibrord much wanted to keep him as his coadjutor and successor; but Boniface was too essentially a pioneer and founder to be able to stop in regions already half won. He returned to Thuringia, and on his way back, as he passed through the land of the Rhine and the Moselle, one story is told of him which illustrates the winning charm by which he drew fellow labourers around him and kept them faithful to the end.

On the banks of the Moselle, near ancient Roman Treves (where St. Athanasius had sojourned, and where St. Augustine's soldier friends had found the life of St. Anthony which changed their lives and gave the final enkindling touch to his conversion), Boniface was received hospitably by the venerable abbess Addula. At table, according to the custom of the times, a boy of fifteen, fresh from school, the abbess's grandson Gregory, read a passage from the Latin Bible.

'You read well, my son,' said Boniface, 'if you understand what you read.'

The boy, not catching his meaning, said he perfectly understood.

'Well then,' said Boniface, 'tell me how you understand it?'

The boy began to read the passage again.

Then Boniface said, 'No, my son, that is not what I mean. I want you to translate what you have read into your native language.'

The boy at once acknowledged that he could not do this. So when he had read it again distinctly Boniface translated it into German and preached on it to the whole company. And the words sank so deep into the boy's heart that nothing would satisfy him but to go himself with Boniface, to learn from him to understand the Holy Scriptures.

'If thou wilt not give me a horse,' he said to his grandmother, the abbess, 'I will go with him on foot.'

The abbess saw that a Divine Power had touched the lad's heart, and she gave him a horse and a servant, and suffered him to go away with Boniface, whom he followed thenceforth whithersoever he went, among the heathen in the forests, to Rome, and finally to his martyr death.

And after his master's death Gregory continued to follow his footsteps till he also was an old man of seventy, teaching the young, and making his monastery a training school of missionaries.

In Thuringia Boniface baptised many thousands of idolaters, destroyed their temples, and built churches.

The form of renunciation which he demanded of these German converts indicates the discrimination and thoroughness of his work. He was not content merely with the usual form, 'I renounce the Devil and all his works.' He asked, 'Dost thou renounce Woden, Seator, and Friga?'

No vague promises of general goodness would satisfy him. The especial temptations of each were to be especially renounced.

From Thuringia he wrote to Pope Gregory speaking of his success and asking his counsel about some practical difficulties.

In reply the Pope congratulated him and desired him to repair again to Rome. That second visit was doubtless of great importance in Boniface's life.

This time he looked out from the Seven Hills on no new work, no unexplored land. He had surveyed his ground, tried his weapons, found out his difficulties, and trained many of his fellow labourers.

From Rome Winfried went forth the second time, as Boniface (the new name given him then), bishop (*regio-*

narius) of the new lands, with authority to claim the obedience of all Christians already existing there, or to be converted.

From the ancient trophies of past victories he went forth ; from the dethroned Jove of the Capitol, to cut down the Sacred Oak of the Teutonic Thor in Hesse.

Soon after his second return to Germany he found many of his apparent converts hopelessly mixing up the new faith and its sacred rites with the old. He determined, therefore, that the moment had come for a visible manifestation that the two could not be combined. There was an enormous oak in the forests of Hesse, near the village of Giesmar, sacred to Thor. Boniface went forth with his clergy to fell it publicly to the ground. It was regarded on both sides as a trial of strength. The heathen must already, in spite of their menacing attitude, have been in some measure shaken to allow of such an attempt being made at all. Boniface bravely took the axe in his own hands. The heathen multitude awaited the result in silence.

After a few strokes a mighty wind seemed suddenly to sway its lofty branches, and the grand old tree crashed down, splitting with its weight into four huge pieces.

Then the heathen confessed their gods to have been vanquished, and at once acknowledged themselves subjects of this new Lord whom they saw to be so strong, and whom Boniface declared to be so merciful and ready to forgive.

A little forest oratory was built at once of the wood of the fallen shrine. It was the first church of the country.

But great as the victory was, it was only the beginning of the conquest.

It is remarkable that this event is almost the only approach to miracle in St. Boniface's life. He never claimed to work miracles. The claim to miracle-working was made by Adalbert, one of the unattached monks whose opposition was one of his chief difficulties.

One characteristic of Boniface's work seems to have been its resemblance to the methods of working in our own times. Around the story of the earlier Irish missionaries plays far more of the glow and twilight mystery of legend. They were principally hermits and recluses, like the Fathers of the Desert. They went into the wilderness not so much to seek for the heathen, as to find solitude and freedom for a disciplined life. They became centres of civilisation simply by being civilised. They spread the light of Christianity by simply gathering it into a focus and shining. They felled the trees in the forest depths and made them into dwellings and chapels; they tilled fields, sowed and reaped, made nets, and fished in the lakes and rivers, while the wild tribes around them looked on and learned. They said to themselves or to each other in raptures of contemplation and devotion (seeing Jesus as He walked among them), 'Behold the Lamb of God;' and the heathen people around drew near and listened, and found the Christ.

They settled (like St. Gall) among the ruins of some ruined Roman city, again lapsed into wild forest, taking the stones of the deserted temples to build their churches and breaking in pieces the gilded images which the wild tribes around had dreaded or worshipped as relics of vanished supernatural beings. On Sundays and holy days St. Columban would carry a heavy volume of Sacred Scriptures on his shoulder into the forest depths to hold converse with God, and the people, watching, came to perceive that these mysterious parchments had voices and that there is an unseen God and Friend who can speak to us and be spoken to.

The writings of St. Columban and others of these monks are full of deep spiritual piety.[1] 'God dwells in us as the soul in the body,' he wrote. Who can indeed be happier than the man whose death is life, whose life is Christ, whose reward is the Saviour, to whom the heavens bow down, whose Father is God, whose servants are angels?' Again, 'It behoves pilgrims to hasten to their home. We are pilgrims; therefore let us hasten to our fatherland. For our whole life is a day's journey.'

[1] Neander, *Denkwürdigkeiten*, and Montalembert, *Moines de l'Occident*.

And again, 'Love is no labour; it is, on the contrary, a sweet and wholesome and healing thing to the heart. Unless the soul is diseased within, its life is love. He tramples on the world who renounces himself. What should we render to the Creator of the world who died for us sinners, for us His creatures? Surely we should die to sin. No one can die to himself if Christ does not live in him. If thou hast overcome thyself thou hast overcome all.'

And so, carrying on this inward combat, leading this inward life, they were doubtless also combating and conquering for the world around them. An intense fire of self-renouncing and enrapt devotion shines out from these early missionaries, these new Fathers of the Desert, in Burgundy and Switzerland, and along the frontiers of old Rome, lapsed again into wilderness, and also a tender glow as from the paradise and childhood of the world. The 'spirit of the mountain,' speaking from his lonely height to the 'spirit of the waters,' acknowledges the mystic power of these strangers. Savage beasts, wolves and bears, fawn on them; birds of prey bring them food; timid hunted creatures trust them and take refuge with them. Their story comes to us like soft music across the wide waters of the past.

But with Boniface we seem to speak in the language of to-day, and, in some ways, the contrast may seem like coming from poetry to prose, from some lovely quaint old ballad to the less fascinating literature of a missionary report. We have, however, but to recover the poetic gold by digging deeper for it; and if we do we shall certainly find it not in grains but in nuggets.

Boniface worked no physical miracles, unless we except the fall of the Sacred Oak of Thor. Once indeed, it is said, a huge bird opportunely dropped a fish above his table when he had not much on it; but the attention does not seem to have been repeated. The sources of his supplies were not ravens or angels, but contributions from friends in his old English home, of books, and clothes, and food, and money. The miracles wrought for him were in hearts moved to help him. His one great miracle was the conversion of Germany. Before all and through all he was a missionary. He went into the wilderness not for its solitude, but because the wandering sheep were there.

From this great purpose he never seems to have swerved for a moment.

If he seeks from the Abbess Eadburga 'a beautiful manuscript of the Epistles of St. Peter, written in golden letters,' it is to 'move the admiration of his Germans.' For himself another kind of gold was more beautiful. As he said at the Council of Tivoli, 'Formerly the priests were of gold and they used chalices of wood. Now the chalices are of gold and the priests of wood.'

And in his conflicts, whether mistaken or not, with some of the earlier monks, Irish and others, it was, as with Cyprian, the safety, the very existence of the scattered flock which he sought in his contests for unity and his efforts at gathering them together.

For his fellow labourers, and for his sustenance, Bishop Boniface looked chiefly to his old English home; and thence they were liberally sent. 'As he worked unremittingly, the fruits of his mission so increased from day to day, that he obtained many new fellow-labourers from England. And also from the convents of Great Britain came a swarm of widows, virgins, mothers, sisters, cousins of the missionaries, eager to share their labours and their perils. Chriemhild and Berathgilt, her daughter, stayed in Thuringia; Chiudrad was sent to Bavaria, and Thekla remained at Kitzingen on the Main; Lioba, beautiful as the angels, of a ravishing eloquence, learned in the Scriptures and the sacred Canons, governed the Abbey of Bischofsheim. These ferocious Germans, who had formerly delighted in blood and battles, came to kneel at the feet of these gentle teachers ('ces douces maîtresses'). Their own silence and humility have hidden their labours from the eyes of the world; but their place is at the origin of German civilisation. Providence has placed women beside all cradles.'[1]

St. Lioba was herself a poetess. She studied the Old

[1] Ozanam, *Etudes Germaniques*, quoted by *Les Petits Bollandistes*.

and New Testaments deeply, also the Fathers; ruled her convent firmly and tenderly; was dearly beloved by her pupils, and exercised a free hospitality to court and peasants, serving her guests with her own hands. She was a cousin of Winfried of Crediton, and came from near his own old home. Many of the letters of St. Boniface are to women; but with Lioba it seems as if the double tie of natural and spiritual kindred, the double association of early memories and high common aims, had made the tie very close. Brief as the glimpses given us are, she seems to stand as a helpmate beside him, as St. Scholastica beside her brother St. Benedict, and St. Clara by St. Francis d'Assisi.

His power of attaching disciples to himself was great, the true spiritual power of winning hearts, not to a helpless clinging, but to a brave following; so that when he died, he left not a wailing group of forlorn orphans, but a valiant, capable company of teachers and missionaries, ready to be martyrs in their turn.

So the years passed on, occupied in penetrating further and further among the heathen tribes, in founding monasteries to be centres of Christianity and civilisation, in organising the new converts to be instructed within the Christian Church.

Boniface (like Bishop Patteson) never returned to his native England. But his heart never left it. Many of his letters are to English women, abbesses of various monasteries.

To one, the royal abbess Eadburga, when she had sent him some manuscripts of the Scriptures, he writes thanking her that she had 'consoled the exile by Divine light, for he who had to visit the dark recesses of heathenism would fall into the jaws of death, if he had not the Word of the Lord as a lamp to his feet.'

To another: 'Pray for me that He who dwells on high, yet hath regard to the lowly, may forgive me my sins, that His Word may arm me with joyful liberty of speech, that the Gospel of the glory of Christ may have full access among the heathen.'

To some nuns : ' Pray diligently that we may be delivered from unrighteous and cruel men, that the Gospel of Christ may be glorified. I would not die unfruitful. I would not go home without leaving some sons and daughters behind me.'

To the English clergy : ' Seek to obtain by your prayers that our one God and Lord Jesus Christ, who wills that all men shall be saved and come to the knowledge of the truth, may convert the hearts of these heathen Saxons to the faith. Have confidence in them, for the people are wont to say " We are of one flesh and one blood with you." '

To an English abbot : 'I need your prayers, because the sea of Germany is so perilous to navigate, that I may not, while I seek to enlighten others, be myself covered with the darkness of my own sins. Pray the beloved Champion of us all, the only Refuge of the distressed, the Lamb of God Who taketh away the sins of the world, that our gracious Father may place burning torches in our hands that we may enlighten the heathen to see the Gospel of the glory of Christ.'

And on the other hand, to Ethelbald, King of Mercia, he writes a letter in which, while rendering honour to what was good in him, his strict prohibition of theft and perjury, his preserving peace and befriending the widow and the poor, he boldly reminds him how all was marred by the unchastity of his own life.

'The heathen Saxons,' he says, 'might be an example to the Christian king in this. Though a ruler of many he is making himself a slave of sin.' He entreats him to ' have compassion on the perishing multitude his evil example is misleading to their destruction,' and nobly warns him how ' if the sanctity of marriage is dishonoured the result is a degenerate race, ever sinking lower and lower.'

The character of his preaching seems to have been discriminating and practical ; no mere rhetoric or commonplaces, but plain words pressed home. He seems to have followed the advice of his friend Daniel, Bishop of Winchester, to 'learn accurately what the religion of the heathen was, acknowledging all that was good in it, or in them' (for instance, their great virtue of chastity); 'seeking, not to irritate them by violent denunciation, but by gentle and patient questioning to let them find out for themselves the unreasonableness of their belief in comparison with the Christian faith.'

Fifteen of his sermons are preserved to us. In one he says,[1] 'See, my beloved, what a message we bring you; not a message from one from whose service you may purchase exemption' (as in the German system of atoning for wrong by fines), 'but a message from Him to whom you are indebted for His Blood shed for you.'

And then he passes on to the sacredness of marriage.

Again, in meeting the objection so often made, that if Christianity were so necessary, surely God would not have left the world so long without it, he passes on from the theoretical difficulty to the practical remedy. 'Know that he who, however late, refuses to be healed has no right to complain of the dilatoriness of the physician. Wherefore dost thou murmur at the Sun of Righteousness having risen so late, when even after His rising thou still walkest in darkness?'

In another sermon to the newly-baptised, after speaking to them as to children, of 'the great city of Rome and the mighty chief called Augustus, who once reigned in it, who made peace in all the world,' he goes on: 'Listen, my brethren, attentively, to what you have abjured at Baptism. You have renounced the Devil, his works, and his pomps. But what are the works of the Devil? Pride, idolatry, luxury, homicide, slander, lying, perjury, hatred, fornication, adultery—in a word, whatever corrupts man. Theft, false witness, gluttony, foul language, quarrelling, using incantations, believing in witches and were-wolves, wearying and turning back from God; these works and those like them are the Devil's works, and the Apostle says those who do such things shall not inherit the kingdom of God. But as we hope by God's mercy that you have renounced all those things in deed as well as

[1] Neander, *Denkwürdigkeiten.*

in intent, it remains for me to remind you, my dearly loved ones, of what you have promised to Almighty God. Now, in the first place, you have promised to believe in Almighty God, in Jesus Christ the Son, and in the Holy Ghost, One God, but Three in One. And the commandments you have to observe are these : You must love God with all your heart and with all your strength, and your neighbour as yourself. Be patient, merciful, kind and chaste. Teach your children and servants to fear God. Reunite those who are at enmity ; let judges not take presents, which blind the eyes to justice. Keep the Lord's Day, and go to church to pray, not to gossip. Give alms as you are able. If you have feasts, invite the poor, exercise hospitality, visit the sick, succour widows and orphans, give tithes to churches. Do to others as you would like them to do to you. Fear none but God, but fear Him always. Believe in the Coming of Christ, in the Resurrection of the flesh, and in the General Judgment.'

The practical method and character of his teaching is illustrated by the especial renunciations (of Woden and Freya) which are added to the baptismal formulas.

As to the other portion of his work, the bringing into the order and unity of the Church of those who had chosen what seemed to them better ways of serving God, the history is very complicated. The story of defeated heresies and schisms must have the onesidedness of all history written only by the conquerors. And Pope Zacharias himself seems to have thought that some of the condemnations of Boniface needed reconsidering.

Of the two opponents who most perplexed him, Adalbert the Frank is accused of having pretended to a direct revelation from an angel, of having accepted almost Divine honours from his disciples, of having taught wild and mystical things, and in general used his gifts to gain honour for himself, rather than to contribute to the common service.

Against Clement, Boniface's other opponent, a teacher of Irish extraction, no accusations of mysticism or self-exaltation are brought. The controversy in his case seems to have turned on questions of discipline, connected with the marriage of the clergy. Also, Clement was said to have declared that our Lord in His descent into Hell redeemed not only the Jewish patriarchs, but heathens and others who had no means of learning of Him in their lifetime.

Whatever may have been Boniface's wisdom as to these minor controversies, in which the Pope and his devoted missionary Apostle of Germany seem to have differed, any complete unravelling of the tangled threads is scarcely to be hoped for in these later days. Boniface's acts, as those of Cyprian, doubtless proceeded from the instinct of the shepherd guiding his scattered flock through a wilderness infested by wild beasts—the instinct of unity; the one essential, it might well seem to him, being to keep the flock together.

And, therefore, even to imprison those who would have divided the Christian forces, as he did imprison Adalbert, would doubtless seem to Boniface mercy to him who would have misled as well as to those who were misled. His 'new Christians' were always first in his heart, his unfledged new converts. For their sakes he even wrote a stormy remonstrance to Pope Zacharias on his encouraging superstition at Rome, by sanctioning amulets, as things that through their old heathen faith still had power over his Germans.

So the fifteen years of ceaseless, fruitful work passed away, until, in 738, Boniface once more made a journey to Rome, to see the face of the new Pope Zacharias. He was welcomed, as a victorious general would have been welcomed in the old days, who had saved the republic.

The tidings of his 100,000 Germans won to the Christian Church had preceded him. To create one, who was indeed already the Apostle of the Germans, Archbishop of Maintz and endue him with the Pallium, was merely a recognition of power already wielded, of triumphs already won.

And at this very time (A.D. 738) when Boniface was receiving at Rome the reward of his lifelong warfare in the commission to further service, his patron and helper Charles Martel was achieving at Chalons that great victory over the Saracens which stemmed the destructive torrent that had ruined the Christian East, utterly laid waste the Church of Perpetua and Cyprian, and swept over Spain.

From the heathen masses in the North and the Moslem hosts of the South and East, Christendom was saved by the different yet co-operative work of the two heroes.

Boniface went back to Germany to carry on the combat for fourteen years more. He founded six new bishoprics, presided at the Councils of Soissons and of Germany, crowned King Pepin le Bref, son of Charles Martel, first of the Carlovingian kings, at Soissons, and in all things did the work of a great metropolitan bishop.

But always in his heart glowed the old missionary fire, always the Apostolic passion for 'the regions beyond;' until at seventy-five he obtained permission of the Pope to lay aside his archiepiscopal dignity and go forth once more, in the Benedictine habit, to the country of his first missionary labours, the northern part of East Friesland.

He named an English monk of Malmesbury his successor as archbishop, and wrote a touching letter to the Frankish court chaplain, Fulrad, committing to his care those he left behind. 'I beseech his Majesty, the King Pepin,' he writes, 'in the name of Christ the Son of God, that he would deign to show me in my lifetime what reward he will hereafter bestow on my scholars, for they are almost entirely strangers' (chiefly, no doubt, his own compatriots). 'Some are priests, appointed in various places to the service of the Church in the congregation; some monks who are supported in our cells to teach children to read; some old men who have laboured with me long and sustained many.

'I am anxious on account of all these, lest after my death they should be scattered as sheep that have no shepherd, and lest the people who dwell on the borders of the heathen should lose their Christianity again. The clergy on the frontiers of the heathen lead a wretched life. Bread to eat they can obtain, but clothes they cannot, if they do not get advice and support from other quarters, as they have from me, that they might be able to remain in such places, in the service of the people.'

King Pepin granted his request.

And then once more girding around him his Benedictine habit, he went forth with a little missionary company of eight, one a bishop, three deacons and some monks. Among them was Gregory, who had followed him since boyhood from his grandmother's monastery on the Moselle.

He took with him one book-chest, containing the Holy Gospels, St. Ambrose's *De Bono Mortis* (On the Gain of Death), a book he loved much, and also an altar-cloth and a shroud; the martyr's death being always a possibility for which he was prepared.

When he arrived in Friesland all at first seemed to go well; he baptised many new converts, and reclaimed some who had relapsed into heathenism since the death of his old friend Archbishop Willibrord. On Whit Sunday he pitched his tent in an open field near Dockum, on the river Burda, and erected an altar. There he awaited the arrival of the newly baptised, on whom he was to lay his hands in confirmation. He was waiting quietly in his tent at prayer, when, instead of the Christian converts he expected, a swarm of fierce heathens, armed and shouting for battle, appeared on the plain. They rushed to the tent of Boniface. His friends and attendants would have fought in his defence. But he would not suffer any resistance to be made. 'We are to render good for evil,' he said, 'and as for me, this is the day I have long waited for. The hour of my deliverance is come.'

Then he went forth from his tent, surrounded by his clergy, encouraging them not to fear the brief passage before them into the celestial kingdom and the 'City of the Angels.'

In an instant the fierce band of the heathen overwhelmed and slew him, and many others with him.

The Devonshire man, who seventy years ago had listened as a boy of five to the Gospel story from the monks in his father's house near Crediton, now lay, at last, in his grey hairs, slain by those he had spent his life in serving. They knew not what they did. When he was dead they rushed into the tent for the booty they had expected of gold and silver vessels and precious vestments ; but they found only a few books, a little wine for the Sacrament, and a few sacred relics ; and, enraged at their disappointment, they turned against each other.

It is said that Boniface died with a book of the Gospels in his hand, that it was pierced with a sword and stained with his blood, but that not a letter of the sacred text was injured.

His body was wrapped in the shroud he had laid among his books, and taken first to Maestricht, where Bishop Lambert had died for purity and righteousness a century before ; and then it was borne, finally, to his beloved Abbey of Fulda, the English Apostle of Germany resting among his Saxons. And there was laid, in time, his cousin, the English Abbess St. Lioba, after she had faithfully carried on his work for twenty years, dying at a great age, the friend of high and low, of the suffering, the aged and the little children. Side by side the noble Devonshire man and woman were laid to rest in the Saxon land they had helped to win for Christ.[1]

[1] V. Sir James Stephen, *Ecclesiastical Biography*, 481. ' His copy of Ambrose's *De Bono Mortis*, covered with his blood, was exhibited during many succeeding centuries at Fulda as a relic. It was contemplated there by many who regarded as superstitious and heretical some of the tenets of Boniface. But no Christian, whatever might be his own peculiar creed, ever looked on this blood-stained memorial of him without the profoundest emotion. For, since the Apostolic age, no greater benefactor of our race has come among us than this Monk of Nutcell, unless it be the Monk of Wittenberg, who, at the distance of seven centuries, appeared to reform and reconstruct the Churches founded by the holy Benedictine. To Boniface, the heart of Germany and Holland still looks back as their spiritual progenitor, nor did any uninspired man ever add to the permanent dominion of the Gospel provinces of such extent and such value.'

Three of the books which were in his chest when he was martyred are, Alban Butler says, still kept at his Abbey of Fulda : a copy of the Gospels written with his own hand, a Harmony of the Gospels, and a copy of a discourse of St. Ambrose on the Holy Ghost, as well as a treatise on the ' Advantage of Death.'

Dedications of Churches : 2. Represented in art with book pierced with sword, a club, a scourge.

St. Edmund the Martyr.

November 20.

(Born A.D. 840; martyred A.D. 870. Calendars: Sarum, Scotch, Hereford. Sarum Ep. and Gosp.: Eccles. xxxi. 8–11; St. Luke xiv. 26–33.)

Four English martyrs are in our Calendar, from four successive centuries, who fell on English ground, besides the great missionary bishop who died by the hands of the heathen in Friesland. Of these four, three marked three successive campaigns by which Christianity was won and kept for England.

Nowhere in Europe was the fight for Christianity harder and more repeated than in England. Three times was the battle fought and won, with the persecuting forces of Imperial Rome and with the Saxon.

The protomartyr Alban marks the union of England with the Continent, and the period of Roman rule. Of Roman name, educated at Rome, he was slain, a victim to the ancient paganism, with its temples to Jupiter and to Diana, in the last desperate conflict of the decaying empire with the rising Church.

Over that early Roman civilisation the tide of northern barbarism swept, and utterly destroyed it. Pagan temples and Christian churches, Roman cities and villas, with the surrounding world of British peasants and slaves, vanished so entirely that when, 400 years after, Bede gives the story of Alban, though he preserves the tradition of a Christian man who, no doubt, really lived and died at Verulam, it is a tradition garlanded with flowers of legend from a world as foreign and far off as the stories of the virgin martyrs of Rome or Sicily.

From the next deadly battle between Saxon heathenism and Roman-British Christianity no martyr's name has survived in our calendars. Yet that conflict also had its spiritual heroes.

Two thousand monks were gathered at Bangor in one of those vast religious settlements which were characteristic of Celtic Christianity, and after a three days' fast a crowd of these ascetics followed the British army to the field near Chester. Æthelfrith, the Saxon chief, watched the wild gestures of these monks as they stood apart from the host with arms outstretched in prayer, and bade his men slay them in the coming fight. 'Bear they arms or no,' said the king, 'they war against us when they cry against us to their God.' And in the surprise and rout which followed, these monks were the first to fall.

Something of the martyr glory surely must be given to those whose prayers the enemy felt to be a warfare so real. This the final defeat of the early British Christians was in 593, nearly 300 years after the martyrdom of St. Alban. Four years afterwards Augustine of Canterbury won the Saxon kingdom of Kent to the Christian Faith. But it was as a foreign conquest. The links with the earlier Christianity were broken.

The next English martyr marks another wave of heathenism which swept from the barbarian North over England.

The Danish pirates in Scandinavia, uniting with those who had settled in Ireland, had conquered Northumbria, and, being beaten back in Mercia, threw themselves all the more fiercely on East Anglia.

There was reigning at the time the young king Edmund, not yet twenty-nine. Young as he was, he had been king, 'under-king, landlord, and duke' of East Anglia, Suffolk, and Norfolk for fourteen years. When King Offa went to end his days in piety and penitence at Rome, his boy successor was crowned, in 855, by Bishop Humbert, on Christmas Day, at Sudbury, a royal country house on the Stour.

Generous and just, peaceable and devout, he seems from the first to have entered on that especial conflict with the especial perils of his own position, which has been said to be the note of saintliness. '.He hated flatterers, and would see with his own eyes and hear with his own ears, so much did he dread one-sidedness in his judgments, inaccuracy or falsehood of reports, and the manœuvres and subtleties of human passions.'

His love of his people was rooted deep in the love of God, and his piety was fed by learning, marking, and inwardly digesting the Holy Scriptures. It is said that he lived as far as he could in solitude for one whole year in a tower which he had built for a country retreat at Hunstanton, in Norfolk, that he might learn the Psalter by heart, so as to be able to repeat it at night, when travelling, or in the intervals of his regal work.

The kingly ideal of the seventy-second Psalm seems to have moulded his life. He judged his people with righteousness and the poor with judgment. He judged the poor of the people and saved the children of the needy. He delivered the needy when he cried, the poor also, and him that had no helper. He redeemed their soul from deceit and violence, and precious was their blood in his sight. The widow and the fatherless found in him their protector. Thus it was in his peaceful days; and when the dark days of warfare came he sought with all the strength he had to 'break in pieces the oppressor.'

'And,' so says Carlyle, 'there is clear evidence that his people honoured, loved, and admired him to quite an astonishing degree, and indeed at last to an immeasurable and inexpressible degree; for finding no limits or utterable words for their sense of his worth, they took to beatifying and adoring him. "Infinite admiration," we are taught, means worship. His life has become a poetic, nay, a religious mythus, though undeniably enough it was once a stern fact, as our poor lives are, and even a very rugged and unmanageable one, and clearly he had contradictory speeches and contradictory facts not a few to reconcile with himself. No man becomes a saint in his sleep. Edmund, for instance, instead of reconciling these same contradictory facts and speeches to himself, which means subduing and in a manlike and godlike manner conquering them to himself, might have merely thrown new contention into them, new unwisdom into them, and so have been conquered by them, much the commoner case. In that way he had proved no saint or god-like man, but a mere sinner, and unfortunately blamable, and more or less diabolic-looking man.

'How then, may it be asked, did this Edmund rise into favour? Really, except it were by doing justly and loving mercy to an unprecedented extent, we do not know. The man, it would seem, "had walked," as they say, "humbly with God," humbly and valiantly with God, struggling to make the earth heavenly as he could, instead of walking sumptuously and pridefully with Mammon, leaving the earth to grow hellish as it liked.

'On this people of Norfolk and Suffolk, living in industry and peace under their beloved young king, burst the Danish heathen hordes, under two of the fiercest of their chiefs, Hincmar and Hubba, sons of Ragnar Lodbrog. They seemed to have had an especial hatred of Christianity. They had destroyed and plundered towns and monasteries in Northumbria and Mercia. In the Fens they razed to the ground the great abbeys of Crowland, Bardney, Peterborough, Ely, and Huntingdon. They massacred the clergy and the nuns with fierce mockeries. At Peterborough Cathedral is shown the stone once placed over a pit in which fourscore murdered monks were buried.

'From the Fens these pirates rushed down on Suffolk and burned the town of Thetford. There King Edmund gathered all his forces, encountered them in battle, and defeated them. But after their defeat large reinforcements so increased the Danish hosts that Edmund, wishing to avoid useless slaughter, disbanded the few troops he had and retired towards his castle of Framlingham.

'The Danes seem to have held him personally in some consideration, for they endeavoured to make a separate truce with him, separating him from his compatriots; but the terms they offered not being such as could save his people or defend their Christianity, the King rejected them without hesitation.

'Then a band of Danes took him prisoner at Bosor, on the Waveney, and brought him loaded with fetters to the tent of the chief, Hincmar.

'Here again safety was offered him and certain terms of peace; but they involved the betrayal of his people and his faith, and the young King would not listen to them for a moment.

'"Cannot we kill you?" cried they.

'"Cannot I die?" answered he.

'And so he was martyred—beaten and cruelly tortured, and then bound to a tree, shot to death as a mark for countless arrows, 'the St. Sebastian of England.' 'Seen and felt by all men to have done a man's part in this life pilgrimage of his; and benedictions and outflowing love and admiration from the universal heart were his meed. "Well done! well done!" cried the hearts of all men. They raised his slain and martyred body, washed its wounds with fast-flowing and universal tears; tears of endless pity, yet of a sacred joy and triumph—the beautifullest kind of tears; indeed, perhaps the beautifullest kind of thing; like a sky all flashing diamonds and prismatic radiance, all weeping yet shone on by the everlasting sun. And this is not a sky, it is a Soul, a living Face. Nothing like this *Temple of the Highest*, bright with some real effulgence of the Highest, is seen in this world.'

'Now might all Anglia laud and follow a hero martyr and great true son of Heaven.

'In this manner did the men of the eastern counties take up the slain body of their Edmund where it lay, cast forth in the village of Hoxne; seek out the severed head and reverently reunite the same. They embalmed him with myrrh and sweet spices, with love and pity and all high and awful thoughts; consecrating him with many stories of melodious adoring admiration and sun-dried streams of tears; joyfully yet with awe, as all deep joy has something of the awful in it, commemorating his noble deeds and god-like walk and conversation while on earth; till at length the Pope and cardinals at Rome, summing up the general verdict of mankind, declared with their *Advocatus diaboli* pleading and their other forms of process that he had in very fact lived a hero's life in this world, and, being now *gone*, was gone, as they conceived, to God above, and reaping his reward *there*. Such, they said, was the best judgment they could form of the case; and truly not a bad judgment, acquiesced in and zealously adopted, with full assent of " private judgment," by all mortals.

'Pious munificence provided him a shrine, a wooden chapel, a stone temple, ever widening and growing by new pious gifts. Such the overflowing heart feels it a blessedness to solace itself by giving. The wooden chapel has become a stone temple; stately masonries; long-drawn arches, cloisters, sounding aisles buttress it and girdle it far and wide. The united companies of men devote themselves in every generation to meditation on man's nobleness and awfulness, and show forth the same as best as they can, thinking they will do it better here in presence of God the Maker and of the so Awful, so Noble made by Him. In one word, St. Edmund's body has raised a monastery around it. New gifts, houses, farms come ever in. King Canute with his crown and gifts; many other kings, queens, wise men, and noble, loyal men. Beodric's Worth has become St. Edmund's Bury, and lasts visible to this hour.

'Certain times do crystallise themselves in a magnificent manner. Let *us* withal be hopeful.'[1]

---

[1] Carlyle, *Past and Present*.
Dedications of churches: 55 (15 being in East Anglia), unless any be to St. Edmund the Archbishop. Represented in art crowned and pierced by many arrows, bound to a tree as above, a wolf guarding his body or crowned head, an arrow in his hand.

King Edward the Martyr.

March 18; Tr. *June* 20.

(Born A.D. 962; martyred A.D. 978; tr. 980. Calendars: Sarum only. Sarum Ep. and Gosp.: Ecclus. xxxi. 8–11; St. Luke xiv. 26–33.)

About 200 years had passed since the Devonshire Bishop Boniface had fallen, martyred by the heathen Frisians, and the whole of the time England had been fighting for life, working her way from a group of divided tribes into a nation.

And at the heart of all the strife of races and dynasties had always been that deeper struggle for a higher unity, the combat for the Universal Kingdom of God through the faith in the unity of God and the unity of men in Christ.

For England at all events her very existence as a nation had been bound up with her Christianity, and her incorporation into the unity of the Christian Church.

The struggle had been first between the divided tribes of successive settlers from the Continent; then, especially between Wessex, Mercia, and Northumbria, which it seemed as if nothing could have united into one nation but the external pressure of the invasions of the Danes and Northmen. In confronting these Northern pirates the men of Wessex, Mercia, and Northumbria began to feel they were one England. In combat with these heathen persecutors and destroyers of cities, churches, and monasteries this one England felt the throb of her common Christianity.

In 730 England was so christianised that she could send out missionaries from her convents and monasteries north and south.

For the next two centuries the Northmen swept down on all her coasts, pillaging the abbeys in the north, where Bede and the Abbess Hilda had sown and watered the first seeds of our English literature; razing Peterborough, Crowland, and the great monastic houses in the Fen country to the ground, and massacring all within their walls; destroying all traces of the Benedictine abbey and school of Nutcell, in Hampshire, where Boniface had learned and taught, and whence he had gone forth to evangelise Germany.

A hundred years after Boniface we have indeed another English martyr in our English Calendar, but it is a young English king, dying for the faith on English soil. And King Edmund had scarcely fallen beneath the heathen arrows in Suffolk when another king among the greatest in all the history of our English Church and nation began the great fight with the heathen in the west—Alfred the Truth-teller, Deliverer, and King.

It is a curious problem why King Alfred's name is absent from the Calendar. It cannot have been only because of the preference for monks and clergymen. Three other English kings are included. Nor can it have been because of any want of sympathy on his part with Rome. He recognised Rome as the centre of ecclesiastical unity, the link between Christian nations, the link between the present and the past of Christianity, visited its shrines with a pilgrim's devotion, was recognised and received by the Pope, and received from him a portion of the Lignum Domini, the Wood of the True Cross. Nor could it have been because the form of his piety was out of harmony with his times; the religious books he loved and used and translated into the language of his people were the devotional manuals of his time; and he himself was moved by a fervent and intense love to God, which was the inspiration of all his work and the solace of all his sufferings. Nor can the omission be explained by any want of popular enthusiasm for his memory. Upward, indeed, usually from the hearts of the people have the names of the saints been lifted to their places in the Calendar; they have been consecrated by the tears and benedictions of the multitude before the ecclesiastical seal has been stamped upon them; and deep in the hearts of the people was enshrined the name of Alfred. Why, then, had he no place in any Calendar, no shrine in any city, no festival in the year?

Perhaps one reason chiefly accounts for the blank. Nothing but martyrdom seems to have placed any names save those of priests and monks in our ancient Calendar.

Nothing but the enthusiasm enkindled by the martyr's death seems to have given force enough to the popular voice to enroll any but those within the consecrated orders in the number of the saints. The tomb had to be the grave of a martyr that it might become the shrine of a saint.

And Alfred's life was not of the monastic type; nor, whatever the martyrdom of his life, did he die the martyr's death.

But in this omission there is more to inspire than to sadden. It simply emphasises the truth that beyond the few names on which the seal of human recognition has been set in the Calendar expands an infinite world of light. These stars, as the little child said of the stars in the sky, are but 'little pricks to let the glory through,' the glory of the boundless heavens around and beyond.

Alfred with his unwearied kingly rule, his holy home life, his thirty years of toiling and battling, shepherding and teaching, for his people, may represent for us a whole heaven of uncanonised saints, toilers, and warriors, working for others in castles and camps, in lonely hovels, in dingy streets, thinking nothing of themselves, fathers and mothers, teachers and patterns of saints. Alfred, uncanonised, lives between our two canonised English royal saints. The shrines of Edmund and Edward the Martyrs shine over Christian England, jewelled and decorated. Alfred enabled Christian England to *be*, and that is honour enough for him.

King Edward the Martyr has his own sacred lesson to teach in his brief boyish life. Archbishop Dunstan had been labouring for years under King Edgar to fulfil the work of King Alfred by pacifying the Danelagh and turning the heathen Northmen and Danes into Christian Englishmen.

At the death of Edgar Edward was a boy of thirteen,

WARFARE WITH BARBARISM OF THE NORTH 225

guided by the counsel of Dunstan. His stepmother, Elfrida, had intrigued in vain to set him aside in favour of her own son Ethelred, then seven years old. Dunstan faithfully guarded the rightful heir, and he was solemnly crowned.

The boy seems to have had a marked character of his own—gentle and affectionate, generous to the poor, thoughtful for the weak and suffering, and never moved by his stepmother's jealousy and injustice from his generous brotherly affection for his little brother, her son, nor yet turned aside from his respectful deference to her.

So he lived and reigned three years and a half. His early death at seventeen was the result of his own trustful, affectionate character. He had been hunting all day in a forest near Wareham, and, weary with the chase, rode up in the evening through the narrow little rocky pass called Corfe Gate to pay a visit to his stepmother and his little brother in Corfe Castle. At the castle door he asked to see his young brother, and waited outside till he should come.

They gave him a cup of wine to drink. He had emptied it and was courteously bending forward to give it back, when he was treacherously stabbed by Elfrida's orders. Finding himself betrayed and wounded, with a dying effort he put spurs to his horse and rode away; but after a few steps he fell from his horse, dead. His body was cast into a marsh to be hidden and forgotten. But the people loved their young king; it was believed that a pillar of light revealed where his corpse was laid; it was removed to the church at Wareham, and afterwards translated to the monastery of Shaftesbury.

The long thin knife with which he was stabbed was kept at Faversham till the suppression of the monasteries.

There are two festivals connected with that boy king in our Calendar, commemorating these two translations of his murdered body.

The Anglo-Saxon Chronicle reveals the depth of popular indignation felt at his death. After the quiet record, 'A.D. 979. This year was King Edward slain at eventide, at Corfe-gate, on the 15th before the Kalends of

April, and then was he buried at Wareham without any kind of kingly honours,' it breaks into a poetical dirge :—

> There has not been among Angles
> A worse deed done
> Than this was
> Since they first
> Britain's land sought.
> Men him murdered,
> But God him glorified.
> He was in life
> An earthly king;
> He is now, after death,
> A heavenly saint.
> Him could not his earthly
> Kinsmen avenge,
> But him hath his heavenly Father
> Greatly avenged.
> The earthly murderers
> Would his memory
> On this earth blot out,
> But the lofty Avenger
> Hath his memory
> In the heavens
> And in earth wide spread.
> They who would not erewhile
> To his living
> Body bow down,
> They now humbly
> On knees bend
> To his dead bones.
> Now we may understand
> That men's wisdom
> And their devices
> And their counsels
> Are all nought
> Against God's resolves.

The young life, so full of promise, was suddenly cut off in this world; but not till he had engraven in our English Calendar the great lesson that death met in the carrying out of everyday duties, such as an act of affection to a little brother or of courtesy in return for unkindness, may lift the sufferer to a place among the martyrs.[1]

---

[1] Dedications of churches: 21, either to him or to St. Edward the Confessor; that at Corfe Castle certainly to the 'Martyr.' Represented in art as a king with dagger, falcon, or cup.

St. Alphege of Canterbury.[1]

April 19.

(Calendars: Sarum, Aberdeen. Born A.D. 954; consecrated bishop A.D. 984; martyred A.D. 1012. Sarum Ep. and Gosp. : Heb. xiii. 9-16 ; St. John xv. 1-7.)

The lesson of the next and last of our martyrs is not unlike that of King Edward. Alphege fell in the fulfilment of his Christian duties to his flock and to his trust, in a raid of the heathen Northern pirates against England, just before the reign of Canute, the Christian Danish king.

His successor, Lanfranc, doubted if he could be termed a martyr, not having been called on to deny the name of Christ ; but St. Anselm decided that death in the discharge of Christian duty was death for Christ.

St. Alphege was born of noble and virtuous parents, who gave him a good education. 'Fearing the snares of riches, he renounced the world while he was yet very young, and though most dutiful to his parents in all things, in this one thing he did not yield even to the tears of his tender mother.'

'He served God first in the monastery of Derherste, in Gloucestershire. His desire of greater perfection taught him always to think that he had not yet begun to live to God.'

'After some years he left Derherste and built himself a cell in a desert place near the Abbey of Bath, where he shut himself up, unknown to men. His virtue, after some time, shone to men the brighter through the veil of his

---

[1] Alban Butler and *Les Petits Bollandistes*. 'From his genuine Life, written by Osborn, a monk of Canterbury, in 1070, but finished by Eadmer.' Dedications of churches : five, one being the parish church of Greenwich, on the supposed site of the murder. Another is in London. Represented in art with stones in his chasuble ; a battleaxe in his hand.

humility, and many noblemen and others addressed themselves to him for instructions in the paths of perfection, and he was at length obliged to take upon himself the direction of the Abbey of Bath. Perfection is with difficulty maintained in numerous houses.'

'St. Alphege lamented bitterly the irregularities of the tepid among the brethren, especially little junketings, from which he in a short time reclaimed them; and God, by the sudden death of one, opened the eyes of all the rest. The good abbot would not tolerate the least relaxation in the community, being sensible how small a breach may totally destroy the regularity of a house. He used to say that it would have been much better for a man to have remained in the world than to be an imperfect monk, and that to wear the habit of a saint without the spirit was a perpetual lie, and an hypocrisy which insults Almighty God, but can never impose on Him. St. Ethelwold (Bishop of Winchester) having died in 984, St. Dunstan (being admonished by St. Andrew in a vision) obliged Alphege to quit his solitude and accept of episcopal consecration. His virtues became more conspicuous in this high station, though he was no more than thirty years of age when he was first placed in it. In winter, how cold soever it was, he always rose at midnight, went out, and prayed for a long time barefoot and without his upper garment. He never ate flesh except on extraordinary occasions. He was no less remarkable for charity to his neighbours than for severity to himself.' And his charity was so effectually organised that it is said to have had the remarkable result, so earnestly sought to be obtained in our own days by various methods, not of increasing beggars, but of abolishing beggary! 'During his time there were no beggars in the diocese of Winchester.'

After the death of Archbishop Alfric in 1006, he was translated to Canterbury, being then fifty-two years of age.

The Northmen at that time, under Sweyn of Norway, were once more ravaging England. Sweyn's fleet reached the coast in 1003, and for four years he marched through southern and eastern England, burning towns and homesteads and monasteries, and massacring the inhabitants.

At last, joined by the traitorous Edric, he invested Canterbury. Before the city was surrounded, the English nobility entreated the archbishop to save himself by flight.

But he refused, saying it was the part of a hireling to abandon his flock in danger.

During the siege he often sent out to his enemies to desire them to spare the innocent people; and meantime he endeavoured to animate his flock against the worst. He exhorted them to suffer the worst rather than renounce their faith; he gave them the Blessed Eucharist, and recommended them to the Divine protection.

Whilst he was thus sustaining and encouraging his people, Canterbury was taken by storm. The heathen invaders, as they entered the city, made a dreadful slaughter of all that came in their way, without distinction of sex or age. The monks would have kept the archbishop in the church, where they thought he might be safe, but he broke from them, and pressed through the Danish troops to the scene of slaughter.

Then turning to the enemy he cried out, 'Spare these innocent persons. There is no glory in spilling their blood. Turn your indignation rather against me. I have reproached your cruelties; I have fed, clothed, and ransomed these your captives.'

Enraged at his bold freedom of speech, the fierce Northmen seized the archbishop and treated him with great barbarity. They made him the spectator of the burning of his cathedral and the decimation of his monks and of the citizens; they wounded his face, beat and kicked him unmercifully, laid him in irons, and confined him several months in a filthy dungeon. But being themselves afflicted with a fatal epidemic, a terror came on them lest it might be a vengeance from heaven for their cruel usage of the archbishop, and they drew him out of prison. He prayed for them and gave their sick bread which he had blessed. 'By eating this their sick recovered, and the epidemic ceased.'

The chiefs returned thanks to the servant of God, and deliberated about setting him at liberty; but covetousness prevailed in their council, and they exacted for his ransom three thousand marks of gold.

He replied that the country was all laid waste, and that he would not squander the patrimony of the poor on his ransom.

He was therefore bound again, and on Easter Sunday was brought before the commander of the fleet, which lay at Greenwich, and threatened with torments and death unless he paid the ransom demanded. He answered that he had no other gold to offer them than that of true wisdom, which consists in the knowledge and worship of the Living God; which, if they refused to listen to, they would one day fare worse than Sodom; adding that their empire would not long subsist in England.

The barbarians, enraged at this answer, knocked him down with the backs of their battle-axes and then stoned him. Like Stephen, among the stones, he prayed our Lord to forgive his murderers and to receive his soul.

At last, raising himself up a little, he said, 'O Good Shepherd, O incomparable Shepherd, look with compassion on the children of Thy Church, whom I, dying, recommend to Thee.'

The death stroke came from a friendly hand. One of the Northmen whom he had lately baptised, grieving to see him tortured in that slow agony, clove his head with a battle-axe, and so gave the finishing stroke to his martyrdom.

Thus died St. Alphege on April 19, 1012, in the 59th year of his age, at Greenwich, as near the opened heavens as at Jerusalem, not a step further from the Master's footsteps for the thousand years between him and St. Stephen amidst his stones.

His body was borne to St. Paul's, in London, and translated, eleven years afterwards, to his own Cathedral at Canterbury, King Canute the Dane following in reverent homage down the narrow street to the river-side and himself holding the stern of the boat as they laid the martyred body in it.

Better close the glorious martyr story can scarcely have than in this brave and loving man dying as he was pleading for his flock ; dying for fidelity to his trust for the poor ; dying among the stones, pleading for his enemies, like Stephen the first martyr. Not once or twice in the great story of the Church,

> Not once or twice in our rough island story,
> The path of duty was the way to glory.
> For he who walks it only thirsting
> For the right, and learns to deaden
> Love of self, before his journey closes
> He shall find the stubborn thistle bursting
> Into glossy purples, which outredden
> All voluptuous garden roses.
>
> Not once or twice in our fair island story
> The path of duty was the way to glory :
> He that ever following her commands,
> On with toil of heart and knees and hands,
> Through the long gorge to the far light has won
> His path upward, and prevail'd,
> Shall find the toppling crags of duty scaled
> Are close upon the shining table-lands,
> To which our God Himself is moon and sun.[1]

' Earl Thurkill, a Christian Dane, offered gold and silver, all that he had, save only his ship, to save St. Alphege's life.'—Blunt's *Annotated Prayer Book.*

Another Account of the Martyrdom of St Alphege.

(From the Anglo-Saxon Chronicle.)

1011. 'And, nevertheless, for all the truce and tribute they' (the Northmen) 'went everywhere in bands and plundered our miserable people, and robbed and slew them. And then, in this year, between the Nativity of St. Mary and St. Michael's Mass, they besieged Canterbury, and got into it through treachery, because Elfmar betrayed it, whose life the Archbishop Elphege had before saved. And there they took the Archbishop Elphege, and Elfward (the king's steward), and the Abbess Leofruna, and Bishop Godwin. And Abbot

[1] Tennyson, *Ode on the Duke of Wellington.*

Elfmar they let go away. And they took there within all the men in orders, and men and women : it is not to be told to any man how many there were. And they remained within the city afterwards as long as they would. And when they had thoroughly searched the city, then went they to their ships, and led the Archbishop with them.

> Was then captive
> He who erewhile was
> Head of the English race
> And Christendom.
>
> There might then be seen
> Misery, where men oft
> Erewhile saw bliss
> In that hapless city,
>
> Whence to us came first
> Christendom and bliss,
> 'Fore God, and 'fore the world.

And they kept the Archbishop with them so long as until the time they martyred him.'

1012. 'In this year came Edric, the ealdorman, and all the chief witan, clergy, and laity of the English people to London, before Easter; Easter-day was then on the Ides of April, and they were there so long as until all the tribute was paid, after Easter; that was eight-and-forty thousand pounds. Then, on the Saturday, was the army greatly excited against the Bishop, because he would not promise them any money; but *he forbade that anything should be given for him.* They had also drunk deeply, for wine had been brought there from the south. Then took they the Bishop, led him to their hustings on the eve of Sunday, the octaves of Easter, which was on the 13th before the Kalends of May; and there they shamefully slaughtered him. They cast upon him bones and the horns of oxen, and then one of them struck him with an axe-iron on the head, so that with the blow he sank down; and *his holy blood fell on the earth, and his holy soul he sent forth to God's kingdom.*

'And on the morrow the body was carried to London, and the Bishops Ednoth and Elfhun and the townsmen received it with all reverence.'

PART II.

SAINTS NOT MARTYRS.

CHAPTER I.

THE FOUR LATIN FATHERS AND ST. BENEDICT.

OF the fifty-five Saints in our Calendar, twenty-five at least were martyrs, bearing witness to the principle of counting not their lives dear unto them, for Christ's sake, by dying. At this high level they set the standard for the whole Church.

But whether martyrs or not, all were soldiers, and every soldier goes into the battle with his life in his hands ; that he does not fall is an accident of warfare. Or, in other words, the true soldier's life is a life of obedience. Doing the duty of the moment, at every moment, at any risk, makes the hero, not the accident that the risk proves fatal.

In the Christian warfare it is the laying down the life all through that is the service, the offering up of the life all through that is the sacrifice, not the moment or the manner of its close. For, moreover, the *universal* close, not the *exceptional*, is dying ; and unless the dying is a continuance of the long sacrifice of living, it is no martyrdom.

The 'Into Thy hands I commend my spirit' of every moment, does, for each loyal heart and true, culminate in the 'Into Thy hands' of the last moment.

And yet for every Christian's life, the whole level is raised by the 'noble army' of martyrs, whom we acknowledge as our leaders and our princes, our white-robed body-guard.

We cannot but observe in entering on the second range of our subject that all the Saints not martyrs in our

Calendar were more or less monastic; consecrated, as was believed, entirely to God, as priests, monks, and nuns.

The one apparent exception, King Edward the Confessor, is no exception, being more monastic in spirit than many monks, a monk in the home, a recluse on the throne.

In the larger and later Calendars this is not so absolutely the case as in ours, which closes in the thirteenth century. Our Calendar, in fact, represents the mediæval ideal of saintliness, and probably no section of Christendom would construct such a Calendar now.

In all ages, saintliness must mean entire unreserved consecration to God. In the ages to which our Calendar belongs, this entire consecration was represented by the renunciation not only of sinful passions, but of the affections which create and constitute homes. It is not a question between one section and another of Christendom, in our age, but between one age and another. No one in the world now, however devoted to the memory of St. Jerome, St. Augustine, or St. Ambrose, or of some of the mediæval saints, would write as they did then about the respective merits or demerits of married and unmarried life.

How far the overstrain of the monastic ideals in the monastic literature may have contributed by the law of reaction to the corruption of the secular literature in the romances is a question worth considering, though not the one before us now.

In all ages, and with regard to all kinds of moral evil, the noblest have often sought refuge from the corruption of the good creatures of God in the renunciation of the good on account of its possible corruption. And these monastic saints, like the Puritans, were surely, with whatever exaggerations, pulling against the stream of the especial sins and dangers of their own times. The highest devotion, and therefore the most effective energy, were among them. Those in our Calendar were almost all founders or reformers of an Order, or of an Abbey, or great missionaries; missionaries of civilisation and of mercy as well as of religion; men of letters, poets, artists, schoolmasters, founders of colonies, clearers of wildernesses, inheritors of the past, and teachers of the future; torch-bearers in a great procession, carrying on the light of the past into the future, diffusing light, not hiding or quenching it.

If these monks and nuns had not preserved the secrets of learning and the arts of civilisation for us, preserving all scriptures written of old for our learning as well as the Holy Scriptures of our faith, amidst the successive floods of barbarism, there would scarcely be a civilised Europe now to complain of the way in which they did it.

The second portion of our story of the Saints seems naturally to divide itself into three groups.

Our Calendar closes in the middle of the thirteenth century with St. Richard of Chichester, A.D. 1250; and this not on account of omissions made at the Reformation, but because it follows the old English Calendars, especially that of Sarum, which were not increased for a century or two before the Reformation. It is peculiarly insular; after the seventh century entirely English, not even Scotch or Irish.

Of the monastic orders, only the Benedictine is represented in it, with the exception of the Carthusian, which sent us from the Chartreuse St. Hugh of Lincoln. The Friars, Franciscan or Dominican, are not there at all.

The second portion of our story of the Saints seems, therefore, naturally to divide itself into three groups; the great Latin group, still within the limits of the language and laws of ancient Rome, including the four great Latin Fathers, Ambrose, Augustine, Jerome and Gregory the Great (linked so especially with England), and also Benedict, founder of the Benedictines, who belongs by descent to Rome, and by influence to the Middle Ages; the five French and Gallican Saints, Hilary of Poictiers, Britius (St. Brice), Remigius (St. Rémi) Machutus (St. Malo), St. Leonard and St. Giles (Egidius); lastly, the Saints especially belonging to our own island, either by birth or work.

St. Ambrose

Of Milan.

April 4.

(Calendars: all. In the Roman and Monastic Calendars, as in the Eastern Church, his feast is on Dec. 7, the day of his ordination. Born A.D. 340; consecrated bishop, 374; died about midnight before Easter Eve, April 4, A.D. 397. Sarum Ep. and Gosp.: Ecc. xlvii. 8-11; St. Matt. xxiv. 42-47.)

Of the three great Latin Fathers, Ambrose, Augustine, and Jerome, Ambrose seems the most essentially Roman. Jerome, if, on one side, like the Oriental monks in fiery vehemence, is also Greek in his breadth of literary sympathy, fearlessly seeking the aid of Jews in translating the Hebrew Scriptures, as Plato might have listened to the ancient lore of Egyptian priests. Augustine, with the genius and the grace which made him a theologian for all ages of Western Christendom, glows also with a tropical African fervour. But Ambrose has the balance and moderation, the courage and reasonableness of a Roman senator or general of Rome's noblest days. If Augustine's words were, for centuries, in themselves deeds, moving the inmost hearts of Christian men, Ambrose's were deeds in another sense, as part of his combat against the vices and sins of his own generation; and his denunciation of the unmerciful act of the Emperor Theodosius; his attack on the last remnant of paganism, the Altar of Victory in the Roman Senate; his defence of Jews and heretics against persecution, are part of the great battle for righteousness and mercy for all time. His hymns also are like trumpet calls to arouse the combatants from sloth, to direct the battle or to proclaim the victory. They cannot be read truly apart from his life.

The sketches given here of these three men of old can

but be brief indications and suggestions to recall well-known pictures, or to lead those who wish to know more to the larger biographies, or to their own writings, which are their best biographies.

St. Ambrose was the youngest child of Ambrosius, Pretorian Prefect of the Gauls, under Constantine the younger. With the exception of military command the whole power, under the emperor, over half Europe, including ancient Spain, France, Belgium, Rhenish Prussia and the British Isles, was in his hands. His chief residence was at Treves, the metropolis of the Northern Empire, with its amphitheatres, basilicas, baths, and all the essentials of a great Roman city; and at or near Treves it is generally believed Ambrose's family lived many years, enjoying the double honours of great secular office and of a Christianity dating to the heroic ages of the persecutions. They gloried to include in their pedigree the name of Sotheris, a virgin martyr who refused to burn incense to the gods, and was put to death with torture under Diocletian.

There were three children in this family, Marcellina, the eldest, Satyrus, and then Ambrose the youngest, ten years younger than his sister.

The relations subsisting among these three are very beautiful. All three were canonised. Of the father and mother we know little. Marcellina seems to have been mother and sister to both her brothers. She being the firstborn was consecrated to God in infancy in baptism. But according to the custom of the times neither of the brothers was baptised until he had reached middle age. The salt, 'symbol of wisdom and incorruptibility,' was indeed laid on Ambrose's lips in infancy, and the cross was signed on his brow, but baptism was deferred. His secretary relates that when Ambrose was lying a babe in the cradle in the court of his father's palace, a swarm of bees settled on his lips (as on Plato's), flying in and out of his mouth. The nurse, in a panic, would have driven them away, but the father, walking near, with the mother and the little sister, would not have them disturbed. In a little while the bees flew up so high that they could not be seen, and the father said, 'This child will be something great.'

The expectation took root in the heart of the little sister and perhaps helped to fulfil itself. From the first to the last Ambrose was kept up to high aims by having much expected from him by one whose own ideal was of the highest.

When Ambrose was a boy and Marcellina a girl of nineteen or twenty, in the quiet of their father's country house, she seemed to hear the voice of the martyred maiden of her house, Sotheris, martyred only fifty years before, calling her to follow her by renouncing the world in her youth and devoting herself to the service of God. Marcellina obeyed, and went to Rome, probably to her father's house near the Capitol.

The following Christmas (453) she received the veil of virginity from the aged Pope Liberius, with other young maidens, in the Vatican Basilica. A great crowd was present at the ceremony. The old man spoke words of warning and encouragement.

'The Christ will receive your vows,' he said, addressing himself especially to Marcellina, whom no doubt he knew; 'love Him much, my daughter, for He is good. The Scriptures say none is good but God. May your soul have wings and your youth be renewed like the eagle's!'

About this time the father died, and the widowed mother returned to Rome to the family palace near the Capitol.

The vowed virgins in those days did not abandon their homes. The mother's house was Marcellina's cloister, and there the four lived together, with a friend of Marcellina's, also dedicated to the especial service of God; a beautiful family life, mingling in all simply natural ways with each other, yet the whole tone raised by the consecration of the only daughter of the house. On one occasion the boy Ambrose, seeing the ladies of his house, according to custom, kiss the hand of the bishop, is reported to have said, 'Kiss my hands; I shall be bishop one day,' for which badinage and presumption Marcellina seems to have administered a little lecture. Doubtless the presence of the widowed mother hallowed and pervaded all the family life, but the chief inspiring and moulding influence seems to have been that of the sister.

'Great enough to understand Ambrose, strong enough to sustain him, tender enough to console him,' he called her his 'holy, his venerable sister.'[1] She watched by his cradle; she survived to kneel by his grave.

The two brothers were nearer each other in age. They studied at school and worked at home together; indeed, were scarcely ever seen apart. If one was seen alone, it was thought the other must be ill. They had endless talks as they read Greek together, and as they took long walks over the hills, so that when in after years Ambrose was reading alone, he would often look up from habit and begin to speak, seeking his brother's sympathy. They studied Greek—not yet fallen, for the West, into its medieval sleep. Cicero, Virgil, Livy were in their mother tongue.

Especially also they studied Roman law and rhetoric, eloquence being then the key of civil and political careers, the rhetoric not free from the florid exuberance of that decaying age. Their society in Rome was mixed. Two hundred and fifty pagan temples were still open in the city, with their priests and sacrificial rites. One of the great houses the brothers frequented, that of Symmachus, prefect of the city, was pagan. The son, a lifelong friend of Ambrose, was one of the latest defenders of paganism, pleading against him for the Altar of Victory in the Senate House. Thus the brothers touched the last growths of a still living (or dying) paganism, with its allegorisings of late Greek philosophy and its strange grafts of Oriental mysticism, represented in temples of Isis and altars to Mithra.[2]

Another great house at which they visited was that of Petronius Probus. This was Christian. Instead of the faint breath of yesterday's pagan incense, the fresh air of new life breathed through it. It was allied with the great

[1] Abbé Baunard.
[2] *Rome sous les Sévères*, par Jean Réville.

house of the Anicii. Among the women of the family or connected with it were Marcella, Paula, Eustochium, Juliana, Fabiola, of the community of the Aventine, Jerome's 'Ecclesia domestica.'

Jerome, the young Dalmatian, full of enthusiasm, might be met there. Christianity in its youth and first flush of victory, encountering paganism, hollow, painted, vainly propped up, dying.

Over Ambrose's youth passed also the shadow of Julian the Apostate, with his attempt at a pagan revival.

The friendship of the brothers and sisters was no exclusive family cult of one another. They lived in a wide world with many to honour and love. There was Priscus, Ambrose's friend in youth and age, and especially there was Simplician, older than the brothers, lifelong friend of Ambrose, and his successor in the see of Milan. And there was the renowned professor Victorinus, translator of Plato, and teacher of generations of the noble youths of Rome, whom Simplician had rescued from heathenism. It must have been among the inspiring stories of Ambrose's youth how his friend Simplician, then young, had been moved to win this great pagan professor to Christianity; how he placed the sacred Christian books in his hands; how Victorinus read, admired, believed, and came step by step towards the Christian faith and the Christian Church, till at last he could tell Ambrose he was a Christian, and at the next great festival they had the great joy of seeing the aged professor, clothed in the white robes of the neophytes, like a child, ascend the steps of the tribune of the Christian Basilica, and publicly renounce paganism, so that there ran a loud murmur through the mouths of all the rejoicing multitude of 'Victorinus, Victorinus;' for all knew him.

Soon after this Julian the Apostate forbade any Christians to teach the classics, and Victorinus resigned the chair he had held for forty years, rather than betray Him 'who can render the lips of children eloquent.'

At the games in the amphitheatre Ambrose was, as a

boy, disgusted by seeing a victorious athlete, when he had overthrown his adversary, strike his face with his heel, ungenerously insulting the vanquished. But while still in early manhood Ambrose was called away from this brilliant corrupt society, and made consular of the Emilia and Liguria, of what is now Piedmont and Lombardy.

The seat of his government was Milan. His old friend Petronius Probus, in bidding him farewell, said to him, 'Act not as a judge but a bishop,' meaning only that he should judge with Christian equity and mercy, but unconsciously uttering a prophecy.

Milan was at that time the Italian residence of the emperors, the virtual metropolis of the Western Empire. Ambrose found the city disturbed with the Arian controversy, under the rule of the Arian bishop Auxentius. He had been only one year in office when Auxentius died. This brought the controversy to a crisis. There were tumults, and especially in the churches. The clergy were assembled for the election in the choir of the great Basilica. The people gathered in crowds in the nave, separated from the choir by a veil, in the Oriental method.

Angry debates arose. There was danger of a riot in the Basilica, and Ambrose, as governor, came to quell it. At his entrance, a sweet clear voice, which seemed that of a child, was heard above the angry din, '*Ambrose is bishop. Ambrose is bishop.*' The position, the faith, the just and merciful character of Ambrose were well known. With tumultuous enthusiasm the whole assembly joined in the call for Ambrose; and in spite of reluctance, resistance, and flight, Ambrose had to yield.

It is interesting, as a token of the link, yet unbroken, between East and West, to observe that Ambrose received a letter of congratulation on his election from St. Basil of Cæsarea.

The archbishop elect was not yet baptised. He received baptism from his old friend, the priest Simplician, of whom he said, 'I may have friendship with many, but my friendship with him is as that between father and son.' With the triple immersion of the Milanese rite he was received into the Church. In little more than a week afterwards he was consecrated bishop (A.D. 375). No worldly advancement was it to him, but a most heavy and real burden, and one from which once taken up he never sought repose during the forty-two years which remained of his life.

His sister Marcellina and his brother Satyrus rejoined him at Milan. His sister left Rome to be with him, often living in his house, and when she retired for quiet and prayer to her country house near Milan, the intercourse between them was constantly maintained by letters, so that she was always really with him, sharing his alms, his prayers, his study of the Scriptures. Satyrus administered the episcopal household and revenues, and a most rare and blessed companionship there was between these two hearts, entirely united in devotion, in their different ways, to the service of God and man. It did not last long on earth. In 378, three years after the consecration of Ambrose, Satyrus went to look after some property in Africa, and on the journey suffered shipwreck, from the shock of which his health never recovered. His great longing in his peril of shipwreck was to live to be baptised. He threw himself into the sea; his prayers were heard; he reached the shore, and, very soon after, the shores of the heavenly country. Just after rejoining his brother and sister at Milan he died.

His body was laid on the bier in the Basilica. Kneeling beside it, Ambrose's sermon on his brother's death, in its conflict between grief and hope, reveals his inmost heart.

'Why should I weep for thee, my beloved brother? It is only place that is changed. Henceforth our souls are always together. Thou gavest up the pleasantness of thy native city only to be near me, and now it is thou who wilt open to me one day the gates of our true country. Henceforth heaven possesses the best part of me. When I was alone, I was never all myself. The best part of each of us was in the other, or rather each of us in the Christ, in Him who is altogether in both and in each.'

And again: 'But now where shall I find thee? What

will become of me, O my brother? The ox misses his yoke-fellow, and thou, my brother, can I forget thee with whom I ploughed the long furrow of life? I worked less than thou, but I loved as much. For thou, surrounding me with tender solicitation like a father, hadst for me the interest of an elder brother, and the respect of a younger. So that in losing thee I lose all with thee.'

And again: 'At every moment I see thee, I speak to thee, I press thee in my arms day and night. I used to dread sleep because it interrupted our communion; now I love it, for in sleep, which is the image of death, I find thee again.'

The sister Marcellina was beside the bier. Ambrose turning to her said: 'Our holy sister is left to me—she who like me placed in thee the happiness of our existence. Thou only canst comfort her. She will feel thy presence, she will feel thy life, she will learn not to regret thee too bitterly, for thou wilt assure her of thy bliss.'

The moment of the solemn 'last farewell' came. According to the ancient rite, three times they called on the dead; the last words were spoken. Ambrose looked on him once more in silence amidst the sobs of the great congregation, and then Ambrose spoke once more.

'Why delay? Call me, I beseech thee, soon to thee. I am impatient to see thee again. O Lord God Omnipotent, accept the oblation of this poor soul, receive my sacrifice as brother and as priest. Let this immolated life be a pledge of the life I would offer wholly to Thee.'

And so on that summer day they bore the body of the brother to the tomb. And eight days afterwards by that tomb, Ambrose preached a great sermon on 'Faith in the Resurrection.'

In seventeen years Ambrose rejoined Satyrus. In a few more Marcellina. But happily for Ambrose, at the beginning of his episcopal life, within all its toil and battle, he had the rest of a home lit up by a brother's and sister's love as deep and pure as the world has ever known.

It was a world of wild confusions in which Ambrose

lived and ruled. All kinds of incongruous beliefs were there, sometimes chemically mixed in new compounds, often mechanically conglomerated in tumultuous confusion.

There was an altar at Milan with the impossible combination of 'Jupiter Adonai ;' another to the 'Deo Pantheo.' The heresies were altogether unlike anything surviving now ; Persian dualisms with long processions of angels or Emanations, melting into Manichæism. The Arianism of those days, as has been said by one [1] given to the most liberal interpretations, was virtually an inroad of polytheism into Christianity ; paganism was still fighting the Church openly in temples and altars ; or secretly penetrating it with immoral heresies ; or corrupting it by lowering the festivals of the saints into revels like those of the old gods, kept with wild excitement ; or by such superstitions as degrading a reserved portion of the Blessed Sacrament into a kind of amulet against shipwreck or other perils.

In the State, nominally Christian, cruel old laws and customs survived, such as a father selling his children into serfdom for his debts ; torture ; the gladiatorial games sanctioned by the emperors. In society, the corruption of the luxury of the decaying old Roman world was mixed with the unutterable miseries of repeated invasions and desolations of barbarous hordes from the North.

Thus the episcopal life of Ambrose was one long toil against the stream, one ceaseless campaign against foes within and without, above and below, always changing, yet never relaxing in the attack.

His three great victories—over paganism, represented in the altar of Victory in the Senate ; over Arianism, aggressively annexing the churches in the assaults of the Empress Justina and her soldiers; over tyranny in the Emperor Theodosius—were no isolated storms in a life of peace. They were moments of manifested victory in a life of ceaseless warfare against wrong of all kinds.

The altar of the goddess Victory had been more than once taken from its place in the Roman Senate House and

[1] Dean Stanley.

restored. It represented not only Olympus, but the patriotic associations of ancient Rome. Not only the corruption of the old heathen world but a chivalrous fidelity to the past was enlisted on its side. The orator who attempted the final defence before the Emperor Valentinian was Symmachus, an old friend of Ambrose. But there could be no truce with falsehood, however picturesque. Ambrose prevailed, and the last political symbol of the vanquished paganism was for ever banished.

In the contest for the Basilicas with the Arian Empress-mother Justina, the method of the conflict was as much a victory as its issue. It was a victory of popular conviction. The people were with Ambrose. They kept the Basilicas for the Faith by simply staying in them.

Waiting night and day in the great Basilica, with its cloistered court, the Milanese people remained, singing the new Ambrosian church music, and Ambrose with them, holding the fort against the Arian emperor.

The soldiers outside, themselves part of the people, were moved, the Empress was vanquished, and the churches were saved.

And in all that highest Church history, which is the story of the struggle between light and darkness, justice and wrong, mercy and oppression, there are few nobler passages than the story of the penitence of Theodosius, which tells how Ambrose conquered the evil by enabling the wrongdoer to conquer himself.

The crime of Theodosius had been very great, however provoked. The populace of Thessalonica had murdered one of his high officers for inflicting just punishment on a wretched charioteer of low character, whose skill in the races had fascinated them.

Theodosius was at Milan at the time. His temper was impetuous and violent, and in a fury fanned by the flatterers around him, he sent orders that the populace of Thessalonica, who had done the wrong, should suffer what they had inflicted. As a city they had offended; as a city they were to be punished. But as a furious avenger indeed, not as a sovereign and judge, did Theodosius award the punishment. The citizens were invited into the arena to see the games—there was perfidy mingled with the ferocity. At once, in the crowded arena, the massacre began. Thousands perished by the hands of the soldiery.

The tidings of this treacherous and ferocious act sent a thrill of horror through the Empire.

Theodosius, still persuaded and persuading himself that he had but avenged justice and the imperial honour, would have continued his attendance at the services of the Church as usual.

But that one faithful voice of Ambrose was not to be stifled. The bishop refused himself to enter the imperial palace, and refused the Emperor an entrance into the Church, until he had made public confession of this great sin, and such reparation as was possible.

Yet while dealing externally with the imperial criminal as an inflexible judge, as a wandering sheep straying from the fold, nothing could be tenderer and more earnest than Ambrose's efforts to restore him; the tenderest father could not have dealt more gently with an erring child. He had to condemn the sin before the world; he had to win back the sinner to the Saviour. He did both.

'Emperor Augustus,' he wrote, 'you have zeal, you have the fear of God, I deny it not. But there is in you an impetuosity which if roused knows no limits.' Then recognising the conflict in the Emperor's conscience, he goes on, 'I deliver you up to yourself. *Become again what you really are.* Let the strength of piety become in you victorious over the violence of nature.'

He brings before him his crime, displays it in all its horror, reminds him of the appeals to mercy he had rejected, of the combat in his own mind in which he had allowed the worst to overcome.

'You can only wipe out this shame by humiliating yourself in the presence of God. You are a man. As such temptation has come to you. Come out of it a conqueror. We can only come out of sin by a path wet with tears. It is not any angel or archangel who can efface this crime. It is only the Lord, who says "I am with you," who gives forgiveness at the cost of repentance.'

Again blaming himself he writes: 'If I had foreseen better I might have spared you this fall. Would that I had obeyed my inspiration instead of confiding in your usual clemency!'

And again with tenderest words he speaks of his own affection: 'How could I not love you, you who were as a father to Gratian' (the young emperor whom Ambrose had so faithfully served)?

For some time the bishop retired from the city, probably to the country house of his sister. But when he returned, the courtiers persuaded the Emperor that if he presented himself at the Basilica, Ambrose would not dare to hold his ground.

With all his imperial suite he came. But before he could cross the outer vestibule of the penitents and catechumens, the bishop confronted him.

'Emperor,' he said, with dignity, 'you know not, I see, the gravity of the murder you have committed. Do you forget that you are made of dust like the rest of us? Perhaps absolute power blinds your eyes. Take care lest the purple make you lose sight of the infirmities it covers. Those you rule are men, your brothers, your fellow-servants, for there is but one Emperor, the Creator of all. How, with the stains of blood unjustly shed on your hands, can you come to the body of Jesus Christ? Rather fear to add to your crimes the crime of sacrilege.'

'But David sinned and God pardoned him,' said the Emperor.

'Accept then the yoke that God will lay on you,' said Ambrose; 'you have imitated David in his fault; follow him in your repentance.'

The Emperor went back in tears to his palace.

For eight months longer, within Theodosius and around him the severest combat went on. Most genuinely he lamented his crime; but the original wrong to his justice, the insult to his dignity, the flattery of courtiers excusing his severity or sometimes in their irony smiling at his repentant tears, the apparent hardness of Ambrose in not retiring a step from his demands—all made the struggle hard. Then came Christmas with all its sacred associations. The Emperor sat in his palace 'shedding floods of tears.' Rufinus his minister came to him and asked him, half in irony, the cause of his griefs.

'You laugh,' said the Emperor, 'for you feel not my misery. The Church of God is open to slaves and beggars. To me only is it closed; the door of the church and the door of heaven.'

Rufinus proposed to go and obtain the bishop's absolution. Theodosius hoped little, but let him go.

It was in vain; Rufinus came back baffled, and, meeting the Emperor on his way to the Basilica, counselled him to advance no further. But with the true dignity of true repentance, Theodosius said at last, 'I will go to Ambrose, and accept the affront I deserve.'

The victory was already won in the heart and conscience of the penitent. He had accepted the deepest humiliation at the tribunal of his own conscience, and external humiliation was little after this.

Ambrose met him in the court of the Basilica. The Emperor accepted his rebukes, the long delay imposed on him as on all penitents; he also made the only reparation demanded, or possible, of enacting a law interposing a delay of thirty days between a sentence of death and its execution; thus guarding himself and his successors against the temptations of despotic power.

And at length readmitted to the church there, not standing or kneeling but prostrate on the floor, in tears, he cried, 'O Lord, I cleave to the dust of Thy house; restore life to me according to Thy word.'

This was indeed no mere victory of sacerdotal power over imperial. It was a victory in the inmost citadel of the heart.

Restored to his true self and influenced by Ambrose, the

Emperor, never forgetting his fall, after this made many merciful laws for the defence of the poor and helpless; for instance, restoring freedom to children sold on account of their parents' poverty into slavery, and defending the weak against the oppression of officials, civil or military.

While this combat was going on Ambrose was also engaged in another battle for toleration and mercy within the Church. By a council of Gaulish bishops assembled at Milan, chiefly through his influence, was pronounced the deposition of certain bishops of their province for having caused the death of the heretic Priscillian. Ambrose had advanced, indeed, more than a thousand years beyond his time; if we should not rather call it a *return* through four centuries, to the words of the Beatitudes by the sea of Galilee, to the Cross outside Jerusalem on Calvary.

The conflict between the bishop and the Emperor ended in a friendship unbroken till death. It is good to have such a glimpse into the possible 'beauty of souls' as this story gives us; not only the fidelity which inspired the rebuke, or the generous truthfulness which accepted it, but the nobleness on both sides which made permanent trust and friendship the result. It was to Ambrose that noble Christian Emperor turned in every subsequent event of his life.

After his victory of Aquileia—the last victory over professed heathens—Theodosius wrote at once to Ambrose (to whom he said he owed his success); and Ambrose took the letter to the altar, and 'even,' he wrote to the Emperor, 'kept it there during the Sacrifice, that your faith might speak to God at the same time as my prayer.'

Anxious that the victory should not be followed by needless bloodshed, and full of pity for the frightened multitudes in Milan who had wavered in their allegiance, Ambrose went to meet the Emperor at Aquileia. He threw himself at the knees of the Prince, humbly beseeching him to spare the vanquished. Theodosius at once lifted him up, pardoned all, and then himself knelt before the Archbishop and protested that it was to him he owed his victory.

Ambrose returned to Milan in time to receive the Emperor, who made his triumphal entry the next day amidst an unbounded enthusiasm, not only for the victory which united east and west under one sovereign, but for the mercy which left the victory unsullied by an act of vengeance.

Nevertheless Theodosius, perhaps remembering Thessalonica, waited some weeks to participate in the Holy Communion, deeming the bloodshed of this necessary battle a stain which rendered him unfit for the Sacrament of sacrificing love.

The gates of a Temple no human hand can open or shut were soon to open on the Christian Emperor. His health was failing, and on the 19th of January, 395, five years after his public repentance, and a few weeks after the victory at Aquileia, Theodosius died, sustained by Ambrose, with the name of Ambrose often on his lips. And in him the Archbishop lost his greatest friend and his truest fellow labourer for the Church.

'He is gone,' said Ambrose from the pulpit, 'this great man, to take possession of a kingdom greater than that he has left. He has made his entry into the Holy Jerusalem whither for his piety Jesus Christ has summoned him.

'He has left us, the great Emperor, but he has not left us altogether. He leaves us his children. It seems to me I hear him say to God, like David, "Dilexi, I have loved." Yes, indeed, he loved with the most supreme devotion, he who saved his enemies, and pardoned those who assailed him. He has loved. Is there a higher praise? For love is the fulfilling of the law. Behold his ardent soul; see him rising above the earth, filled with the Holy Ghost, meeting in his passage other souls, who ask why he is mounting so high, and only answering them in these words, "I have loved." Seeing him reach up to them, the angels and archangels ask of him, "What, then, have you done on earth to deserve this place?" And always he answers, "I have loved."

'That means, "I have fulfilled the law, practised the Gospel, offered myself up to death; and behold, neither death nor life can separate me from Jesus Christ."'

And so the great Emperor, in whom Ambrose had hoped to see his ideal of the relations of Church and State realised, passed away from earth. Two years longer Ambrose lived, giving his counsel to the young emperor, as he had to Gratian and Valentinus before. But the splendid hope of his life for his age had set; and thenceforth his public life reads like a supplement, feeble and prosaic, to a great drama. There were still words and works of mercy and judgment; the proud rebuked, the luxurious warned, the poor consoled, the weak protected, as always by that faithful shepherd; the lambs carried in his bosom, the feeble gently led. Or, if we change the image, the old battle is still carried on by the great soldier of Jesus Christ; the veterans are honoured, the wavering won back, the uncertain kept together, the noblest inspired to ever nobler achievements, and the heavenly life shines more and more; but as an earthly story the climax is past.

In the midst of the battle of his life occurs the beautiful pastoral episode of his intercourse with Augustine.

The great African had reached the farthest point of his descent into the cold and darkness when he arrived at Milan about 384, where Ambrose had been bishop seven years.

He was a declared Manichean; he had abandoned his mother at the little seaside oratory, with that cruel deception which nothing but the fact that we should not have known of it save for his own confession could in any degree excuse. The chains of his old sins held him fast. He deemed the faith of the Church, of his mother, of his childhood, a dream.

As professor of rhetoric he came to Milan; the pagan friend of both Augustine and Ambrose, Symmachus, gave him an introduction to the Archbishop, and in doing so gave into his hand the thread which was gently to draw him back into the fold.

Ambrose's reception, gracious and courteous to the young foreign rhetorician, won Augustine's confidence. Himself an orator he recognised and welcomed the eloquent young African. Himself a true shepherd, he recognised in the wanderer not an enemy, but a lost sheep, whom the Good Shepherd would not rest till He found.

Monica came over from Africa, her heart full of fears, but never desponding like his own. Ambrose soon understood the mother's heart.

Augustine often went to the Basilica to hear the eloquence of Ambrose, 'not for what he would say but to know how he would say it.'

The sermons Ambrose was then preaching were mystical interpretations of the life of Abraham, 'of Isaac and the soul,' of Jacob and the life of benediction.

'All that the religious man can represent to himself highest, most beautiful, most powerful, all that is sovereign and infinite,' said Ambrose, 'that is God ! filling all things, yet never confounded with them ; penetrating all, but unfathomable ; incomprehensible, yet accessible to the adoration of the faithful.'

Very soon Augustine became convinced that the reproaches of the Manicheans against Christian doctrine were misrepresentations, and he felt a generous remorse for having joined in their slanders.

He went first to give his mother this first gleam of joy.

He had ceased to be a Manichean, he told her, although he was not a Catholic Christian.

'Monica redoubled her prayers and tears,' he writes, 'O God, to conjure Thee to succour me without delay. Her visits to the church became more frequent. She hung on the lips of Ambrose.'

And Ambrose observed her. When Augustine sought him, wishing to enter into discussion, the Archbishop avoided controversy and would send him with a simple wise message back to his mother, or would speak to him of the blessing of having had such a mother.

The wisdom and tact of Ambrose come out in a passage of the 'Confessions.'

'I regretted,' writes Augustine, 'not to be able to consult him. The troubles of my heart needed his leisure. But I never found Ambrose at leisure.' It is evident the bishop avoided discussion, and by degrees his goodness penetrated Augustine's heart. 'I found Ambrose happy and surrounded by honour. I envied him all but his celibacy. And yet I knew not his true happiness. The high hopes which guarded him against the seductions of his own greatness, the Voice which spoke to his heart, the delight he tasted in the Bread of life.'

Slowly the light came to Augustine. The Manichean contempt for the flesh was answered in Ambrose's sermons. 'Sin,' he said, 'was in the soul which had served the flesh. Subject to earthly desires this flesh was like a tortoise creeping on the ground. In the regenerate soul the tortoise-shell became the framework of the musical strings.' The words of Ambrose in the pulpit and in private penetrated to the core of Augustine's doubts, to the moral corruption at the root of his intellectual difficulties.

His association with the woman who had been faithful to him for ten years, the mother of his boy, yet not his wife, weighed on his conscience.

'She, more generous than he, only quitted Augustine to give herself to God.'[1]

His chains to sin and through sin to falsehood began to be broken.

The example of the life of Ambrose won him back to Christ.

He listened to his eloquent words and observed his life, which proved more than words the peace of goodness; his daily life among the children, the poor, the wretched. 'Thou art sick,' Ambrose said in his sermons: 'seek the Physician. He will not tear open thy wound. He will heal it with a word.'

Augustine's conscience was touched, his heart was won,

[1] Abbé Baunard, *Life of St. Ambrose.*

and at last his whole being turned, as he has told, to God, and immediately after he went to Monica to pour all the repentance and joy into her heart, proving the truth of his conversion to God by his reverence to true human affection.

His baptism was deferred a few months. The close of that year he spent in quiet near Milan, near the country house of Marcellas, studying the Scriptures, to which Ambrose and his sister were so devoted, especially, by Ambrose's advice, the Book of Isaiah, as a preparation for the Gospel.

During the following Lent, he was constantly in the basilicas, joining in those inspired Ambrosian hymns and listening to the discourses of the Archbishop, whose subjects that year were 'De Fuga Seculi' and 'De Bono Mortis.' 'Let us leave the shadow,' he said, 'we who seek the sun. Let us despise the smoke, we who are sons of light. The smoke is sin; the shadow is this life itself.'

And in the sermon on the 'Advantage of Death' (centuries afterwards the viaticum of the martyr Boniface) Ambrose spoke of bodily death as the liberation of the soul and the revelation of God, in words which recall Plato (for Ambrose had the advantage over Augustine of knowing Greek). Then he goes on to speak of 'spiritual death,' meaning by that expression the actual 'putting off of the perishable in us.' 'We shall enter into the paradise of Thy gentleness,' he says, 'where there are no more clouds, no more storms, winter or night, no more sin; for the brightness of God shines there always, the God who enlighteneth every man who cometh into the world. He has promised to prepare a place for us. O Lord, direct us, unite us to Thee, who art the Way, Truth, Life. Let us rise to Him who says, "Whoever cometh to Me shall not taste death."'

'I could only breathe in the basilicas,' writes Augustine. 'What torrents did those hymns of our Church cause to flow in my heart! The words strike my ear, the truth sinks into my heart; tears flow, and in these was delight.'

At last on Easter Eve (April 24 or 25, 387) came the

longed-for day of baptism. In the octagonal 'Basilica of the Baptistery' Ambrose baptised Augustine ; a meeting of two great souls by the rivers of life, which has embodied itself in the poetical legend that the Te Deum sprang into life in an outburst of responsive adoration between Ambrose and Augustine.

Soon afterwards Augustine left Milan with his mother, and he saw Ambrose no more ; but his sermons and sacred song and his faithful life lived on in the heart and life of his disciple. A very short time after her son's baptism Monica departed in peace ; and in his agony at her loss 'I found my grief not a little softened,' Augustine writes, 'as, alone in my bed, I remembered those true words of Thine Ambrose—

   Æterne rerum Conditor
   (Eternal Maker of the world).[1]

' Listen to the blessed Ambrose,' he says again, 'whom I call my father, because he instructed me in the faith and has begotten me in Jesus Christ. I have heard his discourse ; I have seen in part his labours, his constancy, his perils. The Roman world knows also and proclaims them, and joins me in paying him homage.'

It is most interesting to see how the wonderfully manifold activities of Ambrose's life were nourished through very deep roots. He touched his age at every point, with a variety of capabilities bewildering to think of. Statesman, he made journeys to negotiate peace between empires ; Churchman, he resisted imperial wrongs ; pastor, he patiently guarded souls. In writing, for instance, to a widow contemplating a second marriage, he gave advice as remarkable for point and wit as for wisdom. While writing treatises in praise of celibacy his heart is nevertheless open to sympathise with all the perplexities and troubles of family life. Judge of the Episcopal Court, he set the noblest example of patient investigation and disinterested decisions, setting aside legacies to the Church in favour of the rights of the family.[1] His letters are a history of the public life of

[1] Abbé Baunard.

the period, and also give glimpses into the secret life of countless unknown toilers and sufferers.

Against the oppression and selfish luxury of the rich he spoke with a passionate indignation. 'Ahab is not altogether dead,' he said. 'Every day some Naboth is immolated. Did the angels divide the heavens among them?' he asks. 'The birds freely share the air; the fish swim freely in the sea. Only man takes his delight in excluding others from his delights.'

Yet in the midst of all these labours he found time to be the creator of a new Church music, the first singer of a new era of sacred song, and a commentator on the Scriptures. Doubtless, in these risings of the heart in hymns to God, in these daily bathings of his spirit in the Sacred Word, he found the wings of his soul grow strong and fresh for the flights of every day.

'If we cannot soar like an angel,' he said, 'let us at least fly like a swallow.' Because he did soar as an angel to God he could also take the humble little swallow flights to feed his nestlings.

His hymns were no mere dainties of spiritual literature. They were the household bread of the people of his city and his time. At their work, in their homes, as in the siege of the Basilica, his sacred words and music rang in their hearts. Their character is either objective or occasional. They are inspired by the great objects of the faith.

> Æterne rerum Conditor,
> Veni, Redemptor gentium.

They are designed for the various hours of the day, days of the month, or seasons of the Christian year, recalling the events in sacred history which characterise each day or season.

Sunrise and sunset naturally form the prevailing images of the morning and evening hymns. Christ, the Sun of Righteousness that never sets, the Light that never fades, in Himself at once our Day and Light, is the great theme. The hymns called Ambrosian are all in a short iambic measure, in itself a monotonous one, and are unrhymed.

The language of the early Latin hymns comes into the Church fresh from the market, the battlefield, or the court of justice. There is a calm and steady glow in them—a straightforward plainness of speech. They have a Roman majesty of their own. The imperial dignity of the great language of law and war has passed into them.

When undisguised paganism still lingered in Christendom, and books were scarce and reading rare, there was a beautiful natural meaning in linking the passing hours with heaven, thus making Time himself read aloud the Gospel history and illuminate the seasons of the year into a kind of pictorial Bible for the poor. For they were sacred popular songs, varying from the common speech of the people then, probably, not more than the literary Italian of to-day from the various spoken dialects of Milan, Genoa, or Venice. As St. Ambrose and St. Augustine tell us, they were murmured by the people at their work and in their homes as well as sung in grand choruses by the great congregation in the basilicas.

Ambrose evidently studied and delighted in nature.

His book on the Hexaemeron, or The Six Days of Creation, has beautiful thoughts about the sea, and flowers, and all creatures. 'God saw that it—the sea—was good, good, indeed, and beautiful, with its white waves of foam, its fringes of snow, its surface tinged with the sunset. How melodious its many voices! What proud moanings! What gentle murmurings!' 'The creation is good—lilies, roses, walnuts, chestnuts, all the trees of His planting that He loved.' And thus he closes:

'Then God *rested*. Thanks to Him, He had found a work in which He could rest. He made the heavens; but I read not that He rested. He made the earth; but I read not that He rested. He made the sun, the moon, the stars; I read not that He rested. But I read that He made man, and that then He rested; for He had one to *forgive*.'

And so Ambrose drew near to his rest. He was not yet fifty-seven; but the body, worn with many severe illnesses, with labour, with battles, with disappointments, was at last worn out.

In 397, two years after the death of Theodosius, he had to cease his writing, but he continued his reading and meditation. And as he meditated, his secretary, Paulinus, thought he saw his face irradiated as with the tongues of fire of old.

He was dictating a Commentary on the 44th Psalm.

'It is painful to wait so long for the day when mortality shall be swallowed up of life,' he said, 'but, happily, the torch of the Word of God does not quit our eyes.'

'Up, Lord, why sleepest Thou? for our soul is brought low, even into the dust. Arise, help us, deliver us for Thy mercy's sake.'

And then his strength failed; he taught and spoke no more. The God he called did indeed 'arise,' and delivered him for ever.

It was the end of March. From that time the old friend of his youth, Simplicianus, never left him.

One day, when they were together in the Bishop's room, both were in prayer, and Ambrose saw Jesus Christ approaching him with a divine smile, inviting him to rejoin Him in heaven and to unfasten the last links which bound him to earth.

The Imperial Court, knowing his value, was in terror at the thought of his death, and sent a deputation of his friends to him, with the anxious entreaty, 'Go and ask him to pray God to prolong his days.' They came, and with tears weeping around his bed, entreated him not to leave them.

He thanked them fervently, and replied in the well-known words, 'I have not lived among you so that I am ashamed to live longer; but I fear not to die, for we have a good Master (Non ita inter vos vixi ut pudeat me vivere, nec timeo mori, quia Dominum bonum habemus).'

Marcella sought by her prayers and tender care to retain her brother; but his soul was departing. Marcella, the eldest, was the survivor of the three.

Earth was disappearing from his gaze, in all except the shepherd's undying care for his flock. Some of his deacons were gathered together at the farthest end of his room, asking who should succeed Ambrose. One named Simplicianus; another said he was too old. The dull ear of the dying bishop caught the words which might concern the people he so loved. 'He is old, but he is good (Senex sed bonus),' Ambrose said, three times.

The deacons, frightened at having been overheard, disappeared instantly; but the dying words told. Simplicianus succeeded Ambrose.

On Good Friday, April 3, about 1 P.M. in the morning, his secretary, Paulinus, writes, 'He extended his arms in the form of a cross to pray. This suppliant attitude he never quitted until his last sigh. We followed his prayer by the movement of his lips, but we could not hear the words he said. Honoratus had retired in the evening to the upper story, when towards midnight he heard himself called three times. A voice said to him, "Make haste and arise, for he is going." Honoratus arose and came down, bringing the Body of the Lord Jesus. And when Ambrose had received it into his heart he yielded up his soul.'

On Easter Day they bore his body into the great Ambrosian basilica. Crowds pressed around, men and women of all ranks and all ages; Jews and pagans mixed among the Christians, all united in a common feeling of grief and gratitude.

But for him had begun another Easter festival on high.

When 'any one is the first in anything he gives the impulse, and in that first stroke gives the direction also. Ambrose was certainly one of the first men; a whole world proceeds from him.'[1]

---

[1] Abbé Baunard, *St. Ambroise.* There is a touching story that the Marcomanni, a German tribe on the Elbe, having heard of Christianity from an Italian missionary, and of a great Christian named Ambrose, their queen, Fritigil, sent to seek instruction from him, and the Bishop found time to write a catechism for her and her people. This she learned, and longing to speak to her teacher set off on a journey to Milan, but arrived too late, just as the eloquent voice she had come so far to hear was silent for ever.

Dedications of churches: one, Ombersley, in Worcestershire. Represented in art with beehive, or with a scourge repelling the Emperor.

St. Augustine

OF HIPPO.

August 28.

(In all the Calendars. Born A.D. 354; died A.D. 430. Sarum Ep. and Gosp. : Ecclus. xlvii. 8-11 ; St. Matt. v. 18-19.)

No contrast can be more marked than that between St. Ambrose and St. Augustine. Between them they seem to embrace the whole range of Christian life.

The political history of his times is inextricably bound up with Ambrose, as a statesman, judge, prophet, friend and counsellor of emperors, reformer of laws, tribune of the people, great shepherd of the flocks of Christ.

His life flows through his age as a great river through a great city, reflecting and refreshing.

St. Augustine, on the other hand, as a poet, while mirroring like a lake the world in which he lives, is swayed hither and thither by its breezes and its storms.

In reading the history of Ambrose we read the history of East and West, Church and State. In reading the story of Augustine we learn chiefly the story of a mother finding her son, of a lost soul finding its God ; a story deeper indeed than the secular history amidst which it moves ; not of the age but of eternity, because it is of the depths of human affection and Divine communion. The character of Ambrose moved and controlled his own age ; the heart of Augustine beats through the hearts of all ages.

The treatises of Ambrose are on the shelves of students. The 'Confessions' of Augustine are among the springs of devotional life to all of us to this day. And whilst his theories about the methods of Divine rule and the origin of human sin are in a great measure out of the sphere of any section of Christendom of our times, his story of his mother touches our hearts, and the flames of aspiration in which his spirit goes up to God enkindle our souls now.

The intense individual devotion of his Confessions breathes, and glows for us and in us still. The City of God, of which he speaks with such a fervour of patriotic love and hope, is our city still, the mother of us all. It is because the story is so individual that it is so universal.

His exclusions, his limitations vanish with the narrow horizon to which they belong. The revelations and expansions live on as the heavens from which they came.

His story leads us once more back to the luxuriant fertility of the granary of Rome—North Africa—to the narrow strip of coast bounded by the sea on one side and on the other by desert and wild mountains, where Rome and Carthage fought for the empire of the world, where Perpetua, with a heart bleeding for her old father and her little child, died for Christ, to the little oratory by the seaside which kept up the memory of the martyred Cyprian shepherd and bishop of souls.

The little town of Tagaste was Augustine's birthplace. All we really know of him is from himself, what he tells us of his history in his Confessions and what he reveals of himself in his prayers. His autobiography is written not to us but to God.

'Great art Thou,' he begins; 'great is Thy power, Thy wisdom infinite, and Thee would man praise, though but a particle of Thy creation. Thou awakest us to delight in Thy praise, for Thou madest us for Thyself, and our heart is restless till it rests in Thee. Narrow is the measure of my soul; enlarge Thou it, that thou mayest enter in. It is ruinous; repair Thou it.'

Then he traces back his life to its beginning, how the food was stored for him in a mother's breast, 'for then I knew but to sleep; to repose in what pleased, to cry at what offended my flesh; nothing more. Afterwards I began to smile, first in sleep, then in waking; for I see the like in other infants, though of myself I remember it not. Thus little by little I became conscious where I was, and came to have the wish to express my wishes to those who could content them; for the wishes were within me and they without; nor could they by any perception of them enter within my spirit. So I flung about at random limbs and cries, making the few signs I could, and such as I could, like, though in truth very little like, what I wished. And when I was not presently obeyed (my wishes being hurtful or unintelligible), then was I indignant with my elders for not submitting themselves to me, and avenged myself on them by tears.

'And lo, my infancy died long since, and I live. Passing from infancy, I came to boyhood, or rather it came to me, displacing infancy; for I was no longer a speechless infant, but a speaking boy. By constantly hearing words I collected gradually for what they stood, and being broken in my mouth to these signs, I thereby gave utterance to my will, and so launched deeper into the stormy intercourse of human life.

'Next I was put to school to get learning, in which I, poor wretch, knew not what use there was, and yet if idle I was beaten. So I began as a boy to pray to Thee, praying Thee, though small, with no small earnestness that I might not be beaten at school.

'As a boy I had already heard of an eternal life—promised us through the humility of the Lord our God stooping to our pride, and even from the womb of my mother, who greatly hoped in Thee, I was sealed with the mark of His Cross, and salted, like Ambrose, with His salt.

'Thou sawest, Lord, how, while yet a boy, being seized with a sudden oppression of the stomach, and like near to death, with what eagerness and faith I sought the baptism of Thy Christ. Whereupon the mother of my flesh, since she even more lovingly travailed in birth for my salvation, would in eager haste have provided for my consecration and cleansing by the health-giving sacraments, confessing Thee, Lord Jesus, for the remission of sins, unless I had suddenly recovered. And so, as if I must needs be again polluted, should I live, my cleansing was deferred. I then already believed, and my mother and the whole household, except my father.

'I would fain know for what purpose my baptism was deferred. Why does it still echo in our ears on all sides, "Let him alone, let him do as he will, for he is not yet baptised"? But as to bodily health, no one says, "Let him be worse wounded, for he is not yet healed."

'How much better, then, had I been at once healed; and then, by my friends' diligence and my own, my soul's recovered health had been kept safe in Thy keeping who gavest it. Better truly. But how many great waves of temptation seemed to hang over me in my boyhood. These my mother foresaw, and preferred to expose to them the clay whence I might afterwards be moulded rather than the cast itself when made.

'In boyhood I loved not study and hated to be forced to it; yet I was forced. But why did I so much hate the Greek, which I studied as a boy? For the Latin I loved, not indeed, reading, writing, and arithmetic, but the story of Virgil, weeping for dead Dido because she killed herself for love, the while with dry eyes I endured my miserable self dying far from Thee, O God, my Life. Why, then, did I hate the Greek classics? For Homer, who cunningly wove the like fictions, and is most sweetly vain, yet was he little to my boyish taste. And so I suppose would Virgil be to Grecian children. The difficulty of a foreign tongue dashed all the sweetness of Grecian fable. Latin I learned without fear and suffering, amidst the caresses of my nursery and jests of friends, smiling and sportively encouraging me.'

Then he speaks of the 'hellish torrent' of the stories of the crimes and vices of the gods, 'into which the sons of men are cast, to learn eloquence and how to maintain opinions.' He wonders at the shame felt at some barbarism of grammar, men being more offended at the *h* being left out in 'homo' (a human being), than if that human being hated a human being in despite of God; he wonders at the patience of God with those who observe so strictly the covenanted rules of letters and syllables, and break His covenant of salvation. He sees sin in his boyhood, enslaved by idleness, seeking unfair victories and games while fiercely upbraiding those who did the like. Yet he also admires the gifts of boyhood, the hating to be deceived, the vigorous memory, the delights of friendship.

Next came youth and early manhood, with their fierce new temptations. His mother's prayers and patience had won his father at all events to the threshold of the Christian Church, notwithstanding all the faults and impetuosities which had made her husband a trial to Monica.

Augustine bears affectionate and grateful testimony to the sacrifices made for his education. 'For that year (his sixteenth) were my studies intermitted, whilst after my return from Medaura (a neighbour city whither I had journeyed to learn grammar and rhetoric) the expenses for a further journey to Carthage were being provided for me, and that rather through the resolution than the means of my father, who was but a poor freeman of Tagaste. To whom tell I this? Not to Thee, my God, but before Thee to my own kind, even to that small portion of mankind which may light on those writings of mine. Who did not extol my father for that beyond the ability of his means he would furnish his son with all necessaries for a long journey for his studies' sake?'

That year at home was a year of idleness and excess.

'I ran headlong into sin with such blindness that among my equals I was ashamed of a less shamelessness. But I made myself out worse than I was.' Also he 'had a habit of swearing,' as he told his people afterwards at Hippo when warning them against it.

Curiously, amidst all his sins he dwells at great length on one small theft committed by him and his companions on a neighbour's pear-tree near his father's vineyard. They stole quantities of pears and then threw them wantonly to the pigs.

'I loved my own fault,' he says; 'not that for which I was faulty, but the fault itself, not impelled by any hunger but through a cloyedness of well-doing. Foul soul, fallen from thy firmament, not seeking aught through the shame but the shame itself.'

From this he penetrates to the truth, how envy, covetousness, prodigality, and all vices are perversions of the original good, seeking in the false images and empty shadows of good what is only to be found in God, the only good.

For one thing he reproaches his friends, and his parents. His father, though a Christian catechumen, won at last by Monica's patience and prayers, scarcely blamed his vices, 'he had no care that I was chaste or grew towards Thee.' His mother indeed mourned and wept, 'but I heeded not Thy voice in her, thinking those but womanish advices.'

And even Monica feared a wife might be a clog and hindrance to his hopes—'not the hopes of the world to come, but of learning in this world, which both were too anxious I should attain. So from the muddy concupiscences and bubblings of youth mists fumed out and clouded and overcast my heart, that I could not discern the clear brightness of love from the fog of lustfulness.

'Oh!' he continues, 'that some one had then attempered my disorder, and, turning to account the fleeting beauties of these the extreme points of Thy creation, had put a bound to their pleasurableness, that so the tides of my youth might have cast themselves on the shore of marriage if they could not be calmed, and kept within the object of a family, as Thy law prescribes, O Lord!'

And so the last year of his life in his father's house passed recklessly by. When he was seventeen his father died, and Augustine left home, with an allowance from his mother, to pursue his studies and his profession at Carthage.

'To Carthage I came, where there sang all around me in my ears a cauldron of unholy loves. My God, my mercy! with how much gall didst Thou in Thy great goodness besprinkle for me that sweetness, fettering joy with sorrow-bringing bonds, that I might be scourged with the burning rods of jealousy, and suspicions, and fears, and anger, and quarrels. Stage plays also carried me away, full of images of my miseries and of fuel to my fire.'

In the midst of his company of 'Subverters,' who gloried in this 'devilish name,' mocking and enticing others, that earnest, fiery spirit still found an outlet in work. 'I was chief in the rhetoric school. I learned books of eloquence. In the ordinary course of study I fell upon a certain book of Cicero, whose speech almost all admire; not so his heart. This book of his contains an exhortation to philosophy, and is called 'Hortensius.' But this book altered my affections and turned my prayers to Thyself, O Lord, and made me have other purposes and desires. Every vain hope became at once worthless to me, and I longed with an incredibly burning desire for an immortality of wisdom, and began now to arise that I might return to Thee. For, not to sharpen my tongue (which thing I seemed to be purchasing with my mother's allowances, in that my nineteenth year, my father being dead two years before), not to sharpen my tongue did I employ that book, nor did it infuse into me its style, but its matter.

'How did I burn then, my God, how did I burn to remount from earthly things to Thee! Nor knew I what Thou wouldst do with me. For with Thee is wisdom.'

Thus through the aspirations of the earlier age before the morning of Christianity had dawned, not through that morning itself, did the light begin to shine on Augustine.

'And since at that time (Thou, O Light of my heart, knowest) Apostolic Scripture was not known to me, I was roused to love, and seek, and obtain, and hold, and embrace not this or that sect, but wisdom itself wherever it were; and this alone checked me, thus enkindled, that the name of Christ was not in it. For this name, according to Thy mercy, O Lord, this name of my Saviour, Thy Son, had my tender heart even with my mother's milk devoutly drunk in; and whatsoever was without that name, though never so learned, polished, or true, took not entire hold of me.

'I resolved, then, to bend my mind to the Holy

Scriptures, that I might see what they were. But, behold, I see a thing not understood by the proud, nor laid open to children, lowly in access, in its recesses lofty, and veiled with mysteries, and I was not such as could enter into it or stoop my neck to follow its steps. For not as I now speak did I feel when I turned to those Scriptures; but they seemed to be unworthy to be compared to the stateliness of Tully; for my swelling pride shrank from their lowliness, nor could my sharp wit pierce into the interior things. Yet were they such as would grow up with a little one. But I disdained to be a little one; and, swollen with pride, took myself to be a great one.

'Therefore I fell among men proudly doting, in whose mouths were the snares of the Devil, limed with the mixture of the syllables of Thy name and of our Lord Jesus Christ, and of the Holy Ghost, the Paraclete, our Comforter. I knew not God to be a Spirit.' (The 'abysmal deeps of Personality,' the simplicity of the 'I,' and 'Thou and I' were hidden from him). Not one whose being was bulk; for every bulk is less in a part than in the whole; and if it be infinite it must be less in such part as is defined by a circle of space than in its infinitude; and so is not wholly everywhere as Spirit, as God.

'And what that should be in us by which we are like to God, made in the image of God, I was altogether ignorant.

'They cried out, "Truth, truth," but it was not in them. O Truth! Truth! how inwardly did my soul pant after Thee, when they in many and huge books echoed of Thee to me, though it were but an echo!'

So he went from depth to depth in Pantheistic and Dualistic whirlpools. But all the time the true mother's love was ceaselessly watching over him, and for him, though unconscious, representing the love of God.

'And Thou didst send Thine hand from above and drewest my soul out of that profound darkness; my mother, Thy faithful one, weeping to Thee for me more than mothers weep the bodily deaths of their children. For she discerned the death wherein I lay; and Thou heardest her and despisedst not her tears when streaming down they watered the ground under her eyes in every place wherein she prayed; so that Thou heardest her. For whence was that dream wherewith Thou comfortedst her; so that she allowed me to live with her and eat at the same table in her house, which she had begun to shrink from, abhorring and detesting the blasphemies of my error? For she saw herself standing on a certain wooden rule or plank and a shining youth coming towards her, cheerful and smiling upon her, herself grieving and weakened with grief. But he having (in order to instruct, as is their wont, not to be instructed) enquired of her the causes of her grief and daily tears, and she answering that she was bewailing my perdition, he bade her rest contented, and told her to look and observe that *where she was there was I also.*

'And when she looked she saw me standing by her on the same plank.

'When she told me this vision I would fain bend it to mean that she rather should not despair of being one day where I was. She presently, without any hesitation, replies, " No; for it was not told me that 'where he is there thou art also,' but 'where thou art there he also is.'"

'I confess to Thee, Lord, that to the best of my remembrance this Thy answer, through my waking mother, that she was not perplexed by the plausibility of my interpretation, and so quickly saw what was to be seen, even then moved me more than the dream itself, by which a joy to that holy woman was so long before foresignified. For almost nine years passed in which I wallowed in the mire of that deep pit; all which time she, now more cheered by hope, yet no whit relaxing in her weeping, ceased not to bewail my case unto Thee.

'Thou gavest her meantime another answer by a priest of Thine, a bishop well studied in Thy Book, and who, when she entreated him to vouchsafe to converse with me and refute my errors, refused, wisely, as I afterwards perceived; for he answered that I was yet unteachable and puffed up with the novelties of that heresy.

'" Let him alone awhile," said he. "Only pray God for him; he will find out for himself by reading what that error is."

'Yet she would not be satisfied, and urged him with many tears, when he, a little displeased at her importunity, said, "Go thy way, and God bless thee. It is not possible that the child of these tears should perish." Which answer she took, as she has often mentioned in her conversations with me, as if it sounded from heaven.'

Then as to his own life meanwhile.

'In those years I taught rhetoric, and made sale of a loquacity by which to overcome others. Yet I preferred honest scholars. And Thou from afar perceivedst me stumbling in that slippery course, and amid smoke sending out some sparks of faithfulness. In those years—not in that which is called lawful marriage—when I had found one out in a wayward passion, yet but one, remaining faithful to her.' For ten years; she was the mother of his son, Adeodatus, the son whom they with such illogical pathos called God-given.

As another 'spark of faithfulness' when he was asked by a 'wizard' what he would give if he would secure him a prize by killing some living creatures to propitiate the devils, he, detesting such foul mysteries, answered, 'Though the garland were of imperishable gold, I would not suffer a fly to be killed to gain it for me.'

Next he plunged deep into astrology, in spite of the warnings of a wise old man, Vindicianus, who with his own proconsular hand put the agonistic garland on his head, and told him he had studied that art, but found it so false he would not get his living by deluding people. 'But thou,' he added, 'hast rhetoric to maintain thyself by.' In spite also of his 'dearest Nebridius,' a youth singularly good and of a holy fear, who derided divination altogether.

He was again at Tagaste now, in his mother's house in his native town, and had a friend who had grown up with him from a child ('they had been both school-fellows and play-fellows'), whom he had warped to those pernicious fables.' 'But Thou wert close on the steps of Thy fugitives.

Thou tookest that man out of this life when he had scarce filled up a whole year of my closest friendship—sweet to me above all sweetness of that my life. For long, sore sick of a fever, he lay senseless in a death sweat, and his recovery being despaired of, he was baptised unknowing. He was refreshed and restored. Then I essayed to jest with him at that baptism he had received when utterly absent in mind and feeling; but he so shrank from me as from an enemy, and with a wonderful and sudden freedom bade me, as I would continue his friend, forbear such language to him. I suppressed my emotions till he should grow well; but he was taken away from my frenzy that with Thee he might be preserved for my comfort. A few days after, in my absence, he was attacked again by fever and so departed.

'At this grief my heart was utterly darkened, and whatever I beheld was death. My native country was a torment, and my father's house a strange unhappiness; and whatever I had shared with him became a distracting torture. Mine eyes sought him everywhere, but he was not granted them; and I hated all places, for they had not him, nor could they now tell me "he is coming," as when he was absent and alive. For I wondered that others subject to death did live, since he whom I loved as if he should never die was dead; and I wondered yet more that myself, who was to him a second self, could live, he being dead. Well said one of his friends, "Thou half of my soul," and therefore my life was a horror to me, because I would not live halved, and bore about a shattered and bleeding soul. At once I loathed exceedingly to live, and feared to die; the more since when I thought of Thee Thou wert not to me any solid or substantial thing; for Thou wert not Thyself, but a mere phantom, and my error was my god. If I offered to discharge my load thereon, that it might rest, it glided through the void and came rushing down again on me, and I had remained to myself a hapless spot where I could neither be nor be from thence. For whither could my heart flee from my heart? Whither could I flee from myself? whither not follow myself? And yet I fled out of my country, for so should my eyes less look for him where they were not wont to see him; and thus from Tagaste I came to Carthage.

'Times lose no time, nor do they roll idly by; through all our senses they work strange operations on the mind. Behold, they went and came day by day, and by coming and going introduced into my mind other imaginations, and other remembrances, and little by little patched me up again with my old kind of delights into which those my sorrows gave way. I had poured out my soul upon the dust in loving one that must die, as if he would never die. Hence that mourning and darkness of sorrow, that steeping of the heart in tears, all sweetness turned to bitterness, and upon the loss of life of him dying, the death of the living. Blessed whoso loveth Thee, and his friend in Thee, and his enemy for Thee. For he alone loses none who are dear to him, to whom all are dear in Him who cannot be lost. Thee none loseth but who leaveth. In Him, then, love things beloved, and carry unto Him along with thee what souls thou canst, and say to them, "Him let us love; Him let us love." Stand with Him and ye shall stand fast. Rest on Him and ye shall rest. There is no rest where ye seek it. Seek what ye seek, but it is not there where ye seek. Ye seek a blessed life in the land of death; it is not there.

'But our true Life came down hither and bore our death and slew him out of the abundance of His own life. He lingered not, but ran calling aloud by words, deeds, death, life, descent, ascension, crying aloud to us to return to Him. And He departed from our eyes that we might retire into our heart and there find Him. For He departed, and lo, He is here! He would not be long with us; yet left us not, for He departed thither whence He never parted, because the world was made by Him; and in this world He was, and into this world He came to save sinners. O ye sons of men, how long are ye so slow of heart? Even now, after the descent of Life to you, will ye not ascend to Him?'

A long digression from the autobiography, and yet no digression, since the autobiography is a great poem of Divine love, a continual returning and upspringing of the heart to God; and as well might we understand Dante's 'Vita Nuova' without Beatrice, as these Confessions without this continual 'departure of the heart' to God. 'By one who loveth is another kindled.'

'And man himself is a great deep, whose very hairs Thou numberest; and yet are the hairs of his head easier to be numbered than are his feelings and the beatings of his heart. I erred through pride, and was tossed about with every wind, but yet was steered by Thee, though very secretly.'

Very secretly, leading him on to the light he sought, by the hand of one still in the darkness. Faustus, a 'bishop among the Manichæans, was then at Carthage, exquisitely skilled in the liberal sciences and in all valuable learning,' from whom Augustine 'expected wonders, many having been entangled by his smooth language.' But the truths Augustine 'had before learned from the astrologers of the succession of times and the visible testimonies of the stars,' helped to disentangle for him the errors of the Manichæans. When Faustus 'was proved to have taught falsely of the moon and stars, and of the motions of the sun and moon, his sacrilegious presumption would become evident.'

He found Faustus 'a man of pleasing discourse.' '*But what availed the utmost daintiness of the cupbearer to my thirst for a more precious draught?*' He found him also 'utterly ignorant of the liberal sciences,' and despaired of solution from him. And yet in Faustus he sees much good. 'For this man had a heart, though not right towards Thee. For he was not altogether ignorant of his own ignorance. And fairer is the modesty of a candid mind than the knowledge of those things which I desired.' He had also a good wit and a natural gracefulness.

Augustine studied literature with him, which he himself at that time was teaching the young students at Carthage. 'But all my efforts, whereby I had proposed to advance in that sect through that man, came utterly to an end—not that I delivered myself from them altogether.

'Thus that Faustus, to so many a snare of death, had now, neither willing nor witting it, begun to loosen that snare wherein I was taken. For Thy hands, O my God, did not forsake my soul; and out of my mother's heart's blood, through her tears day and night poured out, was a sacrifice offered for me unto Thee.'

No rest was in his heart yet. He was persuaded to go to Rome, hearing that young men studied more steadily there, under regular discipline, than in 'the unruly licence of Carthage.'

'But why I went hence and went thither, Thou knewest, O my God, yet didst show it neither to me nor to my mother, who grievously bewailed my going, following me to the sea.'

And then follows the desertion and deceit, which, but that we should not have known it except through his Confessions more than anything would alienate our hearts from him.

'But I deceived her, holding me by force, that either she might keep me back or go with me, and I feigned that I had a friend whom I could not leave. And I lied to my mother, and such a mother, and escaped; for this also hast Thou mercifully forgiven me; preserving me, thus full of execrable defilements, from the waters of the sea for the water of Thy grace, whereby when I was cleansed the streams of my mother's eyes should be dried, with which for me she daily watered the ground under her face. And yet refusing to return without me, I scarcely persuaded her to stay that night in a place hard by our ship, where was an oratory in memory of the Blessed Cyprian. That night I privily departed, but she was left behind in weeping and prayer. And what, O Lord, was she with so many tears asking of Thee but that Thou wouldst not suffer me to sail? But Thou, in the depth of Thy counsels, and hearing the main point of her desire, regardedst not what she then asked, that Thou mightest make me what she ever asked. The wind blew and swelled our sails, and withdrew the shore from our sight ; and she on the morrow was there, frantic with sorrow, and with complaints and groans filled Thine ears, who didst then disregard them; whilst through my desires Thou wert hurrying me to end all desire, and the earthly part of her affection to me was chastened by the allotted scourge of sorrows. For she loved my being with her, as mothers do, but much more than many ; and she knew not how great joy Thou wert about to work for her out of my absence. She knew not, therefore did she weep and wail, and by this agony there appeared in her the inheritance of Eve, with sorrow seeking what in sorrow she had brought forth. And yet, after accusing my treachery and hardheartedness, she betook herself again to intercede to Thee for me, went to her wonted place, and I to Rome.'

At Rome he was seized by grievous sickness. 'And now the fever heightening, I was parting and departing for ever into fire and torments, such as my deeds deserved, with which wound had my mother's heart been pierced, it would never be healed. This she knew not, yet in absence prayed for me ; but thou, everywhere present, heardest. For I cannot express the affection she bore me, nor with how much more vehement anguish was in labour for me now than at my birth.

'Thou restoredst me then of that sickness and healedst the son of Thy handmaid.'

Yet even still, at Rome, he joined himself to the Manichæans, being more in friendship with them than with any, especially since he despaired of finding the truth. Evil and good he conceived of as 'two masses, contrary the one to the other, both unbounded, but the evil narrower, the good more expansive ; of our Saviour himself as ' reached forth out of the mass of lucid substance of God,' not really born, nor incarnate, nor crucified, His body a phantom.

Yet the nobler philosophy attracted him 'of those whom they called Academicians.' Plato, though in translation and imperfectly understood, moved his soul. And, moreover, even at Carthage the words of one Holpidius, as he had disputed from the Scriptures against the Manichæans 'had begun to stir him.

His hopes of a satisfactory career as a teacher of rhetoric at Rome were not quite fulfilled. There was not the wild licence of Carthage among his students, but they would band together to avoid paying the master's stipend, and wander away to another.

'When, therefore, they of Milan had sent to Rome to the prefect of the city (Ambrose's old friend, Symmachus) to furnish them with a rhetoric teacher for their city, to send him at the public expense, I made application that Symmachus would try me by setting me some subject, and so send me.'

And Symmachus, himself a pagan, did send Augustine with instructions, which linked his life for ever with Ambrose.

'To Milan I came, to Ambrose the bishop, known to all the world as one of the best of men. To him was I unknowing led, that by him I might knowingly be led to Thee.

'That man of God received me as a father, and showed me episcopal kindness on my coming. Thenceforth I began to love him. At first, indeed, not as a teacher of the truth (which I utterly despaired of in Thy Church), but as a person kind towards myself. And I listened diligently to him preaching to the people, not with that intent I ought, but as it were testing his eloquence, whether it flowed fuller or lower than was reported; but as to the matter I was a careless and scornful looker-on. And I was delighted with the sweetness of his discourse, more recondite, though with a manner less winning and harmonious, than that of Faustus. Yet was I drawing nearer little by little and unconsciously. For though I took no pains to hear what he spake, but only how he spake (for this empty care alone was left me, despairing of a way open for men to Thee), yet together with the words which I would choose came also into my mind the things which I would refuse, for I could not separate them. And while I opened my heart to admit, "How eloquently he spake," there also entered, "How truly he spake," but this by degrees. Especially after I had heard one or two places of the Old Testament solved, and ofttimes in a figure, which, when I understood literally, I was slain spiritually. I now blamed my despair that no answer could be given to such as scoffed at the Law and the Prophets, yet the Catholic cause seemed to me in such sort, not vanquished, as still not yet to be victorious. Hereupon I earnestly bent my mind to see if I could in any way by any certain proof convict the Manichæans of falsehood.

'So then after the manner of the Academics (as they are supposed), doubting of everything and wavering between all, I settled so far, that the Manichæans were to be abandoned.' And yet 'to the philosophers, notwithstanding, for that they are without the saving name of Christ, I utterly refused to commit the care of my sick soul.

'I determined, therefore, so long to be a catechumen in the Catholic Church, and where I had been recommended by my parents, till something better should dawn upon me, whither I might steer my course.'

All this time Monica had been still in Africa, but her son was indeed nearing the threshold. He began to cherish a flickering hope that something certain might dawn on him. He was a catechumen with Ambrose.

'O Thou my hope from my youth, where wert Thou to me, and whither wert thou gone? Hadst not thou created me and separated me from the beasts of the field and fowls of the air? Thou hadst made me wiser, yet did I walk in darkness and in slippery places. My mother had come to me, resolute through piety, following me over sea and land, in all perils confiding in Thee. For in perils of the sea she comforted the very mariners, assuring them of a safe arrival, because Thou hadst by a vision assured her thereof. She found me in grievous peril through despair of ever finding truth, but when I discovered to her that I was no longer a Manichæan, though not yet a Catholic Christian, she was not overjoyed as at something unexpected, although she was now assured concerning that part of my misery for which she bewailed me as one dead, though to be reawakened by

Thee, carrying me forth upon the bier of her thoughts that (as at Nain) Thou mightest say to the widow's son, "Young man, I say unto thee, Arise," and he should arise and Thou shouldst deliver him to his mother.

'Her heart was shaken by no tumultuous exultation, when she heard that what she daily with tears asked of Thee was in so great part realised, assured that Thou who hadst promised the whole wouldst one day give the rest: most calmly, with a heart full of confidence she replied to me, "She believed in Christ, that before she departed this life she would see me a Catholic Christian." This much to me, but to the Fountain of Mercies poured she forth more copious prayers and tears that Thou wouldst hasten Thy help and enlighten my darkness, and she hastened the more eagerly to the church, and hung on the lips of Ambrose, praying for *the fountain of that water that springeth up to everlasting life*. But that man she loved *as an angel of God*, because she knew that I had been brought by him to that doubtful state of faith I now was in, through which she anticipated most confidently that I should pass from sickness to health, after the access, as it were, of a sharp fit, which physicians call "the crisis."'

Following the African custom, Monica took cakes and bread and wine to the churches built in memory of the saints, to give to those who were there. 'The door-keeper forbade her. As soon as she knew the bishop had forbidden this, she at once embraced his wishes. Not willingly would she have relinquished this little service if forbidden by another whom she loved not as Ambrose, most entirely, for my salvation, and he her again for her most religious life, so that when he saw me, he often burst forth into her praises, congratulating me that I had such a mother, not knowing what a son she had in me!'

'Ambrose himself, as the world counts happy, I esteemed a happy man, whom personages so great held in such honour, only his celibacy seemed to me a painful course. But what hope he bore within him, what comfort in adversities, what sweet joys Thy Bread had for the hidden mouth of his spirit, I could not conjecture. Nor could he know the tides of my feelings, nor the abyss of my danger, for I could not ask of him, being shut out both from his ear and speech by multitudes of busy people whose weaknesses he served. With whom when he was not taken up, he was taking absolutely necessary sustenance, or reading to himself. For no man was forbidden to him, nor were any that came announced to him. I had no opportunity of inquiring what I wished of that so holy oracle of Thine his breast, unless the thing might be answered briefly. But those tides in me to be poured out to him required a full leisure.'

Meantime probably Ambrose with his insight and reticence knew quite well what he was doing. And every Sunday Augustine heard the bishop preach, and found the knots those deceivers knit against the Divine books could be unravelled. 'With joy I blushed at having so many years barked not against the Catholic faith, but against the Manichæan fictions. But as it happens that one who has had a bad physician fears to trust himself with a good one, so was it with the health of my soul, which could not be healed but by believing, and lest it should believe falsehoods, refused to be cured, resisting Thy hands who hast prepared the medicines of faith, and hast applied them to the diseases of the whole world.

'Then Thou, O Lord, little by little, with most tender and merciful hand, touching and composing my heart, didst persuade me. Considering what innumerable things I believed, which I saw not, of places, cities, of friends, of other men which, unless we should believe, we should do nothing at all in this life; lastly with how unshaken an assurance I believed of what parents I was born, considering all this, Thou didst persuade me, that not they who believed Thy books (which Thou hadst established in so great authority among almost all nations), but they who believed them not, were to be blamed. No contentiousness of self-contradicting philosophers could wring this belief from me '*that Thou art*,' whatsoever Thou art, and that "the government of human things belongs to Thee." This I believed sometimes more strongly, more weakly other whiles; yet ever that thou art and hast a care of us. For now what things sounding strangely in the Scriptures were wont to offend me, having heard divers of them explained satisfactorily, I referred to the depth of its mysteries, in that, while it lay open to all who read, it reserved the majesty of its mysteries within its profoundest meaning; stooping to all in the plainness of its words·and the lowliness of its style, yet calling forth the utmost application, that so it might receive all in its open bosom, and through narrow passages waft some few over to Thee.

'I panted after honours, gains, marriage. In these desires I underwent most bitter crosses. Thou being the more gracious the less Thou sufferedst aught to grow sweet to me which was not Thou.'

Once he saw a drunken beggar 'joking and joyous,' and learned thence how the lower the joy the more easily it may be laid hold of.

Two young men, his pupils formerly at Carthage, shared his struggle and his earnest search for true life. 'Thus were the mouths of three indigent persons sighing out their wants one to another and waiting on Thee that Thou mightest give them meat in due season.' Alypius, a young advocate, of a passionate nature like Augustine's, who, once tempted reluctantly into the ampitheatre to the gladiatorial games, had been swept away with a frenzy of excitement by the sight of the bloody combats; and Nebridius, who had left a large family estate to come to Milan to seek for truth and wisdom. 'Where shall truth be sought?' they said to each other. 'Ambrose has no leisure; we have no leisure to read; where shall we even find the books?' More joined them, till a little company was gathered of seekers after truth. They thought of banding themselves into a community. But one was already married, and this project fell through.

His mind was tossed about still amongst the old metaphysical puzzles, pantheistic, dualistic, and another practically pervading them all, *Whence is evil?* which stood out more and more vividly.

'I strained to perceive what I now heard, that free-will was the cause of our doing ill, and Thy just judgment the cause of our suffering ill. I knew as well that I had a will as that I lived. I saw that I was not unjustly punished. But again I said, "Who made me? Did not my God, who is not only good, but goodness itself? Is not evil indeed *nothing*, all things being *good* as far as they *are*?"'

Now certain books of the Platonists came into his hands, translated from Greek into Latin (his boyish dislike of Greek never having been quite conquered), which books brought to him, as in a reflection, the light of the theology of St. John, that 'the Word was with God' and 'is light.' 'And Thou didst beat back the weakness of my sight, streaming forth Thy beams on me most strongly, and I trembled with love and awe, as if I heard this voice from on high, "I am the food of grown men; grow, and thou shalt feed on Me; nor shalt thou convert Me, like the food of thy flesh into thee, but thou shalt be converted into Me.'

Such were Augustine's mental struggles. But underneath and through these still rushed the restless torrent of his passions, his yieldings, his repentances. 'I was borne up to Thee by Thy beauty, and soon borne down from Thee by mine own weight.'

The mother of his son was still with him—'faithful to each other,' he writes, 'if but the honourable name of marriage were added,' an omission surely not her fault. But of this no one seems to have thought as a possible solution. We only know of that poor mother for whom the best and tenderest around her seem to have had so little pity or consideration; that she was faithful to him through dishonour and desertion; that they called their only child, with a pathetic inconsistency, 'God-given,' and that he says of the boy, '*We* brought him up in Thy discipline.'

His friend Alypius sought to prevent him from marrying, but Monica, deeming a house and family life best for him, persuaded him to let her arrange a marriage for him with a young girl, to be waited for two years; though she told Augustine, afterwards, she never felt as if God were leading her in this, in spite of the strong cries of her heart to Him about it. Meantime the mother of his son was torn from him, as a hindrance to the marriage. 'I allowed myself to be torn from her who shared my life,' he says; and 'as my soul was one with hers, my heart shed tears of blood.'

And she returned alone to Africa, vowing to be faithful to him till death. But he less generous and patient than she, waiting thus bereaved for his child-bride, fell lower yet. 'Dead now was my evil and abominable youth,' he writes. He was thirty years old, yet his life sank into a deeper gulf than ever.

At length, broken in heart and spirit, he crept to a gate he had not yet tried. He took up the Scriptures themselves; chiefly, at first, St. Paul.

From the infinite spaces and the all-filling Divinity, and the majestic Word, he came down and so up to Him who is meek and lowly in heart.

'Whatever truth I had read in those other books, I found here amid the praise of Thy grace, that whoso sees may not only be admonished to behold Thee, but healed to hold Thee. *The handwriting contrary to us blotted out*, this these other writings contain not. Those pages present not the image of this piety, the tears of confession; Thy sacrifice a troubled spirit and contrite heart; the salvation of the people, the Bridal City; the earnest of the Holy Ghost; the cup of our redemption. No man says there, *Shall not my soul be submitted unto God? For He is my God and my salvation.* No one there hears Him call *Come unto Me all ye that labour.* They scorn to learn of Him, because He is meek and lowly in heart.

'For it is one thing from the mountain's shaggy top to see the land of peace, and to find no way thither, and in vain to essay through ways impassable, opposed and beset by fugitives and deserters under their captain, the lion and the dragon, and another to keep in the way that leads thither, guarded by the host of the Heavenly Commander.'

Still, for his temporal life all was yet wavering. 'The Way, the Saviour Himself, well pleased me, yet I shrank from going through its straitness. The agony of the conflict deepened, for 'everywhere the deeper joy is ushered in by the deeper pain.'

It was then that Simplicianus (the friend of Ambrose, and his successor, '*senex sed bonus*'), told him of the conversion he helped to accomplish, in his youth, of Victorinus, the rhetorician, and his generous confession and renunciation of all for Christ.

The conflict with himself still lingered on. 'I had nothing to answer Thee calling to me, "*Awake, thou that sleepest,*" but only those dull and drowsy words, "Anon, anon, presently, leave me but a little." But "presently, presently," had no present, and my "little while" went on for a long while.'

Yet the moment of victory was approaching. One day a young Carthaginian countryman of his, Pontitianus, once high in office in the emperor's court, came, and fell into discourse about the writings of St. Paul, and then he told Augustine how he and three other young fellow-soldiers of his in the imperial service, one afternoon at Treves, went out to walk near the city walls, and found in a humble cottage there a life of Anthony the hermit, and were moved by the story of his devotion and renunciation of all.

By Anthony's example the mind of Pontitianus was 'stripped of the world; bitter he felt and full of perils was all the glory they had been seeking,' and together the three friends resolved to forsake all, and partake of the glorious reward of Anthony.

'The discourse also turned on the flocks of the monasteries and their holy ways, and the fruitful deserts of the wilderness, whereof we knew nothing; and to a monastery at Milan, quite near, outside the city, full of good brothers, fostered by Ambrose, whereof we knew nothing. We listened in intent silence. Such was the story of Pontitianus.

'And Thou, O Lord, whilst he was speaking didst turn me round towards myself, taking me from behind my back where I had placed me, that I might see how foul I was. And I beheld and stood aghast. And if I sought to turn mine eye off myself, Thou didst thrust me before my own eyes.' He remembered how at nineteen he had been stirred to an earnest love of wisdom by Cicero's Hortensius, how he from early youth had prayed for chastity, 'only not yet!'

Pontitianus went his way, but the arrow was deep in Augustine's heart.

'What ails us?' he said to Alypius. 'The unlearned take heaven by force, and we with our learning, without heart, we wallow still.'

'Alypius gazed in astonishment and kept silence. This was not my wonted tone; my forehead, cheeks, eyes, colour, tone of voice, spoke my mind more than the words that I uttered.' He went into the little garden, as far as might be from the house. 'Alypius followed, not able to leave me in my anguish. Only I was healthily distracted, dying to live. Thus soul-sick was I and tormented, rolling and turning in my chain, till that were wholly broken. And Thou, O Lord, pressedst on me by a severe mercy, redoubling the lashes of fear and shame lest I should again give way.

'Be it done, now,' he said within himself, 'now.' The old temptations rushed back on his imagination, a controversy of self with self, Alypius waiting near in silence.

'But when a deep consideration had, from the secret bottom of my soul, hunted up all my misery, there arose a mighty storm, bringing a great shower of tears. I rose from Alypius. Solitude seemed fitted for the blessedness of weeping. I cast myself down under a fig-tree. I sent up these sorrowful words, 'How long? how long? to-morrow, to morrow? Why not now?'

'So was I speaking and weeping in the most bitter contrition of my heart, when lo, I heard from a neighbouring house a voice as of one, boy or girl I knew not, chanting and oft repeating, "*Tolle, lege,* Take up and read." Instantly my countenance altered; I began to think intently whether children were wont in any kind of play to sing such words, nor could I remember ever to have heard the like.

'So checking the torrent of my tears, I arose, interpreting it to be no other than a command from God to open the book and read the first chapter I should find. For I had heard of Anthony, that, coming in during the reading of the Gospel, he received the exhortation as if what was being read was spoken to him, " *Go sell all thou hast,*" and by such oracle he was forthwith converted unto Thee. Eagerly then I returned to the place where Alypius was sitting, for there I had laid the volume of the Apostle, when I rose thence ; and I seized it, opened, and in silence read that sentence on which my eyes first fell :

" ' *Not in rioting and drunkenness, not in chambering and wantonness, not in strife and envying; but put ye on the Lord Jesus Christ and make not provision for the flesh.*"

' No further would I read, nor needed I, for instantly at the end of this sentence, by a light as it were of serenity infused into my heart, all the darkness of doubt vanished away.

' Then putting my finger between, or some other mark, I shut the volume, and with a calmed countenance made it known to Alypius. He asked to see what I had read, and I showed him ; he read on further, and I knew not what followed. This followed : "*Him that is weak in faith receive,*" and by a good resolution and purpose, wherein he did always differ from me for the better, without any turbulent delay, he joined me.

' Thence we go unto my mother ; we tell her. She rejoiceth ; we relate in order how it took place. She leaps for joy, and triumpheth, and blesseth Thee, *who art able to do above what we ask or think* ; for she perceived that Thou hadst given her more for me than she was wont to beg by her pitiful and most sorrowful prayers. For Thou didst convert me unto Thyself so that I sought neither wife, nor any hope of this world, standing on that rule of faith, that plank where Thou hadst shown me unto her in a vision so many years before. And Thou didst convert her mourning into joy, much more plentiful than she had desired, and in a much more precious and purer way than she had erst required by having grand-children of my body.

' O Lord, I am Thy servant, Thy servant and the Son of

Thy handmaid,' he begins the morning hymn of his renewed life. 'Thou hast broken my bonds in sunder. And this Thy whole gift was to nill what I willed, and to will what Thou willedst.' His free-will not crushed; now first it was awakened. 'But where through all those years, and out of what low and deep recess was my free will called forth in a moment, whereby to submit my neck to Thy easy yoke, and my shoulders to Thy light burden. How sweet did it at once become to me to want the sweetness of those days! For Thou didst cast them forth for me, Thou true and highest goodness.

'Now was my soul free from the biting cares of canvassing and getting and weltering in filth. And my infant tongue spake freely to Thee, my brightness, my riches and my health, my Lord and my God.

'And I resolved in thy sight, not tumultuously to tear, but gently to withdraw the service of my tongue from the marts of lip-labour. Moreover, it had at first troubled me that in this very summer my lungs began to give way, amid too great literary labour, and to breathe deep with difficulty, and by the pain in my chest to show they were injured, and to refuse any full or lengthened speaking; this had troubled me, for it almost constrained me to lay down that burden of teaching. But when the full wish for leisure that I might see *how that Thou art the Lord* arose and was fixed in me, I began to rejoice that I had this secondary, and no feigned excuse, which might somewhat moderate the offence taken by those who for their sons' sake wished me never to have the freedom of Thy sons.'

He kept, however, manfully to his engagements till the vintage legal vacation, and then he accepted the offer of his friend Verecundus to stay at Cassiacum, his country house, 'a noble mansion standing amid the lower slopes of the mountains, some two days' journey from Milan, with lovely views all round of lake and wood, and flowery glades, the pure air cooled by breezes from the snowy heights in the distance, while the mantling vines hung from tree to tree, and the song of the birds came sweetly from the thickets near at hand to break the stillness which reigned in that peaceful and secluded spot.'[1]

'There from the fever of the world we reposed in Thee, with the freshness of Thy Paradise, my mother cleaving to us, in female garb, with masculine faith, with the tranquillity of age, motherly love, Christian piety, and the boy Adeodatus, not yet fifteen, and in wit surpassing] many grave and learned men, and Alypius, the brother of my heart, and a most valiant chastener of the body;' and other friends.

The little company stayed there in this hallowed quiet through the winter, from September 386 to Easter 387. 'With what ardour I read the Psalms of David, those faithful songs and sounds of devotion.' They sang the new hymns and new music of Ambrose. They conversed under the shade of a large tree after the manner of Plato and the Academicians, Dialogues on 'The Blessed Life.' Out of these grew among other things, the book in which his boy's words formed for him such a precious part. 'There is a book of *ours*,' he writes, 'entitled " The Master;" it is a dialogue between him and me.' It was a sweet breathing space, and time of rest, a kind of peaceful and holy childhood of the new life; not unmoved by troubles as of childhood, among others by a fearful toothache, so bad that 'he could not speak, and wrote on waxen tablets asking his friends to pray for him to the God of all manner of health.' 'Presently, so soon as with humble devotion we had bowed our knees, the pain went away.' 'When shall I recall all that passed in those holy days? In what accent spake I unto Thee, my God, when I read the Psalms of David, those faithful songs of devotion, which allow of no swelling spirit! As yet a novice in Thy real love, how was I by them kindled towards Thee, and on fire to rehearse them if possible through the whole world against the pride of mankind!' And saying this his heart went out in pity to his old comrades and misleaders. 'With what vehement and bitter sorrow was I angered at the Manichees! And again I pitied them, for

[1] *St. Augustine*, by the Rev. R. Wheler Bush.

that they knew not those sacraments, those medicines, and were mad against the antidote which might have recovered them of their madness. How I would they had been somewhere near me, and, without my knowing that they were there, could have beheld my countenance, and heard my words when I read the Fourth Psalm in that time of my rest! *When I called Thou heardest me, Thou God of my righteousness. Thou hast enlarged me in my distress.*'

So the quiet hours passed swiftly on, until, late on Easter Eve, he was baptised in the Basilica of the Baptistery at Milan, by Ambrose, with the triple immersion and the triple confession of the name of the Father, the Son, and the Holy Ghost, and then anointed with holy oil, for the wrestling and the reigning of the new life; also the feet washed according to the Milanese rite. With him were baptised Alypius, his friend, and his son Adeodatus, 'our contemporary in grace,' baptised by Ambrose; a day of fulfilment and a morning of promise, out of which might well indeed have burst forth, according to the legend, the great Te Deum to be the matin hymn of the Church throughout the ages.

The boy Adeodatus did not long survive. 'Soon didst Thou take his life from the earth; and I remember him without anxiety, fearing nothing for his childhood or youth, or his whole self.'

'Nor was I sated in those days with the wondrous sweetness of sounding the depth of thy counsels for the salvation of mankind.

'How did I weep in Thy hymns and canticles, touched to the quick by the voices of Thy sweet-attuned chant.'

He had come from the solitary wanderings, the lonely longings of the far country through the 'individual kiss' to the Father's house, to the Blessed company of all faithful people, to the City of God.

They kept together, this little brotherly company, but did not stay long at Milan.

Yet not long to be together in this life. The sorrow was near at hand which was to close that tender story of a mother's love destined to move the hearts of all generations.

'We sought where we might serve Thee most usefully, and were returning to Africa, whitherward being as far as Ostia, my mother departed this life.'

Then he goes back into a long review of her life, all she had been in herself and to him. He speaks of her early Christian training, of 'the decrepit maid servant,' well respected by the heads of that Christian family, who had carried Monica's father when a child, to whose faithful discipline she felt 'a deeper debt than even to her mother's diligence;' the humility which took to heart the rebuke of a young maiden of her father's household, the patient sweetness and ready acknowledgment of faults and mistakes which overcame slander and cleared away the misunderstandings of her mother-in-law, winning the constant respect of her impetuous husband, and at last winning his soul; the life of gentle peace-making which had won the love of all.

The long services of that generous and lowly heart were all but over. At Ostia, still, 'she so took care of that little company as though she had been the mother of us all, so served us as though she had been child to us all.'

The lifelong converse of mother and son was drawing to a close, and tenderly he recalls the last moments.

'The day now approaching whereon she was to depart this life (which day Thou well knewest, we knew not), it came to pass, Thyself, as I believe, by Thy secret ways so ordering it, that she and I stood alone, leaning in a certain window, which looked into the garden of the house where we now lay, at Ostia, where removed from the din of men, we were recruiting from the fatigues of a long journey, for the voyage. We were discoursing then together alone, very sweetly, and *forgetting those things are behind, and reaching forth unto those things which are before*, we were enquiring between ourselves in the presence of the Truth, which Thou art, of what sort the eternal life of the saints was to be, *which eye hath not seen, nor ear heard, nor hath it entered into the heart of man.* But yet we gasped with the mouth of our heart after those heavenly streams of Thy fountain, *the fountain of life,* which is *with Thee,* that being bedewed thence according to our capacity, we might in some sort meditate upon so high a mystery.

'And when our discourse was brought to that point, that the very highest delight of the earthly senses, in the very purest material light, was, in respect of the sweetness of that life, not only not worthy of comparison, but not even of mention, we raising up ourselves with a more glowing affection towards the "Self-same," did by degrees pass through all things bodily, even the very heaven, whence sun and moon and stars shine upon the earth; yea, we were soaring higher yet, by inward musing and discourse and admiring of Thy works; and we came to our own minds, and went beyond them, that we might arrive at that region of neverfailing plenty, where *Thou feedest Israel* for ever with the food of truth. . . .

'We were saying then: If to any the tumult of the flesh were hushed, hushed the images of earth, and waters, and air, hushed also the poles of heaven, yea, the very soul be hushed to herself . . . and He alone speak, not by them, but by Himself, that we may hear His Word, not through any tongue of flesh, nor angel's voice, nor sound of thunder, nor in the dark riddle of a similitude, but might hear Him Whom in these things we love, might hear His very self without these . . . could this be continued on, and other visions of kind far unlike be withdrawn, and this one ravish, and absorb, and wrap up its beholder amid these inward joys, so that life might be for ever like that one moment of understanding which now we sighed after; were not this, *Enter into thy Master's joy . . . when we shall all rise again?* Such things was I speaking, and . . . my mother said, "Son, for mine own part I have no further delight in any thing in this life. What I do here any longer, and to what end I am here, I know not, now that my hopes in this world are accomplished. One thing there was, for which I desired to linger in this life, that I might see thee a Catholic Chris-

U

tian before I died. My God hath done this for me more abundantly, that I should now see thee withal despising earthly happiness, become His servant : what do I here ?"

'What answer I made her unto these things, I remember not. For scarce five days after, or not much more, she fell sick of a fever ; and in that sickness one day she fell into a swoon, and was for a while withdrawn from these visible things. We hastened round her, but she was soon brought back to her senses ; and looking on me and my brother standing by her, said to us enquiringly, "Where was I ?" And then looking fixedly on us, with grief amazed, " Here," saith she, " shall you bury your mother." I held my peace and refrained weeping ; but my brother spoke something, wishing for her as the happier lot, that she might die, not in a strange place, but in her own land. Whereat she with anxious look checked him with her eyes, for that he still *savoured such things*, and then looking upon me ; " Behold," saith she, "what he saith," and soon after to us both, " Lay," she said, " this body anywhere ; let not the care for that any way disquiet you : this only I request, that you would remember me at the Lord's altar wherever you be." And having delivered this sentiment in what words she could, she held her peace, being exercised by her growing sickness. . . . I, considering Thy gifts, gave thanks to Thee, recalling what I before knew, how careful and anxious she had ever been, as to her place of burial (beside her husband), but now when asked whether she were not afraid to leave her body so far from her own city, she replied, "Nothing is far to God ; nor was it to be feared lest at the end of the world He should not recognise whence He were to raise me up." On the ninth day, then, of her sickness, and the fifty-sixth year of her age, and the three-and-thirtieth of mine, was that religious and holy soul freed from the body.

'I closed her eyes ; and there flowed withal a mighty sorrow into my heart, which was overflowing into tears ; mine eyes at the same time, by the violent command of my mind, drank up their fountain wholly dry ; and woe was me in such a strife! But when she breathed her last, the boy Adeodatus' (evidently taken to the grandmother's heart) 'burst out into a loud lament; then, checked by us all, held his peace. In like manner also a childish feeling in me, which was, through my heart's youthful voice, finding its vent in weeping, was checked and silenced. For we thought it not fitting to solemnise that funeral with tearful lament and groanings; for thereby do they for the most part express grief for the departed, as though unhappy, or altogether dead, whereas she was neither unhappy in her death, nor altogether dead. Of this we were assured on good grounds, the testimony of her good conversation and her *faith unfeigned*.

'What then was it which did grievously pain me within, but a fresh wound wrought through the sudden wrench of that most sweet and dear custom of living together? I joyed indeed in her testimony, when, in that her last sickness, mingling her endearments with my acts of duty, she called me "dutiful," and mentioned, with great affection of love, that she never had heard any harsh or reproachful sound uttered by my mouth against her. But yet, O my God, Who madest us, what comparison is there betwixt that honour that I paid to her, and her slavery for me? Being then forsaken of so great comfort in her, my soul was wounded, and that life rent asunder as it were, which, of hers, and mine together, had been made but one. .... I blamed the weakness of my feelings, and refrained my flood of grief, which gave way a little unto me, but again came as with a tide, yet not so as to burst out into tears, nor to a change of countenance; still I knew what I was keeping down in my heart. And ... with a new grief I grieved for my grief, and was thus worn by a double sorrow.

'And behold, the corpse was carried to the burial; we went and returned without tears. . . . Yet was I the whole day in secret heavily sad, and with troubled mind prayed Thee, as I could, to heal my sorrow, yet Thou didst not. . . . It seemed also good to me to go and bathe, having heard that the bath had its name (balneum) from the Greek βαλανεῖον, for that it drives sadness from the mind. And this also I confess unto Thy mercy, *Father of the fatherless*, that I bathed, and was the same as before I bathed. . . . Then I slept, and woke up again, and found my grief not a little softened; and as I was alone in my bed, I remembered those true verses of Thy Ambrose. For Thou art the

> Maker of all, the Lord
> And Ruler of the height,
> Who, robing day in light, hast poured
> Soft slumbers o'er the night,
> That to our limbs the power
> Of toil may be renew'd,
> And hearts be rais'd that sink and cower,
> And sorrows be subdu'd.[1]

And then by little and little I recovered my former thoughts of Thy handmaid, her holy conversation towards Thee, her holy tenderness and observance towards us, whereof I was suddenly deprived: and I was minded to weep in Thy sight, for her and for myself, in her behalf and in my own. And I gave way to the tears which I before restrained, to overflow as much as they desired; reposing my heart upon them; and it found rest in them, for it was in Thy ears, not in those of man, who would have scornfully interpreted my weeping. And now, Lord, in writing I confess it unto Thee. Read it, who will, and interpret it, how he will, and if he finds sin therein, that I wept my mother for a small portion of an hour (the mother who for the time was dead to mine eyes, who had for many years wept for me that I might live in Thine eyes), let him not deride me; but rather if he be one of large charity, let him weep himself for my sins, unto Thee, the Father of all the brethren of Thy Christ.'

The human story is ended, the story of Augustine's natural human relationships, as far as we know it, save for the brief mention of the boy.

Not long afterwards the boy Adeodatus also died, whose bitter weeping at his grandmother's death it had not been easy to still.

[1] *Æterne rerum Conditor.*

'Excellently hadst Thou made him. He was not quite sixteen, and in wit surpassed many grave and learned men. I confess unto Thee Thy gifts, O Lord my God, Creator of all, and abundantly able to repair our deficiencies, for I had no part in that boy but the sin. For that we' (the poor, banished mother and Augustine) 'together brought him up in Thy discipline, it was Thou, and none else, had inspired us to it. I confess unto Thee Thy gifts. There is a book of ours' (his and the boy's) 'entitled "The Master." It is a dialogue between him and me. Thou knowest that all therein ascribed to the person conversing with us were his ideas in his sixteenth year. Much besides and yet more admirable I found in him. That talent struck awe into me. And who but Thou could be the master-maker of such wonders? Soon didst Thou take his life from the earth, and I now remember him without anxiety, fearing nothing for his childhood or youth or his whole life.' One sentence of the boy's, quoted in the book 'The Master,'[1] may express what he was. 'He possesses God who has a pure heart, 'the boy said as they were discoursing on the Blessed Life. And Monica, it is said, approved this much.'

The human story is closed.

But the divine poem, the history of the Soul and the City, goes on.

'Let me know Thee, O Lord, who knowest me. Let me know Thee as I am known.' He questions the earth, the sea and its deeps, the heavens, sun, moon and stars, in all their beauty—all the light and fragrance, and all things 'that encompass the door of the flesh:' searches his own soul, 'its fields and spacious palaces of memory.' 'What, then, do I love, when I love my God?'

"But Thou precedest all things past by the sublimity of an ever present Eternity. In the Eternal, nothing passeth,

---

[1] *Moral and Metaphysical Philosophy*, by Rev. F. D. Maurice, for the sketch of this book and for the analysis of Augustine on the philosophical side.

For three years he lived in retirement near Tagaste, his native town, on a little estate left him by his father, with a band of devoted Christian men who gathered around him.

but the whole is present. Thy years neither come nor go; Thy years are as one day; and Thy day is not daily, but To-day, for Thy To-day gives not place to to-morrow, and neither does it replace yesterday. Thy To-day is Eternity.'

'Love knoweth what that Light is. He that knows it knows Eternity. O Truth, who art Eternal; and Love, who art Truth; and Eternity, who art Love.'

'Too late I loved Thee, Thou Beauty of ancient days, yet ever new. Too late I loved Thee. And behold Thou wert within, and I abroad, and there I searched for Thee; deformed I, plunging amid those fair forms which Thou hadst made. Thou wert with me, but I was not with Thee. Things held me far from Thee, which unless they are in Thee are not at all. Thou didst call, and shout, and burst my deafness. Thou didst flash and shine and scatter my blindness. Thou didst breathe odours, and I *drew in my breath and pant for Thee.* I tasted, and *hunger and thirst.* Thou didst touch me, and I burned for Thy peace.

'When I shall with my whole self cleave to Thee, I shall nowhere have sorrow or labour; and my life shall wholly live, as wholly full of Thee.' 'Lo I hide not my wounds. Thou art the Physician if I be sick.' '*Da quod jubes et jube quod vis*—Give what Thou commandest and command what Thou wilt.'

'How hast Thou loved us, good Father, *Who sparedst not Thine only Son but deliveredst Him up for us ungodly!* How hast Thou loved us, for whom *He that thought it no robbery to be equal with Thee, was made subject to the death of the Cross!* For us to Thee both Victor and Victim, and therefore Victor because the Victim; for us to Thee both Priest and Sacrifice, and therefore Priest because the Sacrifice; making us to Thee of servants sons, by being born of Thee and serving us.'

Monica died in 387 and Augustine in 430, forty-three years afterwards.

Those intervening years were years of ceaseless activity for Augustine; as bishop of Hippo, as a great defender of the faith against Pelagians, Manichæans and Donatists, and as the great theologian of Latin Christendom.

The shadow of the many evils he combated, of the Dualism which had penetrated so deep into his own being, the shadow of the very sins he conquered, may have been thrown from his soul athwart the centuries. But the fire of his genius, the love of his heart, have glowed through Christendom ever since. The theological theories he made, as far as they were his own, being human are corruptible and must decay; what he *was*, being of God's making, is immortal and lives and works for ever.

His second great book, from a biographical point of view, is the 'City of God' (*De Civitate Dei*).

From the same great heart and intellect which poured out in the Confessions the intensely individual story of the love of the mother and her son, of the search of the soul for God, came that other great poem on the Universal Society, the Heavenly Kingdom, the Church, the City of God.[1]

It was begun, as he explains, when, in 410, Rome was taken and sacked by Alaric and his Goths.

For centuries these Gothic tribes had been making attack after attack (led on, it would seem, by a hand they knew not) line after line '*en échelon*' to assault point upon point of the frontiers of the Empire.[2] But now at last the City which to them had been as an unknown glorious city of the gods, lay despoiled, trampled and ruined under their feet. The capture of Rome, it is said, struck the Roman world to the heart. What then must it have been to Rome itself? The remnants of the old Roman houses which had clung to the old gods, disgraced and ruined, fled to the Roman colonies, which then studded the coasts of North Africa. And there they broke into bitter complaints against the new religion which they said had driven away the im-

---

[1] 'The *City of God* was unquestionably the noblest work both in its original design and in the fulness of its execution, which the genius of man had yet contributed to the support of Christianity.'—Milman's *Latin Christianity*, vol. iii., p. 83.

[2] *The Roman and the Teuton*, Rev. Charles Kingsley.

mortal gods, and had been the ruin of Rome. The occasion of the book, *De Civitate Dei*, was the defence of Christianity against these Pagan accusations, to show how powerless their gods had been to defend Troy of old, as their own Capitol now; how, indeed, instead of being Protectors they needed to be protected. But the intention of Augustine was not, from the beginning, limited to this temporary meaning. And during the thirteen years which the book took to grow, the two cities, the earthly and the heavenly, the evil and the good, rose with ever clearer distinctness before his vision from the beginning of the world, and from before the beginning of our world to beyond its end.

'Most glorious City of God,' he begins, 'whether through the course of the ages, whilst living by faith, she makes pilgrimage among the godless, or whether in the stability of that Eternal Dwelling which she, now, patient, expects.'

Then, after the first ten Books devoted to the defence of Christianity against the pagan onset of the moment, he launches on his great subject of the Two Cities, of the World and of God; and in doing so unfolds to the world in its world-wide aspect the whole of the Christianity which had been unfolded to him through the slow learning of the 'Confessions;' the eternal unity of God in the 'essential Trinity of the Loving, the Beloved, and Love; the Revelation through the Son, God and man; the Rest of God not from toil, but in the goodness and beauty of His Creation. All originally created good; the fall of the high angels through their rebellious will; the fall of man through delusion and temptation; the Incarnation and the Redemption; the two great divisions beginning before and extending beyond all earthly history, through all ages and all nations, in the earthly City, and in the City of God.

He traces the great dual story from the first earthly City of Cain, and the heavenly life of Enoch who walked with God, through the history of Assyria, Athens, Rome, as parallel and contemporary with that of the City of God amidst the Patriarchs and the nation of Israel. But he does not limit the citizens to Israel; nationally, Israel was of God, but none could deny that there were holy men of all kindreds and nations destined and trained to that heavenly citizenship. Job was but one instance revealed to represent numbers which might be hidden.

To Roman virtue and Greek wisdom he renders full testimony. Augustine did not forget his debts to Cicero and to Plato.[1]

And so he traces the long procession through the ages, on one side to the final destruction of all corruption, typified in the terrible ruin of Rome (that corrupt city that had ruled over the earth), still ringing in their ears; and on the other side to the Resurrection of the just, the eternal felicity of the City of God, 'where nothing evil will be, where nothing good will be hidden, where glory will be given to all who are worthy, and to none who is unworthy;' where the body shall be wherever the spirit wills, where 'the first freedom of being able not to sin shall be exchanged for the fuller grace of not being able to sin; where men shall not indeed be as gods, but shall be partakers of God, where shall be the true peace, which nothing is suffered to break from within or without, where God Himself shall be to each what each desires, life and health, and good, and liberty, and glory, and love, and heaven, and all good things;' where reasoning hearts shall delight in the reasonable beauty of such a Creator; where all members of the Incorruptible Body now necessarily scattered shall be gathered together in full eternal society, in the presence of Him Who shall be all in all, 'Himself the reward of the virtue He gave.'

In these two great books, the 'Confessions' and the 'City of God,' Augustine lives before us, son of Monica, prodigal son returning from the far country to the Father, citizen of the City of God. Such he is for all ages.

In his own age much of those remaining forty years at Hippo was spent in a ceaseless warfare; no strange destiny for the Saints. The warfare of Ambrose was mostly

[1] 'Augustine, Latin as he was, is emphatically the great Latin Platonist.'—Maurice, *Moral and Metaphysical Philosophy*, i. 601.

against tyranny, and intolerance, against the vices of luxury and the wrongs of poverty; the battle of Augustine was chiefly with heresy and schism, but with heresies which eat out the very heart of Christianity, and with schisms which threatened the very existence of the Church. Manichæism as he knew it made a 'phantom' of Christ and God, of right and wrong. Pelagianism seemed to him to make a phantom of sin and grace; while nominally asserting free-will actually withdrawing men from dependence on Him who only can make the feeble and fettered will free and strong for good.

And the Donatist schism, which was distracting Hippo when he became bishop, was separatist, not by accident, but in its essence, a practical heresy against the mercy of God, such a denial of pardoning love to the lapsed and lost, as is really a denial of the essential meaning of Christianity, a negation of the essential purpose of the Church.

He had also a controversy with St. Jerome, Augustine defending St. Paul against what seemed to him an attack on his truthfulness; a controversy very hot at first, but ending in a continuance of affectionate esteem.

But in external things, those forty years at Hippo were peaceful. The tide that had broken against the Empire had not yet touched Africa.

Augustine's house, as a bishop, was a training home for the young clergy. It was also a house of mercy for the poor and suffering.

His sermons were, it is said, of the simplest, laying aside all philosophy and rhetoric; so personal and practical in their assaults against actual sins, that the sinners recognised their own portraits, wept, and repented.

In times of distress or pestilence, he deemed the highest use of his own income, of the revenues of the Church, and even of the sacred vessels, to be the succour of the destitute, or the redemption of captives. His visits were almost all to the sick, the widowed, the fatherless, and friendless. He spent long hours in patient peace-making, inheriting the tact and grace of his mother. But he preferred to arbitrate between strangers rather than between his own friends. 'Of the two strangers,' he said, 'I make one a friend. Of the two friends I make one an enemy.' His dress was simple, but not ascetic. He wore, like other people, a linen garment underneath, and a woollen one above. He also wore shoes and stockings, and he said to those who thought to obey the Gospel better by walking with bare feet—'Let us observe charity. I admire your courage. Do you condone my weakness.' His table was open and hospitable, but frugal; always vegetables, seldom meat, except for guests or for the infirm. The service of his table was of wood or marble; the spoons of silver. Calumny and detraction he could not bear. On the table, which was without a cloth, according to custom, he had these verses inscribed—

> Quisquis amat dictis absentem rodere vitam,
> Hanc mensam indignam noverit esse sibi.

His disciple and biographer Possidius, afterwards a bishop, says it mattered not what their rank or position, if any talked scandal at his table, he immediately rose from his seat and left them.

But at length this time of peace for the African Church was broken up, never to return. The Vandals came, invited by Count Boniface, to avenge himself against the ingratitude of the Imperial Court of Ravenna. Boniface, himself a Christian and a friend of Augustine, was misled into this revolt by treachery. He would not listen in time to the aged bishop. But he would have given everything to avert the fatal consequences when it was too late.

The fierce Vandals rushed eagerly on the fertile shores, so long the granary of Rome, and the fair cities so long unplundered. Destitute fugitives from all sides, clergy and people, from ruined cities and burnt villages, took refuge at Hippo. At last the barbarians gathered around Hippo itself and began the siege. Augustine would not desert his flock.

But within the beleaguered walls of his episcopal city,

the gates of the City he had so loved and longed for were standing open for him. He was sound in limbs and in sight and hearing, but he had never been strong; he alone had done the work of many; and he was now seventy-five. Moreover his disciple Possidius writes that he found the last days of his life very bitter and sorrowful. He had borne the burden of the shepherd for his people forty years; whilst sounding the depths of Divine truths, and bringing thence treasures for all ages, he had fed the little ones of his flock with simplest words of faithful love. And he would not abandon them now.

'It happened,' writes Possidius, ' that as we were sitting at table and talking together, he said to us, "You know that during the time of our calamity, I have asked God either that He would deign to save this city out of the hands of the enemies that surround it, or, if He judged otherwise, that He would make His servants strong to endure His will, or certainly that He would take me to Himself."'

Not long after this, his breath began to fail; yet he continued to preach till his last illness. It was not long. At the end of the week after he was taken ill fever came on. He knew this meant death. Those around him seemed to see his face shine like St. Stephen's. ' He was unable,' says Possidius, 'to restrain his desire to be with his Lord. He broke forth into words of longing for the City of God. It was a plain and barely furnished room in which he lay. He ordered the Seven Penitential Psalms to be written out against the wall, and placed where he could see them, as he lay in bed; and these he looked at and read in his days of sickness, weeping often and much. And that he might not be restrained, about ten days before his death he asked of us who were present, that no one should come in except at those hours when the physician came to see him, or when refreshment was brought. And so it was done as he wished; and he had all that time for prayer.'

And all the time, while the citadel of his life was being undermined, the enemy was proceeding with the siege of his city, which day by day drew nearer its fall. The siege lasted six months.

But for Augustine the gates of the heavenly City opened first. At last his friends stood weeping around his bed, joining their prayers with those that came from his own dying lips, conscious as he was to the last.

And so, continuing his penitential confessions to the very threshold, he entered the Gates of the City of God. He died August 28, 430. Afterwards the Vandals swept over his Africa, followed by the Mahomedans, and swept away his beloved African Church; but not before it had let its light shine before men in all lands and ages in the life and death of Perpetua, Cyprian, Monica, and Augustine.[1]

[1] Dedications of churches: twenty-nine. Represented in art with a burning heart, a heart with one or two arrows, and with an eagle.

St. Jerome,[1]

OF AQUILEIA.

September 30.

(Born early in 4th century; died A.D. 420. Sarum, Ep. and Gosp.: Ecclus. xlvii. 8–11; St. Matt. v. 13–19.)

Not 'less' but 'diverse,' not by comparison of size and quantity, but by diversities of gifts mutually fulfilling each other, are the saints and the many members of the One Body distinguished. Otherwise we might feel as if we were descending to a lower level in turning from Augustine to Jerome, from the poet to the man of letters, from philosophy to rhetoric, from substance to form, from Plato to the school-men. But we should lose by any such disparagement. The Church needs Ambrose the statesman as much as Augustine the theologian, and Jerome the commentator and faithful translator of Holy Scriptures, as much as Augustine. Ill could we spare that rugged rock, with its rough crevices full of wild flowers; that man of impetuous loving nature, with his legendary friend and likeness, the lion, fawning at his feet.

This fierce denouncer of womankind and chivalrous friend of so many good women, Eusebius Hieronymus, was born at the village of Stridon, in Dalmatia, on a slope of the Illyrian Alps, near Aquileia, the great seaport of the Adriatic, predecessor and also parent of Venice, since it was from Aquileia the little band of exiles fled to the Island of Torcello and the other Venetian islets when Aquileia was destroyed by Attila and his Huns. Of his kindred we only know that his family were Catholic Christians, rich enough to send him to Rome to complete his education. Rome,

---

[1] Represented in art, with red hat and robe, later as a cardinal; with lion, ink-bottle, wallet and scroll, church, hour-glass, skull-stone; beating his breast with a stone, kneeling on thorns, or wearing a garment interwoven with thorns.

thirty years before its sack by Alaric, though for a hundred years it had ceased to be the residence of the emperors, was as glorious in mere external splendour of architecture, and even luxury of living, as ever before or since. All the wholesome activity and discipline of real rule had vanished, but the wealth and pomp remained.

Launched on this sea of corruption in his youth, Jerome says he made more than one shipwreck, until his father sent him from these perils into Gaul. But at Rome there were also great memories of martyrs; and the Catacombs, where but recently these recent martyrs had been laid, Jerome and his fellow-students reverently visited. And also there were the more recent traces of a later Confessor, 'Athanasius, against the world'—for that great Father had been at Rome only twenty years before—filling it with all the inspiration of his own heroic life, and with the story of his friend Anthony and the Fathers of the Desert.

Already a company of men and patrician women were gathering in the luxurious palaces on the Aventine, with a devotion as real as that of the martyrs of Diocletian or the monks of the Thebaid. And from Gaul where in the cottage near Treves the 'Life of Anthony' had conquered the young Pontitianus, and through him Augustine, Jerome himself returned to Rome, himself moved to the ascetic life, to find that same 'Life of Anthony' by Athanasius transforming the lives of the noblest men and women there. At that second visit Jerome was baptised; and then his life first became interwoven with this ascetic movement among the patricians.

At that time the impulsive Melania, widowed at twenty-three, and bereaved of two of her little children, swept away by this rising tide of ascetic enthusiasm, left her third child to the care of the Prefect of Rome, and set out on a pilgrimage to the monks of Nitria, in Syria; and in some way Jerome's name was mixed up with her story as one of the influences which moved her, so that, with his peculiar faculty for making enemies as well as friends, bitter and unjust things were said of him, and he went back to Aquileia in 360, and did not return to Rome again for fifteen years.

At Aquileia he gathered around him a band of young men of the higher ranks, devoted to the ascetic life, many of whose subsequent lives proved good and capable. These tried to emulate the Fathers of the desert in their own neighbourhood. Bonosus went to a little island to live on shellfish; Jerome and his brother retired to a solitude on some neighbouring hills. But the Bishop Lupinus opposed them, perhaps only antedating the long mediæval conflict between the Seculars and the Regulars; perhaps also carrying out the longer conflicts between the worldly-holy and the whole-hearted. Jerome, as usual, has vigorous epithets for his adversary: 'brutal, wicked, feeble pilot of a scuttled ship (perforatæ navis debilis gubernator).' The bishop, however, succeeded in exciting the people against the audacious young reformers, and the little ascetic community of Aquileia was dispersed.

Jerome went eastward by the Danube, Constantinople, Pontus, Galatia, Bithynia, and Cilicia to Antioch; and there found himself plunged in a chaos of ecclesiastical strife about various schisms and heresies. In Antioch he found a hermit, who told him of the holy Cœnobites and Solitaries of the desert of Chalcis. And there Jerome took refuge with one of his Aquileian friends from the conflicts without and within. He stopped at the first 'zone' of the desert where the monks lived in community; the two further 'zones,' of a more tropical fervour of asceticism, being marked by a deeper solitude in its remote recesses.

There his two Aquileian comrades, Marobius and Hylas, died, and Jerome's own health gave way under the austerity of the rule.

But still he had not found the inward victory he sought. He fled further into the bare sandy wastes. 'There, withdrawn into this vast solitude, burnt with the sun, I kept far from men; my soul filled with bitterness; covered with hideous sackcloth, my skin black as an Ethiopian's. I spent days in tears; my bones scarcely held together. When overcome with sleep, I fell on the bare earth. My flesh was already dead, and yet my passions surged upon me.' Evil memories of his life in his early youth at Rome rushed back on him. 'I threw myself at the feet of Jesus. I bathed them with tears.' He hated his very cell as the witness of his thoughts. 'If I found some dark ravine, or steep precipice, that was the place I chose to pray in, and to imprison this wretched body.'

It was to this period of his conflict in the desert of Chalcis that belongs the well-known, often-told, and often-painted mediæval legend that one day he saw a great wounded lion enter his cell, with fiery eyes, and wide-open mouth, holding up his bleeding paw. Jerome approached him, caressed him, staunched his wound, and the terrible beast became his devoted slave.

Deeper and deeper Jerome plunged into the desert, and at times, through the tempest, broke on him the songs of angels, the perfumes of Paradise.

Then he had a dream that he was caught up to the Judgment Seat and there rejected, as 'no Christian, but a Ciceronian,' because of his delight in the classics, and also that he was scourged until he vowed never to read the classics more. 'Was it a vision or a dream?' A dream, he finally concluded, and continued to read the classics, and taught them to little boys and youths of Bethlehem, in after years.

From his books, his beloved library, he had never parted, even in the depths of his anguish. They were with him in the desert. 'Miserable that I was,' he said, 'I fasted; then I read Cicero; and if I tried to read the Prophets the simple style repelled me' (like Augustine).

The true vocation of his life recalled him from solitude to the community of monks. A converted Jew, who had become a monk, taught him Hebrew. At first he hated the rough gutturals, but he persevered and conquered. Then a longing for old friends came back to him. He wrote to his friend Heliodorus, entreating him by every argument to rejoin him and embrace the monastic life, 'even if his father threw himself across the threshold to oppose his departure.' 'Pass on, without a tear. Thou art a soldier, thy banner is below, it is the Cross. Leave the smoky prison of the towns. Here is fresh air, here is light.' Heliodorus did not come. But the terrible appeals of Jerome's letter were circulated among the admiring ladies of the Aventine, and repeated to him fifteen years after, at Bethlehem by Fabiola.

But peace was not long Jerome's portion, in the desert or anywhere. The monks of Chalcis accused him, as a Western, of heresy, angrily demanding whether he was for one contending bishop or another, furiously insisting on his using the latest Oriental formula of doctrine, and deriding his explanations. Finally they called him 'a liar,' 'a heretic' and 'a pagan,' and took away his paper, so that he had to write on a castaway rag. At last, when the spring made the journey practicable, he left them and went away, 'regretting the deserts but not the monks.'[1]

After four or five years of the desert he returned to Antioch, and eagerly resumed his literary work, wrote the Life of Paul, the first hermit, won admiration for his learning and ability throughout the East, and, finally, reluctantly suffered himself to be ordained priest by Bishop Paulinus. It is said he never, or at least but once, celebrated. The next three years he spent at Constantinople, where he became the friend of Gregory Nazianzen. Then he returned through Greece to Rome, everywhere gathering material for his work as a commentator and translator of Holy Scriptures, observing customs, idioms, the aspect and names of places. He ascended the Acropolis of Athens by the steps of the ancient Processions, stood in the Parthenon, saw a large globe at the feet of the statue of the goddess (which it was said to have been the test of the strength of the athletes to lift), and at last, with the Oriental bishops, reached Rome in time for a great Council.

Amongst the community of distinguished and devoted women, mostly patricians, who met for prayer and confer-

[1] Amédée Thierry, *St. Jérôme.*

ence in Marcella's palace on the Aventine, some could remember him in his younger days, fifteen years ago, and all knew him already well by his letters (especially that to Heliodorus from the Desert), and his praises of the ascetic life to which they were devoted.

The widowed Marcella must then have been about forty-seven years of age She remembered listening as a child of seven to the great Athanasius, when he was in Rome, and left there his Life of Antony, a seed of higher life in so many hearts. The only child of her mother Albinia, they lived together in blessed companionship to the old age of both. Ten years afterwards, when Albinia's death had left a great blank in Marcella's home, Paula and Eustochium wrote from Bethlehem, entreating her to rejoin them and Jerome there.

Once only a difference had crossed that hallowed home, when the widowed mother wished to save her young widowed daughter from the perils of a lonely life in that corrupt city (which she knew from experience) by a second marriage with a relative of the Emperor. But Marcella would not listen to this.

Marcella's palace was the meeting-place of the ascetic community, 'la petite Thébaïde dorée.' There Jerome was installed as the most honoured guest, leader and teacher of them all ; and there he worked tranquilly for the next four years at his literary work.

Pope Damasus was his constant friend. The tumults and bloodshed, in churches within and without the walls, especially in the Church of St. Agnes, which had preceded the election of Damasus, were over, but the calumnies against him still lingered. His name was at last carried before a council, and he was acquitted. To Jerome he was always a zealous friend, suggesting and sympathising with his work, inducing him to accomplish the Revision of the Psalter, which is still the basis of the Latin Psalter, and chanted in ' all the Churches of the Latin rite.'

Pope Damasus made Jerome the Secretary of the Cancellariat, and was with him not only in his literary labours, but in his endeavours to reform the morals of the clergy, the deaconesses and the Roman Christians generally. The Christian emperors had already made a law that ecclesiastics were not to receive heritages or donations. 'It is not at this law,' Jerome writes, 'that I grieve, but that we have deserved it.'

Jerome's life at Rome, as elsewhere, was one of conflict. He had always a controversy on hand, in which he was, probably, usually right in the main, yet as usually put himself apparently in the wrong, and added unnecessary bitterness to the necessary strife, by his vehement satire, and the terrible glitter and edge of his weapons. However great may have been his provocations, it is clear he spared no bitter epithets, no stings of sarcasm; and unfortunately for him, his epithets were strong and pointed enough to survive. The echo of whatever bad names adversaries called him, might long since have perished; but when Jerome calls one opponent 'a two-legged ass,' and says of another, who was ignorant and ugly, that 'he should be afraid in future to speak of owls, monkeys, crocodiles, or any other hideous creature, lest Onosus should take it to himself;' when he calls his opponent Vigilantius 'Dormitantius,' and believes he (Vigilantius) 'may be forgiven when (as Origen hopes) the devil is forgiven,' the echo unfortunately lingers.

Yet in the midst of all this strife his heart was always trusted, and his counsel sought by that band of good men and women gathered on the Aventine which was the last blossom and fruit of all that was noblest in the Rome of the heroes, and of the martyrs, and which was always attracting to itself what was best and highest in the Rome and Italy of that age.

Not bound by any monastic rule, as a community, they yet held together in most affectionate unity, meeting daily in the oratory at Marcella's palace for reading the Scriptures and prayer, and chanting the Psalms, often in Hebrew. They lived a life of real work, mental and bodily, visiting the poor, tending the sick, founding the first hospitals, studying the Scriptures with enthusiasm, in Hebrew and Greek ; seeking to penetrate their meaning.

Alaric and the sack of Rome left to this beautiful garden of holy souls no time for decay or division.

The noblest Roman heroes are represented among them, the Fabii and the Scipios. But the first place, amidst all their wealth and rank, seems to have been yielded to Asella, a widowed matron who had long since sold her possessions and lived in poverty, still sharing with the destitute the little she had retained.

We do not hear of her learning ; but her gentleness and inexhaustible charity made her beloved even by the followers of the ancient gods.

If the natural ambition of Jerome's character was for 'affection and fame,' and since the work of his life certainly was the explanation and translation of the Holy Scriptures, and the promotion of the ascetic life which then seemed to all the higher Christian life—here, in Rome, with the approval of the Pope, and the devotion of this little community of disciples, he found all he wanted.

But the friendship which formed the inner core of his life was that with Paula and her children. The event which knit this friendship with cords never to be broken was the death of Paula's daughter Blesilla, though at the time it was the occasion of his abandoning Rome for ever, occurring as it did when his friend Damasus had died, leaving him exposed and unprotected to all the calumnies from the various sections of society whom his piety, or the clever and bitter satire with which he defended it, had made his enemies.

Paula, herself the daughter of a high-born Greek of Athens and a lady of the house of the Scipios, to whom Greek was a native tongue as well as Latin, was an enthusiastic student of sacred literature, a devoted friend of Marcella, and a friend of Jerome, though still retaining many of the dependent and luxurious habits of her earlier life with its Oriental softness and helplessness. She had three daughters, one of whom, Eustochium, resolute and brave as any of her Roman forefathers, was the first of the Roman patrician families who took the vow of celibacy, but continued always devotedly attached to her mother, whom she never left.

In his letters, especially to Eustochium, Jerome was continually using satirical expressions, which gave mortal offence; describing with terribly graphic force the disorders of the clergy, the young priests or deacons with perfumed robes and jewelled fingers who studied the tastes, the hours, the habits of the great ladies, and frequented sick rooms and deathbeds, with sympathetic voices, in search of legacies;' the worldly deaconesses and virgins 'gossiping from house to house,' with their 'little thread of purple, by way of expressing their vows,' their hair flowing in graceful carelessness, 'the long hyacinthine scarf floating in the breeze,' or, on the other hand, their 'ostentatious rags, their languishing countenances, and steps faint as if with fasting,' 'their infantile simplicities of goat's-hair hood, and lisping speech,' 'their ostentatious alms at the doors of churches, attended by troops of servants.' Nor was he more sparing in his monastic sarcasms on the annoyances of domestic life, the wailings of children, the tyranny of husbands. All the Roman society of the time might be depicted from Jerome's letters, as our own from a comic paper of our own days; and Jerome's satires, not being anonymous, naturally made him not a few enemies.

It was through Paula's daughter, Blesilla, newly married and widowed, and taken from her by death, that the friendship between Paula and Jerome was deepened.

Blesilla, after a married life, apparently not happy, had been widowed at twenty. Her disposition resembled her mother's—ardent, impetuous, rather what we might call Italian, than of the firm old Roman type of Eustochium.

Jerome, with his satirical touch, describes the usual course of those early widowhoods of opulent matrons at Rome. First a 'mourning mitigated by jewels; a sober costume as becoming as possible,' 'then the gradual disappearance of sombre tints, a return to silken robes, and golden tresses, with recurrences of grief and despair at intervals;' in the third stage, placid undisguised freedom and pleasure; lastly a second marriage. Of these stages Blesilla had only reached the second—a reviving delight in her toilette and her mirror, and in pleasure; 'blameless,' Jerome says, 'in all else.'[1]

At this point she had a serious illness. One night, in a dream or vision, it seemed to her that our Saviour appeared to her, approached her bed, took her hand and said, as to Lazarus of old, '*Arise, come forth.*' And, waking, she seemed to arise and sit at the table like Mary of Bethany with the Lord. Her whole life was changed from that night; she gathered together her embroidered robes and jewels and sold them for the poor; instead of 'torturing her innocent head with a mitre of curls' she found a veil enough; 'the simple woollen cord, the dark linen, the common shoes, replacing the glistening silks, the gold embroidered girdles and sandals.' She rested only on a hard couch, which she often left early to weep for her sins or to lift up her 'silvery voice' with the alleluias.

Both the recovery of health and the conversion seemed miraculous. Intelligent and studious like the rest of her family she became one of the 'apprentices' of Jerome, who wrote for her a commentary on the book of Ecclesiastes, 'Vanity of Vanities,' and a letter, whose triumphant tone much offended her worldly relations.

But though Blesilla's conversion was enduring, her recovery was not. In a few months another attack of fever laid her low. As her friends were gathered around her dying bed, she said, 'Pray the Lord Jesus to pardon me, because I have not been able to fulfil what I had resolved.' Once again the life-giving voice said to her, '*Arise, come forth.*' But this time it was not to Rome with its corruptions and its calumnies, but to the City of God.

Her funeral was magnificent. An immense crowd followed the bier. Paula, according to Roman custom, accompanied her child to the tomb of her ancestors, wild with

[1] Amédée Thierry.

grief, lamenting, sobbing, and at last fainting, so that she was borne away as one dead.

The people were enraged; they accused the monks, especially Jerome, of killing the young matron with austerities. They cried, 'Let those accursed monks be stoned, and thrown into the Tiber.'

Paula continued weeping and uttering cries of despair for days, refusing to eat, or to see her friends. She consented to see Jerome, because he had understood, loved, and reverenced her child; but the very sight of him only recalled her loss and deepened her grief. At length he wrote her a letter.

He begins with dwelling on all Blesilla had been, her fervent faith, her fine intelligence, the touching details of her death. 'But what am I doing? I would stop the tears of a mother and I weep myself. But did not Jesus weep for Lazarus because He loved him? He can never be a true comforter who does not weep whilst he consoles. Do you think the waves of revolt do not heave often in my heart, when I see impious old age enjoying the good things of this earth, while innocent youth and childhood are taken away? Take care, Paula, lest the Saviour should say to you, "Of what do you complain? That your child has become mine? You refuse nourishment, not from love of fasting, but from love of sorrow."

'Leave these senseless self-tortures to a proud philosophy. The Spirit of God descends only on the humble, not on those who are in revolt. These tears, which bring thee to the threshold of death, are full of sacrilege and of unbelief. Thou utterest piercing cries, as if being burnt alive. But at thy cries the compassionate Jesus comes to thee and says: "Why weepest thou? The child is not dead but sleepeth." Thou castest thyself in despair on the tomb of thy daughter. But the angel is there who says to thee, "*Seek not the living among the dead.*"'

Paula listened, and submitted to God. She arose, and lived. And nothing ever interrupted that friendship which made the joy of her life and of Jerome's.

It was soon after this that Jerome's friend Damasus died, and his successor Siricius, yielding to the clamour of Jerome's enemies, withdrew from him the secretaryship of the Pontifical Chancery.

The calumnies which buzzed about Paula and the Aventine community were redoubled. At last one of the worst slanderers was brought before the magistrates, and, under torture, confessed he had spoken falsely.

But the end of the calumniators was gained; the reform of the worldly clergy and Christians was never accomplished. Instead of the reformation of Rome came her ruin under Alaric.

Jerome, once spoken of as the probable successor of Damasus, was driven from Rome, which he denounced as the Babylon of the Apocalypse. An affectionate company of friends followed him to Ostia; and from Ostia he wrote, amidst many tears, a farewell letter to the aged Asella. 'Would it not have been easier,' he wrote, 'to attract applause by a worldly life? Yet what have I suffered after all, being a soldier of the Cross? Salute Albinia my mother, Marcella my sister, Paula and Eustochium, mine in Christ (whether the world will it or not), Marcellina, Felicitas. Tell them we shall be reunited before the judgment-seat of Christ, where the secrets of all hearts shall be made known.'

Soon afterwards Paula calmly prepared for her departure, dividing her patrimony among her children. She freighted a ship at Ostia and went to Cyprus with Eustochium and a company of consecrated virgins. They rejoined Jerome at Antioch.

She parted without tears from her friends who accompanied them to Ostia. But at the last Paula felt her heart torn in two as she saw her boy Toxotius on the shore, and her young daughter, betrothed to Pammachius, standing silent and motionless, and seeming to cry to her, 'Mother, wait till I am married;' and she would have fainted but for the support of her daughter Eustochium.

The boy was long in forgiving his mother's desertion. In a few years he married the daughter of a pagan Pontiff.

But his bride herself was a Christian. And just at the time of the death of Paula, a little girl was born to them, called after her grandmother, and dedicated to the monastic life, the first word she was taught to lisp being Alleluia; so that (strange to say), at the last, it was the child of the son left on the shore at Ostia, who watched as a tender grandchild by the death-bed of Jerome.

It is not indeed the ascetic monasticism, found in many other religious developments, which is the Christian element in this story. It is the wholesome force of Christian love, bringing back pure human affection into the void.

If an Oriental asceticism broke up Paula's natural ties, the Christianity for which, however mistaken her interpretation, she intended to make the renunciation, created, through her, a home in the solitude of Bethlehem. The monk Telemachus, seeking Christ in the desert, *found Him*, and, with Him, that compassion for the wrongs and miseries of the world he had forsaken, which drove him from the desert, across the sea, to Rome, to put a stop to the gladiatorial games. Jerome, with all his sarcasms against family life, *sought Christ* in the monastic life, and, *finding Him there*, found there, also, in the equal companionship of good women, in the call for fatherly care to the young, in the response of childlike devotion, much of what we mean by a Christian home.

Paula and Eustochium, with their companions, after leaving Rome, rejoined Jerome at Cyprus, and for a year the little company travelled through Egypt and Syria, making one of those pilgrimages or religious tours, so frequent among ladies of distinction then, and scarcely possible since then until these very recent days.

They visited the monasteries of Nitria, wondering at the solitaries in their holes or eyries, and perhaps perplexing them by their enthusiastic admiration and the abundance of their alms.

Paula, fascinated by the desert, would have stayed there always, and founded a convent. But Jerome had tried the desert for some years, and knew its perils, and prevailed on her to return to Bethlehem, where she founded a community, in which, laying aside the luxurious habits of her life, she set the example of a simple and industrious life by washing floors and cleaning lamps and other common household works. Paula's convent became a hospice for pilgrims, and Bethlehem, through their united work, a home of countless kindnesses. And here the last thirty-four years of Jerome's life were spent; years (as was inevitable for him) of almost ceaseless controversy, but of ceaseless activity. His dwelling was a large cave, which he called his paradise, and which, in many respects, must have had about as many glimpses of paradise as have been known since its gates were first closed. Sunlit from above, with prayer and the music of alleluias sounding there night and day, brightened by the glow of pure home affections, from it flowed rivers of water to refresh the earth. Although, indeed, on the other hand, storms thundered over it, again and again.

Once a band of fierce robbers besieged Paula's convent, and forced the inmates to take refuge in a strong tower attached to Jerome's monastery.

Another time the great advancing tide of the Huns threatened to burst over the Lebanon and lay everything waste, and Jerome went hastily to Joppa and chartered 300 ships and boats to transport all the communities, brotherhoods, and sisterhoods from the country. But the terrible host turned westward towards Europe, and Bethlehem escaped.

Yet on the whole the days passed tranquilly in fruitful labour. Jerome held a school for boys and young men, in which he taught the classics. But his great work was the Vulgate, the translation of the Bible into what was then the vulgar tongue 'understanded of the people.' For this he spared no pains or cost, and shrank from no calumny.

He added Chaldee to his Hebrew and Greek. For the Book of Job, he paid a learned Jew to come and help him from Lydda; for the Chaldee of Tobit he had a rabbi from the great Jewish school at Tiberias; and for the

Book of Chronicles another teacher from Tiberias, with whom he compared word by word.

For all this labour he had naturally the reverse of praise from the more narrow-minded and ignorant of the religious world of his time, monastic or other. They said he was turning a Jew, 'degrading the sacred text by consulting the rabbis.' But he never faltered in his purpose, though his difficulties were increased by broken health and by weakness of sight.

In all this work Paula and Eustochium gave real help. They had conferences in their cave day by day as to the most accurate renderings possible; for Jerome had great respect for their scholarship and acuteness, and dedicated his translation to Paula.

Meanwhile there was always a running to and fro of enquirers and devotees at Paula's hospice from all parts of Christendom. Sulpicius Severus, from Gaul, stayed there six months. Fabiola came from Rome with her cases of conscience. And besides visits there was a flood of correspondence about spiritual difficulties, family quarrels, questions of criticism, always pouring in on Jerome from Spain, Gaul, Italy, Africa.

No man can thus become a refuge for human hearts and minds without having in himself a wonderful force of sympathy and help, such as Jerome must have had.

He had, indeed, many controversies. His controversies, moreover, were no light foamings of a shallow brook; they were the impetuous rush of a mighty river, making whirlpools and cataracts around every obstacle. It is pleasant, however, to think that his last important controversy, which was with St. Augustine about the straightforwardness of the Apostles Peter and Paul, ended in a friendship of twenty years.

Pale, meagre, dim-sighted, in that cave at Bethlehem, with its bare sides, its hard couch, clothed with no especial authority, civil or ecclesiastical, Jerome himself, by the simple force of what he was, through his books and letters, became guide and spiritual tribunal to souls through all parts of Christendom; interpreter of the words of God to men, of the hearts of men to themselves. To him monastic life was indeed no isolation. And *because* it was not, the natural shadows of humanity fell heavily on its close.

In 403 the aged Paula had sad tidings of the death of her daughter Paulina, in giving birth to her only child. Paulina's husband, Pammachius, in fulfilment of her bequest, at her death distributed all her fortune to the poor, proclaiming by trumpet a great funeral feast in the Basilica of St. Peter, on the Vatican, to the destitute. After this he himself took the monastic habit, to the amusement of his fellow-senators. But, says Jerome, 'it was in reality the monk who could laugh at them.'

Little as the mother and daughter had seen in later years of each other, Paula was much moved by this bereavement.

After this came a gleam of joy to her old age in the birth, after many years of marriage, of the little Paula, daughter of her son Toxotius and Leta.

The young mother, looking forward with much rapidity of imagination to the baby's future, at once wrote to Jerome for directions as to her education.

Jerome's first thought, in his answer, amidst his joyous congratulations, is the probable conversion of the baby's maternal grandfather, the pagan pontiff Albinus. 'Albinus is already a candidate for the faith,' he writes. 'A crowd of sons and grandsons besiege him. I believe, on my part, that if Jupiter himself had such a family he would be converted to Jesus Christ.' Then he gives, with tender detail, the counsels as to education which Leta had asked for. But he adds, 'It will be difficult to bring up thy little daughter thus at Rome. Send her to Bethlehem; she will repose in the manger of Jesus. Eustochium wishes for her; trust the little one to her. Let this new Paula be cradled on the bosom of her grandmother. Send her to me; I will carry her on my shoulders, old man as I am. I will make myself a child with her; I will lisp to fit her speech; and, believe me, I shall be prouder of my employment than ever Aristotle was of his' (as tutor to Alexander).

The invitation was accepted. The little maiden was

indeed sent to Betlehem in a few years, though not till after the death of Paula the grandmother. And it was this child, the younger Paula, who at last closed the eyes of Jerome. Paula the grandmother did not long survive the birth of her little namesake. Her last illness was beginning. Eustochium watched her night and day, entrusting to no one else the tender last cares, sustaining the drooping head, warming the cold feet, feeding her, and making her bed. If the mother fell asleep for a little while, the daughter would go for a few minutes to the manger of the Saviour, so close at hand, with its tender associations of sacred motherhood, to carry on there her loving ministries by interceding prayers.

But the precious life slowly ebbed away. Knowing that her end was near, Paula began to repeat with great joy the verses of the psalms she knew so well. ' Lord, I have loved the habitation of Thy house, and the place where Thine honour dwelleth.' ' *How amiable are Thy tabernacles, O Lord God of hosts! My soul longeth, yea, fainteth, for the courts of the house of my God.*' '*Better to be a doorkeeper in the house of my God than to dwell in the tents of wickedness.*' When she had finished, she began to say these songs of the threshold over again. She did not answer when spoken to, until Jerome came and asked gently why she did not speak, and if she suffered. Then she replied in Greek, the language of her father and of her childhood, that she had no discomfort, but was 'beholding in a vision all quiet and tranquil things.' ' I feel already an infinite peace,' she said. She kept her finger on her lips, making constantly the sign of the Cross. And still she continued to murmur at intervals the words of that ancient song of pilgrimage until her voice grew fainter and fainter, and with the sigh of longing for His presence on her lips she entered it for ever.

' All Palestine may be said to have assisted at her funeral. A chorus of psalms and lamentations sounded forth in all languages—Hebrew, Greek, Latin. Hermits crept out of their caves, and monks came in throngs from their monasteries to bewail this generous friend, this great Roman lady, this devoted Christian. During her last days bishops had gathered around her from the neighbouring dioceses, and her coffin was borne on their heads into the Basilica of the Manger of our Lord.'

And there all the poor, the widowed and orphans lamented 'their foster-mother,' 'their mother,' and showed the gifts she had given and the garments she had made for them.

Eustochium never left her, kissing the cold lips, and at last, her passion of grief breaking through the usual calm of her disciplined life, throwing her arms around the unconscious form, and praying to be buried beside her.

Paula died at fifty-six. She had spent the last eighteen years of her life in Palestine.

Jerome, for the first time in his laborious life, lost his appetite for work. He could do no more. 'I have been able to do nothing, not even from the Scriptures, since the death of the holy and gracious Paula,' he wrote. 'Grief overwhelms me.' In her death he saw 'the death of her monasteries.'

Eustochium, with the instinct of true affection, drew him out of this stupor by inducing him to write a memoir of her mother for her.

In two sleepless nights he dictated it. 'He could not write himself. Each time that he took up the tablets his fingers stiffened, and the style fell from his hand. He would not dwell,' he said, 'on her great pedigree from the Scipios, the Gracchi, from Agamemnon, nor on her splendid opulence and her palace at Rome. She had preferred Bethlehem to Rome. Her praise was that she died poorer than the poorest she had succoured. At Rome, she had not been known beyond Rome. At Bethlehem 'all Christendom, Roman and barbarian, revered her.'

With the comprehension of that long and hallowed friendship he gave details of her life from childhood. It is from him we know her history.

'We weep not her loss; we thank God to have had her. Nay! we have her always; for all live by the Spirit of God;

and the elect who ascend to Him remain still always in the family of those whom He loves.'

Eustochium quietly took up the guidance of her mother's convents and hospice, and gently won Jerome to resume his work.

One day she entered his cave with the Book of Ruth in her hand, asking him to explain it to her, as to her and her mother of old. Paula had asked him to translate Isaiah and Esther, and to Paula and Eustochium together he dedicated all these translations, as a memorial of the double friendship, ' not separating,' he said, ' those whom he loved from those he had loved.'

Sixteen years of Jerome's life had still to flow, fourteen of Eustochium's. They were years of many storms within and without, the barbarians always penetrating farther and farther into the heart of the Empire, and at last accomplishing the capture of Rome, with the terrible sack and agony of three days and three nights. Marcella was still at Rome. Twenty years before, on the death of her mother, Albinia, Paula and Eustochium had written a touching letter entreating her to 'come out of Babylon' and take refuge with them at Bethlehem. 'When the breathless courier shall announce that Marcella has landed in Palestine, what joy in all the choirs of the convents, the battalions of virgins! When will the day dawn when together we shall weep at the Holy Sepulchre—weep with a sister, weep with a mother, our lips pressing together the wood of His Cross, our hearts rising together in Christ with the ascension of our Lord?' And Jerome had written, 'We offer thee a port from the storms of this life of perils. Dry bread, herbs our hands have watered, milk, our rustic dainties. In summer, freshness and shelter under the branches of a tree; in winter, a bed of dry leaves. In spring, when the flowers paint all the fields and the birds warble above us, the chant of the psalms around us is yet sweeter. In winter the forests give us fuel for fires by which to sleep or to keep vigil. Let Rome keep her tumults, her cruel gladiatorial games, her luxuries. Here we feel it good to find our joy in God.'.

But Marcella never came; she had her poor and her labours of love. She clung to the last to the Rome her friends had forsaken; to the last, when in her palace on the Aventine, where so many sacred tranquil hours had been passed in holy reading and converse and prayer, the barbarian soldiers ill-treated her household, and, irritated at not finding the wealth she had given to the poor, inflicted wounds and bruises on the aged mistress, of which she soon died, in a church near at hand, in the arms of her adopted daughter Principia. She indeed died, at her post, if in 'Babylon.'

Jerome could not get the misery of that story of outrage out of his thoughts night or day. 'The world is crumbling away,' he wrote; 'yet we will not bow our heads. All that has grown ripe must indeed grow old and die.—But Rome!'

Many of the fugitives took refuge at Bethlehem, some of them, unfortunately, bringing the manners and morals of 'Babylon' with them, and introducing grave disorders into Eustochium's convent.

There were also other storms around the old age of Jerome.

The controversy with Augustine ended in a stronger friendship, but the friendship of Rufinus and of Melania had turned to hatred. Augustine's adversaries, the Pelagians, had penetrated into Palestine. Pelagius himself came thither. The Bishop of Jerusalem, moved by him, turned against Jerome. And some of the peasants of the neighbourhood, incited by the monks, besieged and plundered the convents. Rome might be 'Babylon;' but certainly Bethlehem was no 'haven of rest.'

And, through all these storms and controversies, not only did Jerome's labours as a translator and commentator on Holy Scripture never relax, but the mere table of contents of his letters to all parts of the East and West—letters of social and practical advice, of spiritual counsel, of historical instruction, of literary criticism, many of them to distinguished women—indicates correspondence enough, apparently, to employ any one mind and heart. And in those vivid pages, those who know them say,[1] can be seen as in a mirror the manners and conditions of social life throughout the Empire, and traced step by step the decline of the Empire towards its ruin.

Many who had before been estranged from Jerome gathered around him in this hour of trial. From Bishop John of Jerusalem no redress was to be found; but after his death his successor took a juster view, and peace was restored.

His voice became so feeble he could scarcely be heard; at the best his flesh seemed scarcely to cover his bones, and now he grew too feeble to lift himself from his hard couch in his cave, his 'paradise' of holy work and sacred converse. He had to pull himself up by a rope fixed to the roof. In that posture he repeated many psalms, and gave his last instructions to his monks, until at last, on September 30, A.D. 420, the restless, ardent spirit passed away, his failing breath tenderly watched to the last by the young Melania, granddaughter of the impetuous Melania, who had been a friend of his youth, and by the young Paula, of the third generation of that great Roman house in which he had found his 'guardian angels in the desert.'

He was buried, as he wished, in a hollow of the rocks of Bethlehem, where his name can still be traced graven in the rock.

---

[1] Amédée Thierry, *Saint Jérôme*, the chief source of this biography.

St. Benedict[1]

OF MONTE CASSINO.

March 21.

(Born A.D. 480; died A.D. 543. Calendars: all. Sarum Ep. and Gosp.: Ecclus. xxxix. 5-9; St. Luke xi. 33-36.)

We enter with the two last of our Italian saints into a new world.

The great group of the three contemporary Latin Fathers belongs to the old Roman world, amidst the wreck of which they stood. Gregory the Great, the last of the four Latin Fathers, and St. Benedict, belong rather to the wild new shores slowly rising out of the northern deluge, on which they began to rebuild the past, rearing constructions which endured; St. Gregory intentionally, once more making the city whose dirge St. Augustine sang, the great central and centralising metropolis of the West;—St. Benedict, half unconsciously, organising the great monastic system, in which the Greek and Latin classics (which he valued little) and the learning of St. Jerome and St. Augustine, the ancient Sacred Scriptures, and the new Christian theology were to be kept above the waves.

That the continuity of ancient and modern history was not broken by the irruption of the barbarous hordes was, we know, greatly owing to these two great men preserving, in a Christian form, the substance of the earlier civilisation.

The whole attitude of the Church as regards the nations

---

[1] Dedications of churches: sixteen, unless any be dedicated to St. Benedict Bishop. Represented in art as a Benedictine monk, with devils; rolling in thorns; thorns near him; in a cave, food let down to him by a monk; a cup on a book; a cup breaking and spilling liquor; a cup with serpents on a book; a raven at his feet; or with a loaf in its bill; a stick in his hand, the raven on it; a sprinkler; a pitcher; a ball of fire; a book with the beginning of his rule, AVSCULTA, FILI, VERBA MAGISTRI.

changed between Jerome and Gregory, and even Benedict. Both stood in a world of fragments. But to the first three great Latin Fathers (Ambrose, Augustine, and Jerome), these fragments were broken pieces of a wreck. To Benedict and Gregory these broken pieces were rafts on which they came safe to land, and of which they made the scaffolding of a new civilisation.

Benedict indeed was like many of the greatest, in not knowing the full significance of what he did.[1] His aim was simply to flee from the corrupt and corrupting world and live for God.

Born about 480, fifty years after Jerome's death, at Noricum, in Nursia, his parents were people of consideration; his mother of the race of the 'seigneurs' of Nursia, his father of the old Roman house of the Anicii.

Sent to Rome at seven years old for his education, apparently under the care of his nurse Cyrilla, a devoted old servant of the family, the wickedness of the city repelled him, and at fourteen, 'with wise folly and holy ignorance,' St. Gregory, his biographer, says, he fled from the vices with which he felt unable to cope into the solitudes of the Sabine hills, to a wild gorge where the Anio falls from basin to basin, in cataracts which Nero had once ponded back into a lake, building near it a luxurious villa, called *Subiaco,* or the Villa 'below the Lake.'

The beauty and sublimity of the place were not the attraction to the boy, at least not consciously. He was simply a fugitive. What he sought was a refuge from an evil world, a citadel wherein he might keep under his lower self. He met a monk or hermit called Romanus (one of the solitaries moved by the story of Antony and the Thébaïd), who gave him a hair shirt and a goat-skin cloak. With these Benedict buried himself in a deep hollow of the rocks, with no view except upward towards the sky. His only food

---

[1] 'Les maîtres de la vie spirituelle ont toujours remarqué que l'homme qui commence une œuvre bénie de Dieu ne s'en rend pas compte. Dieu aime à bâtir sur le néant.'—Montalembert, *Moines de l'Occident.*

was a portion of Romanus' own scanty fare, thrown down to him at the end of a rope with a bell attached to it, to be rung when it was to be pulled up again. Into this natural oubliette he descended (about A.D. 494), and there he spent three years. But even thither the world followed him; even there he had to roll himself on the thorn-bushes till his flesh was all torn and bleeding, to tear away the memory of a beautiful Roman woman which haunted him in his solitude.

Seven centuries afterwards St. Francis of Assisi came to see this thicket of thorns and planted there two rose trees. Now, the thorns are gone, but the roses of St. Francis remain.[1]

The peasants at first took him for a wild beast, but soon learnt to know him, by his gracious words, as a teacher, and servant of God.

His solitude, with its perils and its rescue, did not last long. As always, around a heart which seemed to have found the Fountain of Life gathered multitudes of human hearts which had perhaps scarcely before known their thirst.

Some monks of a neighbouring convent, seeing his dawning fame, asked him to come and be their superior; but his austerity soon fatigued them, and they gave him a cup of poison, which, by making over it the sign of the Cross he is said to have shivered in pieces. He had to leave these treacherous brethren. But by degrees there gathered around him enough recluses to fill twelve monasteries with twelve monks in each. He thought this the right number. Among them were men of all ranks and characters. One was the son of the Lord of Subiaco, who was content to draw water from Nero's lake for his brethren. Another was a simple-hearted Goth, one of the invading northern hosts, ready to use his strong limbs for the rest, whose pickaxe having fallen into the water, St. Benedict is said to have made it float towards him by his prayers, and presented it to the owner with the words, 'Ecce labora, et noli contristari,' words typical of the great Benedictine rule, and the hope and joy

[1] Montalembert.

it brought, through labour, to the Goth's Gothic kindred throughout Europe.

One day as the young son of the Lord of Subiaco was carrying his heavy pitcher up the steep hill he stumbled with the weight and fell back into the lake. One of the brethren, St. Maur, at St. Benedict's request, is said by legend to have walked on the waves and saved the boy. Bossuet allegorises this story into a sign that obedience and faith can walk through all the uncertainties and storms of life as on solid ground.

But here, as everywhere, the bitterest enemy of the saints was the religious world. A 'wicked priest' of the neighbourhood harassed these young communities in every way, finally sending among them a troop of dissolute women to bewilder them by wild songs and dances.

St. Benedict resolved at last to depart, and with those of his disciples who chose to accompany him, he went farther along the range of the Apennines till he came to the Monte Cassino, then crowned by one of the few surviving shrines of paganism, a temple wherein the neighbouring peasants still worshipped Apollo. To these lingering adherents of a dead religion he made known the Living God, the Light of the world and Healer of men. They listened, cut down the sacred grove, and broke the statue of the sun-god in pieces.

> Quel monte, a cui Cassino è nella costa,
> Fu frequentato già in su la cima
> Dalla gente ingannata, e mal disposta.
> Ed io son quel, che su vi portai prima
> Lo nome di Colui, che 'n terra addusse
> La verità, che tanto ci sublima.
> 　　　　　　DANTE, *Paradiso*, xxii. 37.

And there, in the native country of Juvenal and Varro, arose the great Monastery of Monte Cassino, the mother house of the many thousands of the Benedictines.

It was a time of chaos in many ways, the 'old order changing, giving place to new;' chaos among nations, one northern horde rushing over another, and all against the crumbling Empire; chaos in the Church; wild reactions of paganism, Oriental or classical; wild excesses of disorder, wild excesses of austerity, as Benedict's life shows.

Benedict's convent and his rule, and most of all his hidden life with God, his 'living with himself,' as St. Gregory says, retiring from all the chaos of the world, the Church, the monasteries, to the inner truth of his own spirit, the sanctuary of the presence of God, attracted countless fragments of the flotsam and jetsam of this world of wreck; men of the noblest ancient families, repelled, like Benedict, by the decay and corruption of the Roman world; Goths struggling, in their simplicity, like bewildered children, through the splendours and the wickednesses so new to them, of this new world, at once so much *above* and so much *below* them, to the ideal of the Christianity which was the only life left in it. Oppressed peasants, weary men of that weary old world, Roman nobles, and Gothic kings, came to enquire of this Seer in his shrine among the mountains. And he had messages, different yet alike, for all.

Often also Benedict was a mediator between oppressor and oppressed. Once a fierce Gothic chief named Galla, after plundering the poor Italian peasants near Monte Cassino, had especially tortured one to make him yield up the little left him to live on. At last the poor man, driven to bay, declared he had nothing of his own, having given all to Benedict. Then Galla bound the peasant's arms behind him and rode up the steep of Monte Cassino, driving the plundered man before him.

They found the abbot sitting reading before the gate of his monastery. 'See,' said the peasant, 'here is the Father Benedict of whom I told thee.' 'Rise, rise,' roared the Goth from his saddle to Benedict, 'and restore what thou hast had from this peasant.' At these words Benedict, without moving or speaking a word, looked at the tyrant and at the poor bound peasant till the cords seemed to break of themselves, and the furious Goth, cowed by this majestic quiet and silent indignation, fell trembling from his horse at the feet of the abbot and entreated his prayers. Then they took him into the convent, and gave him some of their food. Afterwards Benedict spoke to him of his cruelty and injustice. The peasant left the monastery a free man; and the oppressor crept quietly away, rebuked and subdued.

Totila also, greatest of the successors of Theodoric, in 442, on his triumphal journey towards Naples to restore the Ostragothic kingdom, after a great victory over the Byzantine army at Faenza, desired to see this prophet of the mountains, revered alike by Roman and Goth. Wishing (as afterwards Charles of France with Joan of Arc) to test Benedict's prophetic insight, he sent one of his attendants before him in his own royal dress and escorted by his royal guard, to pretend to the abbot to be the king.

'Lay aside that dress,' said Benedict, as soon as he saw him; 'it is not thine.' The envoy returned to Totila, who then went himself up the mountain-side; and when he saw, afar off, the abbot seated at his convent gate, he threw himself prostrate on the ground and would not rise. Three times Benedict bade him arise, and finally came forward himself and lifted him up.

Then Benedict said to the king, 'You have done much evil; you are doing it still every day: it is time you should cease your injustices. You will enter Rome. You will cross the sea. You will reign nine years, and in the tenth you will die.'

The king, utterly subdued, entreated Benedict's prayers, and went quietly away. But it is said that the rebuke penetrated his heart and softened it, so that afterwards he treated his prisoners as his own soldiers, the conquered people as his own children, and severely punished every outrage wrought by his own followers.

Austere as Benedict was to himself, he was no promoter of self-torture for its own sake. Once he was told of a solitary in the neighbouring mountains who (like an Eastern fakir) lived in a narrow cavern, chained by one foot to the rock. He told him to break the chain, saying, 'If thou art a servant of God, be bound not by a fetter of iron, but by the chain of Christ.'

His 'living with himself' was indeed no isolation; it

was merely living in the true unseen reality ('the buried life').

Though not a priest he was a great preacher and missionary and apostle among the pagans still left in those neglected recesses of the mountains.

The sick as well as the sinful came to him, and many stories of miracles gathered around him.

From that shrine of his own consecrated heart, cleared from all films and mists of self and self-pleasing, he looked through the hearts of other men. One of his monks, son of a man in high office, relates of himself that one evening, when it came to him in his turn to hold the candelabrum at the abbot's table, he was thinking in his heart, 'Who, then, is this man, that I should stand before him candle in hand, like a slave?' when suddenly Benedict, as if he had heard his thoughts, commanded the candle to be taken from him and that he should retire to his cell; thus, said the rebuked monk, 'turning the candle of the Lord on the pride of my heart.'

His monastery was also a refuge for fugitives, and a house of mercy. With the gifts sent him by the rich he fed the poor and paid the debts of those who were ruined by the many invasions and wars of that tumultuous time. Once in a terrible famine which devastated Campania, in order to feed the starving people, he left his monasteries with only five loaves. 'Never fear,' he said, 'not enough to-day. To-morrow there will be too much.' And, accordingly, on the morrow came in 200 bushels of corn from an unknown benefactor.

So he lived for fourteen years at Monte Cassino, teaching and training his monks, instructing them on his preaching tours among the hills, labouring with them at masons' work or at tilling the slopes of the mountains.

Fourteen years he lived this life of beneficence at Monte Cassino. But his chief work was that of a Founder; and of this he was probably altogether unconscious. Even of this beloved monastery which he had founded he foresaw and predicted the ruin. It was in making practical rules for the daily life of his own monks that he was actually founding the great Benedictine Order.

He had seen and felt the disorder among the scattered cœnobites and hermits, gathered and kept together by various loose and shifting rules; and with the legislative faculty of his nation he determined to organise his own house with Roman stability. The first condition was to be *stability*. The consecration was to be for life. '*Ausculta, fili*,' he begins, 'fear not to be the son of a good father, that obedient *labour* may lead thee back to Him from Whom disobedience and luxury had estranged thee. Wherever thou art, *renouncing thine own will*, to fight under the true King, Jesus Christ, take in hand His glorious and valiant weapons of *obedience*.'

Obedience, labour, humility, the threefold cord of the Order. The postulant was to be tested by being kept four or five days outside the convent gate.

With meditation and prayer seven times a day was to be combined steady, regular work, manual or mental.

The government was monarchical and absolute, but the abbot was to consult the chapter, the council of the brethren. The obedience was to be absolute, without 'murmur,' *beyond* the limits of strength, trusting to God to give strength. The way heavenward was to be like Jacob's ladder, planted in humility, every step upward, a step of humility and discipline.

The Prayers of the Seven Hours were to be chanted together daily; vigils at night from two till dawn. The whole Psalter was thus to be sung through every week. And this was not to supersede mental prayer, which St. Benedict wished to be 'short and simple.'

Each monk was to renounce, and his relations for him, all individual property or inheritance. Whatever was given as his 'dower' was to be for the monastery, 'with a life-charge, if wished, to the donors.'

The monastery, in that world of confusion, was to be self-contained, was to contain its own garden, mill, bakehouse, workshops. The largest and most considerate hospitality was to be exercised, yet the solitude of the monks was to be strictly respected. The dress was to be the tunic and cowl for the choir, and for work the scapulary which was in fact the hooded shepherd's cloak of the mountains.[1]

The meals were to be simple but sufficient: one uncooked and one cooked dish; a weighed quantity of bread; a measured portion of wine; no flesh of four-footed beasts. Fasts frequent, but no excess of austerity, so as to injure health. Meals common, but mostly in silence.

It has been said that the rule is in substance evangelical and in form feudal, having throughout also a strong military stamp.

The Order founded on this rule has endured 1,300 years; its followers needing reform again and again, but the rule never.

Of the founder it is related that towards the close of his life a neighbouring seigneur whom he had converted, and with whom he was very intimate, found him one day weeping bitterly, as if struck with a mortal sadness. The nobleman asked why. The saint replied, 'All this monastery that I have built, all that I have prepared here for my brethren, has been delivered to the heathen by the judgment of God. Scarcely have I been able to obtain the favour of the lives of the brethren.'

And less than forty years afterwards the Lombards fulfilled his prediction in the destruction of his Abbey of Monte Cassino.

The monastery was destroyed, but the Order of which the monastery was the cradle has existed 1,300 years, creating oases in the wildernesses, preserving learning in the midst of the deluge of barbarism; with all its human

---

[1] Montalembert says the habit was originally of white wool; afterwards a woollen or coarse linen shirt was added, and the colour of the outer garment was changed to black. The cowl, the large cloak with sleeves worn in the choir, was always black. The scapulary consists of two strips of stuff joined at the head, with a hood, one strip hanging down before, the other behind. They wore shoes and stockings, and were clothed and *chaussés*, &c., at night. They wore also a girdle of copper.

(or unhuman) defects and failures keeping alight the torch of Christian truth in the midst of the darkest times.

Benedict was born only sixty years after Jerome died. But there is a great gulf between Jerome with his floods of eloquent speech and St. Benedict with the finger on the silent lips (as he is represented in art), withdrawn to the depths within, 'living with himself;' between the kind of monastic life Jerome lived, in close and sacred friendship with numbers of good women, Paula and Eustochium, and Paula of the third generation, and Benedict, only allowing himself to see his own holy and beloved sister Scholastica, who lived in a convent on the slopes of Monte Cassino, once a year.

But a lovely light of human affection shines on the close of Benedict's life. In that meeting once a year the sister used to go from her own gate to meet her brother on the mountain-side, when he would return with her to her convent. The place of their meeting is kept in memory to this day.

At the last meeting Scholastica's health was failing. They spent the whole day in sweet and holy converse. Towards evening, as they were at table eating together, she said to him, 'My brother, leave me not to-night, that we may speak of the joys of heaven till to-morrow morning.'

'What sayest thou, my sister?' he replied; 'at no price can I stay a night outside my monastery.'

On her brother's refusal Scholastica laid her head down on her clasped hands on the table and shed torrents of tears. The weather was calm and bright; but scarcely had she risen when thunder was heard and a violent storm burst on them. The rain, thunder, and lightning were such that neither Benedict nor any of his monks who accompanied him could leave the shelter of the roof that night.

Then he said to Scholastica, 'God pardon thee, my sister, but what hast thou done?'

'I have done well,' she said, 'I prayed to thee, and thou wouldst not listen. Then I prayed to God, and He is hearing me. Go forth now, if thou canst, to thy monastery.'

Then he resigned himself to remain, and they passed the rest of the night in spiritual converse.

His biographer St. Gregory's comment is as beautiful as the story he has told us. 'We are not to be astonished,' he says, 'if the will of the sister was granted by God rather than that of her brother, because of the two it was the sister who had loved most, and with God the more we love the more powerful we are.'

In the morning they parted, never to meet again in this life. Three days afterwards Benedict, being at the window of his cell, 'saw the soul of his sister entering heaven under the form of a dove.' Ravished with joy, his gratitude broke out in hymns to God. Then he went and had her body transported to Monte Cassino and laid in the sepulchre he had prepared for himself. He only survived her forty days. He announced his own death to many of his disciples. A violent fever having seized him on the sixth day of his illness, he had himself carried into the chapel consecrated to St. John Baptist. He had already had the tomb opened where his sister had been laid. There, leaning on the arms of his monks, he received the holy viaticum ; then placing himself on the edge of the open grave, and thus also at the foot of the altar, with his arms stretched towards heaven, he died standing, breathing out his soul with his last prayer. A soldier's death, leader and standard-bearer as he was of a great army which was for centuries to render the Church many services in her ceaseless Holy War.

St. Gregory the Great

OF ROME.

March 12.

(Born A.D. 540; died A.D. 604. Calendars: all. Sarum Ep. and Gosp.: Ecclus. xlvii. 8-11; St. Matt. xxiv. 42-47.)

'Great; and Saint.' Great in the world, whose greatness is ruling; Saint in the Church, whose greatness is serving. The Rome into which Gregory was born was divided by a great gulf from that in which St. Ambrose lived, in which St. Augustine taught rhetoric and St. Jerome directed the community of the Ecclesia Domestica, on the Aventine.

Two hundred and fifty temples, shrines on the Capitol, gladiatorial games in the Coliseum, afterwards that austere, yet beneficent Christian patrician community on the Aventine—all were gone. Africa had fallen a prey to Vandals and was moreover torn by schism. Spain was Arian; England swept bare by the Saxon invaders not only of her Christianity but of her Christians, driven into the mountains and caves of Wales and Cornwall; in Gaul the Catholic faith dishonoured by its professors, the fierce and barbarous successors of Clovis, Brunehild, and Frédégonde, with all the iniquity, impurity, and savage ferocity implied in the existence of such a court; in the East the Empire threatened by the Persians, and Italy itself sinking under war after war of invasion, Goth and Lombard contesting with the Byzantine Court the right to plunder and enslave her.

In few of the Lives of the Saints are legend and history so quaintly interwoven as in that of Gregory. He is at once a great legendary hero of the Middle Ages and a great historical Saint; half the story is like a hard Byzantine portrait, the other half is seen through the flickering firelight of mediæval fancy.

The son of a great Roman house, on one side connected with the Anician, his mother, his sisters, and his father were all canonised. The portraits of both his mother and father are still to be seen: the father with a long, grave, oval face, and considerable beard; the mother with a pleasant mouth, large blue eyes, retaining in age the curves and colour of youth. Gregory resembled them both. From his own description, when worn by illness, of the contrast between his then dried-up form and his former 'mass' (*molem*) it would seem he was of tall and large build. Always trained in earnest Christian life, his first thirty years were spent in diligent study of the classics, grammar, rhetoric, and all that then constituted a liberal education. At thirty he was made prætor of the city. His dress had the splendour of his rank and office, silken robes, purple stripes, and jewels. When his father died his mother retired into a convent, and Gregory sold a large portion of his patrimony to found and endow six monasteries in Sicily.

St. Benedict's monastery on Monte Cassino having been ruined by the Lombards, the monks were at this time in refuge at a house near the Lateran Gate, and Gregory was intimate with some of them. Before long, in his fortieth year, he himself embraced the monastic life; not so much turning away from his previous life in some fierce spiritual crisis as, in the endeavour to balance between secular and religious duties which he had found perplexing, at length dropping the lower and embracing what he believed the higher. The silken robes were exchanged for the black woollen Benedictine dress and hood; his family palace on the Cœlian Hill he turned into a monastery, building a hospice at its gates for the reception of pilgrims.

In this seclusion, though often interrupted by public claims, he remained till 490; a period of quiet to which he looked back as to a sunny haven from the stormy sea through which the rest of his life was cast.

Yet he earnestly insisted on the dangers of the contemplative life to many characters, lengthened the period of noviciate which was to test the vocation of the monks, and strongly enjoined on all the wisdom of trying the active, before the contemplative, side of life.

To this period of comparative seclusion belong some of the legends which embody the effect of his character as a Saint on subsequent ages. We will look a little at these, before entering on the part of his story which rather gives him the name of Great.

His charity was so abundant in Rome, then so wretched with famines, invasions, and inundations of the Tiber, 'tossed,' as he himself said, 'like an old rotten and shattered ship, letting in the waves on all sides,' that one day when a poor shipwrecked sailor appeared to ask alms at his hospice on the Cœlian, at the moment there was not anything to give. But the shipwrecked sailor came again and again, and at last Gregory remembered a silver basin in which his mother was wont to send him vegetable soup—the last remnant of the splendours of his father's table. Gregory at once gave it to the beggar. Afterwards, when he became Pope, it was his custom every evening to entertain at his own table twelve beggars. One evening he perceived that instead of twelve there were thirteen, and called his steward to ask how this was. The steward could only see twelve. Then Gregory himself addressed the additional guest whom only he could see. 'Who art thou?' he asked. 'Dost thou not remember the poor shipwrecked man to whom thou didst once give the silver vessel?' was the reply. 'My name is Wonderful, and through me God will refuse thee nothing.'

Another day, according to the story known to every English child, Gregory was walking through the Roman slave market, when his eye was arrested by a group of fair-haired boys. He was told they were 'Angli' and pagans, from the once Christian island of Britain. They were well named Angeli, he said, those fair strangers. 'Angels they were in countenance and should be coheirs with the angels in heaven.' Being further told they were natives of the province of Deira, 'De ira Dei,' he replied, 'by the mercy of God they shall be delivered.' And hearing that the king of the country was called 'Ella,' his final pun was, 'Alleluia, for alleluia shall yet be sung in that land.'

It was no shallow, transient sympathy which moved him thus. It is said he ransomed these boys and had them at once brought to live in his monastery to be taught. And then without delay he went to the Pope, demanding to be sent himself to bring the name of Christ to the land of these fair slaves. He obtained the mission he sought, and went three days' journey on his way to England, when the Roman people were warned of his departure. At once their old affection for their former prætor and constant benefactor revived. They rose tumultuously, surrounded the Pope as he went to St. Peter's, and cried to him, 'You have offended St. Peter. You have ruined Rome by letting Gregory go.' And Gregory was pursued and brought back. But the longing to serve this England of ours never died out of his heart amid all the toils and battles of his life. He wrote to one he had sent on a mission to Paris not to forget the needs of England in his collections of money. And to Gregory we owe the mission of Augustin of Canterbury.

The next story gives a glimpse into another region of his manifold gifts and works.

It was much on his mind to enrich the liturgy in words and music. Once he had been thinking much of the attractions of profane music and debating in his mind how, like the harp of David, it could be consecrated to God. When he fell asleep, his thoughts passed into his dreams. He had a vision of the Church as of a queen gorgeously apparelled, writing her songs, and at the same time gathering her children under the folds of the mantle. And on this mantle he saw written, in musical notation, many chants and symphonies. He prayed God that he might remember them when he woke; and it came to pass that when he awoke, a dove appeared and dictated the music which became the chant of the Church; a poetical version of the birth of the Gregorians. The singing school was shown for three centuries, near the Lateran, where Gregory himself, when too feeble to stand, would nevertheless from his couch, lead the choir-boys as their precentor, armed with a whip.

The last legends to be given here are ascribed to the few days at the close of his monastic retirement, when he was struggling hard to escape the Pontificate.

During the interval between his election and the imperial confirmation, Rome was suffering from one of the frequent pestilences which devastated the world in those unhappy times. By Gregory's influence all the monks and nuns, and also the matrons and laymen, made processions, with Litanies, for three days through the streets of the city. And while they thus passed before him, looking up to the mausoleum of Hadrian, he saw the vision of an angel on the summit, sheathing his sword, on what has since been called the Castle of Saint Angelo, and crowned with the image of the angel of Gregory's vision.

The two other best-known legendary stories of Gregory, with their contrasts of severity and pity, fill up the features of his mediæval portrait.

A monk of his convent who had much medical skill, and had assisted Gregory himself by his knowledge and kindness, was found, on his deathbed, to have concealed about him three gold pieces, contrary to his monastic vow of renunciation of all individual property.

Such a disloyalty could not, the Abbot thought, be passed by without a punishment which should be a terrific warning to the community. The body of the poor monk who had so feebly clutched at a fragment of all he had voluntarily renounced was cast on the dunghill, with its three pieces of gold; and every member of the community, old and young, instead of chanting the Benedictus at the funeral, was commanded to repeat the awful Apostolic sentence, '*Thy money perish with thee.*'

But this public sentence once executed, Gregory's heart turned tenderly back to his strayed sheep. The touch of the kind hands which had ministered to his own many ailments before they clutched the forbidden gold, probably came back to his heart. Masses and prayers were offered daily for the poor disobedient monk for thirty days, and at the end of these days he appeared in a dream to his brother and told him his soul had been in anguish but now was relieved.

The other legend is the well-known story represented in countless pictures, and beheld by Dante engraven on the walls of Purgatory. The story is variously told. One version is that the Emperor Trajan, going forth to war, was stopped by a widow who threw herself before him and grasped his horse's bridle, entreating vengeance on the murderers of her only son. The Emperor promised to do her justice on his return from the war. But she persisted in imploring immediate redress ; and at length the Emperor alighted and listened to her story, gave her a rich dowry, and said his own son should be to her as the son she had lost. One day as Gregory was meditating on this act of the Emperor, he was cut to the heart, and wept bitterly that such a generous and great soul should be lost. And turning into a church he prayed most fervently that Trajan might be delivered. That night in a vision it was revealed to him that his prayer was granted, but that he himself must suffer for the rescued emperor; either two days in the fires of purgatory, or in a sick and ailing body all the rest of his life. Gregory chose the latter and was a sufferer to the end.

This combination of severity and tenderness, of generosity and self-denial, of width of grasp and fidelity to detail, which made the great Bishop think any trouble worth while to teach children to sing the praises of God in tune, and embraced the widest far off possibilities of conquest for the kingdom of God, was the high ideal which the history of Gregory stamped on the heart of the Middle Ages. It is like coming from an oratory illuminated by sunset into ordinary daylight to turn from these legends to the history.[1]

[1] There is another most significant legend connected with Gregory. A monk who had given up all he had, and had gone through great austerities, once prayed to know what his reward should be. It was revealed to him : 'As great as that of Pope Gregory of Rome.' He was much disappointed. Was Gregory, with all his pomp and praise and wealth on earth, to have as rich a reward as one who had renounced all this? Then it was shown him that Gregory had not valued all his treasures and honours, as much as he himself valued his cat, which was fond of him ; and that it was not possessing treasures but coveting them which was sin.

And yet the history has in it the deepest sources of all the poetry of the legend. In this as in all other true Christian lives, when we see the whole illumined in the light of God, we shall find the simple facts more beautiful than anything ever dreamed of them.

Gregory had to relinquish the calm of his beloved monastery for the labours of the see of Rome. But even whilst still only Abbot of his house on the Cœlian, he had been sent on a diplomatic mission to Constantinople which had given him a close acquaintance with the intrigues of the court, and had won for him the lifelong friendship of the holy bishop Leander of Seville, through whose influence Spain was won back from Arianism to the Catholic faith.

For thirteen years after this (590-604) Gregory lived at Rome a life of ceaseless warfare and labour, with a body always suffering. Italy was torn between the Lombards and the Byzantine empire, represented by the Exarch of Ravenna. Gregory's aims throughout were simply to save the people of Italy from destruction, from Lombard invasion and Byzantine taxation; and to advance the kingdom of Christ among the Lombards and the Italian people; although, beyond this, his missionary zeal for Gaul, Britain, Africa, and Spain never cooled.

Primarily he was Protector of Italy. If there is not the same outspoken frankness in his intercourse with the emperors as was the case with Ambrose, it must be remembered that Ambrose's relations with them were far more personal. Ambrose sought to save emperor and people. Gregory was thinking simply of saving the people from exactions and plunder. With this object he wrote faithful remonstrances on the exactions of his officials to the Emperor Maurice. With this object also he wrote letters (one especially which those who most honour him most deplore) of rhetorical congratulation to Phocas, the murderer of Maurice, and to the wicked Queen Brunehault.

Rome itself he succeeded in saving from another siege and sack. The barbarians, at his entreaty, spared the city, but from that date began the ruin of that fair and fertile country around its gates, which has made the 'Campagna' for centuries a vast and desolate waste, girdling the city with a zone of poisonous malaria.

The devastation and misery which transformed that pleasant land into a poisonous waste may interpret Gregory's sermons. They were no mere pulpit rhetoric. 'Everywhere we see sorrows; everywhere we hear groans. Cities are destroyed, castles ruined, fields laid waste, the land reduced to solitude. In the country is no inhabitant; scarcely any remain in the cities; yet even these small remnants become daily and incessantly smaller. If we love such a world as this, we are in love not with joys but with wounds. Where is she who seemed the mistress of the world? What is Rome now? The senate is no more. Her people perish, her buildings are destroyed. Let us, then, despise this all but extinct world.'

But with him this was no feeble wail. The end of the world he felt sure was at hand. This storm might be the last. But if it were the last, he was the pilot, and would do his best to bring his ship through.

He was not only Protector of Italy but virtually still Prætor of Rome, as well as bishop, and administrator of the lands and revenues of the Church. The whole of Rome was systematically divided into districts, committed to the charge of almoners, whose work was carefully inspected. Yet Gregory felt the whole burden of the care of the poor so personally laid on him that, when once a poor beggar was found starved to death, he is said to have abstained from saying Mass for seven days, as if he were a criminal under sentence of suspension.

As administrator of the lands and revenues of the Church he kept minute accounts, preserved for centuries, bearing witness to his accuracy and fidelity. He gave most careful and considerate directions to the managers of the Church estates not to exact too much of the tenants, but to weigh their difficulties, from war or bad seasons.

He wrote to a steward of ecclesiastical lands in Sicily to restore any sums which had been unduly or harshly exacted from the tenants, and to grant them leases with fixed rents, 'for the coffers of the Church are not to be soiled by unjust gains.'

Like so many of the truest benefactors and reformers, he wrought his great work—little knowing how great it was—by simply carrying out faithfully his daily work; because he was guided in the work of the day, not by conventional rules, but by eternal principles. While he was inspired by world-wide hopes, he was also reforming the abuses and relieving the distress close at hand, and in doing so he was creating unconsciously a code for the new world on the threshold of which he stood.

It took long to work that new world up to the ideal he lived out; for instance, as to the two great wrongs of slavery and persecution. His tolerance was, indeed, like that of Ambrose, no carelessness of uncertainty and indifference, but the patience of hope and love. Especially he showed it towards the Jews, on whom Christians were already beginning to exercise a retaliation certainly not learned at the Cross.

Gregory strictly forbade the bishops of Arles and Marseilles to baptise them by force; and he insisted on the restoration to them of some of their synagogues, which had been violently wrested from them and turned into Christian churches, at Terracina, Palermo, and Cagliari.

As to slavery, in setting free two of the slaves on his own property he signed the decree of universal emancipation,[1] founding that emancipation on the natural rights of man, and on the Incarnation of Christ.

'Since,' he says in the preamble of the Act of emancipation, '*the Redeemer and Creator of the world has willed to incarnate Himself in humanity, to break by the gift of freedom the chain of our bondage, it is to act well and fairly to restore their original freedom to men whom nature made free, but whom the law of nations has bowed under the yoke of slavery.* Wherefore we make you, Montanus and Thomas, servants of the Holy Roman Church, which we also serve by the help of God, from this day freemen and Roman citizens.'

In the midst of all his public work he found time for letters of intimate friendship and spiritual counsel. His

[1] Montalembert.

letters to Bishop Leander of Seville still glow with heart-warming words.

'Your countenance is engraven on my heart. I send you my books. Read them; and weep for my sins; since I know so well what to do, yet do so ill. My letter is very short; you will judge from this how the work and the storms of my Church occupy me, since I can write so little to the one I love best in the world.' And again, 'Your letter is indeed written with the heart; no one kindles this sacred flame in others without its first burning in his own heart.'

To a lady of the Byzantine Court, who wrote to him that she would give him no peace until he told her he had received a special revelation that her sins were forgiven, he replied that he was unworthy to receive a special revelation.

'I know,' he said, 'that you fervently love the Almighty God, and I confide in His mercy that those words from the lips of truth are spoken to you also, " Her sins which are many, are forgiven, for she loved much."'

And through all, he was not only the great bishop, but the great preacher of Rome, though he preached sometimes with a voice faint with illness, and one great course of his sermons he gave during the siege of Rome by the Lombards. He was also the reviser of the Liturgy, the reformer of Church music, the author of books which were the devotional and practical guides of Christendom for centuries. His 'Regula Pastoralis, on The Life of the Pastor,' was the text-book of the Reforming Church Council in Charlemagne's time, and was translated by our own king Alfred. But he thought little of his own books, recommending an Egyptian bishop who wrote to ask for a copy of one, to learn rather of his great fellow countryman, Augustine.

While believing in revelations through dreams, he constantly directs all for guidance to the Holy Scriptures. 'That best alms of the bread of life,' he said, ' we can all give to each other.' 'God does not,' he said, 'answer individual needs by special voices; but He has so arranged His Word as to answer all questions thereby. A general answer is given there to us all about that which each in particular suffers. "*His grace is sufficient for thee*" was said to the Apostle Paul in his particular infirmity, in order that it need *not* be repeated to each one of us. The Scriptures are constructed so as to mould the life of later times by the example of the earlier.'

Again, he believed in the continuance of external miracles. But he placed the interior miracles, which he said all could perform by God's grace, high above these. 'Why, O Paul, do you restore the sick unbeliever (the father of Publius) by your prayers, and for so great a fellow-labourer as Timothy only say this, "*Drink no longer water but a little wine for thine often infirmities*"? Timothy needed no such miracle, because he had already the inner life complete. These visible miracles glitter as the signs of holiness, but spiritual miracles are the essence of holiness itself.' 'The proof of holiness is not working miracles, but loving all as we love ourselves.'

And so ruling, and so serving, with the wide outlook, the firm grasp, and the tender, accurate touch, he left the Rome which he ruled and rescued, once more a great centre for the new world; he left Christendom the one organised and organising power in a tumultuous chaos; and all this work was done in a weak and suffering body, and in fifty-five years.

At last, his originally powerful frame, early injured by the excess of his early fastings, and worn out by the ceaseless work of years, was giving way. In many of his intimate letters, a cry of pain bursts from that brave heart. 'For two years I have been confined to my bed,' he writes to the Patriarch of Alexandria, 'by such suffering from gout that I can only keep up for three hours to celebrate mass at the great festivals. These maladies will neither quit me nor kill me.'

Again: 'My body is dried up as if already in the coffin. Death is the only remedy for me.'

At length the remedy came, and on March 12, 604, he died.

That keen and watchful eye and firm hand were no more at the helm; but Christendom little knew what storm was gathering on the Eastern horizon. Already while

Gregory was dying in Rome, in Arabia Mahomet was beginning to have his visions, and to see his destiny. After Gregory's death, the destructive flood of Mahomedanism swept over the Thebaid of Antony, the churches of Chrysostom, and Augustine, of Jerusalem, and Antioch. But, though the great human steersman was gone from the helm at Rome, the ship he had helped to save and to pilot held her own.

He has been accused of destroying relics of Greek and Roman art; some reproach him with scorn of learning and culture. But he disregarded the past, only as a mere past; his gaze was on the present and towards the future. What of the old could be carried over into the new, he prized. He writes: 'The demons know well that the knowledge of profane letters helps us to know the sacred. In dissuading us from learning them, they do as the Philistines did when they forbad the Israelites to fashion swords and spears, and obliged them to come to them to sharpen their ploughs and harrows.'

In his own person he carried on the past into the future, bearing on the order and learning of the old Rome into the new Rome he helped so much to found.

Was all his work good? What human work is? Will it all endure? What human work can?

Poet, preacher, peacemaker, prince, priest, judge, father of the poor, reformer of abuses, defender of the oppressed—was all his work, man of letters, literary, or statesman of the highest type? Was it not singularly like the work of the great Roman race to which he belonged, of which he was one of the last? Not on the level of the fountains, but on the level of the aqueducts. In Judea and Greece we look for the perennial springs. But Rome, that great builder of aqueducts, with her solid architecture carries the waters of the eternal fountains across the perilous wastes of the Middle Ages to our very doors. And St. Gregory the Great was surely one of the great aqueduct-builders.[1]

---

[1] Dedications of churches: Twenty-five, and one, with St. Mary. Represented in art as a pope, with double or triple crown and book, a dove at his ear, an eagle before him chained to a rock, Christ appearing to him as he says Mass, Christ and the Blessed Virgin appearing to him.

CHAPTER II.

THE SAINTS OF FRANCE.

St. Hilary of Poictiers.
Jan. 13.

(Chosen Bishop of Poictiers A.D. 353; died 368. Calendars: all except Aberdeen. Sarum Ep. and Gosp.: Ecclus. li. 9-12; St. Matt. xiii. 44-52.)

In turning to the cluster of the seven Saints of France (besides the martyrs) who are commemorated in our Calendar, we go back nearly three centuries. With St. Hilary of Poictiers, we touch once more on the Eastern Church, its theology and its controversies. St. Augustine calls Hilary 'the illustrious Doctor of the Church.' St. Jerome says he was 'the trumpet of the Latins against the Arians.'

The incidents of his life known to us are few. As usual with the saints, the date of his festival is his birthday to the life above. He died in 368, five years before the great Athanasius, at Poictiers, where probably he was born.

And in our own days, Dorner in his History of the Doctrine of the Person of Christ[1] speaks of him as the most difficult to understand, but also the most original and deep-thinking of the Doctors of the Church, and of his Christology as the most interesting of the early Christian Ages.

It seems probable that his parents were pagans, yet from his own account he evidently early breathed in a Christian atmosphere. He was of an ancient and illustrious house, and had, like Ambrose and Augustine, studied

[1] *Entwicklungeschichte der Lehre von der Person Christi* von Dr. T. A. Dorner.

rhetoric and philosophy. His life from the beginning was honourable and pure.

He relates his conversion thus :—

'I considered that the most delightful condition, according to the senses, is repose with abundance. But this we have in common with the beasts. Thus I comprehended that the happiness of man might be higher, and I placed it in the practice of virtue, and the knowledge of truth; and this present life being but a series of miseries, it seemed to me we have received it for the exercise of patience, moderation, and gentleness, and that God, the All-good, would not have given us life merely to render us miserable in taking it away. My soul, therefore, longed with ardour to know this God, author of all good, for I saw already the absurdity of all that the pagans taught concerning the Divinity, dividing it into different parts of one or the other sex, attributing it to animals, statues, and other inanimate objects. I recognised that there could be but one God, eternal, almighty, unchanging. Full of these thoughts, I read with admiration these words of Moses, "*I am that I am*," and in Isaiah, "*The heaven is my throne and the earth is my footstool*;" and again, "*He holds the heavens in His hands.*" The first figure shows that all is subject to God; the second, that He is above all. I saw that He is the source of all beauty, and is Himself the Infinite beauty. In a word, I comprehended that I must believe Him incomprehensible. I carried my desires further, and wished that these good feelings I had towards God and a good life might have an eternal reward. This seemed to me just. Yet the weakness of my body and even of my soul gave me fear. But then it was that the writings of the Evangelists and Apostles made me find more than I had dared to hope; especially the beginning of the Gospel of S. John, in which I learned that God had a Son eternal and consubstantial with His Father, that this Son, the Word of God, had become flesh that man might become a son of God.'[1]

Whether his family were pagan or not, it is evident that

[1] Hilary, Lib. i. *de Trinitate*, quoted by *Les Petits Bollandistes*.

Christianity was in the air he breathed.[1] Its moral ideal of patience and gentleness is there; the existence of the God who is all good is there, of One not to be sought as if afar off, but simply recognised and embraced as ever near us all; the Holy Scriptures are there, not as a foreign literature but as an easily accessible and familiar source of knowledge, from Moses to St. John.

Two hundred years of Christian life and death, from Blandina to the martyrs of Lyons and France onwards, had evidently penetrated the world into which Hilary was born with the Christian faith, though his family traditions may have continued pagan.

His especial attraction to the theology of St. John also marks the direction of the current of his Christian life and thought from beginning to end.

His heart, his life, his theology, were all centred in the Incarnate Son of God.

Eastern and Western Christendom were then full of the great Arian controversy, and to Hilary Arianism must have meant a reaction of the polytheism he had abandoned.

'The Unity of the Father and the Son, which Athanasius maintained against these (Arian) tendencies, is still needed as the basis of sound representation of the Divine acts. It (the Arian controversy) is a standing witness that in Scripture and theology no less than in philosophy and conscience, there is a marked repugnance to the fancied oppositions between the justice of the Father and the mercy of the Son, which run through the popular systems of the Redemption adopted since the Reformation. Amongst the various figures which Athanasius uses to express his view, one is that of 'Satisfaction.' But this is introduced incidentally and in entire subordination to the primary truth, that the Redemption flowed from the indivisible love of the Father and Son alike, and that its object was the restoration of man to union with God.'[2]

---

[1] 'Christianity counted its converts by thousands, its unconscious disciples in millions.' Dean Merivale, quoted in St. Hilary &c., by Dr. Cazenove, S.P.C.K.

[2] Dean Stanley, *Eastern Church*, 248.

Hilary was married and had one daughter, Abra. A few years after his conversion, when he was still a layman, on the death of the Bishop of Poictiers, the impulse of the Christian people summoned him, like Ambrose and Cyprian, to the episcopate. His humility, which made him shrink from the office, only confirmed them in their choice.

His piety and ability as a bishop, his 'arrowy' 'Rhone of eloquence'[1] as a preacher and commentator, drew the attention of Christian Gaul to him, and made him an object of dread and persecution to the Arians, who had on their side the power of the young Arian Emperor Constantius to confirm their tenets. Julian (afterwards the Apostate) was then the Cæsar ruling in Gaul, and by the command of Constantius Hilary was banished to Phrygia.

In vain he wrote letters of remonstrance to the Emperor, in which were those golden words of toleration. 'God is Lord of all. He has no need of an unwilling allegiance. He seeks no compulsory confession of faith. It is for our own sakes more than for His that we are to worship Him.'

The variety of the places of exile within the Empire gives an idea of its extent. Athanasius had scarcely returned to Alexandria from his exile in Treves, when Hilary was banished from Poictiers to the remote province of Phrygia, that Phrygia which had sent forth its Christian martyrs two centuries before to die gloriously for the faith at Lyons.

In the east Hilary found these original sources from which the Faith had flowed forth to the West divided by various heresies; and he proved such a formidable opponent to these, that his Asiatic adversaries persuaded the Emperor to restore him to his native land.

During his exile he wrote a Commentary on the Psalms, and a letter to his young daughter Abra, entreating her (although leaving her free) to refuse an offer of marriage, and to consecrate her life to God.

His child obeyed his wishes, and died soon afterwards, quite young; but not till she and her mother had welcomed him home.

[1] St. Jerome, quoted by *Les Petits Bollandistes.*

He rejoiced at her going before him into heaven, instead of being left behind in this stormy world. She died in her father's house, and he was with her.

Hilary's return to Gaul was a triumph. On his way he was met by St. Martin of Tours, then a young soldier just won to Christianity, to whom he recommended as his first duty, before undertaking missions among the pagans in Gaul, to go back to his home in Pannonia and convert his own mother.

After his restoration to his own diocese he made a visit to Toulouse and endeavoured to effect the reconciliation of Auxentius, Ambrose's Arian predecessor, with the Church. In this, however, he did not succeed. He effected much in the restoration of many bishops in Gaul. And after two years of repose at Poictiers he died there, among his own people, on January 13, 368.

A suggestion of his as to the way to read the Holy Scriptures may be given as a golden motto from his life to ours: '*He is the best reader who looks for the meaning in the words themselves rather than imports his own meaning into them, and therefore brings away from the reading more light than he brought into it.*'

Some of his hymns remain with us, of which one, *Lucis largitor splendide*, was sent by him to his daughter Abra with the letter from Asia. Also in his comparative leisure during his exile in the East he composed a treatise *De Trinitate*, of which Möhler and Dorner speak with enthusiasm. It is said to have had much influence at the time. It is, of course, impossible here to enter into his metaphysical elaboration of the Christian faith. But with all his subtlety of thought, his theology was deep-rooted in the heart. Dorner says that in his doctrine of the Incarnation he dwells much on the *capacity of humanity* for such a union, and then on the loving condescension of the Son.[1] The *necessity of death*, he thought, did not exist in our Lord's own physical or spiritual nature, but, *outside* His perfect nature, in *us*, to

---

[1] Dorner, *Entwicklungeschichte der Lehre von der Person Christi*, i. 1052.

whom He would and must be made like, if He would redeem us. If He could not have suffered it would have been a limitation to His love. Therefore, by a free act of love He gave Himself up to suffering and to death. His death was truly an *act*. Not only was His suffering voluntary; it was His joy; for the Head loves the members. This delight in suffering love also continues in His members. In them also pain, accepted for God's glory or for the sake of the brethren, is scarcely felt, but is forgotten in the fulness of love.'[1]

[1] Dedications of churches: three. Represented in art on an island among serpents, with three books, or a triangle, pen, staff, or trumpet, with a child sometimes in a cradle at his feet.

St. Martin

OF TOURS.

November 11, and July 4..

(Born, A.D. 317 ; died, A.D. 401. Calendars: all. Nov. 11. Sarum Ep. and Gosp. : Ecclus. xliv. 17, 20, 21-23 ; xlv. 6, 7, 15, 16 ; St. Matt. xxv. 14-23.)

(Translation of St. Martin. July 4. Calendars : all, except Roman and Monastic. Sarum Ep. and Gosp. : Ecclus. xliv. 17, 20, 21-23 ; xlv. 6, 7, 15, 16 ; St. Luke xii. 32-34.)

A greater contrast as to the way in which we learn what we know of any two saints can scarcely be than between St. Hilary of Poictiers and his disciple St. Martin of Tours.

St. Hilary lives to us in his own writings, and legend has scarcely touched him. He stands at the edge of the daylight of the old classical world, so fast to fade away. Of St. Martin we have no writings and few spoken words ; and every incident recorded of him is so touched with the dreamy twilight of the new mediæval world, on the threshold of which he stands, that the whole reads like a series of parables.

While the name of Hilary, with all his thoughtfulness, and his activity, is scarcely known except to students of Church history, the name of Martin has been borne upward on the heart of the people in every country of western Christendom, only less popular than that of St. Nicholas, because his fame extends only through the West.

The first English Church at Canterbury, after the mission of Augustine, was dedicated in Martin's name ; in our common speech, it lives on in Martinmas, and 'St. Martin's summer.' And through his name lives ever a lovely Christian ideal of a 'sweet serious unfailing serenity ; a heart full of piety towards God and pity for man ;' a prompt, observant, generous kindliness for the destitute ; a humility, not of a sad countenance, downcast and self-conscious, but childlike, loving, grateful, indifferent to self; no easy, smooth tolerance of falsehood, but a yearning to save the sinner; a true, tender protectiveness, a large patience of hope; and all this rooted, as in their deepest soil, and steeped, as in their constant element, in the love and following of Him Who was subject to death, even the death of the Cross.

He was born at Sabaria in Pannonia. His parents were pagan, his father a soldier, apparently of the old Roman soldier type. He received what learning he had (and it seems not to have been much) at Pavia. From what influence we know not, the name of Christ had touched him as a child. At ten years old he fled to a desert to become a catechumen, and like St. Catherine of Siena, and so many besides, moved by the life of St. Anthony and the Fathers of the Desert, he desired to become a monk. But at fifteen he was, at his father's desire, enrolled in the army. Once a soldier, he seems to have been as good a soldier as he could.

At eighteen the movements of the Roman army led him to Amiens. And to Amiens belongs the first story which makes his life like one of the episodes of the Pilgrim's Progress of the Middle Ages.

The young soldier was riding out of the Roman gate on the hill-side swept by the east wind, one bitter winter day, wrapped in his soldier's cloak, along the great Roman road which joined Lyons to Boulogne, when he met a poor ragged man. Martin at once took his sword and cut his cloak in two, and gave half to the beggar. 'The bystanders jeered or admired, according to their turn of mind,' and he went on.[1] In the night he had a dream and saw our Lord among His angels clothed in the half-cloak he had put around the poor man. And the Lord said to His angels, 'Know ye who has thus arrayed Me? My servant Martin, though yet unbaptised, has done this.'

And after this vision Martin went at once and was baptised.

He did not hurry out of his place. Fourteen years

[1] Newman, *Historical Sketches*.

longer he remained quietly in his post as a soldier. But at last, when he was forty years old, the longing to devote himself to more direct service of his Lord overmastered him, and he requested to be allowed to leave the army. Julian the Apostate, the legend says, was then Emperor, and he said scornfully that Martin desired to quit the ranks in order to escape an impending battle. But Martin said: 'Place me naked and unarmed in front of the battle; then shall ye see that armed with the cross alone I will not fear to encounter the enemy.' The Emperor took him at his word, and kept him under guard that night lest he should escape. But early the next morning the barbarous foes sent an envoy to entreat peace; and so Martin's faith brought victory in the most Christian way, by making peace.

Freed from military service, he went to seek guidance for his future life from St. Hilary of Poictiers, who sent him back at once to his own people and his father's house in Hungary, to do what he could for them. Martin succeeded in winning his mother to the Faith. On his way to Pannonia across the passes of the Alps, he fell among thieves. One of the bandits raised an axe and aimed a blow at his head, but another of the company intercepted the blow. However, Martin's hands were bound behind him, and he was given in custody to one of the band. This man took him aside and began to ask him who he was. He gave the old answer of Perpetua and the martyrs of old, '*I am a Christian.*' The bandit then enquired if he felt afraid. He answered without hesitation that he never felt so much at ease, being confident that the Lord's mercy would be especially with him in temptation. Rather, he felt sorry for him, his captor, who, living by robbery, was unworthy of the mercy of Christ. Entering then on the subject of the Gospel, he preached the Word of God to him. To be brief, the robber believed, thenceforth attended on him, and set him safely on his way, begging his prayers. 'This man afterwards was seen in the profession of religion, so that the above narrative is given as he himself was heard to state it.'

Illyricum was then almost wholly Arian, and on his

confessing the Catholic doctrine in one of the cities there, Martin was seized, beaten with rods, and driven from the city.

From Illyricum he went to Milan, where he lived some years in solitude, till he was driven thence by the Arian bishop Auxentius. He spent also some months in the little island of Gallina off the coast of the Riviera, living, like the hermits of Thebaid, with one companion hermit, on roots and herbs.

From thence he returned to Hilary, at Poictiers, and there founded the monastery of Lugojé, the first in France.

Four years after Hilary's death the Christians of Tours, sixty miles from Poictiers, sought Martin out to be their bishop; although, as his biographer tells us, some opposed, 'alleging that he was a contemptible person, unworthy of the episcopate, despicable in countenance, mean in dress, uncouth in his hair.'

As bishop of Tours he still kept to the monastic rules and to his simple, austere life, though with a fulness of authority and a graciousness such as corresponded to the dignity of a bishop. Unable to bear the interruptions of visitors in his cell near the church, he made himself a monastery about two miles out of the city; and so secret and retired was the place that he did not miss his beloved desert. On one side it was bounded by the high and precipitous rocks of a mountain; on the other, the little hovel in which he lived was shut in by the river Loire, which makes there a gentle bend. There was but one way into it, and that was narrow. His own cell was of wood. Many of the brethren made themselves cells of the same kind, but most of them hollowed out the stone of the mountain which was above them. No one had aught he called his own; all things were thrown into a common stock. Clad in camel's hair, not touching wine except when compelled by bodily weakness, eating their meals together, otherwise scarcely leaving their cells, except for prayer; the younger occupied themselves in transcribing manuscripts, the older giving themselves up to prayer. There were eighty scholars under training after the pattern of their saintly master, many of them of noble birth. And among these what city or church did not count priests? Many became bishops.'[1]

Once a rich man, who had received benefit from his prayers sent Martin a hundred pieces of silver, which he accepted and spent in redeeming some of the many captives made in the wars of that stormy time.

Yet his duties to his flock in the city, and to the flocks of God in the remote places of his diocese, were never neglected. One day when preparing to celebrate Mass in the Cathedral, he saw a wretched naked beggar, as before in his youth, at the gate of Amiens. He told one of his deacons to clothe the man; but the deacon was too slow for the saint, whose heart was not at all chilled, since in his early days he had cut his mantle with his sword. The Bishop, therefore, with his old love and impetuosity, took off his sacerdotal habit and threw it himself around the beggar, and then, not waiting for other garments, in the very irregular vestments remaining to him he raised the sacred chalice; and 'on his bare arms were seen chains of gold and silver hung there by the blessed angels.'

To this period also seems to belong one of the many legends of his encounters with the devil.

The devil, says the legend, envious of his virtues and especially hating his great charity, one day reproached him mockingly that he so quickly forgave the penitent. But St. Martin answered him sorrowfully: 'O, most miserable that thou art, if thou also wouldst cease to persecute and seduce wretched men; if thou also couldst repent, thou also shouldst find mercy and forgiveness through Jesus Christ.'

With his disciples from the monastery, Martin made the missionary tours throughout Burgundy and around Autun and Chartres which have won him the title of the 'Apostle of Gaul.' The cities were Christian, and pagan sacrifices were forbidden by law; but temples, altars, images and groves, remnants of the various strata of heathenism, Celtic and Roman, and Gothic, lingered in all the country districts,

[1] *Life of St. Marti* by Sulpicius Severus, quoted by Cardinal Newman.

with their ignorant worshippers, among the little-changing peasant stock of all ages. Among these Martin went with his disciples, young and old, and told them of the Crucified Master, the benignant Saviour, to whom his own heart was so wholly given, whose impress was so stamped on his own life; and then destroying their 'vain refuges' of idols, he led them to the 'Rest' which the 'weary and heavy-laden' toilers in all ages so especially need, and so largely find.

But not only among the people; to emperors and courts, to kings and princes this faithful ambassador went, and effectively; because first to the poor.

At his court at Treves Bishop Martin went to plead with the Emperor Maximus for the followers of his murdered predecessor Gratian; and also for the hunted Priscillianist heretics of Spain.

The Emperor and Empress could not do him honour enough. The other bishops courted and flattered them. Martin warned and rebuked them; and they courted him.

For some time Martin refused all the Emperor's invitations, saying he could not accept hospitality from one who had deprived one Emperor of his dominions and another of his life. But Maximus pleaded that his honours had been forced on him, and showed so much penitence that at last Martin yielded.

The Emperor made it quite a festival and triumph when Martin consented at length to sit at his table.

Martin was placed on a couch close to the Imperial seat, and near him was his attendant presbyter. In the midst of the banquet the wine-cup was first handed to Maximus; he presented it to Martin to receive it back with his blessing. Martin took the cup and drank, and then instead of handing it back to the Emperor passed it on to his own presbyter. The Emperor professed to be moved with admiration, and also to be stricken with penitence; and from that time he often sought private interviews with Martin, obtaining absolution from him, and communing on 'the heavens and the immortal life.'

The Empress also humbled herself in the dust before

the aged bishop, believing in the miracle of his holy life, and the external miracles it was said to effect. She listened and wept, at his feet. At length she begged her husband, and they both begged Martin, to allow her, without assistance of attendants, to serve him a repast. 'With her own hands she spreads a seat, she places a table by it, water she offers for his hands, food which she herself had cooked she sets before him. Then at a distance, as servants are taught, she stands motionless as if fixed to the ground. She mixes his draught, she presents it to him, showing in all things the reverence of an attendant and the humbleness of a handmaid.'

'When the small meal is ended, she sweeps up with all carefulness the broken bits and crumbs of bread, preferring such relics to imperial dainties.'[1]

But after all this patience and reverential homage, when the bishop had left, the Priscillianists (those ascetic Gnostic heretics from Spain for whom he had pleaded so fervently, in opposition to almost all the other orthodox bishops) were *not* spared. Soon after his departure, Priscillian and many of his followers were beheaded.

Afterwards, indeed, St. Ambrose and other bishops at the Council of Milan protested against this persecution; and Ithacus, the leader of the persecuting party, was excommunicated and deposed.

But Priscillian and his immediate followers had then already been executed; and moreover a military expedition was to be sent by Maximus to Spain by the Emperor's orders to hunt out and kill all the heretics they could find.

The rough test of heresy adopted by the soldiery being 'paleness of face and peculiarity of dress,' the expedition was likely to end in an access of wealth to the imperial treasures, but also in a great destruction of innocent persons and orthodox believers.

And in the following year Martin again came on a mission of mercy to the Court at Treves. Again, compliments and homage from the Emperor, but at the same time defence of his acts and persistence in the threatened expe-

[1] Sulpicius Severus.

dition into Spain; until at length, irritated by Martin's persistence in not communicating with the persecuting bishops, the Emperor quitted him hastily, in anger, and gave orders for the execution of Leucadius and Narses, the two officers of the condemned Gratian for whom Martin had come especially to plead.

Then Martin's compassion overcame him. He re-entered the palace; he even consented to communicate with the persecutors of Priscillian, on condition that Narses and Leucadius were spared, and the expedition to Spain recalled.

The Emperor was satisfied. But not the bishop. He went on his way home with downcast mind. And about ten miles from Treves, passing through a deep and lonely forest, he remained there alone, in conflict with his conscience as to whether he had done right.

And, as he was thus examining himself, it is said, an angel appeared to him and said: 'Martin, with reason thou art pricked in heart; but no other way was opened to thee. Retrieve thy virtue, resume thy firmness, lest indeed thou risk not thy renown, but thy salvation.'

And that was Martin's last dealing with emperors and courts.

Eleven years longer he lived. And from time to time he used to confess to his friend, Sulpicius Severus, with tears, that from the mischief of that communion which he joined for a moment, and that not in heart but from compulsion, he was sensible of a diminution of his supernatural gift. He had "lost power to rescue those who were possessed of the devil." Never afterwards would he go to great assemblies, nor even entertain great men at his monastery, lest he should give secret entrance to vanity and elation of spirit.

Perhaps it was after this that the most characteristic and significant of all his visions came to him. It is told by Sulpicius.

'While Martin was praying in his cell, the evil spirit stood before him clad in a glittering radiancy, by this purposing more easily to deceive him; clad also in royal robes, crowned with a golden and jewelled diadem, with shoes covered with gold, with serene face and bright looks, so as to seem nothing so little as what he was. Martin at first was dazzled by the sight, and for a long while both parties kept silence. At length the Evil One began. "Acknowledge," he says, "O Martin, whom thou seest. I am Christ. I am now descending upon earth, and I wished first to manifest myself to thee."

'Martin still kept silent, and returned no answer. The devil continued to repeat his bold pretence: "Martin, why hesitate in believing, when thou seest I am Christ?" Then understanding by revelation of the Spirit, that it was the Evil One, not God, Martin answered: "Jesus, the Lord, announced not that He should come in glittering clothing, and radiant with a diadem. I will not believe that the Christ is come, save in that state and form in which He suffered, save with the show of the wounds of the Cross."

'At these words the other vanished forthwith as smoke, and filled the cell with so horrible an odour as to leave indubitable proof who he was. That this so took place, I know from the mouth of Martin himself, lest any one should think it fabulous.'[1]

Martin's life was long spared to the world which so needed him. At eighty he went to a remote place in his diocese to make peace between two of his clergy. On his return his strength suddenly failed him, and he was stricken with fever, and felt his end near. He gathered his disciples together, and told them he was going. And they, like those around St. Ambrose, with passionate laments, entreated him not to leave them as sheep in the midst of wolves.

He was much moved, and said,

'Lord, if I be yet necessary to Thy people, I decline not the labour (*non recuso laborare*). Thy will be done.' But his wish was heard, not his prayer.

The fever held its course. He caused himself to be laid on ashes. His disciples would have persuaded him to accept the beggar's luxury of 'a little straw,' but he replied, 'My sons, it becomes a Christian to die on ashes.'

[1] Sulpicius Severus, *Life of St. Martin* translated by Cardinal Newman.

His old enemy seems to have made a last assault on him in his last hour of darkness, not this time in gold and glitter and angelic serenity, but in unmasked malignity.

'Beast of blood,' Martin said, 'deadly one, thou shalt find nothing in me. Abraham's bosom is receiving me.'

And with these words he died.

His devoted disciple Sulpicius was at a distance when he died, and that very night seemed to see his master in a vision, clad in a white robe, with face like a flame, and with eyes like stars—'And while his person was what I had known it to be, yet what can hardly be expressed, I could not look at him, though I could recognise him. He slightly smiled at me, and bore in his right hand the book I had written of his life. I embrace his knees and ask his blessing as usual, and I feel the soft touch of his hand on my head, while together with the usual words of benediction he repeats the name of the Cross, familiar on his lips ; then, while I gaze upon him, and cannot take my fill of his face and look, suddenly he is caught aloft, till after completing the immense spaces of the air, and following with my eyes the swift cloud that covered him, he is received into the open heavens and can be seen no more.'

And so for centuries his life was felt through Christendom, the soft touch of his kind hand, the words of benediction on his lips, and the familiar name of the Cross in his mouth, enshrined for us in these last days in the eloquent words, 'Many spirits are abroad, and the credentials which they display are precious gifts of mind, beauty, richness, depth, originality. Christian, look hard at them, like Martin, in silence, and ask for the prints of the nails.'[1]

[1] Cardinal Newman, 'St. Martin,' *Historical Sketches*.

Dedications of churches : one hundred and sixty. Represented in art on horseback, dividing his cloak with a beggar, as a Bishop, a Martinmas goose by his side. The chief authority is *St. Martin's Life*, by his contemporary and friend Sulpicius Severus, quoted by Cardinal Newman in his *Historical Sketches*, and also Mrs. Jameson's *Sacred and Legendary Art*, and Professor Ruskin's *Bible of Amiens*.

St. Britius

OF TOURS.

November 13.

(Died A.D. 444. Calendars: all except Roman and Monastic. Nov. 13. Sarum Ep. and Gosp.: Wisd. x. 10-14; St. Luke xix. 12-28.)

St. Britius was one of the scholars and monks of St. Martin of Tours, in his abbey (or collection of cells) of Marmoutier.

He was apparently endeared to St. Martin by the quantity of trouble he gave him.

At first he seems to have profited by St. Martin's teaching, and was ordained priest, but his pride and violence of temper made him a great stumbling-block.

Once Martin had been greatly pained by his ingratitude. The clergy entreated the bishop to suspend him from the priesthood, and to drive him from the town. But St. Martin, serene and quiet, and with the patience of hope, would not consent to abandon him. 'Did not the Lord bear with Judas,' he said, 'and shall I not bear with Britius?'

St. Martin was, moreover, persuaded that underneath that fiery, violent character were gifts and qualities which would yet serve the Church. He believed even that it had been revealed to him that this great trial of his life and perplexity of his ministry was to succeed him in the episcopate.

St. Martin's holiness and patience won the day.

At his death the reclaimed Britius without hesitation was chosen his successor.

The shadow of his earlier sins, however, pursued him into his new life. He was slandered, and finally driven from Tours, to which he only returned after seven years of exile, it is said, through the influence of the Pope, who was persuaded of his innocence.

Seven years longer, as bishop, he rendered faithful service, justifying the predictions of St. Martin, and repaying his generous trust and fatherly patience by his devoted labours for the flock St. Martin loved and served.

And so St. Britius lives in our calendars, one of the countless witnesses to the unconquerable power of patient love, to the possibility of 'the last' becoming 'the first,' and to the fact that Christianity means primarily Redemption.

[1] Dedications of churches: in England one, Brise Norton, and that of Llanverres in North Wales. Represented carrying burning coals in his vestment, an infant on the ground near him.

St. Enurchus or Evortius.[1]

OF ORLEANS.

September 7.

Died circa A.D. 374.   Calendar: York.

No one seems to know for what reason St. Evortius is left in the English Calendar. Of the six remaining French saints, St. Britius stands as the example of the possibility of recovery from depths of failure to heights of sanctity; St. Malo is certainly almost the only name in our Calendar belonging to the earliest Christianity of these islands, before the mission of Augustine; St. Remigius represents the conversion of Clovis, standing in the same relation to France as St. Augustine of Canterbury to England; the hermit St. Leonard, his disciple, is the patron and restorer of malefactors; St. Giles, patron saint of the woodlands, of lepers, beggars and cripples, and of those struck by sudden misery, is most widely venerated in England and Scotland, from Edinburgh to London; and his legend has also its interest as one of those sympathetic links with the animal world of which we cherish the traces.

But for St. Evortius there is nothing in the scanty history or in the legendary growth from it, which explains his being left in our Calendar; and one could wish St. Cuthbert or St. Aidan in his place.

Alban Butler says of him: 'His name is famous in the ancient Western Martyrology, but his history is of no authority. A famous abbey of Orleans bears his name.'

In 'Les Petits Bollandistes' his story is given as having been a subdeacon at Rome in the days of Constantine and having made a journey to Gaul to ransom his brother and

---

[1] Dedications of churches: none.   Represented in art with a dove.

sister from captivity. When he arrived at the city of Orleans, an episcopal election was going on, and (as in other legends) a dove was seen to alight on his head, again and again, which was considered a sign of the election by the Holy Ghost. He was therefore chosen bishop of Orleans and stands a witness to the popular election of bishops in the fourth century.

He converted so many of the surrounding pagans that it became necessary to build a larger church. In digging for its foundations they found a treasure which the bishop at once sent to the Emperor as his due. The Emperor acknowledged the recognition of his rights by returning the treasure doubled in amount. An angel traced the plan of the church for the bishop on the snow, a beautiful tablet for angelic architectural plans. In three years it was finished, and at the dedication a luminous cloud was seen above the Bishop's head as he officiated at the altar, a cloud with a hand extending the three fingers to give the benediction. Therefore the device of the seal of the chapter of Orleans to this day is a cross with a cloud encircling a hand that blesses.

The heavenly hand tracing the church on the winter's snow, and extended over the cross in ceaseless benediction, are beautiful symbols to be associated with any name in any calendar.[1]

---

[1] His name is variously spelt Evortius, Euverte, Evorce, Emirte, Emirce. The Enurchus of our Calendar seems a variety of our own, attributed to no profounder cause than a misprint.

St. Remigius [1]

OF RHEIMS.

October 1.

(Born circa A.D. 439; died A.D. 533. Calendars: all. Sarum Ep. and Gosp.: Heb. vii. 23-27; St. Luke xii. 35-40).

St. Remi (St. Remigius) is said to have been born about 439, and to have died in 533 at the age of 94, having been bishop of Rheims about 70 years.

The genuine sources of information about his biography are said to be scanty, and its decorations bear rather the character of fiction written for edification than of genuine popular legend. That is, they seem rather to give us a smoothed illumination of what a saint in general should be, than any true and characteristic portrait of what this particular saint was. His parents were of that Roman Gallic stock, from which the clergy and saints of France were mostly derived; his father's name was Remigius, that of his mother (also canonised), Cilinia. They were rich, of honourable birth, and of high Christian character. Remi, the son of their old age, was born in their castle of Laon. He had two elder brothers and a younger. His nurse also, Balsamia, is in the Calendar. He was early dedicated to the service of God; was taught all of the old learning to be learned at Laon, and was said to be one of the most eloquent men of his age. The little room in his father's house at Laon, which he made an oratory, was shown with reverence 400 years afterwards. But he sought a deeper solitude at some distance from the city.

At twenty-two (461) he was consecrated Bishop of Rheims. He had, therefore, been bishop twenty years when Clovis, a boy of fifteen, was raised to the chieftainship of his

---

[1] Dedications of churches: seven, unless any be to St. Remigius of Lincoln. Represented in art with the ampulla, or a dove bringing it to him.

4,000 Franks, and a quarter of a century when, in 486 Clovis, at twenty, won his first victory over Synagrius of Soissons, the last representative of Roman rule in the region around Rheims.

Clovis and his Frankish confederation, his confederation of 'free men,' were still pagans; not, of course, pagans of the classic type, but of the old northern worship of force and courage; practising originally rites of sacrifice of human captives; the fiercest, it was said, of any of the northern tribes, except the Vandals; brave, with a light-hearted courage; with military laws of their own as to equality of rights, and subordination to chieftains, and especially as to division of spoil, which were kept with strictest severity. It is the conversion of those Franks ('the most important event in its remote, as well as in its immediate, consequences of European history')[1] which is the triumph and glory of St. Remigius.

In 493 Clovis, still a pagan, married Clotilda, an orphan princess of the Burgundians, whose family were Arians. Clotilda herself, by what influence it is not known, was not Arian, but Catholic. She had been orphaned by her uncle Gundebald, the reigning prince, who had killed his brother her father, tied a stone round the neck of her mother and drowned her in the Rhone, beheaded her own two brothers and thrown them into a well, besides various other family murders.

Amongst all these horrors Clotilda seems to grow apart, like a fair flower, although herself apparently sharing the Frankish ideal of manhood, since when, in after years, her favourite grandsons were tonsured and made monks to unfit them for the throne, she said indignantly, 'Satius mihi est, si ad regnum non venient, mortuos eos videre quam tonsos.'[2] There was courage in this princess evidently, to encounter, as well as charm to win, her Frankish lord.

Her first victory was persuading him to have their firstborn son baptised. The child died in his white

[1] Milman, *Latin Christianity*.
[2] 'If they do not reign, I had rather see them dead than tonsured.'

chrisom robes within a week of his baptism. The king reproached her and said, 'If he had been consecrated in the name of my gods he had not died, but having been baptised in the name of yours he could not live.' The queen replied, 'I thank God, who has thought him worthy of being a child whom He has called to His kingdom.' And she prevailed in having their second son baptised. This child also fell sick, and Clovis said in great anger : 'It could not be otherwise ; he will die presently as his brother did, having been baptised in the name of your Christ.'

But the young queen trusted and prayed, the child recovered, and she continued to seek to turn Clovis from his idols, until at last Clovis went forth to his second great war ; this time not with the falling Roman empire, but with the Alemanni, a German tribe as fierce as his own, who had been laying all the land waste. As he took leave of Clotilda, as the story is told, she said : 'My lord, you are going to conquest, but in order to be victorious invoke the God of the Christians ; He is Lord of the universe.' And in the thick of the fight, when the battle was going against him, and his men were flying in panic, Clovis remembered the parting words, and said : 'O Christ, whom Clotilda invokes, O Son of the living God, I implore Thy succour. Deliver me from my enemies and I will be baptised in Thy name.' With this new hope enkindling his courage he rallied his Franks, and as the result France became French and the Franks became Christians.

When he met his queen again he said, 'Clovis has vanquished the Alemanni, and you have vanquished Clovis.'

'To the God of Hosts is the glory of both triumphs due,' she said. At once Clotilda introduced him to St. Remigius, as the holiest and most able of the neighbouring bishops.

St. Remi exhorted him to speak to his chiefs and endeavour to convert them. Without much hope Clovis gathered his Franks together. But before he could begin his speech they cried out, 'My lord, we abandon mortal gods, and are ready to follow the immortal God whom Remigius teaches.'

For many days the king cast aside his crown and humbled himself in ashes, until the great day of baptism came. Processions with cross and lights and rich vestments went through the streets of Rheims. The church was filled with incense ('like odours of Paradise') and hung with tapestries and blazing with countless lights, when Clovis and 3,000 of his Franks came to the fonts to be baptised and clothed in white—some on Christmas Day, some later on the usual Easter Eve.

'Fierce Sicambrian,' said the Bishop Remigius, 'bow thy neck; burn what thou hast adored, adore what thou hast burned.'

The legend of the descent of the white dove with the ampulla of fragrant oil, compounded by angels, from which the French kings were anointed at Rheims, is of later date.

And it was in one of their conferences afterwards, when the eloquent bishop was dwelling on the barbarity of the Jews and Romans in crucifying our Lord, that Clovis showed his realisation of the event in his famous exclamation: 'Had I and my faithful Franks been there, they had not dared to do it.'

Thus France became French and the Franks became Christians.

A letter of St. Remi's to Clovis is quoted by Alban Butler. 'Choose wise counsellors, who will be an honour to your reign; respect the clergy. Be the father and protector of your people; let it be your study to lighten as much as possible all the burdens which the necessities of the State may oblige them to bear; comfort and relieve the poor; feed the orphans; protect widows; suffer no extortion. Let the gate of your palace be open to all, that every one may have recourse to you for justice; employ your great revenues in redeeming captives.'

At all events, under the influence of St. Remi the idols throughout France were abolished, and the Christian ideal was set up, and exhibited with telling force and conquering power in his own life.[1]

[1] Many miracles are related of St. Remigius, among them that the wild birds used to come and eat out of his hand at table.

St. Leonard, Patron of Prisoners,

OF THE LIMOUSIN.

November 6.

(Died circa A.D. 559. Calendars: all except Roman and Paris.[1]
Sarum Ep. and Gosp.: Ecclus. xxxix. 5-9; St. Luke xi. 33-36.)

St. Leonard, hermit and monk in the Limousin, had been one of the young chiefs of his Franks to whom Clovis was most attached. He was a disciple of St. Remigius, being one of the 3,000 Franks baptised in the cathedral of Rheims after the victory of Tolbiac. Clovis wished to keep him always near himself, in the highest posts. But Leonard aspired to a higher life than he thought could be found in that tumultuous court, and in the prime of his days became a monk in the monastery of Micy near Orleans.

In the legend of his life, written long after, the story is told how, when as a young deacon he was carrying the wine for the Sacrament to the church, a poor man met him, weary and fainting, and entreated in the name of Jesus for a drink of the wine. Leonard remembered the words of our Saviour, '*I was thirsty and ye gave me drink*,' and gave the wine to the weary stranger, who then told him to fill his little pitcher again from a spring close at hand. And as he did so, the first miracle of our Lord, the perpetual miracle of the turning of the water into wine, was repeated for him. The water was made wine, to be poured out again from the sacramental chalice as a draught of life.

St. Leonard's passion for solitude was not satisfied with the monastery. Probably, consciously or not, he was of the order of founders rather than of followers. He left the community of Micy (following a narrow gorge of the river Vienne), made his way through a wild forest, haunted by beasts of prey, and in the depths of the wood, on a solitary hill, built himself a hut with twisted branches, and an oratory, and there lived on wild fruits and roots.

From time to time the thoughts which had burned in his heart in solitude would burst into a flame which must enkindle others, and the hermit would appear in various churches of the villages and cities around, and stir the hearts of the people from the slumber of unbelief and sin to God and the deathless life.

The sick went to him, or were borne to his hut, to be soothed and healed in body and soul. On an opposite height to the hermitage, rose a castle, where the king of the country used to come to hunt the wild creatures of the forest. Once the Queen was with him and was brought into great peril of life at the birth of a child. The castle was full of tumult and despair, and at last the king himself came to Leonard's hut to entreat the help of his prayers. The very sight of his peaceful face serene with the light of perpetual prayer gave hope.

As he entered the Queen's chamber, the Queen revived, and the grateful king would have given Leonard vessels of gold and silver, sacred vestments, purple and gold embroideries, as offerings of his gratitude. But of all the royal gifts Leonard would only accept a portion of the forest, that the sick and the rescued prisoners, the penitents who came to him for counsel and help, might dwell together around him in prayer and peace.

Especially penitents. For from his earliest days of Christian life Leonard's heart had gone out in tenderest compassion, longing to save, towards prisoners, and captives, all captives apparently, but more especially those who were under the double bondage of their own crimes.

In the depth of every hopeless prison and sunless dungeon of those fierce times, it began to be felt that there was a friend near at hand *for whom there were no outcasts*, who did not despair of them, who would welcome them to his heart. The likeness of Him who came to save the lost shone once more through a human life on the hearts and consciences of the most abandoned. The legend says, they called from the depths of the dungeon on the name of Leonard, and their chains dropped off.

So the forest of Leonard's hermitage became peopled with penitents. These he welcomed to the healing discipline of labour, to a simple austere life and to prayer. '*If the Son make you free*,' his life said to them, '*you shall be free indeed*.' Old servants and old friends, also, drawn by the magic of that compassionate heart, sold their patrimonies and came to Leonard in his forest. To all he said, 'My sons, man is born to work as birds to fly. Work for your own need, and that ye may have to give to those that need more.' Thus the forest was cleared of its beasts of prey, and the hearts of men of their sins and sorrows. For neither wild beasts, nor sins, glide away from their haunts *of themselves*. The cheery sounds of axe and plough mingled with hymns of praise. And so Leonard lived on until with a glad heart he could say at last: 'O death, desired so long, I welcome thee.' And then he lay down to rest among the multitudes he had awakened to new life and hope; Leonard, Patron of prisoners.[1]

[1] Dedications of churches: about 150, one with St. John, and one with St. Mary. Represented in art as a monk or abbot, with chains, fetters, etc.

St. Machutus (St. Malo, St. Mawes)

OF BRITTANY.

November 15.

(Calendars: Sarum, York, Hereford, Aberdeen. Died A.D. 564. Sarum Ep. and Gosp.: Ecclus. xliv. 17, 20-32, xlv. 6, 7, 15, 16; St. Luke xix. 12-28.)

St. Machutus has an especial interest for us, because he is the only saint retained in our Calendar of that noble company of Celtic monks, including St. Patrick of Ireland, St. Columba of Iona, St. Columban of Luxeuil, St. Gall of Switzerland, who cleared the forests, and by their preaching and living brought Christian life to Ireland, Wales, Cornwall, Scotland, Burgundy, Bretagne, and many remote recesses of Switzerland, Germany, and France.

Welsh by nation, he was the child of his parents' old age. He was cousin-german to St. Sampson and St. Magloire, and was educated either in Ireland or in Wales, in one of the celebrated Irish monasteries, which were the high schools and also the elementary schools of the age.

The abbot to whose care he was confided was St. Brendan. In the old lections on his festival the story used to be told to the people how, as a child, when his school-mates were playing on the sandy shore, Machutus strayed far away and fell asleep on a bed of sea-weeds and was forgotten, until his playmates, driven back by the advancing tide, regained the monastery, and the child Machutus was nowhere to be found. Then St. Brendan, the abbot, ran to the sea-shore and called 'Machutus, Machutus,' but no answer came. The abbot returned to his cell and passed the night in prayer, and the next morning, not in hope but in the hopelessness of grief, he went down again to the sea. From a point of rock he looked over the waves. In the morning light, and not too far off for his voice to be heard, he saw the lost child standing on a float of seaweed, singing hymns. The abbot and the boy held a joyful dialogue, until the waves bore the child near enough to reach the shore, and the two went back to the abbey together, thanking God.

The incursions of the heathen Anglo-Saxons were sweeping Roman civilisation and earlier British Christianity out of England, and Machutus and many other monks took refuge among the kindred races of Brittany (la Bretagne bretonnante). Among these were St. Sampson, first bishop of Dol, St. Magloire, St. Brieuc, St. Pol, and St. Méen. They landed on the isle of Aaron (now the town of St. Malo). Thence St. Malo made a journey to Luxeuil, to learn from the lips of his countryman, St. Columban, his Rule for his monks. St. Machutus sought solitude, but the Christians of the neighbouring town of Aleth insisted on having him for their bishop.

For forty years he lived as bishop at Aleth, near the present St. Malo. But the Breton princes were covetous and quarrelsome; there were divisions also in the Church between the bishops and their clergy; and the people appear to have been fickle.

And finally they drove their Saint away. On departing it is said he called down on the ungrateful city the maledictions of heaven—'not in vengeance but for their good.'

He took ship with thirty-three monks, who chose to share his exile, and landed on an island near Saintonge, where Leontius, Bishop of Saintes, gave them a large grant of land near his city. The friendly people of the city added the gift of an ass, which was to carry wood for the community. One day, the legend says, this ass was devoured by a wolf, but the wolf, at St. Machutus' command, more manageable than his human flock, thenceforth penitently took the ass's place, and became a beast of burden for the convent as long as the saint lived there.

Another of the glimpses of Paradise Regained, and touches of sympathy with the wild creatures, characteristic of the Celtic legends, is combined tenderly with St. Malo's name. One hot day, when he had laid aside his outer garment for a few hours, a little bird came and made its nest in its folds. The Saint would not have it disturbed until the eggs were hatched and the nestlings fledged.

Another of these legends introduces a new character out of the animal world. St. Malo was once at sea on Easter Day, and, determining to celebrate Mass, he landed on what seemed a small islet, close at hand. The islet proved to be a whale; but the creature remained quite still until the service was finished and the Saint and his company had returned to the ship, when it plunged again into the sea.

Maledictions scarcely seem to belong to such a gentle Christian. But meanwhile his rebellious flock at Aleth, against whom he had uttered those denunciations, had been suffering from famine and pestilence and all kinds of evils; so that, at last, once more they thought of their banished bishop, remembering his blessings and his watchings, and many also of the miracles of mercy he was reported to have worked at Saintonge. And they thus sent and entreated him to return.

The merciful angels counselled him to forgive and yield.

So St. Malo rejoined his repentant flock, and the famine ceased. But after many years he returned to the friendly monks and people in Saintonge to die, at the age of 133.[1]

[1] There are various attempts at attaining this Celtic or Gaelic word in Latin forms—Malou, Macou, Mahout, Machutus. *Les Petits Bollandistes* and Alban Butler think ' Maclow ' the most satisfactory, the *Mac* being in their opinion the characteristic portion.

Dedications of churches: St. Mawes, in Cornwall. Represented in art as a bishop.

St. Giles or Egidius, Patron of Lepers, &c.

September 1.

(Calendars: all. Died circa A.D. 725. Sarum Ep. and Gosp. Ecclus. xxxix. 5-9; St. Luke xi. 33-36.)

The legend of St. Giles leads us back to the East, to a legendary Athens of the seventh century where dwelt his parents Theodore and Pelagia, of royal blood, and where he was trained in Christian piety and love and also in the schools of classical learning.

When he was twenty-four his father and mother died, and the young man, stricken to the heart by the double loss, and penetrated with the sense of the transitoriness of all human joys, sold all that he had and gave it to the poor, and went forth to follow the Master whithersoever He would lead.

Across the seas the young Athenian went till he landed on a lonely island near his Athens. On the shore he saw human footsteps, and following these, he found a cave in which a venerable old solitary had lived for twelve years on herbs and roots, who was content to share his cave, his roots, and his prayers with this young stranger.

But after three days St. Giles began to fear his friends might find him, and accordingly he hailed a passing ship and sailed away to the West, and landed at the old Greek colony of Marseilles. His presence brought a blessing to the sick of the city, and they would have constrained him to be their fellow-citizen. But still seeking solitude, St. Giles secretly and suddenly withdrew, crossed the Rhone, and went towards a rocky steep watered by the river Gardon. Here in a cave, whose entrance was concealed by a thicket, he found another solitary, also a Greek; and great was their joy as they conversed together in their mother tongue and sang the praise of Christ their Lord. But here also the restless sufferers of this troubled world found the saint out, and the tranquil solitude 'à deux' was broken. The two compatriots parted once more, tenderly as a father and a son, and St. Giles went further and further, by all lonely and hidden paths, till finally in the depths of a forest he found a hollow of a rock, in a green glade by a stream, shaded by four gigantic oaks.[1]

There he lived in peace and prayer, his only companion a gentle hind, whose milk he drank. But one day the forest echoed with the noise of horns and hounds, and all the cries of the chase. To the hunters St. Giles's gentle companion was merely part of the wild game.

Pursued by hounds and huntsmen, the gentle creature took refuge with her human friend. St. Giles received in his hand an arrow aimed at her. The creature was rescued, and the huntsmen, touched by the gentle dignity of the Greek hermit, listened reverently as he spoke to them of this life vanishing like a cloud, and the eternal life in the love of Jesus Christ which passes not. The huntsmen, who were of the Court, brought their King Wamba to see the hermit in his cave with this hind.

The king would have given him lands for any foundation he chose. But no entreaties would persuade him to desert his life of solitude and prayer.

Another version of the legend, however, connects him with the invasion of the Saracens, thus curiously linking the traditions of the early Eastern days of the Church with the devastation and deluge which had swept away much of the Eastern Church, and was threatening the West.

St. Giles, it is said, according to this legend, consented to be the founder of an abbey, which flourished greatly till the Saracen invasion. Then far and wide the cities were burned, the fields were laid waste, and among them the Abbey of St. Giles. Thereupon he and his monks took refuge with Charles Martel, and aided him by their prayers in his great battle for the Christianity of the West.

[1] Processions are made to the place to this day.—*Les Petits Bollandistes.*

Their prayers were heard, and the tide of Mahomedanism was stemmed once for all at Chalons, and driven back over the Pyrenees.

St. Giles' monastery was restored, and then he said, 'Lord, now lettest Thou Thy servant depart in peace,' and was content to die. 'Eighty-three years weigh on me,' he said, and on Sunday, the 1st of September, 720, he fell asleep. St. Giles became one of the most popular saints in the West, the patron saint 'of the woodland, of lepers, beggars, cripples, and of those struck by some sudden misery, and driven into solitude like the wounded hart or hind.' One hundred and forty-six churches are dedicated to him in England, frequently on the outskirts of the city, and his name is familiar to us in the old Cathedral of Edinburgh, in the contrast between the St. Giles and St. James of London, and in the St. Giles of 'the people's Earl' of Shaftesbury, one of the nineteenth century successors of the patron of the leper, the sorrowful, and the poor.[1]

[1] Dedications of churches: 146, and one with St. Martin. Represented in art with the hind and the arrow in various ways, with a milk cup in his hand.

CHAPTER III.

SAINTS OF ENGLAND, WALES, AND IRELAND.

St. Augustine

OF CANTERBURY.

May 26.

(Died A.D. 604-605. Calendars: Sarum, York, Hereford, Aberdeen, Monastic. Sarum Ep. and Gosp.: Ecclus. xlvii. 8-11; St. Luke x. 1-7 (during Eastertide); St. John xv. 1-7.)

THE rest of our story lies altogether within the shores of England.[1] For the first time the land of the English is once more a heathen land, swept bare of its Christianity and its Christian people by the overwhelming rush of the three great northern tribes which form the basis of our race, not by a military invasion, scarcely even by a conquest, but by a possession of the land by a new people.

The fair children who touched the heart of Gregory in the Roman slave-markets were English children, not British prisoners of war, but children of their own race, sold by an evil custom, in pursuance of which, centuries after, English slaves were sold from Bristol to Ireland.

Yet the people they were sold from amongst were free, and had among them elements of freedom and unity, lost altogether amongst those races which had been civilised, taxed, corrupted, enslaved under imperial Roman rule. It was on new virgin soil St. Gregory was casting forth his precious seed. It was to a nation, mother of many nations, to a people who were to spread their language and in it the Sacred Scriptures so dear to St. Gregory throughout the world.

[1] With the exception of St. Patrick and St. David.

The Holy Scriptures which St. Gregory sent Augustine, 'in two volumes, the Psalter, the Book of the Gospels, and other books,' were the foundation or beginning of the library of the whole English Church. That Bible has not lain idle ever since, and is sowing precious seed through its hundred recent translations into other languages now.

The name of Augustine is inevitably thrown into the shade by the name of Gregory, the great and holy man as whose messenger he came. It was, indeed, to the heart and also to the wise, directing mind of Gregory that England owed her conversion.

'If not an apostle to others he is an apostle to us.' Yet we must not disregard or disloyally underrate the instrument Gregory chose carefully for the work so dear to him, so incalculably important to us.

Nothing seems known of Augustine's early history; no trace of father, mother, childhood, youth. He appears first as an abbot of St. Gregory's monastery on the Cœlian.

Few of the saints have so little that is individual in their story. We have scarcely a single trait of his character, or a word of simple human intercourse. All seems official and public.

We have not a letter of his. Only through St Gregory's answers can we guess what Augustine's side of the correspondence was.

After that first meeting with the English slave children in the Roman forum Gregory's heart had been especially directed not only to England but to the method of winning her to Christ through the ransom of her captive children.

Among his epistles is one to the presbyter who had charge of the property of the Roman Church in Gaul, directing him to spend part of the money collected in Gaul in the purchase of such Anglo-Saxon youths as might be exposed for sale, and to send them in company of an ecclesiastic, who could baptise them in case of mortal sickness, to Rome, in order that they might be trained and instructed in the monasteries there.

Meanwhile, Ethelbert, King of Kent, and Bretwalda, acknowledged as a kind of chief of chiefs by the rest of his race in England, had married Bertha, daughter of the King of the Franks, in Paris. And at last, six years after he had been elected Pope, Gregory was able to carry out the steadfast purpose of his heart for England.

He chose Augustine, the abbot of his own monastery, in his father's house on the Cœlian, for the mission.

Down those forty steps went the forty monks on their far-off quest to this heathen England, as unknown a land to those Italian monks then, speaking a language as 'barbarian' to their Italian ears, and in bondage to a barbarism as savage, in some respects, as that of the African tribes to which we are sending missionaries to-day. They took a long time reaching England.

On their way they paused at the sacred monastic island of Lerins, with its memories of Vincent, and of St. Patrick; and there so terrible were the reports which reached them of this 'barbarous, fierce, and unbelieving' nation, that they were seized with a sudden panic, and began to think of returning home. Indeed, they sent back Augustine, that he might by humble entreaty 'obtain of the holy Gregory that they should not be compelled to undertake so dangerous, toilsome, and uncertain a journey.'

The fire was originally in the soul of Gregory rather than in theirs. But happily for them and for us, the Benedictine discipline bore them up. There is something especially touching in this glimpse of the rank and file, through whom so much, after all, of the work is done.

Augustine returned from Rome with a letter containing certainly no relaxation of their marching orders.

'*Gregory, the servant of God, to the servants of our Lord.* Forasmuch as it had been better not to begin a good work, than to think of desisting from that which has been begun, it behoves you, my beloved sons, to fulfil the good work, which by the help of our Lord, you have undertaken.

'Let not, therefore, the toil of the journey, nor the tongues of evil-speaking men deter you; but with all possible earnestness and zeal perform that which, by God's direction, you have undertaken, being assured that much labour is followed by an eternal reward. When Augustine, your chief, returns, whom we also constitute your abbot, humbly obey him in all things, knowing that whatsoever you shall do by his direction, will in all respects be available to your souls. Almighty God protect you with His grace, and grant that I may, in the heavenly country, see the fruits of your labour. Inasmuch as, though I cannot labour with you, I shall partake in the joy of the reward, because I am willing to labour. God keep you in safety, my most beloved sons.'

They persevered, Augustine and those poor forty monks, frightened, rather reluctant, not knowing whither they went, and not clear what they were to do, or how they could do it, knowing also that many such enterprises had ended in martyrdom. And on their way through France, after all the work there, of all the Saints, Roman and Gallic, for a century, those forty pilgrims met somewhat of a rough reception. In the forests of Agen they slept on the fallen leaves, and by day 'they were sometimes taken for werewolves, and the women followed them with howlings.' What then might not be expected from heathen Saxons? Yet they went on. They crossed the sea, to them no doubt perilous and unknown, and landed at last on a sandy cove between Ramsgate and Sandwich, where Julius Caesar had landed six centuries before, and Hengist and Horsa, not a century before, leading the heathen pirates into possession of the land.

They found a half-ruined church near Canterbury, dedicated in the name of St. Martin of Tours, where the Christian Queen Bertha with her Frankish bishop had been praying year after year for their coming.

In all this English missionary story, the various individualities are much hidden. Not a word of the Christian Queen, descendant of Clotilda, has reached us. She had sons, but not apparently brought like Clotilda's babes to the font. Yet silent and hidden as she is, something in her steadfast faith and life, had made her husband turn towards what she believed. No rude or cold reception was awaiting Augustine and these forty monks, but a welcoming and a listening nation.

King Ethelbert came to meet them in the Isle of Thanet, at Ebbsfleet, a quiet space of high tableland, 'sitting royally' in the open air. He would have nothing unfair, this straightforward Englishman, no unknown 'rites and spells under mysterious roofs, lest by some magical arts they should get the better of him.'

Sitting royally in the open air, with glimpses of the open sea beyond, King Ethelbert called the foreigners into his presence.

But they came furnished with Divine, not with magic virtue, bearing a silver cross for their standard, ' and the image of our Lord and Saviour painted on a board, and singing the Litany, they offered up their prayers to the Lord for the eternal salvation both of themselves and those to whom they were come.' When Augustine had sat down, according to the king's commands, and preached to him and his attendants there present the word of life, the king answered : 'Your words and promises are very fair, but as they are new to us, and of uncertain import, I cannot approve of them so far as to forsake that which I have so long followed with the whole English nation. But because you are come from far unto my kingdom, and as I conceive are desirous to impart to me those things which you believe to be true, and most beneficial, we will not molest you, but give you favourable entertainment, and take care to supply you with your necessary sustenance ; nor do we forbid you to preach and gain as many as you can to your religion.'

Nobler and more royal welcome to a messenger from heaven than those words can scarcely be shown in the history of Christian origins. It is good to look back to the spiritual ancestry of our church and feel that *noblesse oblige*.

The king's promise was well kept. He gave them a

dwelling in his city of Canterbury, and sustenance, and did not refuse them liberty to preach.

'It is reported that as they drew near to the city after their manner, with the Holy Cross, and the image of our Sovereign Lord and King, Jesus Christ, they in concert sang this Litany, "We beseech Thee, O Lord, in all Thy mercy, that Thy vengeance and wrath be turned away from this city, and from Thy holy house. Alleluia."' [1]

Gregory's music and the 'Alleluia' he had longed for echoed at last on English ground. Soon, with no hasty excitement but with 'swift' and ready 'hearing,' within a year, the king was baptised at Whitsuntide. And at the next Christmas, ten thousand of his people were baptised in the cold waters of the Medway where it flows into the Thames. The Alleluias were spreading well.

The king's generous welcome was as generously met. 'As soon as Augustine and his monks entered the dwelling consigned them, they began to imitate the course of life practised in the primitive church, applying themselves to frequent prayer, watching and fasting, preaching the word to as many as they could; despising all worldly things as not belonging to them, receiving only things necessary; living themselves in all respects conformably to what they preached to others, and being always disposed to suffer any adversity and to die for that truth which they preached. In short several believed and were baptised, admiring the simplicity of their innocent life, and the sweetness of the heavenly discipline.' [2]

St. Gregory had done well not to despair of those forty discouraged monks. At last, in the little church of St. Martin, where the queen had prayed so many years alone, English Christians met together to sing the praises of God. The King undertook the sustenance of the Italian missionaries, gave them a house at Canterbury, and encouraged them to restore the ruined Roman churches, and to build new ones where they could.

Before long Augustine restored the ancient Roman

[1] Bede. [2] Bede.

church at Canterbury, which grew into the Cathedral, and consecrated it 'in the name of our Holy Saviour, God and Lord, Jesus Christ.' It gives an idea of the extent and closeness of the intercommunication of Christendom at that time that St. Gregory wrote to Eulogios, bishop of Alexandria, rejoicing in the baptism of King Ethelbert, and 10,000 of his people. ' The nation,' he said, ' whose tongues had so long been used only to barbarous speech, had now learned the Alleluias.'

He (as also the English converts themselves) attributes the rapidity and number of the conversions to the miracles of healing wrought by Augustine. Certainly, it was no effort of faith for St. Gregory or the men of his age to believe in any amount of miracles ; and when we think of the power of a new interest and a new hope to restore health, and the power of the mind over the body exercised in prayer, without even taking into account the objective help all who pray believe prayer brings, it might seem strange if this miracle of spiritual life and healing for a whole nation, so far greater, as Gregory himself said, than any external wonders, should not have brought also with it the lesser miracles of bodily healing.

St. Gregory, however, was quite as much impressed with the spiritual dangers such miracles might bring to Augustine, as with their beneficial effects on the converts.

'It is necessary that you rejoice with trembling,' he writes to Augustine ; 'you may rejoice that the souls of the elect are by outward miracles drawn towards grace, but you may fear lest among the wonders wrought the weak mind may be puffed up. When the disciples said, "*Lord, in Thy name the devils are subject to us*," they are presently told, "*Rejoice rather that your names are written in heaven.*" *They are recalled from the private to the public, from the temporal to the eternal joy.* For those who are disciples of the truth ought not to rejoice save for that good thing which *all* enjoy as well as they, and *of which the enjoyment shall be without end.*'

He then begs him to recall his sins so as to be freed

from the danger of vanity, and to consider that these miraculous powers are not conferred for his sake, but for the sake of those for whose salvation they were sent.

It scarcely seems fair to conclude from this (as some have done) that Augustine's special danger was spiritual vanity. It seems juster to infer how true the hearts must have been on both sides which could bear such faithfulness of warning and rebuke, given and received. There must surely have been no small amount of the grace of silence and humility in the character on which Gregory could rely for such work as Augustine had to do, and which has yet suffered itself to be so entirely hidden in the greater light.

In the correspondence between Gregory and Augustine only Gregory's answers remain. Much of it touches medical and ceremonial questions; but with glimpses throughout of the widest liberality as to the variety of customs in different churches. For instance :

'You know, my brother, the custom of the Roman Church. But it pleases me that if you have found anything either in the Roman or the Gallican or any other church, which may be more acceptable to Almighty God, you carefully make choice of the same, and salutarily teach the Church of the English, which is as yet new to the faith, whatever you can gather from the several churches. For things are not to be loved for the sake of places, but places for the sake of good things.'

As to pagan customs, St. Gregory thought it wise to substitute Christian festivals for those the people were used to, building booths around the churches and making of the oxen they had been accustomed to sacrifice to the gods a feast of good roast beef for the people.

'For there is no doubt it is impossible to efface everything at once from their obdurate minds; because he who endeavours to ascend the highest places mounts by steps, not by leaps.'

The whole story of the mission of Augustine is a touching picture of the silent work of the rank and file of the army, without whom the victories cannot be won; of the unrecorded masons and carpenters by whose hands the most glorious cathedrals must be built. Augustine seems to stand at the threshold of our history, silent and obedient, on the second level indeed, looking up the forty steps of his Cœlian monastery for the guidance of his Father Gregory, claiming nothing for himself, defending himself against no accusations, content, if in that way he has to learn his lessons, that his difficulties or defects should not be hidden. It may be that his mind was liable to small scruples; the large, expansive answers of Gregory to his questions may imply this. It may be his character moved rigidly in accustomed grooves. His refusal to rise to meet the British clergy may have been a narrow adhesion (as Bede's history implies) to 'Roman custom' rather than any personal assumption. Gregory, we can imagine, might have risen with a fine impulse of courtesy, and come forward with outstretched hands to meet them, and so won them to accede to all he wished. A touch of generous sympathy might have enlisted on his side all that Celtic enthusiasm which had in earlier years enkindled Switzerland and Burgundy. But the subordinates can seldom have the free movement of the chiefs. The very silence of Augustine seems his most eloquent defence.

At least those forty Benedictines did their best for us. And to do the best when it can only be second best is not the easiest lesson to learn.

Already, at the commencement, Gregory, in the ardour of his hopes, had portioned England into two archbishoprics, originally intended to be London and York, and twelve bishoprics.

Both Gregory and Augustine were anxious to secure the co-operation of the ancient British Church from which so many missionaries had gone forth to the Continent. But probably neither of them understood the passion of indignation which the dispossessions and plunders, wrongs and slaughters of the English (Saxon) conquest had created between the races.

Under a grand old oak near the Severn ('to this day,' says Bede, 'called Augustine's Oak') on the borders of Wales, the Roman strangers met the British delegates, bishops, and monks from the mountainous fastnesses which were all the invaders had left them.

The story is variously told, although so much of the telling has necessarily been left to the victorious side.

The questions in debate were chiefly the period of Easter, the adoption of the Roman form of Baptism, and the joint preaching of the word of God to the heathen English (mortal enemies, it must be remembered, and conquerors of the Britons); and, underneath all, the question of supremacy.

Bede records that Augustine appealed to the test of miracles, and proved his claims by restoring sight to a blind man.

The British Christians, apparently moved by this, finally consulted a saintly hermit as to what would be the true test of Augustine's mission and authority, which would make it their duty to forsake their own traditions.

'If he is a man of God, follow him.'

'How shall we know that?' said they.

The hermit replied: 'Our Lord saith, *Take my yoke upon you and learn of me, for I am meek and lowly in heart*; if, therefore, Augustine is meek and lowly of heart, it is to be believed that he has taken upon him the yoke of Christ, and offers the same to you to take upon you. But if he is stern and haughty, it appears that he is not of God, nor are we to regard his words.'

They insisted again: 'And how shall we discern even this?'

'Do you contrive,' said the anchorite, 'that he may first arrive with his company at the place where the synod is to be held, and if at your approach he shall rise up to you, hear him submissively, being assured that he is the servant of Christ; but if he shall despise you and not rise up to you, whereas you are more in number, let him also be despised by you.'

They did as he directed; and it happened that when they came, Augustine was sitting on a chair, which they observing, were in a passion, and, charging him with pride, 'endeavoured to contradict all he said.'[1]

Thus the conference ended in an explosion. Augustine pressed on the British Christians the obvious Christian duty of evangelising their heathen conquerors. But probably he had no conception of the bitterness of mutual resentment and contempt wrought between the races (originally already in many respects so diverse and uncongenial) by a century of warfare and wrong; how little the conquerors would be disposed to listen to the faith which had not saved the conquered; and how hard the conquered, exiled, and hunted Britons must find it to believe in the possibility of pardon and redemption for those who had burned their cities, ruined their homes, and were still chasing them like wild beasts to the caves and crags of the mountains.

At the end of the conference, Augustine threatened the British Christians that if they would not join their friends they would be pursued and destroyed by their enemies; a prophecy too sure to be fulfilled by those fierce and aggressive heathen tribes who were always hemming in the conquered race within narrower and narrower limits. It was, indeed, not long afterwards that those twelve hundred monks of Bangor in Flintshire were massacred as combatants, at the great battle near Chester, by the heathen king Ethelfred, although they kept apart from the combat, in prayer—their prayers being recognised as very real weapons.

Monks of the race of Columba, Columban, and Aidan, only fifty of the twelve hundred fled, and escaped.

After the conference Augustine returned to Canterbury. The conversion of the English, with many ebbs and flows, advanced, and England was gathered into the unity of Roman Christendom, to stand against the floods and storms of the coming centuries, during which the tide of northern barbarism was still to extend itself, whilst Mahomedanism was sweeping away the divided Churches of the East.

[1] Bede.

Augustine died in May 605, two months after his great 'father and friend,' St. Gregory the Great.

He was buried ultimately in the church of the first Benedictine monastery, since called by his name, which he himself had dedicated in the names of St. Peter and St. Paul;—'the Lord Augustine, Dominus Augustinus, first Archbishop of Canterbury,' says the epitaph, 'who being formerly sent hither by the blessed Gregory, bishop of the City of Rome, and by God's assistance supported with miracles, redeemed King Ethelbert and his nation from the worship of idols to the faith of Christ, and having ended his office in peace died the sixth day of May, in the reign of the same king.'

Legendary story has not gathered around his name. Even in his epitaph the first place is given to Gregory, and not to Augustine, as we may be sure Augustine would have wished.[1]

[1] Dedication of churches : Twenty-one, unless in some of them the saint intended is St. Augustine of Hippo. Represented in art as an archbishop.

St. Patrick,

APOSTLE OF IRELAND.

March 17.

(Calendars : Sarum and Modern Roman (not in the Prayer Book Calendar of the Church of England, 1661, but inserted here from the Almanac published with the authorisation of the Archbishops of Canterbury until 1832.[1] A.D. 387-475.)

We come again to the British Isles, and before we touch English England, to the earlier Christianity of Ireland and Wales. 'Ireland, that virgin island on which no Roman proconsul had ever set his foot, which had not known either the exactions of Rome or its orgies, was also the only place in the world of which the Gospel took possession without the effusion of blood.'[2] Two captives, St. Patrick and St. Bridget, brought the liberating faith to Ireland.

St. Patrick was a Gallo-Roman by birth, said to have been born at Dumbarton, on the Clyde. There is a tradition that his mother was a niece of St. Martin of Tours. In his Confessions—the chief authentic source of our knowledge of him—he says, 'I, Patrick, a sinner, the rudest and least of all the faithful, and the most despicable among most men, had for my father Calpurnius, a deacon, son of the late Potitus, a presbyter, who was of the town Bonaven Taberniæ, for he had a farm in the neighbourhood, where I was taken captive. I was then nearly sixteen years old. I knew not the true God and I was carried in captivity to Hiberio '(his name for Hibernia)' with many thousands of men, because we had gone back from His commandments, and had not been obedient to our priests, who used to warn us for our

[1] Blunt's Annotated Prayer Book.
[2] Montalembert, *Moines de l'Occident*. Tod questions the literal truth of this statement, though, no doubt, St. Patrick's method of beginning with the conversion of the chieftains lessened the danger of persecution from above. Nevertheless, his monasteries had to be fortified.

salvation. And the Lord brought upon us the wrath of His displeasure, and scattered us among many nations, even unto the ends of the earth, where now my littleness is seen amongst aliens. And there the Lord opened the sense of my unbelief, that even though late I should remember my sins, and be converted with my whole heart unto the Lord my God, who had regard unto my loneliness, and had compassion upon my youth, and on my ignorance, and preserved me before I knew Him, and before I could understand or distinguish between good and evil, and protected me and comforted me as a father would a son.'

Again : 'I was like a stone lying in the mire, but He who is able came. He raised me up in His mercy.'

He chronicles his perils and trials in captivity, 'to make known the gift of God and spread the fearless confidence in His name among my brethren in Gallia, and the sons whom I have baptised in this land.'

'When I came to Ireland I used daily to keep the cattle and often every day to pray, and the fear and the love of God were ever more and more increased in me, and my faith increased, so that in the day I spoke a hundred times in prayer, and in the night as often, and even when I passed the night on the mountains, or in the forest, amidst snow and frost and rain, I would watch before daylight to pray. And I felt no discomfort ; there was then no laziness in me such as I find in my heart now. For the Spirit was ever burning within me.'

One night, after he had been in captivity six years, he heard in a dream a voice which said, 'Thy fasting is well ; thou shalt soon return to thy country.' And again, in another dream, the same voice told him that the ship was ready, but was distant 200 miles. 'I went in the power of the Lord, who directed my way for good, and I feared nothing until I arrived at that ship.' The captain, however, roughly refused him a passage ; but Patrick prayed, and his prayer was not finished, when one of the sailors called to him to come back quickly, 'for these men call thee.' They were three days at sea, and afterwards twenty-eight days in a desert place till their provisions ran short. Then the leader of the party said to him :

'What sayest thou, Christian? Thy God is great and all-powerful; why, then, canst thou not pray to Him for us, for we perish for hunger, and can find here no inhabitant?'

Patrick answered : 'Turn ye in faith to my Lord God, to whom nothing is impossible, and He will send you food, and ye shall be satisfied, for He has abundance everywhere.' And a herd of swine soon after appeared, of which they killed many. They found also some wild honey. But because some of them had said, 'This is an offering; thank God,' Patrick would not taste of it, fearing that it had been offered to an idol.

The same night an event occurred which he says he could never forget. He felt as if a great stone had fallen upon him. He was unable to move a limb, but he called out 'Helias!' with all his might.

'How it came into my mind I know not, but lo, the brightness of the sun fell upon me, and straightway removed all the weight, and I am persuaded that I was relieved by Christ my Lord, and that His Spirit then cried out for me.' It is suggested that this invocation refers to our Lord's 'Eli! Eli!' on the Cross. In an ancient Irish book of hymns are these lines from a hymn attributed to St. Hilary of Poictiers.

> Tu Dei de corde Verbum, Tu Via, Tu Veritas,
> Jesse Virga Tu vocaris, Te Leonem legimus;
> Dextra Patris, Mons, et Agnus, Angularis Tu Lapis,
> Sponsus idem, EL, Columba, Flamma, Pastor, Janua.

He was restored to liberty. He speaks of himself as being some years after with his parents in Britain. But the yoke of bondage he had borne in his youth had become to him the fruitful yoke of service. His heart was kind for ever to the sufferers and the fellow captives whose miseries he had shared, to the land where he had suffered, always burning to render to his oppressors the Christian vengeance of overcoming evil with good.

The legends and Biographies vary, and tell us many

things difficult to reconcile with each other. In this brief sketch it seems best to give as much as possible of his own words.

In the 'Confessions' he says:

'And there (namely in "The Britanniæ," with his parents)[1] in the dead of night, I saw a man coming to me as if from *Hiberio*, whose name was *Victoricus*, bearing innumerable epistles. And he gave me one of them, and I read the beginning of it, which contained the words, "The voice of the Irish." And whilst I was repeating the beginning of the epistle, I imagined that I heard in my mind the voice of those who were near the wood of *Foclut*, which is near the Western Sea. And thus they cried: "We pray thee, holy youth, to come and henceforth walk amongst us." And I was greatly pricked in heart and could read no more; and so I awoke. Thanks be to God, that after very many years the Lord granted unto them the blessing for which they cried, (præstitit illis Dominus secundum clamorem illorum).'

'Again, on another night, I know not, God knoweth, whether it was within me or near me, I heard distinctly words which I could not understand, except that at the end of what was said, there was uttered, "He who gave His life for thee, is He who speaketh in thee." And so I awoke rejoicing. And, again, I saw in myself one praying, and I was as it were within my body, and I heard him, that is to say, in my inner man, and he prayed there mightily with groanings. And, meanwhile, I was in a trance (stupebam) and marvelled and thought who it could be that thus prayed within me. But at the end of the prayer, he became so changed that he seemed to be a bishop. And so I awoke, and recollected the apostle's words: "The Spirit helpeth the infirmity of our prayer. For we know not what

---

[1] There is nothing said about his brothers and sisters in the 'Confessions,' but the little kernel of truth in the mass of legends about them has been curiously shown lately by the discovery of an ancient tombstone, not later than the beginning of the sixth century, on an island in Loch Corrib, with the inscription, 'The stone of Lugnaed, son of Limania'—the names given in the legend to one of St. Patrick's sisters, and the youngest of her seven sons.

to pray for as we ought, but the Spirit Himself maketh intercession for us, with groanings that cannot be uttered." And again : " The Lord our advocate intercedeth for us."'

The rest of his life was entirely devoted to the country of his captivity and his adoption. His heart burned with the wrongs of her people as with his own. The epistle to Coroticus is the indignant remonstrance of a father for the wrongs of his children.

Coroticus seems to have been the leader of a piratical raid of the Picts and pagan Scots of Argyllshire, in alliance. He speaks to them not as mere pagans but apostates, lapsed Christians, not pagans. They had massacred and enslaved numbers of his lately baptised Christians. At first, Patrick, now missionary bishop of all Ireland, sent a deputation of clergy to the pirates, to whom he speaks not as merely pagan, but as apostates, lapsed Christians. The deputation was sent away with mocking and insult. Then with his own hand, Patrick wrote this Epistle, still existing, which is a solemn episcopal excommunication as well as a deunciation : 'Soldiers' (he says), 'whom I no longer call my fellow-citizens, or fellow-citizens of the Roman saints, but fellow-citizens of the devils, in consequence of their evil deeds ; who live in death, after the hostile rite of the barbarians ; associates of the Scots and apostate Picts, desirous of glutting themselves with the blood of innocent Christians, multitudes of whom I have begotten in God, and confirmed in Christ.'

'I testify before God and His holy angels, that it shall be so as my ignorance has said. These are not my words, but the words of God, of apostles, of prophets, who never lie, which I have translated into Latin : *They who believe shall be saved, but whoso believeth not shall be damned.* God hath spoken. I therefore, earnestly request of every one, whosoever as a willing servant of God may become the bearer of this letter, that it be not withheld from anyone, but rather that it be read before all the people, and in the presence of Coroticus himself. May God inspire them to return to a better mind towards Him, that even though late they may repent of their impious deeds. They have been murderers of the brethren of the Lord; but let them repent, and set free the baptised captive women whom they have heretofore carried off; so shall God count them worthy of life, and they shall be made whole here and for ever. Peace to the Father, to the Son, and to the Holy Ghost. Amen.'

The Biographies give various accounts of his missionary journeys and foundations. His method seems to have been to adopt as much as possible, *i.e.* as much as had good in it, of the customs and laws of those whom he was seeking to christianise.

Devoted as he was to the oppressed, the suffering and the poor, his first converts were often the chiefs of the clans.[1] Their sons became his scholars, and often ultimately his clergy, itinerating with him on his missionary journeys. The bishops were spiritual shepherds of the clans, and the priests chaplains of the chiefs. The ecclesiastical divisions were by tribes and families, rather than by territories and parishes.[2] And as regards the Druids, the priests, teachers and poets of the people, his endeavour was, not to repel, but to enlist them on his side.

In his legend (Montalembert says) 'nothing is more poetical than his meeting with the Irish Bards who formed a sacerdotal caste.' It is among these that he recruits his most faithful disciples. Agreement was not established between them, however, without some previous storms. Patrick is said to have expressed a fear that the too piratical and profane warriors whose glory the Bards celebrated ought to be in hell. 'If thy God were in hell,' the Bard replied, 'my heroes would rescue him thence.' But the triumph of the truth brought peace between poetry and faith. The monasteries founded by Patrick became the asylum and home of

---

[1] Very significant is the story of the King of Munster, who having his foot accidentally pierced by a spear during his baptism, accepted it as a necessary part of the rite of the Sacrament, and never flinched or uttered a sound of pain till all was finished.

[2] The 'roving commissions' of the Irish bishops were long afterwards a perplexity to their English neighbours.

Celtic poetry. 'The song of the Bards,' says an ancient author, 'blessed and transfigured, became so beautiful that the angels of heaven stooped down to listen, and the harp became the badge of Catholic Ireland.'

Also whenever this seemed possible, like Augustine of Canterbury, he endeavoured to hallow the pagan festivals by adapting them to some portion of Christian doctrine or history. And everywhere his house and his hands were open to the poor, and young and old gathered around him.

While such was the spirit and method of his mission, it is most interesting to trace from his own words what the message of that mission really was.

And to this three very ancient Irish manuscripts help us.

His Creed is given thus in his Confessions :—

There is none other God, nor ever was, nor shall be hereafter, except God the Father unbegotten, without beginning, from whom is all beginning, upholding all things, and His Son Jesus Christ, whom we acknowledge to have been always with the Father, before the beginning of the world, spiritually with the Father, in an ineffable manner begotten, before all beginning, and by Him were made things visible and invisible ; and being made man, and having overcome death, He was received into heaven unto the Father, and (the Father) hath given unto Him all power, above every name, of things in heaven and things in earth and things under the earth, that every tongue should confess that Jesus Christ is Lord and God. Whom we believe, and we look for His coming, Who is soon about to be the Judge of quick and dead, Who will render unto every man according to his works, and hath poured into us abundantly the gift of the Holy Ghost, and the pledge of immortality, who maketh the faithful and obedient to become the sons of God the Father, and joint-heirs with Christ, Whom we confess and worship, One God in the Trinity of the Sacred Name. For He Himself hath said by the Prophet, Call upon me in the day of thy tribulation and I will deliver thee, and thou shalt magnify me. And again He saith, It is honourable to reveal and confess the works of God.

His method of evangelising may be gathered from Tirechan, who wrote early in the seventh century, from a story giving at all events what was believed to have been Patrick's way of teaching.

Then St. Patrick came to the well which is called 'Clebach,' on the sides of Crochan, towards the east ; and before sunrise they (i.e. Patrick and his followers) sat down near the well, and lo, the two daughters of King Laoghaire, Eltine the fair, and Fedelin the ruddy, came early to the well to wash, after the manner of women, and they found near the well a synod of holy bishops with Patrick, and they knew not whence they were, or in what form, or from what people, or from what country; but they supposed them to be 'Duine sidhe,' or gods of the earth, or a phantasm. And the virgins said unto them: 'Who are ye, and whence come ye?'

And Patrick said unto them, 'It were better for you to confess to our true God than to inquire concerning our race.'

The first virgin said:—

'Who is God?

'And where is God?

'And of what (nature) is God?

'And where is His dwelling place?

'Has your God sons and daughters; gold and silver?

'Is He ever living?

'Is He beautiful?

'Did many foster His Son?

'Are His daughters dear and beauteous to men of the world?

'Is He in heaven or in earth?

'In the sea?

'In rivers?

'In mountainous places?

'In valleys?

'Declare unto us the knowledge of Him.

'How shall He be seen?

'How is He to be loved?

'How is He to be found?'

But St. Patrick, full of the Holy Ghost, answered and said:—

'Our God is the God of all men.

'God of heaven and earth, of the sea and rivers.

'The God of the sun, the moon, and all stars.

'The God of the high mountains, and of the lowly valleys.

'God who is above heaven and in heaven and under heaven.

'He hath as an habitation the heaven and the earth, and the sea, and all that are therein.

'He inspireth all things.

'He quickeneth all things.

'He is over all things.

'He sustaineth all things.

'He giveth light to the light of the sun.

'And He hath made springs in a dry ground.

'And dry islands in the sea.

'And hath appointed the stars to serve the greater lights.

'He hath a Son co-eternal and co-equal (*consimilem*) with Himself.

'The Son is not younger than the Father.

'Nor is the Father older than the Son.

'And the Holy Ghost breathed in them.

'The Father, and the Son, and the Holy Ghost are not divided.

'But I desire to unite you to the heavenly King, inasmuch as you are the daughters of an earthly king, to believe.'

And the virgins said, as with one mouth and one heart :—

'Teach us most diligently how we may believe in the heavenly King. Show us how we may see Him, face to face, and whatsoever thou shalt say unto us, we will do.'

And Patrick said :

'Believe ye that by Baptism ye put off the sin of your father and your mother?'

They answered,—

'We believe.'

'Believe ye in repentance after sin?'

'We believe.'

'Believe ye in Life after death?'

'We believe.'

'Believe ye the Resurrection at the Day of judgment?'

'We believe.'

'Believe ye the Unity of the Church?'

'We believe.'

And they were baptised, and a white garment put upon their heads. And they asked to see the face of Christ, and the Saint said unto them : 'Ye cannot see the face of Christ, except ye taste of death, and except ye receive the Sacrifice.'

And they answered, 'Give us the Sacrifice that we may behold the Son, our Spouse.'

And they received the Eucharist of God. And they slept in death.

The character of his worship and his spiritual life may be felt from the Hymn, certainly of great antiquity, attributed to St. Patrick himself, appended as one of his Four Honours to his 'Hymnus Scoticus,' written 'in a very ancient dialect of Irish Celtic.'

1. I bind to myself to-day
 The strong power of an invocation of the Trinity,
 The faith of the Trinity in Unity,
 The Creator of the elements.

[1] This hymn, taken from Tod's *Life of St. Patrick*, is a 'lorica' or breastplate to protect those who devoutly recite it from bodily and spiritual dangers.

2. I bind to myself to-day
   The power of the Incarnation of Christ with that of His
     Baptism,
   The power of the Crucifixion with that of His Burial,
   The power of the Resurrection with the Ascension,
   The power of the Coming to the sentence of judgment.

3. I bind to myself to-day
   The power of the love of Seraphim,
   In the obedience of angels,
   In the hope of Resurrection unto reward,
   In the prayers of the noble Fathers,
   In the predictions of the Prophets,
   In the preaching of Apostles,
   In the faith of Confessors,
   In the purity of holy Virgins,
   In the acts of righteous men.

4. I bind to myself to-day
   The power of heaven,
   The light of the sun,
   The whiteness of snow,
   The force of fire,
   The flashing of lightning,
   The velocity of wind,
   The depths of the sea,
   The stability of the earth,
   The hardness of rocks.

5. I bind to myself to-day
   The power of God to guide me,
   The might of God to uphold me,
   The wisdom of God to teach me,
   The eye of God to watch over me,
   The ear of God to hear me,
   The word of God to give me speech,
   The hand of God to protect me,
   The way of God to prevent me,
   The shield of God to shelter me,
   The host of God to defend me
   Against the snares of demons,
   Against the temptations of vices,
   Against the lusts of nature,
   Against every man who meditates injury to me,
   Whether far or near,
   With few or with many.

6. I have set around me all these powers
   Against every hostile savage power,
   Directed against my body and my soul,
   Against the incantations of false prophets,

Against the black laws of heathenism,
Against the false laws of heresy,
Against the deceits of idolatry,
Against the spells of women, and smiths, and Druids,
Against all knowledge which blinds the soul of man.

7. Christ protect me to-day
   Against poison, against burning,
   Against drowning, against wound,
   That I may receive abundant reward.

8. Christ with me, Christ before me,
   Christ behind me, Christ within me,
   Christ beneath me, Christ above me,
   Christ at my right, Christ at my left,
   Christ in the fort,
   Christ in the chariot seat,
   Christ in the ship.

9. Christ in the heart of every man who thinks of me,
   Christ in the mouth of every man who speaks to me
   Christ in every eye that sees me,
   Christ in every ear that hears me.

10. I bind to myself to-day
    The strong power of an invocation of the Trinity,
    The faith of the Trinity in Unity,
    The Creator of the elements.

11. Domini est salus,
    Domini est salus,
    Christi est salus.
    Salus tua, Domine, sit semper nobiscum.

These words, revealing the impression made by what St. Patrick actually taught, are especially valuable when we consider that from the Ireland which after his labours was called 'The Isle of Saints,' from the Irish monasteries which he founded and whose brethren were his disciples, went far and wide for centuries, to Iona, to Scotland, to England, to Switzerland, Burgundy, and Saxony, the first evangelists and teachers of the nations of Northern Europe. Columba, Aidan, Columbanus, St. Gall are spiritual descendants of St. Patrick, who might be called through them the Apostle, not only of Ireland, but of all the pagan North. The Biographies vary as to the period and extent of his missionary work. As time went on, his presence as the founder would naturally be claimed on any possible ground in all directions; and there was the tendency to arrange his life into analogies and parables, such as assigning to it the 120 years of Moses, or dividing it into three even periods.

But of the devotion of his life, whatever its date or duration, there is no doubt.

Of his death, as with so many for whom death could have been but the last upward step of a continually upward life, the step across the threshold, little is said. There is a tradition, that St. Bridget, herself the daughter of a captive slave, who was one of his converts, afterwards associated with him as Patroness of Ireland, foretold when he was to die, and with her own hands prepared his coffin and buried him. The place of his burial is disputed.

A captive, learning from the miseries of captivity to pity at once his own captors and all captives ; a slave, redeeming multitudes from slavery ; robbed by pirates of his patrimony, and through his poverty making many rich, it is said with pathetic appropriateness of the Apostle and Patron Saint of Ireland : ' He always gave till he had no more to give, and rejoiced to find himself poor with his Master.'[1]

---

[1] This legend is too quaint and significant not to give. 'The knight of Daire came after these things to honour St. Patrick, bringing with him a wonderful brazen cauldron from beyond seas, which held three firkins. And Daire said unto the Saint : " So this cauldron is thine." And St. Patrick said : " *Gratzacham* " (Gratias agam). Then Daire returned to his own home and said : " The man is a fool, for he said nothing good for a wonderful cauldron of three firkins, except ' *Gratzacham.*' Then Daire added and said to his servants : " Go and bring us back our cauldron." They went and said unto Patrick : " We must take away the cauldron." Nevertheless, this time also St. Patrick said : " *Gratzacham*, take it." So they took it. Then Daire asked his people, saying, " What said the Christian when ye took away the cauldron ? " But they answered : " He said *Gratzacham* again." Daire answered and said : " *Gratzacham* when I give, *Gratzacham* when I take away. His saying is so good that with those *Gratzachams* his cauldron shall be brought back to him." And Daire himself went this time and brought back the cauldron to Patrick, saying to him : " Thy cauldron shall remain with thee, for thou art a steady and imperturbable man ; moreover, also that portion of land which thou didst desire before, I now give thee as fully as I have it, and dwell thou there." And this is the city which is now named Arddmacha.'

St. David (Dewi), Patron of Wales.[1]
March 1.

(Died A.D. 601. Calendar: Sarum, Hereford, Aberdeen. Sarum Ep. and Gosp.: Ecclus. xliv. 17, 20, 21-23; xlv. 5, 7, 15, 16; St. Matt. xxv. 14-22.)

St. David, with the exception of St. Malo (Machutus), is the only saint of Celtic blood, of that imaginative race of which came so many of the earliest missionaries to Europe, in our Calendar. Of the two national saints, patrons of Ireland and Wales, 'St. Patrick was a gentleman,' born of a good Roman Gallic family, and St. David (Dewi) 'was a Welshman,' and through them Wales and Ireland are united by very real historical links. It is said to be on the Welsh promontory of Menevia looking towards Ireland, now St. David's, that St. Patrick, standing in deep discouragement, had a vision of the Ireland which was to be given to the Christian Church by his labours. On that little elevated tableland, thirty years afterwards, St. David founded the monastery and church which made it thereafter St. David's. And it was through the monastic institutions of St. David that the Irish and Welsh monks were especially united.

St. David's mother was an Irishwoman. His birth was illegitimate, his mother, like St. Bridget's, in those days of violence, the victim of lawless passion. The Church, while sanctioning through one of her early saints the choice of suicide rather than dishonour, suffered no taint of the wrongs of others to bar the sufferers from her highest places.

It is good to have even this one link with those races which have not been vulgarised and made prosaic by success, whose patriotism, tried by so many fires, has given so much of that wild and tender minor to their

[1] Dedications of churches: in England, 9; in Wales, 33. Represented preaching on a hill, a dove on his shoulder.

poetry and music, without which the practical and prosperous races around them would be so much poorer.

The ancient Welsh law which forbad the seizure for debt of any man's sword or harp, or books, throws a vivid light on what the people did most and loved best.

Two of the ancient traditions also bring their thoughts home to us,—one Irish, the other Welsh. 'In one of the voyages of St. Brendan,' says the legend,[1] ' in search of the earthly paradise, he and his companions found a mermaid lying dead of a severe wound. St. Brendan restored her to life, baptised her, and then asked her who she was. 'I am of the inhabitants of the sea,' she said ; 'of the people who implore and pray for the Resurrection.' Brendan asked her what was her wish, whether she would go to heaven at once or return to her fatherland? She answered in a language which none but Brendan understood, and said, 'To heaven, for I hear the voices of the angels praising the Almighty Lord.' And after she had received the Body of Christ and His Blood, she died without disquiet.

The other story is of St. Cadoc, Welsh prince and monk, who took refuge from the heathen Saxons in a little island off the coast of Brittany in the archipelago of Morbihan, and there held a monastic school to which scholars came from the neighbouring shores. He made them learn Virgil by heart. One day when he was walking on the shore with his famous friend and compatriot, Gildas, his Virgil under his arm, he began to weep at the thought that the author of the book he so loved might perhaps be in hell. Gildas reproved him severely for the 'perhaps,' having himself no doubt of the damnation of Virgil. At that moment a gust of wind swept the book into the sea. Cadoc, dismayed, retired to his cell and said to himself, 'I will not eat a mouthful of bread nor drink a drop of water until I know clearly what God will render to those who have sung on earth as the angels sing in heaven.' Thereupon he went to sleep. Soon he had a dream, in which a sweet voice said to him, 'Pray for me, pray for me, be not weary of praying; I will sing

[1] Tod's ' Life of St. Patrick.'

for ever of the mercies of the Lord.' One would much like Dante's Virgil, who left his disciple with words of sympathetic tenderness at the borders of the earthly Paradise he himself might not enter, to have known of St. Cadoc's dream.

There is a tradition that David's father was of the kindred of Arthur of the Round Table, and that in his later years he restored the ancient British Church of Glastonbury, where Arthur was buried.

There is a curious significance in the blending of the legend of Joseph of Arimathea, traditionally the first evangelist of Britain, and the thorns he planted at Glastonbury with King Arthur and his warrior knights, and with St. David and his labouring monks ; the 'secret' disciple whose secret devotion blossomed into open confession, and generous homage at the moment when hope seemed over,—the Confessor whose courage came from the Cross and the Sepulchre,—with the races which knew so much of both.

David's education, again, links him with Patrick's ancient Gallic race. It was in the monastic schools founded by the influence of St. Germanus of Auxerre, when he came twice to combat Pelagianism in Britain, that David learned all that could then be learned of the ancient learning.

The good bishop Germanus, while on his way to Britain, passing through Nanterre discerned the piety of the child shepherdess, St. Genevieve of Paris, blessed her, and picking up from the dust a piece of money stamped with the Cross, gave it her to wear as a badge of her consecration. Those same observant eyes and benedictory hands saw the needs of Britain, and laid the foundation of the schools which were to scatter darkness by diffusing light.

David from his earliest years was under the training of Paulinus, disciple of Germanus. All through his life the heathen Saxon, or English, were sweeping in successive waves over Roman and Christian Britain.

In the beginning of David's century the Romans had withdrawn their legions to defend Italy from the Goths. In the middle of the century (449) Hengist and Horsa landed in Kent, and a century and a half of warfare and plunder, of desperate fighting and desperate defeat followed before the Britons were driven into the wild fastnesses of which they were never dispossessed, and England became England, and the western mountain ranges Wales.

But David's conflicts were not only with the Saxons, but with expiring paganism and with heresy among his own people; with some of the still heathen chiefs and bards of his race (called in the legends 'satraps and magi'); and with the Pelagianism of which one of his compatriots was the originator.

Legendary as his life is, he was in the same line of battle with St. Augustine of Hippo, and was a contemporary of St. Benedict. 'Indeed St. David' (Montalembert says) 'was the St. Benedict of Wales.'

David's monastic rule was very severe. Garments of the roughest, coats of skins, food of the simplest, and scanty supply even of this; bread with no flavouring but salt; for drink, water with a little milk. Labour, manual or mental, with devotions private or common, filled all the hours during which it was possible for mortal eyes to keep awake. The monks were not even to have the aid of the patient beasts of burden, but were harnessed to the plough themselves. Yet their love of knowledge and their imaginative power seemed rather stimulated than dulled by all this toil. Mystical poems and epigrammatic sayings, still left to us, light up their labouring life; and they spent much time in transcribing and in studying the Holy Scriptures. Their eagerness and interest in their intellectual work was such as to make the rule a trial, and a necessity, that at the instant the church bell began to ring they were to lay aside any work, however engrossing, that they were engaged in, *with the sentence unfinished*, or even *the word half written*.

At length St. David died in his beloved monastery on the high tableland near the Irish sea; and this and all his monasteries became a sanctuary and refuge for hunted men of his brave but vanquished race, and in after years St. David's was a shrine of pilgrimage for conquerors and conquered alike.

St. Chad

OF LICHFIELD.

March 2.

(Calendars : Sarum, York, Hereford and Aberdeen.   Died A.D. 672.
Sarum Ep. and Gosp. : Ecclus. xlv. 1–5 ; St. Mark xiii. 33–37.)

We come to a saint of a new tongue and kindred and nation, the first really English saint, belonging to the race, and speaking the language which is the basis of our own. It is interesting, nevertheless, to observe that by spiritual descent St. Chad does not belong to the English, but to the earlier British or Celtic Christianity.

He was one of four brothers, all priests, trained in the Scottish monastery of Lindisfarne, under Bishop Aidan. Cedd and Chad were bishops. By birth they were Northumbrians. Their mission lay among the East Angles and Mercians.

St. Augustine of Canterbury had been dead half a century, and the people of Essex, their faith shaken by a pestilence, had in a great measure relapsed from Christianity. The new impulse of St. Chad's days came from the North. That royal lady, the great abbess Hilda, of Whitby, and the saintly family of St. Chad himself, owed their Christianity to the North, and to the Celtic monks with their fervent diffusive faith, who sent their teachers east and south and west throughout England ; men of humble self-denying life, who went on foot like the Apostles of old, and built churches of wood, but took everywhere the sacred Scriptures. Bishop Cedd founded a monastery at Lestingau in Yorkshire 'among craggy mountains, which looked more like lurking places for robbers and retreats for wild beasts than dwellings for men ;' and his way of founding it was to go and live there alone, fasting and praying through Lent, never eating till evening except on Sundays, and then indulging as his festival fare in one hen's-egg, and a little bread with milk and water. In this way he thought, 'as was the custom of those sent out, those of whom he had learned the regular discipline, to reclaim the place from a habitation of dragons, to be a place where the fruits of good works should spring up.'[1] There he lived and established the religious customs of Lindisfarne, where they had been educated. And there, at last, he fell sick of a prevalent mortality and died, so much beloved that thirty brethren from another monastery among the East Saxons, when they heard of their father's death, came to be near his last resting-place; and there they all took the pestilence and died. He left the monastery to be governed by his brother Chad.

Chad had spent many years of his early life with Egbert, another young Northumbrian monk, among the Irish monasteries, receiving the instruction so freely given there, and sharing the passion of missionary zeal which possessed the heart of Egbert, who intended, if he had been permitted by health, to evangelise the Frisian, Saxon, and other wild German tribes of the north of Europe. The friendship continued till death.

But the Christianity of England was not to flow in the old Celtic channels. The dispute, in form about Easter and the tonsure, and in essence about the unity and obedience of Rome, was decided otherwise.

After the death of the holy Aidan, Wilfrid, the great Northumbrian, at the council of Whitby persuaded the majority of the clergy, with Oswy, the king, to follow the general custom of Rome, and the rest of Western Christendom.

Colman, bishop of Lindisfarne, with his monks, thereupon took the bones of St. Aidan and bore them to Scotland, abandoning what had so long been, indeed, the Holy Island, and a fountain of life to England.

The holy bishop Cedd was among those convinced by the arguments of Wilfrid. The controversy, so trivial in

[1] Bede.

apparent differences, so important in its essential results, was virtually over. England became knit to Rome and to Continental Christendom. And it is from the Benedictine Bede we have the generous and tender record of the lowly devoted lives, the fruitful labours, the humility and holiness of these early missionaries of Scottish training.

About 564, Bishop Colman with his monks left Lindisfarne, and a few years afterwards Benedict Biscop founded the Benedictine abbey of St. Peter's, Wearmouth, where Bede was educated.

England was thus launched on the broad current of Latin Christianity. By the mission from Rome of the Greek archbishop Theodore of Tarsus (introduced by Hadrian, a Neapolitan of African descent, who would not undertake the office himself), our country is curiously linked with the birthplace of St. Paul and of St. Augustine. And it is interesting to think that Greek was spoken by a Greek at the founding of our English Church, and beside the well-springs of our English literature.

Theodore's connection with St. Chad reflects a most pleasant light on both.

Chad had been consecrated in Wilfrid's absence Bishop of York (of the 'Deira' of St. Gregory's 'Angels'), by Wini, bishop of Winchester, before Theodore's arrival.

'Being thus consecrated bishop he began immediately to devote himself to ecclesiastical truth and to chastity; to apply himself to humility, continence, and study; to travel about, not on horseback, but, after the manner of the apostles, on foot, to preach the Gospel in towns and the open country, in cottages, villages, and castles, for he was one of the disciples of Aidan, and endeavoured to instruct his people by the same actions and behaviour, according to his and his brother Cedd's example. But Theodore had arrived at Canterbury, and with Hadrian' (the African monk from Naples), 'both excellently skilled in the Greek and Latin tongues, well read in sacred and secular literature, they went through the land, gathering a crowd of disciples, and there daily flowed from them rivers of knowledge, to water the hearts of their hearers; and together with the Books of Holy Writ, they also taught them the arts of ecclesiastical poetry, astronomy, and arithmetic. The testimony of which is that there are still living at this day some of their scholars, who are as well versed in the Greek and Latin tongues as in their own in which they were born. Nor were there ever happier times since the English came into Britain, for their kings being brave men and good Christians, they were a terror to all barbarous nations, and the minds of all men were bent upon the joys of the heavenly kingdom of which they had heard; and all who desired to be instructed in sacred reading had masters at hand to teach them. 'From that time also they began in all the churches of the English to have sacred music.'

'He was the first archbishop whom all the English Church obeyed.'

'And when he came to York, Theodore upbraided Bishop Chad, that he had not been duly consecrated, and Chad answered with great humility, "If you know I have not duly received episcopal ordination, I will willingly resign the office, for I never thought myself worthy of it, but, though unworthy, in obedience submitted to undertake it."[1]

Theodore by sympathetic insight perceiving his fitness through his humility, would not suffer him to lay aside his episcopal dignity, but completed his ordination, and evidently from that time treated him with reverent love and consideration.

Through Theodore, Chad was summoned from the monastery his brother Cedd had founded (at Lestingau, in Yorkshire), to which he had retired, and appointed to the great diocese of Mercia, then comprising nearly all Northumbria, with Lancashire, Lincolnshire, Shropshire, Stafford, and part of Cheshire.

Of this great territory Chad fixed on Lichfield as his episcopal city, and there he laboured for the rest of his life of two or three years, always with the same simple, self-denying ways as his 'father Aidan.' Theodore endeavoured

[1] Bede.

to guard the treasure of such a devoted life against his own hardness to himself.

'Seeing it was his custom to go about the work of the Gospel on foot rather than on horseback, Theodore commanded him to ride whenever he had a long journey to undertake, and finding him very unwilling to omit his former pious labour, he himself with his own hands lifted him on the horse, for he thought him a holy man, and, therefore, obliged him to ride wherever he had need to go.'[1]

A tender and holy fear and reverence marked his life, and a monk whose name was Trumhere, who had lived in his monastery at Lestingau, told Bede that 'if a storm of wind came while he was reading or doing anything, he would lay aside his book and call on God for *mercy to be extended to all mankind.*' His solitude with God was solitude with the Father and lover of men. If the storm increased, and there were thunder and lightning, Chad would repair to the church and spend the time in prayer and psalms till calm returned. For he thought of the great judgment coming on the world, and felt the Hand lifted through the trembling sky which it behoved us to answer with due fears and love, and to search and clear the recesses of our hearts. But for himself 'he joyfully beheld the day of his death, or rather, the day of our Lord which he had always expected till it came.' And at last when he had become Bishop of Lichfield, 'there came a mortality sent from heaven, which by means of the death of the flesh, translated the stones of the Church from their earthly places to the heavenly building.'

His death was announced 'by a call of heavenly music.' His disciple, the monk Owini, once a great man, chamberlain and councillor of Queen Etheldreda, who had come to his monastery at Lestingau, with an axe and a hatchet in his hand, to renounce the world, and labour with his hands for others, and learn of the humble and holy abbot, heard this heavenly call.

[1] Bede.

'At Lichfield Owini was received by the bishop into the house, and there entertained with the brethren; and whilst they were engaged within in reading, he was without, doing such things as were necessary.

'One day while he was thus employed abroad, and his companions were gone to the church, as I began to state, the bishop was alone reading or praying in the oratory of that place, when on a sudden, as he afterwards said, he heard the voice of persons singing most sweetly and rejoicing, and appearing to descend from Heaven. Which voice he said he first heard coming from the south-east and that afterwards it drew near him, till it came to the roof of the oratory where the bishop was, and entering therein, filled the same and all about it. He listened attentively to what he heard, and after about half-an-hour, perceived the same song of joy to ascend from the roof of the said oratory, and to return to heaven the same way it came, with inexpressible sweetness. When he stood for some time astonished, and seriously revolving in his mind what it might be, the bishop opened the window of the oratory, and making a sign with his hand, as he was often wont to do, ordered him to come in to him. He accordingly went hastily in, and the bishop said to him, "Make haste to the church, and cause the seven brothers to come hither, and do you come with them." When they were come, he first admonished them to preserve the virtue of peace among themselves, and towards all others; and indefatigably to practise the rules of regular discipline, which they had either been taught by him, or seen him observe, or had noticed in the words or actions of the former fathers. Then he added, that the day of his death was at hand; for, said he, "that amiable guest, who was wont to visit our brethren, has vouchsafed also to come to me this day, and to call me out of this world. Return, therefore, to the church, and speak to the brethren, that they in their prayers recommend my passage to our Lord, and that they be careful to provide for their own, the hour whereof is uncertain, by watching, prayer, and good works."

'When he had spoken thus much and more, and they, having received his blessing, had gone away in sorrow, he who had heard the heavenly song returned alone, and prostrating himself on the ground, said : " I beseech you, father, may I be permitted to ask a question ? " " Ask what you will," answered the bishop. Then he added : " I entreat you to tell me what song of joy was that which I heard coming upon this oratory, and after some time returning to heaven ? " The bishop answered : " If you heard the singing, and know of the coming of the heavenly company, I command you, in the name of our Lord, that you do not tell the same to any before my death. They were angelic spirits, who came to call me to my heavenly reward, which I have always longed after, and they promised they would return seven days hence, and take me away with them." Which was accordingly fulfilled, as had been said to him ; for being presently seized with a languishing distemper, and the same daily increasing, on the seventh day, as had been promised to him, when he had prepared for death by receiving the Body and Blood of our Lord, his soul being delivered from the prison of the body, the angels, as may justly be believed, attending him, he departed to the joys of heaven.'

Dedications of churches : thirty-one, all in the Midlands. Represented in art as a bishop, sometimes with a church in his hand.

St. Etheldreda (St. Audrey).

October 17.

(Died A.D. 679. Calendars: Sarum, Hereford. Sarum Ep. and Gosp.: 2 Cor. x. 17; xi. 2; St. Matt. xxv. 1-13.)

It is probably partly on account of an enthusiasm of the people for the daughter and spouse of their kings, and partly on account of her adherence to the Roman rules and rites which prevailed in England—through her counsellor and guide, Bishop Wilfrid, that Etheldreda is in our Calendar, while the name of the great Abbess Hilda of Whitby is absent.

One of four sisters renowned for their piety, as were St. Chad and his four brothers, there is a touching link between her life and his in the story of Owini, governor of her royal household, who told the story of the heavenly music he heard at St. Chad's death.

The first and most popular of canonised Englishwomen, there must have been something to raise Etheldreda and her shrine to the place they held in the heart and imagination of the people. No command from far-off authority would have made the English people love her memory as they did, although without the sanction of that authority she would not have had her place in the calendar. She lived in a world of great abbesses, noble and royal in birth, and noble and royal in generosity and influence. In these early English days her family bequeathed many names of princesses and abbesses to the canonised roll. But neither Hilda, the royal Abbess of Whitby, Etheldreda's aunt, nor Ebba, of Coldringham, aunt of the husband she left for the convent, have left the traces on English popular imagination left by St. Etheldreda (Audrey), Queen and Nun.[1]

---

[1] It is said the word 'tawdry' is derived from trifles bought at St. Audrey's fair.

Yet to us no story of all the saintly histories seems to have so little attraction. No doubt, the old English royal name, like that of Edmund the Martyr, in his own East Anglia, wrought like a spell among the Christians plundered by the Danish pirates, and afterwards among the English people, kept under by Norman lords. The monasteries in the Eastern counties were those which suffered most from the Danes; and in the Fens, the land of Hereward, the last resistance was offered to the Norman conquerors.

And also, doubtless, the victorious Roman party, the powerful defender of which Bishop Wilfrid was her spiritua director, might especially sanction her cult. But also, one cannot but think, there must have been something, originally in her character and personality to win the homage which grew into such a worship, and endured so long, and left traces so wide and deep.

One of four 'saintly' sisters, daughters of Anna, king of the East Angles, the traditions of the family are at once patriotic and monastic. Her grandfather Siegebert had left his crown for a monastery; but when called by his people to lead them against the deadly enemy of Christianity, Penda of Mercia, once more he put on his armour to lead them against the foe, although he refused himself to bear any weapon but a staff, and perished in the field. Her father, Anna, as devoted a Christian, was also as devoted a patriot; he also died fighting at the head of his people against Penda.

Two of the most remarkable men of her time were bound up with the history of her house; Fursey, an Irish monk, whose poetical visions of the unseen world are among the many streams which at last flowed into the great poem of the 'Divina Commedia;' and Felix, the great Benedictine from Burgundy, yet the warm friend of the Celtic St. Aidan, who laboured for seventeen years in the eastern counties, preaching and teaching, and founding schools and monasteries which were in a very real sense the beginnings of the schools and universities of England. One of her sisters,

Emerilda, wife of the King of Mercia, was the Clotilda or Bertha of Mercia; another was married to the King of Kent, destroyer of idols. Her mother's sister was the great Abbess Hilda, 'mother' of the great double Abbey of monks and nuns at Whitby, and discoverer and patroness of the first English poet Cædmon. Etheldreda is said to have been of dazzling beauty, so that her hand was sought in marriage by many of the princes around. Of these suitors the promise of her hand was won from her father by Tonbert. But from her earliest years, the legends say, she had devoted her virginity to God. The prince reverenced her, respected her vow, and dying in two years left her as her dower the Isle of Ely.

In her second marriage, with Prince Egfried, into which she was reluctantly compelled, the prince vainly endeavoured to induce her to renounce her monastic purpose. She won his reverence and affection, and was the Lady of the household from which went forth the good Owini, her chamberlain, to be the disciple of St. Chad.

At this point of the story appears that great Northumbrian noble and Benedictine monk, more Roman than any of the Romans, more a ruler than any archbishop or king then in the Northumbrian land, Wilfrid of York, who influenced the council of Whitby against the Celtic missionaries to whom Northumbria owed its conversion, thus causing the self-exile of Colman of Lindisfarne.

There must have been a wonderful charm about this man. He is said to have been of noble bearing, fair in face, and frank in speech; he won the hearts of old and young, men and women, high and low, from the young son of the king of Northumbria to the aged bishop of Lyons, who would have adopted him as his son. It is scarcely possible, happily, for anyone to receive so much affection without giving much. And it is said that when afterwards, on Wilfrid's homeward journey from Rome, the aged bishop was murdered in one of the frays of that disturbed region, the young Northumbrian would willingly have died with him. 'Why,' he said, 'should not the son die with the father, and be with Christ?'

He is said to have had a noble beauty of countenance
and form, and a most persuasive eloquence. Everything
told of him indicates that personal fascination which is
apt to make spiritual influence so overwhelming and so
perilous. No small or selfish nature would have won the
influence he won. No shadow of the lower kind of calumny seems to rest on his name. And yet it seems too
evident that he fell before the deeper temptations on the
higher levels, so identifying himself with what seemed to
him to be the will of God, that any obstacles of ordinary
human principle which stood in his way were swept out
of it as if they had been revolts against heaven.

Prince Egfried entreated Wilfrid to persuade the queen
to abandon her monastic purpose. Wilfrid, while seeming
from motives of policy to yield to the prince, secretly
encouraged Etheldreda in her purpose, and actually administered to her, kneeling before him, the monastic vow.

'In these days' (says Montalembert) 'it appears happily
certain, that no one in the Catholic Church would approve of the conduct of Wilfrid. It is not less certain,
that in the age in which he lived, no one seems to have
blamed him.'[1]

'The mills of God grind slowly, but they grind ex-
ceeding small.' It took nearly a thousand years before
such a perversion of the Divine ideal of the family led to
the rasing to the ground of the institutions built on it,
with all their beautiful memories of good, and capacities of
service.

Yet, even in Wilfrid's life (Montalembert thinks), the evil
results of this mistake began at once. 'His life, before
that, agitated, but glorious and prosperous, was, after the
consecration of Etheldreda, but one tissue of trials and
storms.'[1]

Etheldreda fled from her home, not to her own aunt the
abbess Hilda, who never yielded to the influence of Wilfrid,
but to the convent of her husband's aunt, Ebba, abbess of
the great abbey of Coldingham. Thither Wilfrid went at

[1] *Moines de l Occident.*

once and gave her the veil and the black robe. Thence Egfried would have removed her; Ebba was powerless to defend her against her husband; and with one attendant the young wedded nun wandered away and lay hidden in lonely places. Legend says that once when she slept exhausted with fatigue, her pilgrim staff struck root in the ground and grew at once into a great tree; that the sea itself swept up in unusual tides, and guarded her on a promontory where she had taken refuge; until the baffled and bewildered Egfried gave up hope of ever recovering her, let her alone, and married again—this time, naturally, as it would seem, choosing a lady who was not too much of a Christian. At last Etheldreda ventured to return to her own territories, the Isle of Ely, dower of her first marriage, and there she founded the abbey of which Wilfrid consecrated her abbess; where she ruled for the remaining seventeen years of her life, over one of the double communities of monks and nuns, such as those of Hilda and Ebba. Many of her old servants and members of her household followed her, desiring to place themselves under the firm and gentle guidance of their beloved queen and mistress.

There she practised austerities as to food and clothing, and also as to washing, which throw rather a consolatory light on the habits of our forefathers with regard to ablutions; it is mentioned as an exceptional merit that she rarely used a hot-water bath except before Easter, Whitsuntide, and Epiphany, having first assisted in washing the rest of the community.

There also she patiently bore pain and suffering from ill health, especially a swelling on her throat and face, saying that such a distemper pleased her. 'For there,' she said, 'I remember, when I was young, I wore a senseless weight of gold and jewels.'

And there she died, a victim to one of the fatal epidemics then so common. She was young when she died and was buried by her sister Sexburga, who succeeded her as abbess, in a white marble coffin, or sarcophagus, most beautifully wrought, opportunely dug by the monks of the neighbouring abbey out of the ruins of an abandoned Roman city.

In less than 200 years the Danish pirates, rowing up the waters of the Fen Country in their huge black boats, burnt the Abbey of Ely and scattered the monks and nuns. But it was restored at the beginning of the eleventh century. It was whilst rowing by Etheldreda's abbey that King Canute, listening to the sacred music brought from Gregory's Rome, made the well-known distich—

> Merrily sang the monks of Ely when Canute king rowed by.
> 'Row, boatmen, near the shore, and hear we those monks sing.'

Etheldreda's memory was kept fragrant through century after century of Danish ravage and Norman tyranny as St. Audrey, granddaughter, daughter, and kinswoman of so many English saints and kings, and mother and benefactress of her people.[1]

[1] Dedications of churches: six, one destroyed. Ely Cathedral dedicated to her with St. Peter. Represented in art in monastic habit, but crowned, and with crosier, book, or budding staff.

The Venerable Bede.

May 27.

(A.D. 673-735.)

There can scarcely be a greater range of monastic life than that which embraces Wilfrid and Bede—the wide ecclesiastical rule of Wilfrid, his dominant spirit, his many journeys to Rome; and Bede, in the humble quiet of his unambitious seclusion, never going more than a few miles from his monastery, in which he was brought up from the age of seven.

And yet while the trumpet sounding to battle echoed far and wide among the battlefields to which it called, that one low strain of the harp which you must be still yourself, and near, to hear, vibrates through the centuries; and on the music of its strings float down to us countless great names, but for that music almost forgotten.

Of Bede's life the incidents are few. Its stillness is needed for the faithfulness of its reflections. Born in a home between the two great monasteries of Wearmouth and Jarrow, at seven he was confided to the care of the abbot Benedict Biscop, the Northumbrian noble, of the royal house of Lincolnshire, who had devoted himself to the gathering together of all the light and wisdom he could for his country. The boy must have seen the Abbot sail away again and again for Rome, and on his return, with his ardent love for books and all kinds of learning, must have watched with eager interest the unpacking of all the treasures collected from Rome, Vienne, and the seventeen monasteries the Abbot had visited.

He was seventeen when Benedict died. 'Spending all the remaining time of my life,' he writes, 'in that monastery, I wholly applied myself to the study of Scripture, and amidst the observances of regular discipline and the daily care of singing in the church I always took delight in learning, and teaching, and writing.' He learned Greek and knew something of Hebrew. 'In the nineteenth year of my age I received deacon's orders, and in the thirtieth those of the priesthood, both of them by the ministry of the most revered Bishop John (St. John of Beverley) and by order of the abbot Ceolfrid; from which time till the fifty-ninth year of my age I have made it my business, for the use of me and mine, to compile out of the works of the venerable Fathers and to interpret and explain according to their meaning the following pieces.'

Then follows the long list of his works, chiefly commentaries and translations of the Scriptures, his martyrology, a book of epigrams, the lives of various saints of earlier ages, the life of the holy Cuthbert in verse and prose, a book 'On the Nature of Things,' his autobiography, and his great Ecclesiastical History, the foundation of our historical literature.

The stages of his ecclesiastical ministry, his ordinations, his books are the incidents of his life. So still and transparent is the medium itself, that at first you seem to see nothing of it but only what is seen through it or reflected in it. Yet as you look closer you find that the story of his Church and nation, of the people he had heard of and the people he knew is no mere mechanical reflection, but a painting and an illumination carefully touched by a human hand, and by a mind always truthful, but lingering with tender detail on what it loves best.

Rare indeed are the qualities which shine through the simplicity of those pages; justice rarest perhaps of all, especially in religious history; justice to opponents from one whose convictions on the other side are strong. Such justice only charity can ensure. From the Benedictine Bede we learn the saintly virtues of Aidan and the Celtic monks, and the readiness to yield with which at first they met St. Augustine of Canterbury. Then, as the *intellectual* side of this great virtue, an accuracy which spares no pains to find the truth and an honesty which never fails to tell it at any risk.[1]

As the *negative cause* of such transparent honesty there seems to be in Bede an absolute absence of vanity, literary or personal (he never once intrudes himself into the narrative except as a listener), which makes his words, in times when the turgid rhetoric of the late Empire was the fashion, fall as simply and naturally around his thoughts and facts as the drapery around a Greek statue; whilst as the *positive* spiritual fountain of his truthfulness and justice, we feel in every page a love of God and of goodness, and therefore of man, which makes detraction impossible to him—because sin in others, as in himself, gives him the deepest pain—and which makes him scent out and bring to light and tenderly unfold everything pure, and loving, and good, with the delight and tenderness of a mother.

It is a large range of comprehensive sympathy which embraces as he does with reverent loyalty St. Gregory the Great and Aidan, one of the Celtic monks and missionaries whom Gregory's missionaries replaced—Aidan, whom he describes as the 'friend of the poor and as it were father of the wretched,' and dwelling on his love of men and his humility, his mind superior to anger, his authority in rebuking the haughty and powerful, his tenderness in comforting the afflicted and defending the poor ('although in no way commending what he improperly understood as to the observance of Easter—nay, very much detesting the same'). Many of Bede's stories vibrate with such sympathetic tones that they are like tender elegies—such as his pictures of the friendship of Cuthbert on his sea-washed Lindisfarne and Herbert on his little isle on Derwentwater, meeting every year at Lindisfarne for a few days for holy converse, and at their last meeting having a vision in answer to their prayers that the 'Heavenly Goodness would let them, as

---

[1] Miracles of course to him needed no *more* evidence to render them credible than any other stories, probably *less*, if they illustrated some Divine truth or human saintliness. Heaven was for him *nearer* than anywhere else on earth to any spot on earth; and the supernatural, the natural law of the Kingdom of Heaven.

they had served Him together on earth, depart together to see His bliss in heaven ; and they saw each other no more in the flesh, but their spirits, from the island on the sea and from the lake, departed together on the same day to the heavenly kingdom :' or of the child who when dying called one of the nurses who had taken care of him, 'Edgitha ! and she soon followed him ;' of the holy abbess who was seen 'very gently drawn up to heaven on a heavenly bed with golden cords, which are her works of charity.' Then there are the stories of the Irish Abbot Fursey, and his visions of the unseen world, 'dark and ice-cold or lurid with the flames ;' of the four fires, which the angels said are the fires of falsehood, of discord, of covetousness, of oppression, which when they drew near, the Abbot feared ; but the angel said, '*That which you did not kindle cannot burn you.*' He gives with delight the story of Father Egbert, severe to himself, enduring in friendship through years of absence, who by his gentle persuasion brought the monks of Iona to the Catholic observance of Easter ; and on the other side, with as full detail and delight, the noble picture of the abbess Hilda, as true a type of queenly womanhood as can be, guiding her communities, 'whom all that knew her called mother from her singular piety and grace ; the first to recognise the first English poet, Cædmon, calling him from the stable to sing the praise of all created things ; passionately loved by the nuns, one of whom heard the bells in the air and saw shining light from above, as she went up to God,' although she remained true to the traditions of Iona to the last.

Through such a history we indeed learn to know the man who wrote it. No small honour is it to England to have the first page of her historical literature illumined with a sympathy so tender and deep and a justice and candour so unswerving.

His letter to Egbert also reveals him as a true statesman, as well as a man of letters and as a saint. In this he earnestly presses on the Archbishop to study the Scriptures, to ordain more priests to preach and administer sacraments in remote country villages, to translate the Lord's Prayer and the Creed into Saxon for the people ; to follow St. Gregory's large plans for increase of bishoprics, so that the remotest towns and districts might be visited ; to abolish the monasteries which had become luxurious and irregular, and thus 'were training none for true religion, whilst they withdrew men from the defence and service of the nation.' The gentle Bede was indeed no mere dreamer seeing the world around him according to his wishes. His letter gives, it is said, a clearer insight into the condition of the church, and the social state of England, than any other document of the time, and unfolds a dark picture of the corruption and luxury of the laity and of the decay of the monasteries so lately founded.[1] One of the remedies he suggested was the foundation of that school of York which may be regarded, with his history, as the Venerable Bede's great legacy to England and to the whole Church. For in this school was preserved the learning, already fading from Greece and Rome. And from this school in the stormy century which followed, when England was ravaged by the Danes, and all the learning swept away, when Bede's own monasteries of Jarrow and Wearmouth were ruined, Alcuin and a troop of young English scholars carried back the learning preserved in England to the court of Charlemagne, and thence to France, Germany, and Italy, once more to flow back into England in later days.

On the last days of Bede sunlight falls from the touch of his devoted disciple Cuthbert.

'He lived joyfully,' his scholar writes in his last sickness, which brought him to the grave in his sixty-third year, 'giving thanks to God day and night—yea, at all hours—until the Feast of the Ascension. Every day he gave lessons to us, his pupils, and the rest of his time he occupied himself in chanting psalms. He was awake almost the whole night

---

[1] In this letter he mentions daily Communion as common in Italy, Gaul, Africa, Greece, and the East, and says there are innumerable boys and girls, as well as young men and women, innocent and chaste, who might well communicate weekly.

and spent it in joy and thanksgiving. And when he awoke from his short sleep, immediately he raised his hands on high, and began again to give thanks. He sang the words of the apostle Paul, "It is a dreadful thing to fall into the hands of the living God." He sang much besides from the Holy Scriptures, and also many Anglo-Saxon hymns. He sang antiphons according to our and his custom, and amongst others this one: "O King of Glory, Lord of Power, who this day didst ascend a Victor above all the heavens, leave us not orphaned behind Thee, but send to us the promised Spirit of the Father. Hallelujah." And when he came to the words "leave us not orphaned behind Thee," he burst into tears. And in an hour he began to sing again. We wept with him; now we read, then we wept; but we could not read without tears. Often would he thank God for sending him this sickness, and often would he say, "God chasteneth the son whom He loveth." Often too would he repeat these words of St. Ambrose: "I have not lived so that I should be ashamed to live amongst you; yet neither do I fear to die, for we have a good Lord." Besides the lessons which he gave us, and his psalm-singing during those days, he composed two important works—a translation of the Gospel of St. John into our native tongue, for the use of the Church, and extracts from Isidore of Seville; for he said, "I would not that my pupils should read what is false and after my death should labour in vain."

'On the Tuesday before Ascension Day his sickness increased, his breathing became difficult, and his feet began to swell. Yet he passed the whole day joyfully dictating. At times he would say, "Make haste to learn, for I do not know how long I shall remain with you, whether my Creator will not soon take me to Himself." The following night he spent in prayers of thanksgiving. And when Wednesday dawned he desired us diligently to continue writing what we had begun. When this was finished we carried the relics in procession, as is customary on that day. One of us then said to him, "Dearest master, we have yet one chapter to translate. Will it be grievous to thee if we ask thee any further?" He answered, "It is quite easy; take the pen and write quickly." At three o'clock he said to me, " Run quickly and call the priests of this convent to me, that I may impart to them the gifts which God has given me. The rich of this world seek to give gold and silver and other costly things; but with great love and joy will I give to my brethren what God has given me." Then he begged every one of them to offer Masses and to pray for him. They all wept, chiefly for that he said that in this world they should see his face no more. But they rejoiced in that he said, " It is time that I go to my Creator. I have lived long enough. The time of my departure is at hand; for I long to depart and be with Christ."

'Thus did he live till evening. Then that scholar (i.e. the writer Cuthbert), said to him, " Dearest master, there is only one thought left to write." He answered, "Write quickly." Soon the scholar replied, " Now this thought also is written." He answered, " Thou hast well said. It is finished. Raise my head in thy hand, for it will do me good to sit opposite my sanctuary, where I was wont to kneel and pray, that sitting thus I may call upon my Father." So he seated himself on the ground in his cell and sang, " Glory to Thee, O God, Father, Son, and Holy Ghost ; " and when he had named the Holy Ghost he breathed his last breath.'[1]

---

[1] Alcuin relates a beautiful anecdote of Bede in a letter to the Monks of Jarrow. 'It is,' he says, 'related that Beda, our master and your blessed patron, used to say, "I well know that angels visit the congregations of brethren at the canonical hours. What if they should not find me there among my brethren? Will they not say, Where is Bede? Why comes he not with his brethren to the prescribed prayers?"'—Blunt, *Annotated Prayer Book*.

St. Swithun
Of Winchester.
July 15.

(Consecrated Bishop of Winchester 838 ; died 862. Calendars : Sarum only. Sarum Ep. and Gosp.: Heb. vii. 23-27 ; St. Luke xii. 35-40.)

St. Swithun's name, as that of other saints whose festivals occur in July, is, as we are all aware, much associated with the weather, with the forty days of rain or sunshine supposed to be inaugurated on his day.

He and St. Edmund the Martyr are the two stars in our English Calendar that shine across the darkness of that terrible ninth century, when the last and fiercest storm burst over the land from the heathen north, sweeping away the monastery of Jarrow, with its carefully collected libraries, where Bede spent his tranquil years of faithful service, and the great school of York, and Etheldreda's Ely.

Swithun was a West countryman of noble birth, and was taught grammar, philosophy, and the Holy Scriptures ; his early life was spent in the prosperous days when Egbert, King of Wessex, was apparently uniting all England finally into one. At his death in 838 he left Swithun prior of the old monastery of Winchester and guardian of his son. During the nineteen years of Ethelwulf's reign St. Swithun, who had educated him, was his counsellor and friend, and two years before Ethelwulf's death Swithun was made Bishop of Winchester, the royal city. Throughout his reign Ethelwulf was fighting off the Danes; yet he found time to consider in other ways the welfare of his people, and it is said to have been by St. Swithun's counsel that he regularly settled the tithe of the land on the Church, and also enacted that on his own hereditary property a group of ten families should support one poor man in meat, drink, and clothes. In 852, after a victory over the Danes, Ethelwulf went on a pilgrimage to Rome with his youngest son, Alfred, and rebuilt the English school at Rome. Five years after, in 857, he died. St. Swithun survived his royal pupil and friend five years, and died in the reign of Ethelbert, second son of Ethelwulf, who became king just before the terrible combined invasion from Scandinavia and Ireland. He is said by William of Malmesbury to have been full of humility and charity. He loved sacred music. He was severe to himself, and, like the Celtic bishop Aidan, he made his episcopal journeys on foot; he liked also to walk barefoot to any special pomp or solemnity, such as the consecration of a church. He built many churches and almshouses. 'His feasting was not with the rich, but with the needy and the poor.' And when he was dying he desired to be buried in no rich shrine within any of the stately churches he had built, but 'in a mean place on the north side outside the door, where men might walk over him and the rain might water his grave.'[1] Thus he chose to rest as well as feast with the poor he had loved and served, unsheltered from any of the storms common to all. It is pleasant to think that this self-denying, beneficent life, which he must have known from his earliest childhood, may have been among the influences which helped to mould the character of Alfred the Truthteller, Deliverer, and King.

[1] 'In 971 his bones were translated to a rich shrine within the church, but it is said that a most violent rain fell on the appointed day and continued for *thirty-nine days.*'—Blunt's *Annotated Book of Common Prayer.*

Dedications of churches: fifty-one, and one with St. Nicholas. Represented in art as a bishop.

St. Dunstan [1]

OF CANTERBURY.

May 19.

(Born 925; died 988. Consecrated Archbishop of Canterbury 959.)

Between the death of Swithun and the birth of Dunstan the glorious reigns of Alfred, of his daughter Æthelflæda, the Lady of Mercia, of his son Edward the Elder, and of his grandson Athelstan, 'whom as a golden-haired child Alfred had girded with a sword with golden scabbard and jewelled hilt,' had beaten back the tide of Danish invasion; and in the Danelagh had begun the blending of that second tide of northern barbarism with the first which had brought Alfred's ancestors from Germany.

The reversal of the harsh judgments of St. Dunstan's character, not long since so generally received without question or hesitation, simply in consequence of the careful investigation of the documents which contain the story of his life, is among the many inspiring previsions given us in these days of the Day ('dies illa dies lucis') when all misunderstandings shall be cleared away, and all false judgments shall be reversed. After calumnies scarcely controverted for centuries, a little more light comes; and at once controversies and calumnies cease, simply because we see.

The completion of the West Saxon realm 'was in fact reserved for the hands not of a king or warrior but of a priest. Dunstan stands first in the line of ecclesiastical statesmen who counted among them Lanfranc and Wolsey and ended in Laud. He is still more remarkable in his own vivid personality after eight centuries of revolution and change.' [2]

---

[1] The authorities chiefly followed in this sketch of St. Dunstan are his five Latin biographies in the Rolls Series, with the introduction by Bishop Stubbs.

[2] Green, *History of the English People*, vol. i.

'The early and more trustworthy writers connect the name of Dunstan with no cruel or barbarous action. The evidence of the laws does, I think, confirm the testimony of the Lives. Dunstan is a constructor, not a destroyer; a consolidator, not a pedantic theorist; a reformer, not an innovator; a politician, not a bigot; a statesman, not a zealot. His merits as a scholar, an artist, a musician, a cunning craftsman, are part of the contemporary picture which ought not to be disregarded. His zeal for education is a far more authentic trait than his zeal for celibacy.'[1]

The history of his biographies is a most interesting chapter in the history of legend. The first Life was written by a priest, who gives only his initial B. and calls himself 'vilis Saxonum indigena.' This was written just after St. Dunstan's death, between 988 and 1000, and was copied and circulated in France immediately afterwards. This 'priest B.,' as he tells us in his prologue, heard much of what he relates from Dunstan's own mouth, and much from the scholars whom he had educated from their childhood. 'We can, without any great stretch of imagination, see the white-haired old bishop sitting with the children of his household, his counsellors and guests, by the fire in winter, and telling the little ones the story of his childhood, as he told the elders the history of St. Edmund, king and martyr, which had been told him when a boy by the King's cupbearer.'

To this primary source (Dunstan himself) we must assign the mention of his Irish teachers; of King Edward's Chase; of his dreams as a child at Glastonbury, his walking in his sleep to the church, his vision of the mystic dove at Æthelflæda's death; of the Devil taking the form of a bear, a dog, or fox, perhaps also told as a dream. 'All these stories bear the impress of the same mind, slightly morbid, very sensitive, but pure, devout, and void of grossness or grotesqueness; stories for the children, magnified in repetition on account of the greatness of the narrator.' This first Life of Dunstan has a 'subjective' value. Its marvels are not miracles, but visions and impressions. 'Such in his inner

[1] Bishop Stubbs, *Introduction to St. Dunstan*, in the Rolls Series.

life, in his rest and meditation, in his talks with the children, was the man who for thirty years was the mainstay of the safety and glory of the English.'

With this first biography, the work of Adelard, written twenty years after Dunstan's death, 'is in strong contrast.' From this are derived the more startling objective marvels. 'Dunstan had already become a legendary hero.' 'The delirious dream of sleep-walking becomes a real journey;' the dreams of the dog, the bear, and the fox become an actual incarnation of the Devil. But to this Adelard we owe the beautifully simple narrative of the last moments.

Seventy years afterwards, years for England of strife and humiliation, a new order had come in, and a new Life was written by Osbern, a disciple of Archbishop Lanfranc. In this Dunstan is represented, coloured by the author's ideals, not so much as a patriotic English statesman as an ascetic monastic reformer, somewhat of the style of Hildebrand. This is compiled, with additions and subtractions, from the two former Lives, and to it is appended a 'Book of Miracles' altogether new.

Then comes a compilation by Eadmer, a disciple of Archbishop Anselm (as Osbern of Lanfranc); and finally the Life by William of Malmesbury, derived from the others, with severe criticisms on the style of his predecessor Osbern, also weaving in notices of the lives of other contemporary saints.

Not a word has reached us of Dunstan's own writings, either books or letters; not many of the words he spoke.

His parents, Heorstan and Kynefrida, were noble, and connected with the royal house of Alfred. Both were Christians. His father took him early to the ancient monastery of Glastonbury, still full of legends of the earlier British saints, and with Irish monks living there or coming and going on their missionary itineratings. It was built on an island surrounded by quiet streams or channels of water, containing fish. But the buildings were 'very poor, without art, and out of repair.' The father stayed the night for the sake of the prayers, and 'in a dream of sweet sleep' the boy saw 'an aged man clothed in white leading him through the pleasant courts of a sacred temple,' which afterwards through Dunstan's influence was indeed built.

At Glastonbury he learned much from the Irish monks, probably, among other things, his skill on the harp, and in illuminating manuscripts. On its imaginative and artistic side his mind would be much akin to theirs. He received the tonsure for minor orders, and as a child served the altar in the church where he had been baptised. Part of his boyhood was spent at King Athelstan's palace, where his dreams and prayers met with little sympathy. His companions accused him of making incantations and using forbidden pagan charms and verses; perhaps Celtic poems, perhaps Latin, which they did not understand.

He took comfort from the Beatitude on the persecuted; and his persecutors made the application more complete by accusing him falsely to the King and entreating his dismissal, and finally by taking the matter into their own hands, binding him hand and foot, throwing him into a muddy pond or marsh and trampling on him. There they left him, and when he struggled out, the dogs of a neighbouring farmer 'rushed on him with fierce barkings,' deeming him in his muddy condition 'rather a monster than a man.' But the dogs were kinder than the boys, and, hearing his caressing voice, they recognised him and at once fawned on him. And among the few words left us of St. Dunstan's are those addressed to these dogs. 'O cruel frenzy of my kindred,' he sighed, 'turned from human kindness to canine rage! And now the irrational nature of dogs shows a true human kindness by the friendly wagging of their tails!'

A fever followed this rough treatment.

It is probably to this period that belongs the story of his somnambulism, when he left his sick bed, crept out of the window of his cell, climbed over the roof of the church, and was found peacefully sleeping in the church below.

The Devil (according to the first biography) 'tempted him to marriage' by representing to him its delights; but the Bishop of Winchester recommended him to become a monk. After his illness the Bishop prevailed, and Dunstan became a monk at Glastonbury.

His third biographer, Osbern, describes a visit to Dunstan's cell at Glastonbury a hundred years after his death.

It was 'five feet long by two and a half feet wide, of the height of a man; more like a grave than the dwelling of the living.' There the young Dunstan worked and prayed. To Osbern that narrow cell seemed 'wider than the walls of spacious cities,' as he thought what healing and teaching and benediction had gone forth from it far and wide. And with tears he knelt in the lowly oratory and workshop, and handled with his 'sinful hands' the works of Dunstan's hands.

The character of Glastonbury, when afterwards it was placed under Dunstan's rule, was (Bishop Stubbs says) rather that of a school, the monks becoming his scholarly disciples.

Near Glastonbury lived then the widowed lady Æthelflæda. She had built a house to be near the sacred services, and for love of the heavenly country. She was of the kindred of King Athelstan.

'She ceased not day nor night to hold blessed communion with Jesus Christ, our Lord. Dunstan (also of Athelstan's kindred) clave to her much, and loved her most truly, for the sake of kindred and religion. She held all her royal kindred dear and was much beloved by them.'

One day, being surprised by a sudden visit from the King and his court, with a supply of mead which she feared would be scarcely sufficient for the thirst of the courtly train, it was believed a miracle was wrought and the mead was increased like the oil of the cruse of old.

To this lady Dunstan was a great comfort in her last illness, and one day when her strength was fast failing, 'as he stood singing at the church door,' he saw a fair white dove descend from the eastern sky ; the tips of its feathers sparkled like fire, and as it struck the air with its wings 'the air flashed as with lightning ; and with swift strokes it flew to the lady Æthelflæda's house.'

St. Dunstan, anxious about his sick friend, followed, and when he entered her dwelling he heard her voice within 'in grave alternate converse, as with a familiar friend. He asked the handmaidens who were watching near their mistress with whom she was speaking,' but they could only tell of 'a beam of glorious light which had filled her room,' and that when the light ceased this voice was heard speaking.

When the voice ceased, and the curtain of the door was drawn aside, the lady told him how 'the mystic dove which he had seen had been speaking with her. Her friends were not to grieve for her, she said ; she desired only to partake of the Body and Blood of the Lord, and then, He Himself leading her, to depart by the common way of all.' Dunstan hastened to do all she asked, and 'after tasting the most salutary Eucharist she ended her blessed life, in Jesus Christ our Lord.'

St. Dunstan added to his study of Sacred Scriptures great skill in music and painting. It happened that a noble lady called Æthelwynn asked him to come and make a design for a stole, that she might embroider it with gold and gems. 'He went and took his cithara with him (which in our language is called hearpa) to entertain her attendants and to refresh his imagination with music.'[1]

And 'as the harp was hanging on the walls of the room beside him, its strings, without being touched, gave out rich tones of music, which seemed to the lady and her maidens to be from the well-known antiphon about the saints who follow the footsteps of Christ and reign with Him for ever, *Gaudent in cœlis animæ sanctorum*.'

He lived much afterwards at the Court of Edmund, in Somersetshire, and elsewhere, and many there, seeing his fidelity and constancy, began to love him as one of their own

[1] First *Life*.

kindred. But some envied ; and once by their evil plots, while the King was near Cheddar, he was driven from the Court. Not long after this, when King Edmund was hunting, the stag with the hounds after it rushed over one of the precipitous cliffs of those rocky ravines. The King was close behind, and his horse's hoofs rang on the edge of the chasm. Then he remembered Dunstan, and making as he thought his dying confession to God, he said in his soul, 'I thank Thee, O Most High, I cannot remember injuring anyone in these last days, but only Dunstan, and if I live I will at once be reconciled to him.'

The horse recovered itself, and the King was saved ; and when he reached his home at once he sent for Dunstan, rode with him to Glastonbury, 'prayed and gave thanks in the church with floods of tears, embraced Dunstan, led him to the sacerdotal seat, placed him in it, and said to him, "Be abbot of this church, and whatever is lacking to the Divine service I will supply by royal largess."'

As abbot, Dunstan was able to fulfil his old boyish dream and enrich Glastonbury with beautiful buildings. And around him gathered many scholars, who were so instructed by his teaching and example that they were sought for, far and wide, to be abbots, bishops, and even archbishops.

Meanwhile it is said the Devil frequently tempted him in various forms, disturbing him at prayer night and day, and even at the altar, as a bear, a dog, or a serpent. One day at church he appeared as a fox, at which the blessed Dunstan, laughing gently (*subridens*), made the sign of the Cross, whereupon the Devil was discomfited and vanished.[1]

---

[1] *Subridens* ; the devil being, as Luther said, 'a proud spirit and never able to bear contempt.' Perhaps the popular story of St. Dunstan's pulling the Devil's nose was an 'objective' version of this 'subridens.' It is given by Osbern, writing a century after Dunstan's death, and about seventy years after his first biography. He gives the story thus : 'That deceiving one, having taken on the deceptive form of a man, sought the cell of the young Dunstan at Glastonbury, peeped in at the window, and, seeing him at work forging metal, asked him to make something for him. Meantime he began to talk, and to mix up the names of women and evil pleasures with religion, and then again to dwell on luxurious delights, so that Dunstan soon came to understand

But meantime Dunstan was also combating the evil one on other fields and with different weapons, scattering darkness by the light of wholesome learning, silencing his malicious suggestions by the music of holy song.¹

And throughout the English land the influence of his wise counsel was felt. After his reconciliation with Edmund the league between Scot and Dane was broken. 'Strathclyde was conquered, and the Danes of the Danelagh, left to themselves without aid from outside, after some years of yet hard fighting became one with the people among whom they had settled.'² Always, in Dunstan, imagination and practical statesmanship, artistic work, music, and song were combined, devotional visions with resolute rule and careful legislation.

King Edred, Edmund's successor, would have made Dunstan Bishop of Crediton, but he could not be persuaded to accept the offer, and procured the appointment of a venerable man in his stead. But it seems that his refusal was thought a shrinking from duty, for the night after his ultimate refusal 'St. Peter and St. Paul appeared to him in a vision of the night with St. Andrew, and showed him many things in intimate converse; but Andrew' (for whom he had always an especial devotion) 'struck him, with no feeble blows, from a rod in his hand, saying, "This thou hast because thou didst yesterday refuse to be consorted with our apostolic company."'

who he was. Then the athlete of Christ held the pincers firm and heated them well in the fire, all the while confessing and calling on the name of Christ, with tightly compressed lips. And when the pincers were well heated, moved by a holy rage, swiftly he drew them out of the flames and seized the spectral face, and with all his might dragged the monster inside, so that with a fearful outcry he fled away, howling, "What has this baldhead done?" (Eadmer reports it this 'bald-headed devil.') 'For Dunstan's hair, though beautiful, was thin. The next morning all the people came to see what all this noise and screaming could have meant. But from that day, more than ever, Dunstan kept himself always fully equipped for battle, by fasting and prayer, knowing that in no other way can the fight be won.'

¹ It is interesting to find Glastonbury, centuries afterwards, in the front rank as to sacred music.

² Green, *Hist. Eng. People*, vol. i.

After this Dunstan became successively Bishop of Worcester and London, and Archbishop of Canterbury.

King after king succeeded to the throne of Wessex during his lifetime. Edmund died only a short time after appointing him Abbot of Glastonbury in 946. Edred, Edmund's brother, a young man of about twenty-one (Dunstan's own age), seems to have trusted him entirely, as also Queen Eadgifa, his mother. The next nine years (946 to 955) were years of prosperity and unity, the allegiance of Northumbria being finally secured. These Dunstan spent in teaching at Glastonbury, in building, and in constant counselling of the King.

Then followed a break in Dunstan's influence during the three years of the reign of the boy King Edwy, crowned at fifteen. Dunstan was one of the two bishops deputed by the Witan (the 'Senate,' as the Life calls it) to recall Edwy at his coronation feast to the grave assembly of his nation and rebuke the 'petulant' wilfulness which had made him choose to retire to the society of the lady Eathelgifu and her daughter. Eathelgifu never forgave Dunstan and procured his banishment. But beyond this faithful fulfilling of the command of the Witan and of his duty as Archbishop and counsellor of the late King, Dunstan had no share in the tragedy of the young King's marriage with Eathelgifu's daughter (prohibited on account of consanguinity), in the rebellion of Mercia which followed it, or in the death of the young Queen, except as far as the exile of the wisest and most patriotic of his subjects ruined Edwy's reign. Dunstan's two years of banishment were spent in Flanders with Count Arnulf. On Edwy's death he was at once recalled by King Edgar to the country and to his place as chief counsellor of the King.

Dunstan proved his zeal on more than one occasion for the sanctity and purity of marriage. It is said he subjected King Edgar himself, his own steadfast friend and the patron of the monastic revival of the time, to a long and severe penance for a sin of his youth, not absolving him till after seven years of penance. And from a powerful Earl who had made an unlawful marriage he refused to withdraw his excommunication at the entreaty of the King, or even in deference to a letter obtained by the Earl from the Pope. 'God forbid,' he said, 'that for the sake of any mortal man or to save my own life I should set aside the law which Christ my Lord, the Son of God, established in His Church.'[1] And at last the Earl, subdued and penitent, came to Dunstan with a rod in his hand, seeking penance and forgiveness, and was received with tears of joy.

Dunstan became Archbishop of Canterbury after Edgar's accession, and no doubt promoted, though he did not originate, the revival of the monastic discipline (so apt to relax in the monasteries), which marked Edgar's reign. 'It was the enforcement of monastic discipline, not the celibacy of the clergy, which was the object of these clerical reforms; and in this Dunstan only partially sympathised. Men's views of what constitutes vice may differ, but any rule which condemns Dunstan condemns John the Baptist also; and if any error on the side of severity is pardonable, it is when the rebuke is addressed to the vices of princes. Why is Dunstan to be blamed for that which is the glory of Ambrose and Anselm?

'Dunstan's work was national, for the whole people and not only for any religious section of it. Throughout Edgar's reign the direction of the state lay virtually in his hands.[2] "The noblest tribute to his rule lies in the silence of the chroniclers."[3] His work was indeed a work of settlement; such a work was best done by the simple enforcement of peace. During the years of rest in which the stern hand of the Primate enforced justice and order Northmen and Englishmen drew together into a single people. The union was the result of no direct policy of fusion. On the contrary, Dunstan's policy preserved to the original Danelagh its local rights and local usages. But he recognised the men of the Danelagh as Englishmen. He employed the

---

[1] Adelard, Osbern, and William of Malmesbury.
[2] Bishop Stubbs's *Introduction to the Lives of Dunstan*, in the Rolls Series. [3] Green, *Hist. of Eng. People*, vol. i.

Northmen in the royal service, and promoted them to high posts in Church and State. It was not till Edgar's reign that the name of Britain passed into the name of Englaland. The same vigour of rule which secured rest for the country told on the growth of national prosperity.'

'Commerce sprang into a wider life. "Men of the Empire," traders of Lower Lorraine and the Rhineland, "men of France," are seen in the streets of London. It was in Edgar's days, indeed, that London rose to the commercial greatness it has held ever since.'[1]

The laws of Edgar's reign doubtless retain the impress of Dunstan's hand, leader as he was of the people through the Witan and also chief counsellor of the King (leader both in Lords and Commons). And among those laws is recorded the great principle of law and order and equal justice : 'I will that every man be worthy of folk-right, both poor and rich, that righteous dooms be judged to him.'

At Edgar's death he became 'the Jehoiada of the boy king "Edward the Martyr,"' warning and guarding and counselling him as a father until his murder (or 'martyrdom') by his stepmother, Elfrida, closed the political life of the Primate, and again began the old weary strife between kingdom and kingdom, class and class, which gave occasion for a fresh invasion under King Canute.[2]

Of those last thirteen years of Dunstan's life, from the age of fifty-one to sixty-four, there are few records.

He resumed at times the employments of his youth, exercising his old skill in various arts and handicrafts, in the making of musical instruments, such as the organ which was long kept at Malmesbury, and the bells that were known at Canterbury as Dunstan's own. The great domains of the Church also gave him much administrative work.

'He spent his time much in prayer and in David's psalms, breaking sweet sleep by vigils, toiling in ecclesiastical

---

[1] Green, *Hist. Eng. People*, vol. i.
[2] When King Canute became a Christian he showed his reverence for Dunstan's memory by ordering the solemn observance of his festival throughout the kingdom.

works, before dawn arising to correct lying books or to erase mistakes in manuscripts; with wise insight judging the true and false between man and man, or with placid words bringing those who were out of peace or at strife to quiet and concord; consoling widows, orphans, pilgrims, and strangers, so that all the English land was filled with his holy doctrine; shining before God and man like the sun and the moon. Or when he was minded to bring to Christ the Lord His due hours of service and the celebration of the Mass, with such entireness of devotion did he labour in singing that he seemed to be face to face with the Lord, even if just before he had been vexed with the quarrels of the people.

'Like St. Martin, he ever kept eye and heart intent on heaven, never letting his spirit rest from prayer.'[1]

To this period belongs his vision of the Church as his Mother, sitting at a glorious bridal festival amidst the mighty sweetness of the singing of angels, singing the Kyrie Eleison. He listened to their strains, and especially to the words of one hymn so often repeated that they lingered in his memory when he awoke: 'O Rex gentium Dominator omnium propter sedem Majestatis Tuæ da nobis indulgentiam. Rex Christe peccatum delinque.'[2]

Another time, it is said, in Edgar's days, he once fell asleep at Mass on Sunday, and in his sleep heard a solemn service in heaven; and after he awoke he dictated to his servants the Kyrie Eleison, which he had learned in his dream.

The music of the antiphon *Kyrie Rex splendens* afterwards sung at his festival, was also said to be his own.

These were days of active and yet tranquil waiting.

'On the Feast of the Ascension he preached for the last time, three sermons, the last (after they had sung the Agnus Dei) commending the lambs committed to his charge, just

---

[1] *Life*, by Priest B.
[2] 'O King of nations and Ruler of all, for the majesty of Thy Throne grant us pardon. O Christ, our King, give us remission of sins.'

delivered from the burden of their sins, to the Good Shepherd, the Lamb, Christ Jesus, who came, in His compassion, to bear the sins of the world, to be kept of Him in peace, without spot and blameless.' 'Wonderful was the power and glow of those last sermons. And on Saturday morning after Ascension Day, when the matin hymns were now finished, he bade the holy congregation of the brethren come to him. In the presence of whom, again commending his spirit to God, he received from the Heavenly Table the viaticum of the sacraments of Christ, which had been celebrated in his presence; and giving thanks to God for it, he began to sing, "*The merciful and gracious Lord hath so done His gracious works that they ought to be had in remembrance. He hath given meat to them that fear Him.*"

'And with these words in his mouth, rendering his spirit into the hands of the Creator, he rested in peace. Oh, happy indeed whom the Lord found thus watching!'[1]

[1] *Life*, by Adelard.

St. Edward the Confessor.[1]

October 13.

In passing from St. Dunstan to King Edward we turn from the council chamber to the cloisters, from the man to the child. Again and again in the records of these monastic saints we find under the monk's frock the statesman, the historian, the poet, the schoolmaster, the professor, the clearer of wildernesses, the artist, the adventurous colonist, the legislator; in King Edward we find the monk on the throne.

In him England, under the yoke of the foreign kings who succeeded him, idealised her own past and the ancient race of her native kings.

The laws of Edward the Confessor, to which the people turned, were, for them, the relics of a golden age. And yet Edward, to his people 'the last of the Saxons,' was in his own tastes and predilections no Saxon at all, but the first of the Normans,' caring chiefly for the kindred of the Norman princess Emma, his mother, who by her second marriage became the widow of Canute the Dane. The French handwriting, in his reign, superseded the old Anglo-Saxon. Norman monks were more to him than the English.

He helped by the influx of Norman strangers to bring England into the current of European culture; he built the first cruciform church in England on a Norman model. 'Destroying the old building,' he says in his charter of Westminster Abbey, 'I have built up a new one from the very foundation.'

It is very difficult to think of him except as in a kind

---

[1] Dean Stanley's *Westminster Abbey*; *Les Petits Bollandistes*; Freeman; Green, &c.
Dedications of churches, twenty-one, either to him or St. Edward the Martyr. Represented in art with a ring, and a purse.

of dream world, so inconsequent and dream-like are the stories of his legend ; so little grasp does he seem to have of the actual world, so much of the child remained in him all through his sixty-four years, with his 'rose-red cheeks, his white flowing hair, his thin transparent hands in whose touch there was supposed to be a kind of magic.' Devoted as he was to his mother's family and people, something in his bearing made him seem 'hard' to his mother, but it was perhaps rather a dreamy absence of mind, a living far off in another world untouched by the interests or passions of this, making a cloister of his home and a dream of his life. 'Often he would smile or laugh suddenly as if in conversation with some one unseen.' If he had a passion it was for hunting. The only vehement expression of his recorded is his swearing in a very unsaintly way at a poor peasant who interrupted him in the chase—'By God and His Mother, I will give you just such another turn if ever it come in my way,' words, one must hope, remembered because so *unlike* himself.

His exiled youth passed among the Norman kindred of his mother Emma, while she was in England with her second husband, Canute the Dane. The temptations of that wild and gay Norman court passed over him like a shadow ; and yet, since the tempter is no shadow or dream, perhaps it was there he won his title of 'Confessor.'

He vowed to St. Peter that if ever he returned to his father's kingdom of England he would make a pilgrimage to his tomb and church at Rome. But this also passed away like a shadow. On his accession he proclaimed this purpose to his Parliament ; they dissuaded him by many arguments, their own need of the king, the perils of the roads to Rome by sea and mountain, ambuscades at bridges and fords, 'the false Romans, who covet the red gold and the white silver as a leech covets blood.'

A hermit at Worcester also had a very opportune dream that the King's vow would be fulfilled by his founding a Benedictine monastery and dedicating a church to St. Peter in the Thorny Islet of the Thames, to be the West Minster of London, as St. Paul's was the East. And so he gave in. Out of this vow arose the most solid monument of his life, the Abbey of Westminster, fifteen years in building, 'at the cost of the tenth of the property of his realm,' which replaced the little chapel which had once (according to the legend) shone across the river 'without shadow or darkness,' illumined from within by angels and consecrated by the Apostle Peter's own hand.

Before that little chapel faded like a flower, to grow into the fair fruit of the Abbey, it is said to have been endeared to King Edward by two miracles.

A crippled Irishman called Michael, a leper, sitting in the highway between the King's palace and the chapel, cried out to the King and said he had made four pilgrimages to Rome in vain, but that St. Peter had told him if the King of England would carry him on his back to the monastery he would recover. The King at once took him on his shoulders, and amidst the scoffs of the court bore the Irish cripple to the high altar, where he instantly stood on his feet once more and walked away cured, a type of what might, even yet, possibly come to pass, if the race to which law appeals in the shape of loyalty, and the race whose strong shoulders were made to bear many burdens could understand each other, and meet at the Altar of God.

Another day, in the same little chapel which the angels had once illumined, the legend says the King's eyes were opened to see, at Mass, on the same high altar whence the Irishman had departed whole, the vision of the Divine Child, pure and bright like a spirit, a vision vouchsafed at the same time to Leofric, Earl of Mercia, and the renowned Lady Godiva, his wife.

Thirty-three years King Edward reigned. Whatever share he took in the rule of his nation, his delights are said to have been chiefly in the chase, in the building of his Abbey, in his devotions, and in such deeds of impulsive kindness as that carved on the screen of his chapel at Westminster, where he is sculptured, resting after the fatigues of the day on his couch, with the brazen money-chest beside him, left open by his steward Hugolin. The scullion, deeming him to be asleep, creeps in and helps himself to the royal treasure. At his third entrance the King, so often dreaming whilst apparently awake, now waking in his apparent sleep, starts up and warns the thief to fly before Hugolin returns, or 'he will not leave you a halfpenny.' And afterwards from that dream world of his, altogether untroubled by laws of property, he pleads for the delinquent. 'He hath more need of it than we. Enough treasure hath King Edward.'

In the sixteenth year of his reign he began his Abbey, and for fifteen years he carried on the building. The solid kingdom of his fathers was falling with him, but the beautiful Abbey was rising stone on stone. The opening of his church and the closing of his life drew near together.

Two legends belong to these closing days—the story of his sitting crowned, in gold-embroidered robes amidst his courtiers as they were feasting hard at Easter, after Lent, when with one of his dreamy laughs he went off into his dream world, and 'saw the Seven Sleepers of Ephesus turn in their age-long sleep from one side to another, and how this boded seventy years of woe and pestilence and famine; and immediately a knight was sent off to the Mount Celion, in the cave of which the Seven Sleepers slept, and he found it even as the King had said.'

The other story is of St. John, whom he loved tenderly, as he honoured St. Peter. On his way to the dedication of the Chapel of St. John a beggar implored him for an alms for love of the saint. King Edward could find no gold or silver (not being at any time, entrusted with much by his steward, Hugolin); so after a moment of silent thought he drew off from his hand a ring, large, royal, and beautiful, and gave it to the beggar, who at once vanished. Two English pilgrims from the town of Ludlow shortly afterwards found themselves benighted in Syria, when suddenly their path was lighted up, and an old man, white and hoary ('tarrying till his Lord should come'), preceded by two torches, accosted them. They told him of their country and their saintly king, on which the old man 'joyously, like to a clerk,' guided them to an hostelry and announced that he was John the Evangelist, the special friend of Edward, and gave them the King's ring to carry back, with the message that in six months the King would be with him in Paradise. The pilgrims returned. They found the King at his palace in Essex, said to be called, from this story, 'Have ring atte Bower.' He recognised the ring and prepared for his death, according to the message.

At Midwinter he came to Westminster, and had the minster consecrated, which he himself had built to the honour of God, St. Peter, and all the Saints.

On Christmas Day the mortal sickness fell on him. On his beloved St. John's Day he grew worse, so that the consecration was postponed to the Childermas, the festival of the Innocents, when he roused himself to sign the charter of the foundation. He had already ordered all as to the gifts and relics. But on the day of consecration he was too ill to be present, and Queen Edith, with her brothers Harold and Gurth, took his place. On that evening he sank into a deep stupor, broken by delirium, from which he rallied from time to time. In his delirious dreams he spoke of a green tree severed, and removed three acres off, which should yet return to its parent stem, again to bear fruit and flower; wandering words afterwards interpreted to mean the marriage of the first Henry with the Saxon Maud. Meantime his queen Edith sate by him weeping, and held his cold feet in her lap, and to her he said at last, 'Weep not. I shall not die, but live. I am going from the land of death to the land of the living.'

And, says his biographer, 'St. Peter, his friend, opened the gate of Paradise, and St. John, his own dear one, led him before the Divine Majesty.' He had waked up at last from his dream world into the world of which he dreamt.

As he lay dead 'an unearthly smile seemed to pass over the pale face, and a soft glow as of youth, and the thin hands looked more transparent than ever.' He was buried in his abbey, in his royal robes, with the crucifix and the pilgrim's ring. Crowds flocked to his funeral from all the country round; and a thrill of dread passed through the land, for old things which all loved were passing away like a dream, with the dreamlike king.

St. Hugh

OF LINCOLN.[1]

November 17.

(Born A.D. 1140; died A.D. 1200. Sarum Ep. and Gosp.:
Eccles. xl. 1-5; St. Mark xiii. 33-37.)

We come out again into daylight and fresh air in a wide and solid world.

St. Hugh was of an old Burgundian house, the lords of Avalon, near Grenoble. 'Early,' says his 'Magna Vita,' written by one who lived long with him in a close intimacy, 'he lost the solace of his mother, bereaved of her when yet a child.' When he was eight years old his father, parting his property among his children, went with him into a house of Canons Regular at Grenoble, near his own castle. From infancy the child was under strict discipline, and yet not cut off from natural duties. There was a school of noble youths at Grenoble, in which his father had always been especially interested. Here he placed his son Hugh, exhorting him with fatherly tenderness. 'The levity of thy schoolfellows, dearest son,' he said, 'is not lawful for thee; thy lot is not such as theirs. Little Hugh, little Hugh, I nurture thee for Christ, and jest and levity are not for thee.'

Quick in wit and work, of a vigorous and keen intelligence and a capacious memory, he studied diligently. Also he was ever ready to listen to the divine voice, like the child Samuel. '*Speak, Lord, for Thy servant heareth.*' Humble in all services to others, he had delight in the Church services, and so he grew up to nineteen. And then the father

---

[1] Chief authority: *Magna Vita St. Hugonis Episcopi Lincolnensis*, in the Rolls Series, edited by Rev. James F. Dimock.

Dedications of churches, one at Quethiock, in Cornwall. Represented in art with a tame swan, holding three flowers in his hand.

was growing old and infirm. The relation between the boy and the old seigneur, genial and gentle, with all his seriousness, had always been especially happy. And now the Prior confided entirely to the son the care of the old man. In this duty he delighted. As he often loved to tell his biographer in later years, 'he led about his father, carried him, put on his shoes and garments, washed him, made his bed, prepared his food and gave it him,' and in doing so received a thousand times his father's blessing, which he loved (in memory) ' to draw up thirstily from his eager heart.' Beloved and blessed was he in this by all. 'The blessing of a father builds up a house.' And so he waited tenderly on his old father till his death.

At nineteen Hugh was ordained, and very early his earnest preaching waked up slumbering hearts to the love of the heavenly country ; and before all he loved to plead with sinners.

But the more secular life of the Canons did not satisfy him. Having taken to the monastic life, he wished for the hardest to be found. The hardest was in all likelihood to be found in the newest Orders. Hugh of Avalon found what he sought on the snowy heights of the Chartreuse and in the monastery founded by St. Bruno about 100 years before. The rule was a combination of the life of the hermit and the cœnobite ; each brother living alone in his cell, cut out of the rock, his bedding being a horsecloth, a pillow, and a skin ; the dress a horse-hair shirt, worn night and day next the skin, and a white sheepskin, combined ; the food a loaf given to each on Sunday morning, to last the week. The brotherhood met at a common table, but silence was strictly observed.

To this Order the young Hugh, brought to the Chartreuse one day by his prior, entreated to be admitted. He was but grimly welcomed. 'The men who inhabit these rocks,' an old monk said, ' are hard as the rocks themselves ; severe to themselves and others.'

This threat of severity was not likely to damp, but rather to stimulate a character like Hugh's. No cause

G G

has won converts worth having, without having some cross to bind on the shoulder or stamp on the heart.

Hugh became a Carthusian, and gained from his rocks not their hardness but their steadfastness; which was to be well tested.

There was a library at the monastery, with abundance of books for reading, and abundance of quiet for prayer. The passion for learning grew on Hugh; and also, to balance this intellectual work, he, trained to such tender ministry by his devotion to his own father, had an old monk put under his care, 'whom he cherished as a mother, serving him as Jesus Christ.' The old monk was occasionally severe with his patient nurse and rebuked him for being so ambitious as to wish to be ordained priest. But another time he said, 'Be not troubled, thou, my son, or rather my lord. When God's time comes thou wilt be a bishop.'

At that time England, after the anarchy of Stephen, and the frightful oppressions and tortures of the barons, let loose from the repressing grip of the early Norman kings, was stirred from end to end by a great religious revival, the first of so many among our English people.

'Everywhere in town and country men banded themselves together for prayer; hermits flocked to the woods; nobles and churls welcomed the austere Cistercians, a reformed offshoot of the Benedictine Order, as they spread over the moors and forests of the North. A new spirit of devotion woke the slumbers of the religious houses and penetrated alike to the home of the noble and the trader. London took its full share in the revival. The very aspect of the city was changed. The Priory of St. Bartholomew rose at Smithfield and St. Giles at Cripplegate.' Then followed the struggle of Thomas Becket with King Henry, his murder, the indignation of Europe and of the English people, lay and clerical, the penitence of the vanquished sovereign at Canterbury, the enthusiastic pilgrimages to the new shrine of the new popular Saint Thomas of Canterbury, which threw the ancient homage to the English Dunstan into the shade.

Henry threw himself into the religious movement so far as to invite some of the Carthusians to England, and endow them with lands at Witham, in Gloucestershire, to be the first 'Charterhouse' in England. The first abbot could not agree with the Saxon peasants already in possession and soon threw up his office. The second died. Henry sent to the Chartreuse for a third. Reluctantly the brotherhood consented to part with their best to found the Order in the new country.

Thus Hugh of Avalon came to England, and won the hearts of the peasants and the King by that true justice, only possible to sympathy, which satisfied both.

'My lord,' he said to the King, 'until the last obolus is paid to these men this place cannot be bestowed on us.' 'Jerusalem,' he said, 'must not be built with blood.' Finally, when the former tenants were removed he restored to them the materials of their houses.

Then after many years, when still the cells and chapel Henry had promised were not built, three of the monks went in deputation to remonstrate with the King. One of them, named Gerard, a man of high birth and fiery temper, receiving but a vague answer from the King, said, 'You think it a great thing to give us bread which we do not need. I leave to you your kingdom, and depart to our desert Chartreuse and our rocky Alps.'

Hugh tried to stay the fiery rebuke. The King was 'philosophising, and did not move his countenance.' 'And what do you think, good man?' he said to Hugh when the fiery Gerard ceased. 'Will you also cede our kingdom to us and depart?' But Hugh in his sympathetic way had been thinking evidently of Henry's labours and of his family troubles, of his struggles with his turbulent barons and his no less turbulent children. And he answered the King submissively and mildly, 'My lord, I do not despair of you. Rather I pity your hindrances and occupations, which weigh against the salutary care of your soul. You are busy; but when God will help, you will finish the good work you have begun.'

'By the salvation of my soul,' swore the King, 'while I breathe you shall not leave my kingdom. With thee I will share my counsels; with thee also the necessary care of my soul.'

Never, those who knew him said, did Henry love and honour any man like this man. They said there was a remarkable likeness between the two, so that Hugh might have been his son; more sonlike indeed to him than any of his own children. His genial talk, his enthusiastic bringing before him the histories of illustrious men, his faithful counsel, and more faithful rebukes,—Henry was pleased with all. Hugh had a remarkable delight in collecting and diffusing the Holy Scriptures, and in this the King assisted him, in the purchase of manuscripts. 'How much money do you want for this?' he once asked. 'One mark will suffice.' Whereupon the King laughed softly and said, 'How reckless you are in your demands!' And then he ordered ten marks to be given. The Bible was Hugh's delight and riches in tranquil days, his weapon in warfare, his food in hunger, his balm in sickness.

Meantime, while the King delighted in him, the peasants of the country round loved him no less, and sought him for teaching and help. He was believed to work miracles, but these, says his friend and biographer, 'he cared for less than anything, in the lives of the saints. He neither desired much to hear of them nor to work any such himself. They were good, he said, no doubt, for those who admired them.' To him, as to St. Gregory, the sanctity of the saints was the miracle; and the example.

Eleven years he remained Abbot of Witham, never seeking any higher post or wider sphere for himself. At the end of that time, he was elected Bishop of Lincoln, then a very large and disordered diocese. The King much desired this, but Hugh refused it again and again. Nothing but the command of his superior at the Chartreuse induced him to accept.

He rode to Winchester with the canons in his ordinary simple style, they on their richly caparisoned palfreys, with sumpter horses and gennets; he with his Carthusian wardrobe, consisting of blankets and sheepskin strapped behind him at the back of his saddle, till the canons, afraid of the ridicule of the crowd, had the straps cut unknown to him and passed his baggage on to the servants.

Soon after his installation he excommunicated the head forester of the King himself for oppressing his tenants about the forest game.

Not long after this the King sent to ask for a rich stall which happened to be vacant, for one of his courtiers. Hugh bade the messenger take back as an answer to the King's letter that the prebendal stalls were for priests, not for courtiers, and that he must find some other way of rewarding temporal services. Henry, who himself had cared so much for Hugh and for his election, was hurt as well as offended, and summoned the Bishop to meet him at Woodstock, intending to show how gravely he was displeased. When Hugh arrived at the park gates Henry rode off with his retainers into a glade of the forest, and there sat down on the ground to receive the delinquent bishop; and when he approached, by the royal command, no one rose or spoke. Hugh saluted the King. There was no answer. No one moved or spoke. The Bishop turned towards the King, but still there was silence. At last Henry, looking up, asked for a needle and thread; he had hurt a finger of his left hand. It was wrapped in a strip of linen rag: the end was loose; he began to sew. Still the awful silence continued.

The Bishop watched him through a few stitches, and then grimly said, 'Quam similis es modo cognatis tuis de Falesia! (Your Highness reminds me of your cousins of Falaise).' Like a light but penetrating dart the daring words went to the King's heart. Alone, of all present, Henry understood the allusion, and with a sudden reaction from his over-acted anger and silence to the old cordial understanding, he clenched his hands, struggled hard to contain himself, and at last rolled on the ground in convulsions of laughter. 'Do you understand the insult this barbarian has heaped on us?' he said. 'My ancestor the great William's mother came of a very middle-class family at Falaise, a town famous for its tanning; and so this mocker, seeing me sewing up my finger, recognises me as a kinsman of the tanners of Falaise.' Then the king demanded explanations of Hugh as to his forester.

The Bishop did not yield the point, but respectfully gave his reasons, saying he knew the King only desired justice in his dominions. Henry was convinced, and gave up the delinquent forester, whom the Bishop first had flogged, and then absolved, and made him his firm friend ever after. But no courtier afterwards asked for a stall at Lincoln.

If a man really honestly enjoyed is cell and horsecloth, with ministering to the suffering poor, more than any riches or honours the King could give—if he was quite free from worldly vanity, pride, and covetousness, and also victorious over the subtler temptations of spiritual vanity, and pride and covetousness, he must obviously have stood on a vantage-ground from which no king could displace him, possessed of a content no king could give him. It must also be remembered that St. Hugh was a Burgundian and no born subject of Henry's, and that the royalty of Henry's house was recent, so that probably his Angevin and Norman blood would seem to Hugh of Avalon no nobler than his own.

Among his own clergy he kept unity and peace, although, or perhaps because, he confessed 'my own temper is sometimes hotter and sharper than pepper. I thank them for bearing with me.'

In the episcopate he kept, as much as possible, to his old Carthusian dress and ways of living, sometimes carrying stones with the masons for the building of his new cathedral and the various religious houses on that fine terrace at Lincoln with its wide outlook.

He had great delight in visiting the sick, and also in paying honour to the dead, especially the poor. 'If they had been good they were worthy of honour; if not, they needed help

---

[1] *Brev. ad Usum Sarum Sanctorale*, St. Hugh, Lectio viii.

the more.' He would never allow any of his priests to perform the last rites if he were near. Once when he found that a poor beggar had been buried by the roadside where he had died, the Bishop stopped in his journey to perform the funeral service. For the sake of rendering this last service he delayed coming to King Henry's table. And once he kept Richard Cœur de Lion (not the most patient of the fiery Plantagenet kings) waiting for dinner, while he was ministering beside a grave at Rouen. 'He need not wait,' said the Bishop to the courtier who came to fetch him; 'let him go to dinner, in the name of God. Better the King dine without my company than that I leave my Master's work undone.' 'It may be observed,' says his biographer, 'that he who neglected two kings to bury the poor, at his own burial, was followed by two kings.'

His compassion was deepest for those who had sunk the lowest; for lepers, then so common in England, he had the tenderest pity. He would spend days under the same roof with them, touch them and kiss them, feeling that in them he touched the hand of Him who touched the leper of old in Galilee.[1] When the Chancellor of Lincoln, 'a very good and learned man,' once said to him, wishing to test whether, on account of the excellence of this work, this just man was elated in spirit, 'St. Martin kissed the leper, and by kissing healed him; but you do not cure the lepers you kiss,' the Bishop at once answered, 'Martin's kiss healed the body of the leper, but my kiss of the leper heals my soul.' 'Bone Jesu,' exclaims his biographer parenthetically, after describing the loathsomeness of these diseased ones, 'forgive my unhappy soul for referring to this.' Yet while living in their lazarhouses, and consoling them with the tenderest words, he would gravely and faithfully reprove them, if needful, and seek to cure them of their sins. His heart went out in a rapture of love to the Saviour for His kindness to such. 'Unhappy those,' he said, 'who feared anything so much as grieving Him, who thought anything sweet in comparison with Him, who thought anything bitter *with* Him.'

[1] *Brev. ad Usum Sarum Sanctorale*, Lectio vii.

Another significant saying of his is worth remembering, as to miracles. Once, in a country town near Troyes, his chaplains were much impressed by the story of a miracle which a priest of the place described as having turned him from unbelief. This priest said he had seen the Sacramental wine at the altar turn visibly into blood. 'In the name of God,' said the Bishop, 'let him keep to himself the signs of his unbelief, let him indeed gaze, if he will, through the little doors of his eyes, on Him whom he would not see by the inward gaze of faith. What have we to do with such things who every day partake of the Heavenly Sacrifice?'

For the diseases of the soul his pity was deepest of all. His sermons are said to have brought back multitudes of sinners. And from the execution of the sentence of death, in those days of cruel severity, he more than once rescued, at any peril, those who took sanctuary with him.

Allusions are also made in his Life, to his courageous quelling of riots in Lincolnshire and Northumbria, encountering a mob when all the rest had fled.

Children and animals also trusted and loved him, the shyest little ones, it is said, creeping fearlessly close to him in the houses which he visited. For them he had always smiles and fun, and yet a tender reverence. 'Suffer the little children to come unto Me,' echoed in his heart.

And there was one especial swan, very fierce and feared by everyone, who felt himself so understood by the Bishop that he accepted food from his hands, waited about for him, and would even poke his long neck into the ample sleeves and folds of his dress, making joyful sounds of welcome and also little soft cries (*mussitare*) for crumbs. Sometimes he would go back for a visit to his old convent of the Grande Chartreuse, where, with his liberal hand and gracious speech and bearing, he had an enthusiastic welcome from all, especially from the poor. At home he was the defender of the orphan and forsaken. And he would never accept fines (as was too common then) as an atonement for any wrong, instead of penitence and reparation.

His relations with Richard Cœur de Lion were as intimate and as original as with Henry. He had studied the English laws, and he absolutely refused to impose burdens on the clergy to furnish soldiers for foreign service, though he recognised the obligation to provide for military service at home. For this offence he was summoned to Roche d'Andely, near Rouen, to answer for his refusal to the King. He found him on a stately throne at the entrance of the choir, hearing Mass. Hugh went up to him and demanded the customary kiss. Richard frowned and turned away; the Bishop insisted. 'You have not deserved it,' said the King. 'I have deserved it,' said the bishop, grasping Richard's robes and shaking him; 'kiss me.' The kiss was given. Then the archbishop and bishops would have placed Hugh in a place of honour, but he went through them all to the corner of the altar and knelt there with humblest devotion.

Afterwards the king yielded to his counsel as to foreign military service. But the bishop sought for deeper things, in his intercourse with the king. He sought to see Richard alone and asked him then if he had no sin on his conscience. Richard said he was conscious of no special sin but being too angry with his French enemies. But the bishop searched deeper. Were there no oppressions of the poor, no unfair exactions of taxes, no unfaithfulnesses to his queen? The king did not fly into a rage, but listened to the admonition and said afterwards: 'If all bishops were like my lord of Lincoln, not a prince among us could lift up his head against them.' Hugh was called with reason 'the hammer of kings.'

But Richard also passed away from the affectionate rebukes of Hugh of Lincoln to another tribunal; and when he died, the bishop, a lion in real danger, insisted on going through a disturbed country, at peril of his life, to pay Richard the funeral honours he had often risked his displeasure rather than not pay to the poor.

And now of that strong royal house only John with his falseness and meanness was left. Between him and Hugh there could be no sympathy. 'I trust you mean what you say,' the bishop said to John; 'you know I much hate lying.' He warned him also against trusting in a stone amulet he wore round his neck. 'Trust not in that senseless stone, but in the living stone, the Lord Jesus Christ,' he said. And at Fontevrault he pointed out to John with significant earnestness a sculpture of the Day of Judgment, 'with a group of crowned kings being led away by devils to the smoking pit.'

But the strong, well-worn frame was failing. He knew it, and prepared with humble confession of sin, but without terror, for death. He would not give up his hair-shirt, but yielded so far to the physicians as to take a little meat. The fever of which he died came on him in London. King John came to visit him on his deathbed, with blandest expressions of respect, but to him Bishop Hugh said little. Archbishop Hubert, who had much thwarted him, also came to see him, and suggested that he should ask pardon of him as his primate and spiritual father for the sharp words he had said to him. The bishop, on the contrary, thought it his duty to apologise, not for what he had said but for what he had omitted to say, 'for your negligence and attachment to the world,' said he, 'do sore damage to the souls placed under your direction.'

And so on the afternoon of March 17, 1200, St. Hugh of Lincoln died. The choristers of St. Paul's were sent for to chant Complin for him for the last time. He had himself laid on the ashes on the floor of his room, and there, in great tranquillity, while they sang the Nunc Dimittis, his spirit 'departed in peace.' His body was carried to Lincoln. The highest and the lowest came to meet him, and the Jews (banished ninety years after from England for nearly four centuries) ventured to come to show their reverence for this just man. King John and three archbishops, Hubert among them, took the bier on their shoulders and waded knee-deep through the mud to Lincoln Cathedral. The king of Scotland stood apart in tears.

St. Richard

OF CHICHESTER.[1]

April 3.

(Died A.D. 1253. Sarum Epistle and Gosp. Ecclus. xliv. 17, 20-23, and xlv. 6, 7, 15, 16; St. John xv. 1-7.)

It is significant that whilst among the saints of the Early English or Saxon Church, three are kings and the bishops work harmoniously with the kings, after the Conquest there are no kings in our Calendar, and the bishops (with St. Thomas of Canterbury carefully expunged by the vigorous hand of Henry VIII.), are all more or less in antagonism with the royal power. St. Thomas of Canterbury and St. Hugh of Lincoln were canonised at all events in the hearts of the English people as leaders in the resistance to absolute power, strong churchmen standing their ground against strong monarchs, between whom the freedom of the nation was wrought out. Richard of Chichester, the latest saint in our Calendar, brings us to another level of time. The great founders of the friars, St. Francis and St. Dominic, were in the world, although they are not in the Sarum Calendar, on which our own is based; but whilst Hugh of Lincoln belongs, through the Carthusians, to the monastic reformation and revival of his day, Richard of Chichester spent some time with his friend Edmund, Archbishop of Canterbury, in the Dominican monastery of Pontigny. St. Richard lived in that great thirteenth century, the century of the great cathedrals, of the foundation of the great Franciscan and Dominican orders, and of the birth and death of so many things; and he belonged to his age. The friars were carrying on their missions among the people of the towns; the

---

[1] Dedication of churches, 1, at Aberford, in Yorkshire. Represented in art with a chalice at his feet, or kneeling with a chalice before him, alluding to a legend that he fell with the chalice without spilling its contents.

monks and hermits were still seeking seclusion from the world in the valleys and forests, but Richard seems to have had no early inclination to the monastic life. His parents had been in good circumstances, but they fell into such poverty that his elder brother was thrown into prison for debt. Richard worked hard to help his brother, doing the roughest manual work of a servant in his house; and moreover he managed the family affairs so well that they rallied, and the elder, with generous gratitude, insisted upon resigning the property to the younger, who he said had saved it for both. Soon after this, a rich marriage was arranged for the younger, which apparently made the elder regret his donation; whereupon Richard yielded up the estate, and the marriage, which seems to have depended upon it, and went forth free and poor among the thousands of poor wandering scholars of that age of intellectual awakening. He studied first at the university of Oxford, and then at Paris. There he lodged with two scholars as poor as himself. They had to wear their one coat, and take their lessons, in turn.

But in the ardour of youth and of the keen pursuit of knowledge he found these, as he often said afterwards, the happiest years of his life. In Oxford he was made Master of Arts. From Oxford he went to Bologna, where he studied law, civil and ecclesiastical, for seven years. His fine intelligence and his pure and affectionate heart won him honour and affection in the great Italian university. When his professor fell ill, it was to the young Englishman he turned to supply his place, and on his recovery he would have given him his only daughter in marriage, and left him heir of all he possessed. We do not hear of any monastic purpose as the cause of Richard's declining this marriage. Throughout his life his renunciations have more the air of a princely indifference than of a difficult self-denial, as if he were simply giving up to others things they cared about, whilst he did not. His heart was English, and he returned to Oxford, where he was made Chancellor of the university. The Archbishop of Canterbury (St. Edmund or Edmé) won his services for his diocese. Edmund himself had shared Richard's passion for knowledge. When a boy of twelve, son of a poor pious widowed mother, he had studied Aristotle at Oxford; but this thirst for secular knowledge was in conflict with a tender mystical piety reflected from his father, who had taken refuge in a monastery, and from his religious mother who had given him, as his inheritance, a hair shirt, which he promised to wear every Wednesday. Edmund probably influenced Richard in many ways. The archbishop was tossed about on many waters; the intellectual conflicts between the old religion and the dawning of the first Renaissance quenched in blood, the stormy combats between king and Papacy, Henry III. and Innocent; the royal gifts of sacred offices to careless courtiers, and the Papal claim of 300 wealthy benefices for 300 Italian priests.

'Seeing that the English church was being daily trampled on more and more,' says Matthew Paris, 'despoiled of its possessions and deprived of its liberties, he became weary of living, and retired with his faithful chancellor, Richard, to the Dominican Monastery of Pontigny, where he died.'

It was after the death of his beloved master Edmund that Richard devoted himself more especially to theology, and was ordained to the priesthood. His subsequent appointment to the see of Canterbury was from Rome, in contradiction to Henry III., who had designed it for one of his own countrymen. Henry was very indignant at the appointment of Richard, knowing that he was of the party of Edmund, who had opposed him, and he sent to Rome to get the appointment annulled. But Richard also went to Rome, and was there consecrated by Pope Innocent IV., though for two years Richard took the charge of his diocese without its revenues, which were withheld by the king. Revenues were indifferent to him, except to administer and give away. When he at length received them, he distributed them in such a bountiful shower, that his elder brother, to whom he had committed the administration of his temporal affairs, complained of his largesses, for which he said no revenue would suffice. But Richard reminded him that 'their father had eaten and drunk out of common crockery, and he had no need of gold and silver plate.'

He was very tolerant of offences against himself; but of immorality, especially in his clergy, utterly intolerant. 'Never,' he said, 'shall a ribald have cure of souls in my diocese of Chichester.' Towards the end of his life he wore out his strength in preaching the Crusade against the Saracens, by order of the Pope, in every village and town throughout the land. He felt ill, but insisted, nevertheless, on going to Dover to consecrate a church and a cemetery for the poor, in the name of his friend St. Edmund.

From the consecration he went back to prepare himself to die. He asked for a crucifix and kissed the signs of the Sacred Wounds with much fervour. An old friend was by his bedside to help him. To him he said with a peaceful countenance, 'I was glad when they said, Let us go unto the House of the Lord.' He entreated 'the Virgin Mother of God and of mercy' to pray for him, and said, 'Lord Jesus Christ, I thank Thee for all the blessings Thou hast given me, and for all the pains Thou hast endured for me, so that to Thee apply most truly those words, "Come and see if there be any sorrow like unto My sorrow." Thou knowest, Lord, how willingly I would endure insult and pain and death for Thee; therefore have mercy on me, for to Thee I commend my spirit.'

And so, from the House of the Lord being built amidst darkness and battles below, to the House of the Lord being prepared in light and peace above, passed away the last of the Saints in our English Calendar.

CHAPTER IV.

OTHER MINOR FESTIVALS.

OF the remaining eleven minor festivals in our Calendar (or twelve, if we include All Souls from the calendar which also includes St. Patrick) three—the Nativity, the Conception, and the Visitation of the Blessed Virgin—are connected with the Mother of our Lord, and St. Anne's festival may also be considered as the commemoration of her childhood.

The Greeks have three festivals of St. Anne. The first mention of St. Anne is in one of the apocryphal gospels, which by their childish and often unlovely stories throw the true Gospels into such strong relief. The legends in those apocryphal gospels are a curious mosaic of Old Testament stories, such as that of Hannah and Manoah, with the very different ideal of the supreme sanctity of the single life. There is a pathetic lament of St. Anne on her childlessness appealing to the little sparrow brooding on its nest in her garden as more blessed by God than she is, and even to the inanimate earth, rivers and seas, as giving more return to God than she could. With a great rapture of joy the little daughter is at length welcomed. The tender reverence of the aged parents for the little Virgin, of whose great destiny they have a prevision, is most touching. The picture of the fearless gladness with which the saintly child ascends the temple steps to be presented for consecration, and also of the aged mother St. Anne teaching the little girl to read, are beautiful features of the legend.

As to St. Mary Magdalene, it is said that one reason of the banishment of her festival from among the major feasts may be the difference of opinion of the Eastern and Western Churches about her history; the Latins believing that Mary of Bethany, Mary Magdalene, and 'the woman that was a sinner,' were one and the same person, while the Eastern Church has held the three to be distinct.[1]

The loss of that wonderful exemplification of how 'the last' may 'become first,' embodied in the Western tradition of the Magdalene, may be lamented, whatever our convictions as to the history.

The collect in the first book of Edward VI. was: 'Mercyfull Father, geve us grace that we never presume to synne, thorough the example of any creature, but if it shal chaunce vs at any tyme to offende Thy diuyne Maiestie, that then we may truely repent and lament the same after the example of Mary Magdalen, and by a lively faithe obtaine remission of all our synnes through the onely merites of thy Sonne our Sauiour Christ.'

In the Greek Church the Magdalene is held to have been the equal of the Apostles, having been the first witness of the Resurrection. She is supposed to have retired to Ephesus with the Blessed Virgin and St. John, and to have been buried there; whilst according to the Western legend, she went with Lazarus and Martha (her brother and sister) to the south of France, there won many by her life and words to Christ, and was miraculously borne to heaven daily by the angels in a rapture of Divine communion.

The mediæval hymns referring to St. Mary Magdalene are among the most beautiful. Such as the '*Pone luctum Magdalena.*' The hymn in the Sarum Sanctorale, if a little touched with monastic or academic play on words, is very expressive:

> Hæc a Jesu Jesum quærit,
> Sublatum conqueritur:
> Jesum intus mente gerit,
> Jesu præsens quæritur.
> Mentem colit, mentem serit
> Jesus, nec percipitur.

And the Sequence in the Sarum Missal presents very finely

---

[1] Blunt's *Annotated Prayer Book.*

the contrasts and resemblances between the Mother of Christ and Mary Magdalene :—

> Illa enim fuit porta
> Per quam fuit lux exorta ;
> Hæc resurgentis nuncia
> Mundum replet lætitiâ.

Two of the remaining festivals, Holy Cross Day and the Invention of the Holy Cross, were called the Holy Rood of May and the Holy Rood of September.[1] The Invention of the Cross (the Holy Rood of May) was sometimes called St. Helen's or Ellinmas Day, in commemoration of the supposed finding of the actual Cross on which Our Lord suffered about A.D. 326.

St. Ambrose relates the discovery by the Empress Helena on Golgotha.

St. Chrysostom, about the same time, mentions the finding of the Cross, but does not speak of the Empress. Eusebius mentions the Empress's journey, but not the finding of the Cross. Gradually the story grew into a very elaborate legend.

The Exaltation of the Holy Cross (the Holy Rood of September) in the Greek Church was and is the Commemoration of the appearance of the Sign of the Cross in the heavens to Constantine, the 'In hoc signo vinces.' In the Breviaries of the West (Blunt's 'Annotated Prayer Book ') the lections mainly relate to the recovery by the Emperor Heraclius (A.D. 629) of a portion of the recovered Cross which had been preserved in a richly jewelled case at Jerusalem, and carried away by Chosroes, king of the Persians. Heraclius entered Jerusalem barefoot and meanly clad, carrying the precious reliquary in his hands. This being opened, was lifted up before the people, whence probably the festival is called the *Exaltation of the Holy Cross.*

Lammas Day is also kept in the Western Church, and commemorated in the Sarum Missal as ' S. Peter *ad Vincula,* in memory of the dedication of the church in Rome where

---

[1] The hymns in the Sarum Sanctorale for the Holy Rood days are, 'Ave crux benedicta,' ' Pange lingua gloriosi prœlium certaminis ' and Venantius Fortunatus's ' Crux fidelis inter omnes.'

one of the chains which fell off St. Peter at the touch of the angel is supposed to be preserved. *Lammas* means really a feast of firstfruits, being hlaf Mass or loaf Mass, a *feast of thanksgiving for the firstfruits of the harvest.* It was customary on this day to consecrate in the Mass the bread made of the new wheat.

The Transfiguration, in August, was also, besides its especial significance, in a sense, *a feast of firstfruits for the vintage.* It was customary on this day for the deacon to press a few drops of the first grapes of the new vintage into the chalice, thus consecrating and offering up the firstfruits of the vintage, as at Lammas the firstfruits of the corn.

The Beheading of St. John the Baptist is commemorated in all the calendars, Eastern and Western.

The remaining minor festivals in our Calendar are all directly connected with our Lord.

The 'Name of Jesus' (in the Sarum Missal 'Festum dulcissimi Nominis Jesu, festum majus duplex') is a festival of late origin[1] in honour of 'the Name which is above every name, at which every knee shall bow.' St. Bernard's hymn, 'Jesu dulcis memoria,' is one of the sequences to be sung on this day, according to the Sarum Missal.

'*O Sapientia*' is simply the first invocation of the first of the seven antiphons to the Magnificat, with which begins the final ushering in of the Advent preparation for Christmas; the first strophe of the great Bridal Hymn with which the Church goes forth to meet her Lord.

Like a trumpet, pealing out the first notes of a great réveillé, it gives us the key of the great Advent hymn.

There could scarcely be a fitter close to these sketches of the blessed ones who shone in His light than this sevenfold song of the glories of Him in whose light they shone.

For as we trace, and seek to follow, that great procession of the saints, we are not looking back to them in the past, but onward with them to the future, and upward with them

---

[1] 'About the beginning of the 15th century.'—Blunt's *Annotated Prayer Book.*

to '*Him who was and is and is to come.*' Not only *Eureka* was the song of each of them, but *Veni*.

Wisdom unfathomable and Incarnate Word of God; Lord and Leader of Thy people; Root and Flower, and fulfilling Fruit, Foundation and Ideal of humanity; Key of all mysteries, unlocking our hearts to ourselves and to each other, and therefore their Sceptre; ever dawning Radiance of the Eternal Light; King of nations and their Desire, because Thou art Emmanuel, God with us for ever! Come! To solve all our perplexities, to heal all our divisions, to liberate from all wrongs, to redeem from all sin! Because we have found Thee, we ever seek Thee; because Thou hast come, Come!

December 16.

(Ecclus. xxiv. 3; Wisd. viii. 1: *comp.* 1 Cor. i. 24; Prov. i. ix.)

O Sapientia quæ ex ore Altissimi prodisti, attingens a fine usque ad finem, fortiter suaviterque disponens omnia, Veni ad docendum nos viam prudentiæ.

O Wisdom, which didst come forth from the mouth of the Most High, reaching from end to end, and strongly and sweetly ordering all things, Come, that Thou mayest teach us the way of understanding.

December 17.

(Exod. iii. 14; St. John viii. 58.)

O Adonai, et Dux domus Israël, qui Moysi in igne flammæ rubi apparuisti, et in Sina legem dedisti, Veni ad redimendum nos in brachio extento.

O Lord and Leader of the house of Israel, Who didst appear unto Moses in a flame of fire in the bush, and gavest Thy law in Sinai, Come, that thou mayest redeem us with Thine outstretched arm.

December 18.

(Isa. xi. 10; Rev. xxii. 16.)

O Radix Jesse, qui stas in signum populorum, super quem continebunt reges os suum, quem gentes deprecabuntur, Veni ad liberandum nos: jam noli tardare.

O Root of Jesse, which standest for an ensign of the people, before whom kings shall shut their mouths, and to whom the

Gentiles shall seek, Come, that Thou mayest deliver us: tarry not, we beseech Thee.

December 19.

(Isa. xxii. 22; Rev. iii. 7; Isa. xlii. 7.)

O Clavis David, et Sceptrum domus Israël, qui aperis et nemo claudit, claudis et nemo aperit, Veni et educ vinctum de domo carceris, sedentem in tenebris et umbra mortis.

O Key of David and Sceptre of the house of Israel, Thou Who openest and no man shutteth, Who shuttest and no man openeth, Come, and bring forth from the prison-house him that is bound, sitting in darkness, and in the shadow of death.

December 20.

(Wisd. vii. 26; Heb. i. 3; Matt. iv. 2.)

O Oriens Splendor lucis æternæ et Sol justitiæ, Veni et illumina sedentes in tenebris et umbra mortis.

O Dayspring of the eternal light and Sun of righteousness, Come, and give light to those who sit in darkness and in the shadow of death.

December 22.

(Hag. ii. 7.)

O Rex gentium et Desideratus earum, Lapisque angularis qui facis utraque unum, Veni, salva hominem quem de limo formasti.

O King of nations, and their Desire, the Corner stone which maketh of both one, Come, save man whom Thou hast formed out of the dust of the ground.

December 23.

(Isa. vii. 14; St. Matt. i. 23.)

O Emmanuel, Rex et legifer noster, expectatio gentium et Salvator earum, Veni ad salvandum nos, Domine Deus noster.

O Emmanuel, our King and our Lawgiver, the Expectation of the nations, and their Saviour, Come, that Thou mayest save us, O Lord our God.

www.ingramcontent.com/pod-product-compliance
Lightning Source LLC
Chambersburg PA
CBHW051858300426
44117CB00006B/442